Directions for Mormon Studies in the Twenty-First Century

Edited by Patrick Q. Mason

DIRECTIONS FOR MORMON STUDIES *in the* TWENTY-FIRST CENTURY

THE UNIVERSITY OF UTAH PRESS
Salt Lake City

The Defiance House Man colophon is a registered trademark of the University of Utah Press. It is based on a four-foot-tall Ancient Puebloan pictograph (late PIII) near Glen Canyon, Utah.

20 19 18 17 16   1 2 3 4 5

LIBRARY OF CONGRESS CATALOGING-IN-PUBLICATION DATA

Name: Mason, Patrick Q., editor.
Title: Directions for Mormon studies in the twenty-first century/edited by Patrick Q. Mason.
Description: Salt Lake City : University of Utah Press, 2016. | Includes bibliographical references and index.
Identifiers: LCCN 2015037633 | ISBN 9781607814757 (pbk. : alk. paper) | ISBN 9781607814764 (ebook)
Subjects: LCSH: Mormon Church. | Church of Jesus Christ of Latter-day Saints.
Classification: LCC BX8608 .D57 2016 | DDC 289.307—dc23
LC record available at http://lccn.loc.gov/2015037633

Printed and bound by Sheridan Books, Inc., Ann Arbor, Michigan.

For Armand Mauss

and all my mentors and colleagues in Mormon studies

Contents

Illustrations

Figures

Table

Preface

MOST OF THE ESSAYS IN THIS VOLUME ORIGINATED AS PAPERS DELIVERED AT A conference called "Beyond the Mormon Moment: Directions for Mormon Studies in the New Century," which I organized and hosted in March 2013 at Claremont Graduate University. The occasion of the conference was to honor the career and legacy of Armand Mauss, a distinguished sociologist of religion and one of the most prominent Mormon intellectuals of the late twentieth and early twenty-first centuries. As I began conceptualizing the conference, it quickly became apparent to me that Mauss's considerable scholarly contributions to Mormon studies were in many ways ahead of their time. In his long career he has anticipated a number of themes and trajectories that other scholars in the field have only recently begun to pick up. As we consulted together about the conference, Mauss insisted that it be neither an extended eulogy nor a simple celebration and review of his (impressive) scholarship, but rather an occasion to genuinely advance the field. I selected the conference themes accordingly and invited an all-star cast of speakers. To round out the volume, I also solicited original essays from other scholars who could not be at the conference due to schedule conflicts or limited space. The collected talent in this book stands as a testament to the respect that Armand Mauss has earned among his peers and to the intellectual inspiration that he has provided to the entire field of Mormon studies.

Mauss's extensive catalog of work is frequently referenced in these essays, but not gratuitously—when taking up the themes herein, which represent some of the important new directions for Mormon studies in the twenty-first century, the foundational and paradigmatic work of Armand Mauss is simply inescapable. The essays here extend Mauss's arguments and at times argue with his findings; as a true scholar, I'm confident he would have it no other way. Though the twelve main essays engage with the scholarly contributions of Armand Mauss, it is also appropriate to appreciate him as a person. Claudia Bushman does so in the volume's coda, which locates the scholar in his time and place and identifies him as a particular breed of "California Mormon."

A personal note of gratitude and acknowledgment is in order. Special thanks are due to the Howard W. Hunter Foundation and Mormon Studies Council at Claremont Graduate University, which generously sponsored the 2013 conference that was the genesis for this book. My colleagues at Claremont Graduate University, especially Dean Tammi Schneider, have been exceptionally supportive of using the university as a gathering place to have important conversations that help grow this emerging field of Mormon studies. I am grateful for the support and assistance of John Alley and his entire editorial team at the University of Utah Press. The authors in this volume were universally gracious, professional, and easy to work with, for which I am profoundly thankful. Two of my graduate students, Amanda Pumphrey and William Floyd, skillfully assisted in the early preparation of the manuscript. This volume is a token of my thanks to and appreciation for the entire community of Mormon studies scholars—past, present, and future—who do such excellent, stimulating, and important work.

Last but not least, it would be impossible to have a more supportive family, which gives me the space and encouragement to do what I love to do. Thanks and love most of all to Melissa, Finn, Rhett, and Lucy.

Introduction | Mormon Studies
The Emergence and State of the Field

Patrick Q. Mason

As we entered the last third of the twentieth century, the number of reputable academic books on Mormons and Mormonism was small enough to fit on one shelf. Now, in the second decade of the twenty-first century, it is almost impossible to keep up with the tidal wave of high-quality scholarship that constitutes the emergence of the academic subfield of Mormon studies. In one sense, scholarship on Mormonism has benefited from a general turn toward religion in recent years; in 2009 the American Historical Association reported that religious history had become its members' most frequently stated area of specialization, surpassing cultural history.[1] In addition to this broader receptivity toward the study of religion on the part of the scholarly community, Mormonism was seemingly thrust onto the national—and at times world—stage by a series of events in the past decade and a half, known popularly as the "Mormon Moment." The confluence of an academy more attuned to the importance of religion, the increased public prominence of Mormons and Mormonism, and the steadily rising number of graduate students and established scholars applying ever more sophisticated methods to the study of Mormonism has produced a new era in Mormon studies.

As a subfield of the modern academy, Mormon studies is both relatively new and old. The term, as a self-conscious designator of a related body of scholarship, is essentially a twenty-first-century creation. In this sense Mormon studies is a relative latecomer in the American academy, following years or decades after the advent of other specialized "studies" areas such as American studies, Islamic studies, African American (later Africana) studies, and women's (later gender) studies. Indeed, the twenty-first-century emergence of Mormon studies speaks to the continuing salience of multiculturalism and identity politics in the academy and the broader culture, even while such notions have become increasingly contested. That Mormon studies has gone beyond a niche enterprise of passionate insiders to become institutionalized in multiple ways within various segments of the secular academy comes as a shock to many veteran scholars who have researched and published on Mormon-related subjects for decades—and who for much of that time struggled to find a hearing in mainstream academic journals, conferences, and professional societies. Now the American Academy of Religion has a thriving Mormon Studies Group; three secular universities have established endowed chairs in Mormon studies, a fourth has an undergraduate program, and others are on the drawing board; Mormonism is regularly covered in religion and history courses across the country; and the editor of a significant (non-Mormon) academic journal has reported to me that he is overwhelmed with high-quality submissions related to Mormonism. Indeed, in the middle of the second decade of the new century, we can safely say that Mormon studies has established a firm foothold and is genuinely coming into its own.

Though many of these particular developments, especially on the institutional level, are novel and in some ways surprising, the intellectual foundations of Mormon studies were laid nearly three-quarters of a century ago by Fawn Brodie in her biography of Joseph Smith, *No Man Knows My History*.[2] Ever since its publication in 1945, Brodie's book has drawn partisan reactions; it has consistently been overvalued by Smith's critics and undervalued by Smith's defenders. To be sure, the book has its flaws, and many of its claims have not held up (both of which are rather unremarkable observations about any seventy-year-old book). But the most lasting virtue of Brodie's work—and the reason why I mark it as a formative moment in the *possibility* of Mormon studies—was its tone and approach. Quite simply, Brodie anticipated what would become the hallmark of Mormon studies, as distinct from its related but ultimately different modes of apologetics (both pro- and anti-Mormon) and denominational history (typically deemed "church history" in Mormon circles).

In Mormon studies, Mormonism and Mormons appear as the subject or object of scholarly study, but the questions, concerns, and issues at the heart of the study are principally generated outside the community of religious believers themselves. In terms of research agenda, approach, and analysis, Mormon studies is attentive to official church institutions but not beholden to them, and goes far beyond (and sometimes contrary to) ecclesiastical concerns and interests. The difference between Mormon studies and church history is less the topics under consideration—though in practice they often do vary significantly—than the orientation of the study: church history primarily faces inward, Mormon studies primarily faces outward. Mormon studies is more engaged with the academy than the church, more oriented to Athens than Jerusalem, so to speak. It is chiefly influenced by and in conversation with the categories, theories, paradigms, and discourse of the secular academy. Generally attracted to non-Mormon university and trade presses and academic periodicals, Mormon studies acknowledges a base of LDS interest and readership but is more concerned intellectually with reception by scholarly peers than ingratiation with ecclesiastical elites (or even laity). The particular faith commitments or academic background of the author matter less than the nature and quality of her scholarship. Four foundational figures illustrate this dynamic: Fawn Brodie was a disenchanted Mormon writer who was excommunicated for her writings; Thomas O'Dea was a sympathetic Catholic sociologist of religion; Juanita Brooks was a devout Mormon marginalized but never disciplined for her historical heterodoxy; and Leonard Arrington was a committed Mormon economic historian who was for a time head of the LDS Church's Historical Department before incurring the displeasure but never official censure of senior church leaders.[3] All this means that although not inherently hostile to Mormon belief and practice, Mormon studies scholarship is generally more useful in the college classroom than the LDS Sunday School classroom.

Building on the work of intellectual pioneers such as Brodie, O'Dea, and Brooks, the historiographical bridge between an older style of apologetics and Mormon studies was the so-called New Mormon History. With Leonard Arrington serving as both a midwife and godfather, most of the practitioners of the New Mormon History, which was the regnant approach from the 1960s to the 1990s, were professionally trained historians and also devout Latter-day Saints. Following the lead of Arrington's classic book *Great Basin Kingdom*, they set aside the contentious debates over the veracity of LDS faith claims to examine Mormons and the Mormon past as social, cultural, intellectual, political, and economic phenomena.[4] History, they discovered, became a safe place for intellectual exploration and revisionism—when controversial matters arose, they could say they were not taking a position, simply stating the facts as they were. Postmodernism has since belied this posture, but conveniently hiding behind the veil of objectivism was and remains useful in the explication and promulgation of historical heterodoxies.[5] Contra its cousin the Reorganized Church of Jesus Christ of Latter Day Saints (now the Community of Christ), in the second half of the twentieth century leaders of the Church of Jesus Christ of Latter-day Saints did not show much of an appetite for historical deconstruction or any other form of normative critical scholarship. Occasional disciplinary actions against intellectuals—including Fawn Brodie, D. Michael Quinn, and Maxine Hanks—proved that well-regarded historical scholarship did not offer its authors a cloak of invisibility or invincibility. Conservative church leaders understood just as well as reform-minded scholars that the construction of usable pasts can always be employed to support a contemporary agenda.

For the most part, however, the New Mormon History was not interested in fomenting ecclesiastical revolution or even substantial reform; though the participants shared a broadly revisionist orientation, most were more interested in preserving and enriching Mormonism rather than fundamentally upsetting it. Because of the temperament of its practitioners as well as the location where much of it was produced (either the LDS Church Historical Department or Brigham Young University), most of the New Mormon History was ultimately concerned with the essential tasks of documenting and recovering various half-forgotten aspects of the Mormon past, as well as updating outdated or inaccurate interpretations. Scholars reveled in plumbing the astounding richness of the seemingly endless primary source materials. The New Mormon History was very much an exercise in exploring Mormon identity—increasingly recognizing that internal conflict disrupted traditional discourses of unity and produced in actuality plural Mormon identities. The historiography was characterized by a near-exclusive focus on Mormonism's formative period until 1890, with important but only limited attention paid to even the early decades of the twentieth century. The contributions of the New Mormon History were on display for the general public and academy, but for the most part only other Mormon academics and a relative handful of enthusiasts—as well as wary church leaders—paid much attention while an impressively robust body of scholarship was generated.

One of the most important interventions in scholarship on Mormonism, which anticipated in many ways the later development of Mormon studies, was Jan Shipps's indispensable 1985 book, *Mormonism: The Story of a New Religious Tradition*.[6] The book's particular arguments remain compelling for serious examinations of the religion. But *Mormonism* was a game-changer in at least two other regards: it ventured away from linear narrative history and opted, instead, in a religious studies mode, to interpret and theorize rather than simply describe and analyze; and it demonstrated how Mormonism could be profitably used to complicate our very notions of what religion is and how it operates. The New Mormon History, generally speaking, imported concepts and narratives from American and Western history to better understand Mormonism. Without abandoning that fruitful approach, Jan Shipps showed how Mormonism could itself become a lens on history and theory.

Building on the foundation of the New Mormon History, Mormon studies is predominantly a humanistic enterprise, with key contributions from the social sciences. The disciplinary scope of Mormon studies research is steadily expanding beyond history—though history remains the core of the enterprise, and the methodological expansion is occurring somewhat more slowly than we might have predicted. Currently, the most active and promising fields (other than history) are religious studies, theology, women's and gender studies, and philosophy, with sociology, folklore studies, literary studies, anthropology, and political theory present but less developed.

The shift in the disciplinary nature and topical focus of Mormon studies is in part a marker of generational transition. We currently stand at a pivotal juncture in Mormon studies in which we are witnessing the metaphoric passing of the torch from one generation to the next. The first generation of those who systematically applied scholarly methods to their study of Mormonism—most of whose work fell in the New Mormon History—were scholars who came of age in the 1960s and 1970s and are now nearing or beyond retirement age. In large part, what should have been the successive generation of scholars—those coming of age in the 1980s and 1990s—was discouraged from engaging in scholarship on Mormonism by the various negative signals and resistance from LDS Church leaders toward independent intellectuals during that era. We are now seeing the rise of a new generation—those trained in graduate school beginning in the late 1990s and 2000s (including myself)—that is indebted to the contributions of the first generation, generally unscarred by the battles of the middle generation, and now poised to take the field in new directions based on the new methods and insights they have acquired in their graduate studies, including but also ranging far beyond history.

The New Mormon History was successful, I would argue, largely because of the institutions that its practitioners created and maintained. The Mormon History Association, with its flagship publication *Journal of Mormon History*, turned fifty years old in 2015. The other leading Mormon studies periodical, *Dialogue: A Journal of Mormon Thought*, was founded only months after the MHA. Other influential periodicals, notably *BYU Studies* (now *BYU Studies Quarterly*) and *Sunstone*, have also published important scholarship—as well as fiction, poetry, personal essays, and book reviews—representing different perspectives and occupying various places on the ideological spectrum. The LDS Church Historical Department housed much of the remarkable output of the Arrington years, followed by the Joseph Fielding Smith Institute for LDS History at Brigham Young University. A mutually profitable relationship between Mormon historians and the University of Illinois Press meant that the best Mormon historical scholarship would be produced and marketed by a respected and nationally distributed university press. Independent Mormon publishers such as Signature Books also produced a steady supply of quality scholarship that many other presses at the time considered to be too niche.

Mormon studies scholars have flourished in the rich institutional and intellectual culture nurtured during the years of the New Mormon History. We are, however, also seeing a shift in the institutional arrangements of Mormon studies compared to its forebears. The most visible development has been the establishment of endowed chairs or programs in Mormon studies at four secular universities (Utah State University, Claremont Graduate University, the University of Virginia, and Utah Valley University).[7] The Mormon History Association and Sunstone Symposium are no longer the principal outlets for the presentation for cutting-edge research on Mormonism. In large part because many of them are in the early stages of their academic careers, most younger Mormon studies scholars focus on presenting at national professional conferences (especially the American Historical Association and the American Academy of Religion) and publishing in non-Mormon venues. This is driven both by intellectual orientation—their inherently outward-facing proclivities—as well as by career considerations, given their need to compete on the academic job market and then satisfy university tenure committees.

In terms of publishing, Oxford University Press has supplanted the University of Illinois Press as the dominant publisher of Mormon-related academic books. Most would agree that this represents a "step up" in prestige in the world of academic publishing, and both reflects and drives the increased respectability of the field. No doubt lured by the fact that American Latter-day Saints, on the whole, are an educated and reading public, other presses have followed Oxford's lead, and one can now find excellent Mormon studies titles published by Columbia, Harvard, Illinois, North Carolina, and Utah university presses. Signature Books has been joined by Greg Kofford Books, among others, in also offering significant and often award-winning Mormon studies scholarship from independent Mormon publishers. Brigham Young University's academic engagement with Mormon studies has been reinvigorated through the Neal A. Maxwell Institute for Religious Scholarship and its associated publications, notably the *Mormon Studies Review*. Authors are increasingly taking their journal-length scholarship to non-Mormon venues. In fact, it has become cause for concern among the editorial teams of the traditional Mormon studies periodicals that the best articles are more often than not being submitted to non-Mormon journals that may attract fewer LDS readers but which are professionally more advantageous for young scholars.

Given the increased prominence of Mormon studies in the academy, perhaps it's fair to ask how its contributions stack up against what we might consider peer subfields, particularly those within American religious history and religious studies. This is not to engage in some kind of ranking system to determine the overall productivity, value, or significance of various literatures and groups of scholars, but rather to act as a kind of interim measure of the vitality and development of this particular subfield at this particular point in time. Mormon studies should, on the whole, be proud of its achievements. This is especially true given that Mormonism provides a far more limited canvass, especially for historians, than do other religious movements that are much larger or whose histories are much longer. Nevertheless, given these constraints and others (including ecclesiastical pressures sometimes brought to bear by the LDS Church), Mormon studies scholars have produced a substantial and sophisticated body of scholarship that is increasingly recognized and cited by their peers outside the subfield. This is most evident in the field of American religious history, where the extant literature on Mormonism certainly lags behind the scholarship on white Protestantism (particularly evangelicalism), Catholicism, and African American religion in terms of depth and richness, but arguably exceeds what is available on any other religious minority group. It should be noted that Mormon studies scholarship has had by far its greatest impact on other scholars interested in religion, especially in the fields of history, religious studies, and sociology. The impact of even the best of the Mormon studies canon has been far more attenuated in nonreligious fields, such as political science, women's studies, or even general American history. One suspects this is both because Mormon studies scholarship has not oriented itself toward those areas (American history being the primary exception), and because Mormonism's limited size and scope mean that its historical and cultural influence have been similarly circumscribed.

Despite its remarkable accomplishments in a relatively short time, Mormon studies still has considerable room to grow and expand. The essays in this volume are designed to build on the contributions of previous scholars in order to gesture toward and suggest possible directions for the next generation of Mormon studies scholarship. The volume captures this particular moment by bringing together a few of the most influential voices of Mormon studies, including those who have been working in the area for decades and others who are newly making their mark in the field. The intent of this collection is not to provide a complete survey of the field, nor to recapitulate research agendas that have dominated the literature in recent decades. Rather, this volume is designed to chart out a few key areas and modes of inquiry that will shape Mormon studies as it continues to mature.

Specifically, this collection begins by addressing three broad areas that scholars agree have received relatively limited treatment in the extant literature but which represent the leading edge of Mormon studies in this century: a (re)assessment of Mormonism in the twentieth century; the dynamic interplay of Mormonism's historical, cultural, and religious roots in the United States with its international expansion and encounter with global diversity; and how Mormonism, as a modern religious and cultural phenomenon, has shaped and been shaped by modern theories and discourses of race. To these themes the volume adds essays addressing two other areas that have not received sufficient attention: more intentional reflections on theory and method in Mormon studies, including a consideration of the utility of social scientific approaches; and new ways of thinking about the individual Mormon subject, including an analysis of autobiographies and memoirs not just as historical sources but as literary creations.

As indicated, Mormon studies in the twenty-first century is increasingly, and appropriately, an interdisciplinary enterprise. Accordingly, the authors who have contributed to this volume bring to bear a range of disciplinary expertise. In addition to American historians (always well represented in Mormon studies), the authors herein hail from religious studies, economics, literature, sociology, linguistics, and anthropology. Important disciplines such as ethics, theology, political science, and philosophy are not represented here, but this was done less out of a desire to exclude than because of the limits of space. In addition to disciplinary expansiveness, to reach its potential Mormon studies must be further enriched by the voices of scholars from around the globe who provide different perspectives than their American counterparts. To that end, this volume includes essays by three non-Americans, offering their expertise on Mormonism in East Asia, sub-Saharan Africa, and Europe. A decision also made for the sake of coherence was that this collection would narrow its focus of study to the Church of Jesus Christ of Latter-day Saints; other scholars will continue to research the diversity of other institutional expressions of Mormonism, including the Community of Christ and various fundamentalist groups.

Part I contains two essays that offer new vistas and reinterpretations of twentieth-century Mormonism. One of the most significant transformations in the twentieth-century LDS Church came about with the priesthood correlation movement, which many scholars have identified (and generally lamented) as a conservative or even fundamentalist retrenchment among the church's mid-century leadership. Matthew Bowman complicates this narrative by locating the roots of LDS correlation in the early twentieth-century progressive movement, which combined a kind of moral perfectionism and faith in human progress with reliance on technical expertise and bureaucratic organizational methods. In Bowman's account, the purpose of correlation was not to stifle spirituality but to enhance it. Proponents of correlation considered it to be the perfection of an ancient patriarchal order; in their minds, correlation thus constituted the fulfillment of Joseph Smith's restoration rather than a betrayal of it.

Jan Shipps traces the development of Mormonism in the early to mid-twentieth century by showing how the concept of Mormon ethnicity became less literal as a result of an increased number of conversions. Nevertheless, ethnicity continued to play an important part in the construction and maintenance of Mormon identity, ultimately taking the form of peoplehood, a concept that Mormons could readily access whether they were blood descendants of pioneers or first-generation converts. The concept of the Mormon people thus became the twentieth-century equivalent of a Mormon ethnos, and provided a powerful shared identity for the LDS Church's increasingly diverse membership.

Part II turns a critical gaze toward the internationalization of Mormonism and the question of whether an American church can become a world religion. Shinji Takagi approaches the subject through a study of the LDS Church's mission in Japan in the first quarter of the twentieth century, generally deemed to be a dismal failure. As opposed to most of the literature on Mormon missionary endeavors that have taken a "supply-side" approach by focusing on the personality, work, and message of the missionaries, Takagi insists that Mormon missionary efforts must be understood from the perspective of the host culture, including a nuanced understanding of local, regional, and national dynamics. Takagi argues that Mormon missionaries' arrival in Japan in 1901 came at the worst possible moment, with the decline of Christian influence in the country and an upsurge of nationalism supported by Shinto and Buddhism. Through a careful study of local context, Takagi provides a helpful model for future studies of Mormon international missions.

Walter van Beek draws upon his long anthropological experience in western Africa to argue that the LDS Church will need to come to terms with real cultural variation if it wants to succeed internationally. The church has tried to adopt innocuous forms of "culture" (such as different foods) without actually taking seriously the diversity of cultures around the globe. Critically examining the official church discourse of a universal "gospel culture," van Beek documents the incongruity of "Deseret" culture with African cultural notions of job rotation, bride price (bridewealth), funeral feasts, polygyny, tribal identity and belonging, and religious inclusivity. Even supposed universals such as "family" and "family values" take on considerably different meanings in the context of various cultural formations. Van Beek provocatively asserts that Africa does life and Mormonism does eternity—and since culture is all about this life, Mormonism, in its present form, does not do culture.

Is Mormonism a world religion? Wilfried Decoo's essay sets the research agenda for future scholars interested in taking up this question, and many others related to the internationalizing of Mormonism. Like van Beek, Decoo emphasizes the American particularities of the contemporary LDS Church, and interrogates the utility of the concept of "gospel culture," arguing instead for the importance of local adaptations, accommodations, and enculturation. Echoing Takagi's call for more of a focus on local communities in the study of Mormon missions, Decoo calls upon researchers to consider the negative dimensions of Mormon proselytizing, particularly the effect on families and communities. Through a series of penetrating questions and insights, Decoo sets before us an ambitious research agenda for years to come.

Part III examines the role of racial theory and discourse in the shaping and contestation of Mormon identity. As an important category of sociocultural analysis in the late twentieth- and early twenty-first-century academy, race has not been neglected by Mormon scholars. However, for the most part the extant scholarship is concerned with race relations, namely how mostly white Euro-American Mormons thought about and treated non-whites, principally African Americans, Native Americans, and Latin Americans, but also Polynesians, Jews, and others. As valuable and even transformative as this scholarship has been, it has reified the notion that Mormonism and Mormons were and are normatively white. What happens, however, when we destabilize that notion?

American religious historian Quincy Newell suggests that we see Mormonism anew when we look *with*, rather than *at*, its non-white members. She uses the autobiography of Jane James, an early and prominent black Latter-day Saint, to reframe given narratives of nineteenth-century Mormon history and, more broadly, race and religion in America. Putting James at the center of the story decenters white ecclesiastical elites, displaces the temple as the spiritual nexus of Mormonism, disperses spiritual authority from the male priesthood, and disturbs official remembrances of the religion's founding prophet. Quincy demonstrates how James's life represents an alternative narrative about the locus and nature of charismatic spiritual power and religious authority in early Mormonism and nineteenth-century American religion.

At the same time that Mormons barred non-whites like Jane James from priesthood ordination and participation in sacred temple ordinances, historian Paul Reeve shows how many Americans argued that Mormons themselves failed to satisfy the demands of whiteness. Reeve traces Mormon upward mobility through their achievement of whiteness, from their being framed as not white enough in the late nineteenth century to too white during the 2012 presidential campaign. An analysis of late nineteenth- and early twentieth-century cultural discourse reveals that Mormon racial identity cannot be taken for granted, but rather is something to be interrogated, critically analyzed, and theorized. Not only does Reeve use whiteness theory to complicate Mormon studies, but he also demonstrates how religion complicates the extant whiteness literature, which has typically focused on categories of labor, immigration, and class.

Part IV features three essays reflecting explicitly on theory and method in Mormon studies. Whereas history has traditionally dominated the scholarship on Mormonism, Mormon studies is intentionally expansive and interdisciplinary in its approach. Two essays by social scientists demonstrate the usefulness of moving beyond, or at least supplementing, the dominant historical approach. Economist Michael McBride's essay is the first use of rational choice analysis (informed by game theory) to examine how authority works in Mormonism. Following a helpful introduction for nonspecialists, McBride examines the workings of authority in the cases of the transmission of authority and leadership through church callings, as well as challenges to and the enforcement of sartorial norms as seen through the episode of "Wear Pants to Church Day." Sociologists Gary Shepherd and Gordon Shepherd illustrate a different social scientific approach by reviewing the methods and findings from their statistical content analysis of LDS General Conference addresses and early patriarchal blessings. Their detailed examination of a particular case (Mormonism) allows them to make claims about more general phenomena, such as the relative effectiveness of "commitment mechanisms" in the success of new religious movements. Together, the essays by McBride and the

Shepherd brothers are richly suggestive of the possibilities of a more robust place for social scientists in Mormon studies.

Though they may be willing to share the stage, historians are not about to yield it entirely. In his meditation on the differences between historical and social scientific methods, historian Richard Bushman reports being caught somewhat off-guard by the intellectual assumptions of social scientists. The historian, he says, is concerned primarily with interpretation of human particularities, while the social scientist strives for the general theory. The two disciplines are not stranded on opposite sides of an unbridgeable chasm, however. Both learn from the insights of the other; historians, Bushman writes, are like "jackals" preying upon the theories of the social scientists when they are useful in making their interpretations. While each scholar will choose his or her own preferred intellectual approach, Bushman argues for methodological diversity and generosity within Mormon studies, all of which will foster greater intellectual expansiveness and creativity.

An area that neither historians nor social scientists have fully explored is the genre of Mormon autobiography and memoir, a genre that Levi Peterson and Jana Riess explore in Part V. Peterson focuses on the distinctive, even idiosyncratic, autobiography of Wayne Booth, who was raised as a Mormon but lapsed from church activity and even called himself an atheist as he went on to become one of the world's foremost literary critics. In his autobiography, Booth sought to find resolution among his many described "Selves," but Peterson questions whether Booth was as successful as he thought in arriving at this harmony. Booth's book does not fit within the established conventions of Mormon autobiography, which Peterson argues is precisely the point: it expands not only the boundaries of the genre but also our very conceptions of what it means for a person to be Mormon. Better capturing and understanding the internal pluralism of Mormonism will be one of the chief tasks of Mormon studies in the twenty-first century.

The diversity of the Mormon experience is a key theme in Jana Riess's examination of the role of memoir in the articulation and shaping of Mormon identity. She traces the distinctive Mormon penchant for record keeping to the belief that individual lives matter because they are part of God's workings in the world; diary keeping and memoir writing thus become testimonial acts of documenting God's dealings with his children. Surveying a number of Mormon memoirs from the nineteenth to the twenty-first centuries, by both female and male authors, Riess demonstrates how they typically serve one of three purposes: as propaganda, in which the memoirist has an agenda and gets the last word; as a vehicle to communicate ineffable spiritual experience, faithfully if incompletely; or to explore the tensions between faith-promoting experience and a more earthbound realism.

Mormon studies will no doubt grow in new and unexpected ways in the coming years and decades. This volume is a modest effort to help spur the field forward at the beginning of what proves to be a century of exciting intellectual discovery.

Notes

1. Robert B. Townsend, "A New Found Religion? The Field Surges among AHA Members," *Perspectives on History* (December 2009), online at http://www.historians.org/perspectives/issues/2009/0912/0912new3.cfm. For similar trends in sociology, see Armand L. Mauss and Stacy A. Hammons, "Attaining a 'Sophisticated Maturity': A Brief History of the *Journal for the Scientific Study of Religion*," *Journal for the Scientific Study of Religion* 39, no. 4 (December 2000): 449–73.
2. Fawn McKay Brodie, *No Man Knows My History: The Life of Joseph Smith, the Mormon Prophet* (New York: Knopf, 1945).
3. See Thomas F. O'Dea, *The Mormons* (Chicago: University of Chicago Press, 1957); Levi S. Peterson, *Juanita Brooks: Mormon Woman Historian* (Salt Lake City: University of Utah Press, 1996); Leonard J. Arrington, *Adventures of a Church Historian* (Urbana: University of Illinois Press, 1998).
4. Leonard J. Arrington, *Great Basin Kingdom: An Economic History of the Latter-day Saints, 1830–1900* (Cambridge: Harvard University Press, 1958). For an excellent overview of Mormon history and historians, including the New Mormon History, see Ronald W. Walker, David J. Whittaker, and James B. Allen, with a contribution by Armand Mauss, *Mormon History* (Urbana: University of Illinois Press, 2001). For a representative collection of essays, see D. Michael Quinn, ed., *The New Mormon History: Revisionist Essays on the Past* (Salt Lake City, UT: Signature Books, 1992).
5. For a broader discussion, see Peter Novick, *That Noble Dream: The "Objectivity Question" and the American Historical Profession* (New York: Cambridge University Press, 1988).
6. Jan Shipps, *Mormonism: The Story of a New Religious Tradition* (Urbana: University of Illinois Press, 1985).
7. At the time of this writing, the University of Southern California had also announced plans to establish the John A. Widtsoe Chair in Mormon Studies.

Part I | Reassessing Twentieth-Century Mormonism

Chapter 1 | Zion

The Progressive Roots of Mormon Correlation

Matthew Bowman

The project called "priesthood correlation" during its time and simply "correlation" by the 1980s was a structural reorganization of the Church of Jesus Christ of Latter-day Saints, designed to streamline lines of authority, systematize curriculum, and gather administrative power within the Quorum of the Twelve Apostles. Its beginnings are normally dated to 1961, when the apostle Harold B. Lee established the All-Church Coordinating Council to develop and initiate the reforms, which were largely complete by the mid-1970s. However, correlation was more than simply a bureaucratic accomplishment: it had a profound theological and cultural impact on American Mormonism as well.

Though Lee completed the task, the first attempts at correlation dated to the presidency of Joseph F. Smith (1901–1918). This was no mistake: Smith initiated the program for reasons both organizational and theological. It fell to him to clean up the debris from the end of plural marriage: the collapse not merely of a social structure, but a soteriology. The growing seriousness with which the Mormon leadership suppressed further plural marriages derived not only from the process of extracting plural marriage from Mormon institutions and practices, but also from their dawning awareness that the religion itself would now require restructuring in both form and aim. To extract polygamy was to remove much of how Mormons imagined their relationship with the afterlife. Correlation, broadly defined, came to replace plural marriage as the animating force of the Mormon quest for salvation: the structure through which they imagined what gaining heaven looked like.

By the time of Joseph F. Smith's administration, institutional Mormonism had grown large and unwieldy. By 1880, the five auxiliaries of the church—the children's Primary, the Sunday School, the Relief Society, and the Young Men's and Young Women's Mutual Improvement Associations—were established on a churchwide level, and for the next generation each vigorously pursued similar agendas but more or less neglected to coordinate. That state of affairs drove Smith in 1908 to organize a General

Priesthood Committee on Outlines and in 1912 to organize a Correlation Committee, both chaired by David O. McKay. The first committee coordinated curriculum only among priesthood quorums, while the second committee was supposed to coordinate curriculum among all the auxiliaries, but failed to implement lasting changes.[1]

That failure troubled McKay and Smith existentially, because they understood the task before them to be sacred, even salvific. It was not merely procedural, not merely about eliminating waste and defining lines of authority, but affected the ways Mormons related to God. In 1921 the next attempt, called the "Correlation–Social Advisory Committee," chaired by the apostle Stephen L. Richards and including representatives from each of the church auxiliaries, sent their report to the First Presidency. They recommended a number of prosaic alterations: the teaching prerogative in the church should be consolidated in the Sunday Schools; the organizations for young people should have more readily defined tasks; the Priesthood should be given definite authority over worship services; social and music committees should be eliminated. However, the committee made these recommendations with this interesting caveat: "These organizations were at their inception, given to the Church through inspiration to its leaders, that to the extent that their original purposes and functions may be discovered, these institutions should be so administered as to subserve the original purposes of their organization."[2] This is not the language of bureaucratic reform; this is the language of religious primitivism, a hint of Mormon restorationism applied to committee work.

This language was appropriate because the Mormons understood the process of reorganizing their church to be basically soteriological. This is because after the end of plural marriage Mormons began to think about the process of salvation less in the dynastic, kingdom language of the nineteenth century and, increasingly, in terms of the cultivation of personal character, moral improvement, and self-discipline. If plural marriages were the route through which dynastic salvation could occur, the social institution of the church became the facilitator of personal salvation.[3] The great theologians of polygamy—John Taylor, Orson Pratt, Brigham Young, Orson Spencer—constructed a heaven of interlocking households, parallel kingdoms made up of great networks of patriarchs ruling over kingdoms whose respective glory depended upon the size of their progeny. As the great advocate of polygamy Orson Spencer argued, "The family order which God established with Abraham and the Patriarchs, was the order observed among celestial beings in the celestial world. . . . It is of perpetual duration." Plural marriage, in short, created the most powerful imagery of what salvation was, placing Mormons into covenantal relationships that they believed would allow them to find exaltation in the hereafter. It drove them to seek separation from the mundane socialities of America, to replace them with a new society laid down along God-indicated lines.[4]

This was all faintly dynastic, even medieval—and certainly was predicated on a premodern, static understanding of the individual. Salvation depended upon entering into the correct relationships and living worthily of them, rather like a nobleman might seek the best marriage for his daughter. The end of plural marriage wrecked those attempts. Historians like Kathleen Flake have pointed out that the end of polygamy caused the Mormons to look back even further, to the rudiments of Mormonism as propounded by Joseph Smith, in order to reinvent their religion.[5] To many Mormon thinkers, what remained was the sheer optimism of Joseph Smith's theology, its grand narrative about human progress and potential. Joseph Smith had emphasized that God and humanity were far closer in nature than traditional Christian orthodoxy supposed; over the course of his life he gradually came to define salvation less and less in terms of God's deliverance of humanity from bondage to hell and sin, and more and more in terms of the exaltation of human capacities and potential. As he said near the end of his life regarding human purpose: "You have got to learn how to make yourself God, kings, priests, &c., by going from a small to great capacity." That language presupposed two things: that humans could become gods, and that the process would come through learning.[6] But while earlier Mormons found the channel of this potential in the sacred network of relationships that Mormon ordinances could create, by the turn of the century Mormons rested their hopes in the cultivation of character.

The Mormons were not alone in this faith. This was the age that historians call the progressive era, an era dominated by educated middle-class American reformers, and it was afflicted with two great confidences: the first in human potential and the second in the capacity of well-designed and efficiently administered organizations to maximize that potential. As Eldon Eisenach has written, "Just as the new industrial economy integrated economic producers and consumers on a nationwide basis, so it created networks of social and psychological interdependence that had to be legitimated and directed."[7] The progressives were a curious combination of technocrats and apostles; they were fascinated with bureaucracy, policy, classifications, and notetaking, but they also believed that these new means and methods of organization modern American society demanded had moral ramifications. They were the first sociologists; the first Americans to systematically investigate what they believed to be the causes of poverty and success; the first to argue that the environment children were raised in might influence their decisions later in life. But at the same time they directed the ends of this rather dry policymaking toward the messianic goals of salvation, spiritual conversion, and moral transformation. They thought both in the private idiom of regeneration, healing, and renewal, and in the public language of scientific precision. These two ideas—trust in institutions and the need to reinvent the soul through education and training—were for the progressives deeply linked.[8]

These ideas penetrated American culture broadly and deeply, and it is interesting to note the ways differing progressive groups might embrace similar strategies and methods while fundamentally disagreeing with one another. For instance, we might call W. E. B. DuBois, the founder of the NAACP and one of the leading African American intellectuals of the century, a progressive (though a melancholy one). DuBois was consumed with the problem of racism, and yet in his masterwork *The Souls of Black Folk* he insisted that education—specifically, liberal arts education—would aid both African Americans and white Americans in overcoming it. Reform also featured a strong institutional dimension: DuBois organized the NAACP and championed legal confrontation of institutionalized segregation. But at the same time, Ben Tillman, the U.S. senator and governor of South Carolina, was also a progressive who championed institutionalized segregation on the grounds that African Americans required the firm hand of a technocratic state in order to progress culturally.[11]

Similarly, many progressive religious thinkers found Mormon doctrine absurd and abstruse, while Mormons like B. H. Roberts snorted at the liberalizing theology of the era. Nonetheless, the Mormons had no hesitation in using progressive language to articulate what their religion meant in a post-polygamy age, and borrowing progressive institutions in order to implement it. Roberts and his great intellectual compatriots John Widtsoe and James Talmage freely drew on progressive philosophy and scholarship, citing frequently progressive thinkers like Herbert Spencer and John Fiske to argue that character was achieved through overcoming odds, and all of humanity tended toward increased sophistication and complexity.[12]

For instance, Susa Young Gates, one of the early leaders of the church's organization for young women, the Young Women's Mutual Improvement Association, observed that the Young Women's organization reflected the demands of American society at the turn of the twentieth century. Given the "great underlying unrest and upheaval in all classes of society," she said, "the present age is the admitted women's age," which demands "as many progressive, intelligent, and capable women as can be found among the Latter day Saints." Thus, she said, the aim of her organization was the "shaping of strong, self-reliant, and original characters," which were best formed through participation in Mormonism itself. Mormonism was uniquely suited to the building of such character for two reasons: first, it was, to use her term, "unpopular," a state Gates embraced as a point of pride; and second, because Mormons "had been and constantly are pioneering," in the sense of building, organizing, and sustaining new communities.[13] "We believe it ignoble," one YWMIA declared in resolution, "to imitate those worthless and inconsistent habits acquired by the world." Instead they declared their goal to be "the cultivation of our immortal minds."[14] For Gates, religion was about training, growth, the shaping of character. Gates did not merely develop these ideas herself. She cited, gratefully, the guidance she received from other women's organizations, citing in particular her experience at the 1893 World's Congress of Representative Women, where she met a woman named May Sewell, a feminist and pioneer in women's education, whom Gates brought to Utah to discuss both the Young Women's organization and female political activism in 1894.[15] At about the same time, Amy Brown Lyman, who served on the Relief Society general board, met the settlement house pioneer Jane Addams in Chicago, and later borrowed much of the technique and theory she used there in implementing social service programs in the Relief Society and Young Women's organizations in Utah.[16]

The other auxiliaries embraced a similar understanding of their purpose and similarly drew on progressive theory and ideas. For instance, in 1898 the General Superintendency of the Deseret Sunday School Union (including the apostles George Q. Cannon and Joseph F. Smith) declared that "the great aim of Sunday School work is to insure right action . . . a desire to obey . . . doctrines and ordinances. In short, to make Latter-day Saints out of them."[17] For several years, in his capacity as superintendent of the Sunday School, George Reynolds attended the American Sunday School Annual Conventions, an innovation of the progressive era in which advocates of Sunday school for many denominations met to swap theory, techniques, and ideas, and which Reynolds drew from as he assembled the program.[18] The ASSAC drew upon the theory of progressive educators like John Dewey, which emphasized student initiative, classroom projects, and practical problem solving in order to cultivate students' ability to solve problems and moral dilemmas, all directed to the goal of moral formation, rather than the authoritative impartation of information upon passive students.[19] Just so, Reynolds instructed Mormon Sunday School teachers that "teaching is directing the self-activities of the student," because "the aim of the Sunday School teacher should be directed mainly to the implanting of religious truths by precept and example rather than merely teaching theological facts for the knowledge of facts alone will not make a child religious."[20]

Mormons, in short, fully participated in the American progressive movement; they adapted progressive ideals in order to further particularly Mormon aims. The historian Alan Brinkley has described how progressivism's distinctive fusion of moral idealism and faith in bureaucracy faded in the strain of the Great Depression. But Mormonism carried that particular fusion forward, and the correlation movement was the fullest expression of a distinctive Mormon version of American progressivism. In short, to the extent that Mormonism wed its optimism about human potential to faith that such potential could be maximized through training, education, and bureaucracy, Mormonism continues to embrace the progressive philosophy of the early twentieth century.

I want to make a few qualifications before I proceed.

First, the most common objection to this assertion is theological. That is, as this objection goes, progressive-era Mormon theologians (most particularly, the apostle James E. Talmage, the Seventy B. H. Roberts, and the apostle John A. Widtsoe) were theologically "liberal" in some sense, while the prominent theologians of the era of correlation in the second half of the twentieth century were staunchly conservative—the most prominent being Joseph Fielding Smith, longtime president of the Quorum of the Twelve and briefly president of the church, and his son-in-law, Bruce R. McConkie, who served as an apostle from 1972 until his death in 1985. This argument is true in a limited sense, but placing too much weight upon it overstates the difference between the two groups. First, it is important to note precisely how "conservative" even the progressive theologians were. Roberts publicly disdained the views of prominent liberal Protestant contemporaries such as Henry Ward Beecher, who proposed that at least some of the miracles recorded in the Bible were best understood as metaphors.[21] Talmage, Roberts's friend and sometime theological ally, entirely ignored most contemporary biblical scholarship when he wrote his life of Christ, relying instead on traditionalist works premised on the notion that the gospels could be harmonized. Though Bruce R. McConkie is often considered far more theologically conservative than Talmage, he had nothing but praise for Talmage's work when he wrote his own biography of Jesus.[22] None of these men differed appreciably on their basic assumptions that scriptural narratives were to be taken as factual, that Jesus Christ was born of a virgin, was literally resurrected in the flesh, performed the miracles ascribed to him, and so on. All of these things made the Mormons in total a fairly conservative theological bunch. On the spectrum of twentieth-century American theology, the Mormons crowded the right.

The primary difference between progressive-era Mormon theologians and their midcentury descendants was their respective openness to intellectual work produced by non-Mormons. Roberts and Widtsoe happily read and tried to assimilate the vast spectrum of human knowledge—a decidedly progressive impulse. As Roberts once said, "It is a pleasure to find one's conclusions sustained by men of recognized ability in any line of work on which they have specialized."[23] McConkie and his fellows, on the other hand, were suspicious of everything but the works of Mormon canon and the teaching of Mormon leaders.[24] The primary disjuncture between early and mid-twentieth-century LDS leaders was a difference of process rather than content—but even there, similarities abounded.

Fundamentally, all of these church leaders, from Roberts through McConkie, held to the basic notions of progressive Mormonism as I have outlined them: they embraced an optimistic view of human nature and rejected absolutely the concept of original sin, but described this potential in terms of cultivation and education of character, emphasizing that it was best achieved through cooperation in institutions. Similarly, they adopted the evolutionary language many progressives adapted from Darwinism through social thinkers like Herbert Spencer and John Fiske, emphasizing the progress of the human character in terms of natural selection, struggle against obstacle, and expanding one's capacities. "Undoubtedly true evolution is true, meaning progress from the lower to the higher, from the simple to the more complex," James Talmage wrote.[25] The language here closely mirrored Spencer, who argued in the late nineteenth century that the principle of evolution held as true for societies and individuals as it did for species and biology: the natural tendency of living things as for species was toward greater complexity, growth, and progress.[26]

Similarly, they emphasized the importance of institutions in fostering that growth by providing opportunities to expand capacities, gain education, and properly direct individuals. Progressives placed great stock in schools, in social work, and in settlement houses; similarly, Mormons in the early twentieth century came to emphasize the importance of regular and routine participation in an ever-expanding church. As John Widtsoe emphasized, "A Church which separates itself from the actual, daily life of man . . . will enable a man or his fellows to test his progress and spiritual condition, which in turn will be his guide for future work."[27]

The second qualification to my argument is that as the twentieth century progressed, the progressive movement itself evolved, and Mormon progressivism to some extent followed that evolution. The traumas of the decades between 1910 and 1940 sharply dampened progressives' optimism. After the First World War, the leaders of progressivism talked less about an America made into a moral middle-class utopia and more and more about the necessary pluralism of American society; less and less about instilling moral virtue and more and more about how to simply manage a nation of such diversity. By 1927 the confidence of the journalist and progressive thinker Walter Lippmann's 1914 book *Drift and Mastery* had given way to *The Phantom Public*, a title that intimated Lippmann's exhaustion. In the former book, Lippmann confidently proposed that bureaucratic reform rightly applied could solve America's social problems. In the latter book Lippmann posited that Americans could "no longer expect to find a unity which absorbs diversity," and instead must settle for "an accommodation of purposes." America, Lippmann wrote, was a nation of "deep pluralism," and the perfect unity progressives dreamed of was impossible.[28] Similarly, during the Great Depression progressives in the Roosevelt administration gradually surrendered the notion that managerial competence could utterly restructure the American economy in order to ensure full employment—the dream of New Dealers like Rexford Tugwell—and instead settled for incremental crisis management. As one Democratic congressman said in 1937, "We have pulled all the rabbits out of the hat and now there are no more rabbits."[29] After World War II, the unbounded confidence in administration that had seemed so appealing two or three decades before now uncomfortably resembled Soviet central planning.

The organizational faith of progressivism thus gradually began to wane after World War I—at least in politics. However, one place where it survived was in American business. Beginning in the 1920s celebrations of American industry commonly saw the bureaucratic and organizational acumen of businessmen as a sign of moral depth of character; Bruce Barton's famous 1925 *The Man Nobody Knows*, which credited Jesus with being "the founder of modern business," is perhaps the best example.[30] Thus, it was only natural for the Mormons to turn to American business for a model. Indeed, when the 1960s church leaders began to institute correlation in earnest, the Quorum of the Twelve hired two consulting firms to help reorganize the church's administration and public relations in the correlation period. Much of what emerged from the process resembled a corporation: a set of committees was erected, regular lines of authority were established, quantitative measures were instituted, and so on.[31]

In 1960, David O. McKay, now president of the church, asked the apostle Harold B. Lee to head the All-Church Coordinating Council to "correlate the courses of study given by the quorums and auxiliaries of the church." Lee was determined this council would not fail like its predecessors. Moreover, Lee took his mandate to be much more expansive than this somewhat modest charge. Over the course of the next decade he began coordinating the curriculum and gradually brought the various auxiliaries of the church under the supervision of the Quorum of the Twelve Apostles, consolidating their once-independent budgets, leadership, and publishing efforts into a unified effort directed by the priesthood quorums. As Lee said as early as 1962, in a meeting of the All-Church Coordinating Council, his goal was "to get the priesthood fully defined and work out the scope of its program . . . [to] bring the priesthood back to where it should be, according to revelations, and then determine the relationship of the auxiliaries to the priesthood."[32] Lee was certain from the beginning that the priesthood had drifted from the center of Mormonism, and he was committed to returning it to that center, because he believed so doing would refocus the salvific character of the church. In early 1963 he told the auxiliary heads that they had three mandates: "(1) simplify the program, (2) stress the priesthood, (3) stress the home."[33]

A number of contemporary observers have critiqued the correlation movement for being, essentially, too secular. One critic has argued that an organic sense of Mormon peoplehood "has died already through a Correlation program," to be replaced with an arid bureaucracy.[34] Even Paul Dunn, formerly of the Quorum of the Seventy, worried that "correlation, like the Supreme Court, is becoming more and more the originator of thought rather than the coordinator of thought."[35] Many liberal Mormons tend to use terms like "uncorrelated" and "pre-correlated" to indicate their sympathies lie with the presumably free-wheeling and romanticized Mormonism that existed before the movement took hold, and the assumption is often that the "original" Mormonism was more "authentic" or "spiritual" than the Mormonism that emerged on the far side of the 1960s. One such critic claims to hold to an "an open, optimistic, pre-correlation world view."[36] Another blasts "today's constrained, correlated approach to religious thought [with] incessant admonitions to be obedient to authority."[37] The implication here is that true spirituality—true Mormonism—is incompatible with the regularized administration correlation created. This is characteristic of post-progressive America: a nation in which individual expression and institutional allegiance have come to seem incompatible. We see this particularly in the post-sixties era, what the sociologist Robert Bellah has called the age of Sheila, after a 1980s nurse who was one of the first to coin the phrase "spiritual, but not religious."[38]

But correlation's organizers believed that their task was nothing if not spiritual, because their progressive ethos taught them that rather than smothering it, organization might facilitate the purest flowering of one's spiritual potential. By the middle of the twentieth century the church leaders who drove forward the correlation program conceived of their task in cosmic, sanctifying, religious terms. We can think of this in two ways. First, the Mormon leaders who built it understood correlation to be another step in the restorationist work they traced back to Joseph Smith. Correlation seen this way was not a modern innovation, but rather the restoration of a scriptural, sacred order of things. It was not bureaucratic procedure; it was as holy as Joseph Smith's creation of priesthood councils, and the logical end of his work. As a result, the second way correlation was a religious phenomenon is that its processes were considered salvific. This may seem counterintuitive in light of the aforementioned critiques of the spiritual aridity of a bureaucratized church. But the people who built correlation intimately bound the institutional structures they created to the processes of perfecting the human soul and completing the journey from premortality to divine exaltation. If exaltation came through building character, correlation was the mechanism through which a particularly Mormon character was formed.

How was correlation a form of restoration? In 1971 the Brigham Young University professor of religion Hyrum Andrus produced a lesson manual called "Priesthood Correlation: The Lord's Battle Plan," which contained a timeline entitled "The 7000 Years," stretching from Adam to the Millennium. Marked on this timeline are three "Zions": the first belonged to Enoch (as recorded in Moses 7 of the Pearl of Great Price); the second occurred in the Book of Mormon (4 Nephi); the third was designated as "Priesthood Correlation Today," with references to various sections of the

Doctrine and Covenants (38–42 and 101–5) pertaining to the modern establishment of the church. Each of the three Zions was characterized as "One Heart, One Mind, Dwell In Righteousness, No Poor." However, Andrus's timeline also indicated progress from Adam to the millennial Zion. Each Zion sought to fulfill commandments given to Adam: "multiply," "industry," "prayer," "obey," and so on. Andrus drew on references in the Doctrine and Covenants to indicate how the Zion of correlation would accomplish these things: the Mormons would be "taught more perfectly," they would "know duty," they would be "sanctified," and hence they would "become very great." While earlier Zions sought to perfect "the individual," correlation's Zion would perfect "the group."[39] The lesson accompanying this chart emphasized "counterparts" between early Zions and correlation, emphasizing the individual nature of the former and the group focus of the latter. While Adam was commanded to eat bread by the sweat of his brow, the modern church has a welfare program; while Adam taught his children, the modern church has "missionary and home and visiting teaching"; while Adam called upon God, the modern church teaches family prayer, and so on. The emphasis of the lesson is outlined in the beginning: "In each dispensation, the Lord has revealed a plan designed to make his people a 'kingdom of priests, and a holy nation' (Exodus 19:5–6). . . . The Correlation Program is not a man-made program, but a divinely revealed plan designed to augment the building of Zion and prepare a people for the coming of Christ."[40] The lesson emphasizes the connection between priesthood correlation and spiritual accomplishment, summarized in a rhetorical question: "Do you know the reason why the City of Enoch was translated? It was because they had the correlation program of the priesthood."[41]

Claiming that correlation was not a contemporary reform effort, but the restoration of a sacred, divinely inspired order of things was common as the new procedures went into effect. Various Mormon leaders traced its roots to Joseph Smith, or, as Andrus had, even further back to the world of scripture. The apostle Marion G. Romney observed that, based on Lee's reforms, "home teaching is moving the way the Lord presented it to Joseph Smith before the Church was organized."[42] Jerry Rose, a student of Andrus's, described the bureaucratic reform of the early Mormon leaders Brigham Young and Lorenzo Snow as attempts at "correlating the priesthood of the church."[43] Dale Mouritsen, a director in the Church Educational System who worked for Lee during the process of correlation, later wrote several books about the reforms. Like Andrus, he declared the biblical city of Enoch to be the prototype for modern correlation. After describing Enoch's city, he wrote, "Zion then is to be eventually established in the present dispensation. The agency through which this is to be accomplished is Priesthood Correlation." Mouritsen claimed that correlation was a priestly program that required certain apostolic keys returned to the earth when "the prophet Joseph Smith was given the charge of establishing Zion."[44]

Correlation's framers repeatedly emphasized that it was a priestly effort, part of the restoration of the biblical priesthood Joseph Smith claimed to have accomplished. Correlation was often described to the church as "priesthood correlation," emphasizing its ritual and sacred implications, as opposed to, say, its procedural functions. As Theodore Tuttle, a member of the Quorum of the Seventy, told an audience at BYU in 1973, "it is not a program—it is not a system, and it is not a procedure. It is an *emphasis* on the priesthood."[45] Harold B. Lee claimed in a General Conference of the church, "My mind has been filled with the realization that in 1964, and the year just preceding, we have been receiving as pertinent and important divine direction as has ever been given to the Church in any similar period of its history through the prophet and leader who now presides as the president of the church. You may recognize it in some of the developments we know as the correlation program."[46] Marion G. Romney—and many other leaders—lent correlation prophetic significance, pointing to statements by church presidents including Joseph F. Smith, who pronounced, "We expect to see the day when every council of the priesthood . . . will understand its duty, will assume its own responsibility, will magnify its calling." Romney claimed that correlation demonstrated the fulfillment of this prophecy and indicated it was one element that demonstrated the winding up of God's work on earth.[47]

This restorationist interpretation of correlation accomplished two things. First, all such priestly language perhaps inevitably lent itself to a patriarchal impulse, because the Mormon priesthood remained restricted to men. Indeed, manuals and leaders routinely invoked that biblical word to describe the nature of the Zion society that correlation would build. Dale Mouritsen speculated that "the whole tone of Priesthood Correlation seems to be the establishment of the divine Patriarchal Order."[48] Jerry Rose concurred, arguing that correlation was designed to organize the church in the following way: "The pipeline of authority was from the individual up through the head of the home, to the home teacher, to the priesthood leader, to the bishop, to the stake president, to the quorum of the Twelve, to the Prophet, and to Christ."[49]

Correlation sought both to integrate the home into priesthood bureaucracy and to establish patriarchal leadership in the home. The church's new (and correlated) magazine for adults, the *Ensign*, carried articles recommending "better correlated family affairs," and encouraging families to take advantage of "the resources and ideas developed through the priesthood correlation program of the Church," including a yearly time capsule buried in the backyard encouraging children to make weekly goals and report to their parents on their completion. One family described in the article affirmed the new *Family Home Evening Manual*'s claim that "fathers may receive guidance [from God] for their family problems as well as in their work," and urged families to follow their example when they "asked for help" from church institutions.[50] The implication was clear: families should see themselves as part of a chain of priesthood authority, and fathers served as the link. Harold B. Lee stated that correlation existed to "strengthen . . . a well-ordered home. If parental leadership is weak, the priesthood home teachers and auxiliaries must give the necessary guidance . . . aiding fathers who hold the holy priesthood in assuming their proper role as the heads of their households."[51] James A. Cullimore of the Quorum of the Seventy said in General Conference in October 1972 that "each family in the Church is really a kingdom or government within itself. The father, by virtue of the priesthood of God that has been bestowed upon him, is the head of that government. This is what constitutes patriarchal office in the family."[52]

The patriarchal, restorationist cast of correlation's language may go a long way toward explaining the marginalization that correlation inflicted upon women's auxiliaries like the Relief Society. Bruce R. McConkie claimed in his book *The Ten Commandments of Priesthood Correlation*, "If attempts are made to transmit the power of the gospel through auxiliary circuits or fringe committees appointed for specific purposes, the Lord's people are denied the blessings that a perfect organization perfectly operated would bring."[53] The auxiliaries were useful only insofar as they were brought under the umbrella of priesthood authority, which was a more sacred, and therefore more perfect, organizational structure than mere human institutions which McConkie deemed the auxiliaries to be. In December 1963 Harold B. Lee's secretary noted that, "Auxiliary leaders [were] advised to observe priesthood line of authority."[54] Describing the importance of the chain of priesthood command from the head of the household to Jesus Christ, Rose stated that "anyone not in that pipeline of authority was an auxiliary to assist the priesthood."[55]

In addition to its patriarchal overtones, the restorationist impulse within correlation bore a strong imprint of mid-twentieth-century Mormon dispensationalism and apocalypticism. In standard millenarian tones, Mouritsen predicted "the collapse of the family, political decay, fiscal irresponsibility and general moral disintegration." However, he promised, "Stability will be maintained in the Rocky Mountains for a time and righteous and honorable men will flee thereunto. . . . There will be an even greater need for religious and moral fortitude on the part of the church members. A mature program of Priesthood Correlation will provide that fortitude." Eventually righteous Mormons would flee back to Missouri where "they will erect a great Temple and commence the building of the City of New Jerusalem. . . . The part that Priesthood Correlation will play in this program will be highly significant."[56]

Though they rarely offered a narrative as detailed as Mouritsen's, higher ranked authorities involved in the correlation program as well as official materials echoed the young man's ideas. S. Dilworth Young of the Quorum of the Seventy declared that correlation would enhance the church's missionary efforts, which would in turn anticipate "the happy day that all men see the glory of the Son of God and witness the fulfillment of his word that the gospel should roll forth until it has filled all the earth."[57] Apostle Spencer W. Kimball declared that correlation was an answer to the question: "Can we turn back the tide and bring back decency and order out of chaos? The answer is yes—a positive, stentorian, yes."[58] The lesson manual "The Lord's Battle Plan" emphasized that "except for Enoch's society and a few other instances, the saints in all previous dispensations have failed to achieve the exalted purpose that the Lord has revealed to them for the establishment of a religious socio-economic system through a spiritually regenerated priesthood." This dispensation, however, would not fail, and correlation was designed to preserve it: "We read the story of Enoch and we think, isn't it marvelous that the great city was taken up out of the wickedness of this world! But brethren and sisters, the correlation program of the church will do exactly the same for you with the coming of Jesus Christ and will take you out of this world and the wicked will be destroyed. That is exactly what the correlation program is designed to do."[59]

The framers of correlation also believed that it would strengthen the spiritual lives of Mormons through regularizing the character-building processes of the church. This task took two forms: education and carefully defined opportunities for service. Both depended upon a progressive confidence that once humanity had been properly instructed in the correct modes of behavior it would be able to implement them. The key was proper instruction, and that is what the leaders of correlation feared had been lost in the church's overfocus upon its auxiliaries. Marion Romney described correlation as fundamentally an educational effort. In order to procure humanity's salvation, Romney said, "The Lord has established a very definite pattern which has been in operation since the beginning." This pattern had three steps: "The first step is divine revelation from God to man. The next step is the teaching of children by parents, and then God set up his kingdom in the earth—the organization of which is now the Church—and he put on the church some very specific instructions to teach the gospel. Now, that's all the priesthood has to do."[60]

For Romney, learning the gospel would allow one to obey the gospel, and obedience to the gospel could secure salvation. The notion of teaching the gospel was not new: however, the leaders of correlation emphasized that instruction in the tenets of the faith had to be done with properly designed manuals, by properly trained teachers, and in a properly supervised fashion to be really effective. This concern for expertise and regular procedure went back to the progressive period; in 1921, for instance, the

Correlation–Social Advisory Committee wrote of a "pronounced need in the Church for a well-organized, well-administered course of study which will be adequate to insure to the membership of the Church a comprehensive coherent conception of the fundamental principles of the gospel."[61] The committee then recommended that Mormons take advantage of Adam Bennion's *Fundamental Problems in the Teaching of Religion*, which invoked the work of Protestant progressive educators like Luther Wiegle, who had studied with John Dewey and William James.[62]

In 1964, in order to regularize and standardize the church's form of education, Lee spearheaded a "priesthood teacher training program," and the overhaul and revitalization of the most important programs priesthood teachers would be administering: Family Home Evening and Home Teaching. In October 1964 the council issued a manual for Family Home Evening, to "be placed in the hands of fathers, with a lesson for each week. There will be a weekly Melchizedek priesthood lesson and a monthly Relief Society lesson to support home instruction. Monthly suggestions are prepared for home teachers to encourage the program."[63] The next March, Lee approved a three-level system of education for the youth of the church and directed it be implemented the following year.[64] All of this training and curriculum was designed with one of the most important principles of progressive education in mind. John Dewey and other progressive educators had posited that children should be instructed differently at different ages, and that the older they got, the more their education should be placed in their own hands, in the form of implementation. As Antone Romney put it, "The gospel will be presented according to the level of each group, moving from the simple to the complex in such a way that the members of the Church will be motivated to understand it and apply it in their lives."[65]

This sort of implementation was reflected in the organization of home teaching, a visitation program that Lee's correlation committee systematized. In the manual for home teachers issued in 1963, Lee wrote that "home teaching is the instrument by which we see to it, through the Priesthood, that every program in the Church is made available to parents and their children."[66] The centrality of the home teaching program, in which Mormon men were assigned in pairs to visit the homes of members of their congregation, cannot be overstated.[67] As Lee stated elsewhere, "Home teaching isn't just one of the programs. . . . Home teachers could represent any or all of the organizations of the church when they visit their families. In the priesthood line of authority home teachers function or communicate as official representatives."[68] Home teaching connected the family to the church, effectively welding the two organizations, but it also functioned as a teaching institution, for those taught but also for the home teachers.

In one of the earliest meetings of Lee's committee, the secretary noted that "need of activities growing out of instructional program stressed."[69] Home teaching was one of these. Therefore in May 1964 manuals that systematized and regularized the church's programs for Missionary Work, Welfare, Genealogy, Family Home Evening, and Home Teaching itself were completed. Lee divided the work of the church into four areas: home teaching, missionary work, genealogy, and welfare, and made the "suggestion that functions of four priesthood committees be tied to the various quorums; i.e., home teaching is the responsibility of every quorum; missionary responsibility of seventies, genealogy responsibility of high priests, and welfare responsibility of elders."[70] Note again that the tasks here are delegated primarily to the priesthood quorums—but at the same time, part of the task of those quorums was making them available to the rest of the church.

The principles being taught required assessment and coordination, and home teaching was designed to do both. Lee directed that "organizations go into homes only as directed by the Home Teaching Program." Thus, home teachers were responsible for carrying new manuals for genealogy work, welfare work, curriculum, and so on into each home, and were also responsible for evaluating how each family was doing in the implementation of these new programs.[71] But at the same time, home teaching was designed to be a form of implemented education to those involved in it. One home-teaching manual declared that home teaching and visiting teaching (the equivalent program for Mormon women) would help those involved "to become better trained for a future role as a family patriarch or mother" and would provide opportunities for them to cultivate their own eternal progress: "Our skill as Home Teachers will be in direct proportion to our desire to be good home teachers. . . . Study, preparation, understanding, training and action are essential to all progress."[72] This slogan might be a good summary of the philosophy behind correlation more generally.

In May 1965 Lee responded to an apparently radical proposal for restructuring the church by saying that correlation "would be organized within the framework of the present priesthood and auxiliary organizations."[73] Though this view is technically correct, in retrospect correlation seems far more transformative than Lee's measured response seems to indicate. It is telling that Harold B. Lee, one of the principal architects of correlation, chose to frame it as an essentially conservative process. Indeed, correlation was basically conservative, in ways both pragmatic and ideological. It essentially institutionalized the progressive philosophy adopted by early twentieth-century leaders such as B. H. Roberts and John Widtsoe. Its emphasis on discipline, the cultivation of character, and strenuous effort directly mirrored the theology synthesized at the turn of the twentieth century. But correlation wed this practical ethos to a deeply

Mormon form of restorationist utopianism: the notion that Zion, long since lost to humanity, was achievable once more. These twin ideas of restorationism and perfectionism meant that correlation was much more than a conservative bureaucratic organization. It was that, to be sure, but it also brought about a cultural revolution whose impact on Mormonism has yet much to wane.

Notes

1. Thomas G. Alexander, *Mormonism in Transition: A History of the Latter-day Saints, 1880–1930* (Urbana: University of Illinois, 1985), 125–57; Gregory Prince and William Robert Wright, *David O. McKay and the Rise of Modern Mormonism* (Salt Lake City: University of Utah, 2005), 139–59; Michael Goodman, "Correlation: The Early Years," in David J. Whittaker and Arnold Garr, eds., *A Firm Foundation: Church Organization and Administration* (Salt Lake City: Deseret Book, 2011), 319–38.
2. "Report of the Correlation–Social Advisory Committee to the First Presidency and the Council of the Twelve on the Definition and Assignment of Auxiliary Functions and Organizations, April 12, 1921," Church History Library, Church of Jesus Christ of Latter-day Saints, Salt Lake City, Utah (hereafter referred to as Church History Library), 1. See also Thomas G. Alexander, "Between Revivalism and the Social Gospel: The Latter-day Saint Social Advisory Committee," *BYU Studies* 23 (Winter 1983): 19–39.
3. For this argument, see Matthew Bowman, *The Mormon People: The Making of an American Faith* (New York: Random House, 2012), 152–84.
4. Orson Spencer, *Letters*, 6th ed. (Liverpool: Budge, 1879), 192. For a great deal more on this theme, see also Spencer's *Patriarchal Order* (Liverpool: Richards, 1853). Discussions of polygamy that reflect this argument include Lawrence Foster, *Religion and Sexuality: The Shakers, the Mormons and the Oneida Community* (Urbana: University of Illinois, 1985), 123–77; and Todd Compton, *In Sacred Loneliness: The Plural Wives of Joseph Smith* (Salt Lake City: Signature Books, 1997), 1–25.
5. Kathleen Flake, *The Politics of American Religious Identity: The Seating of Senator Reed Smoot, Mormon Apostle* (Chapel Hill: University of North Carolina Press, 2004).
6. Andrew F. Ehat and Lyndon W. Cook, eds., *The Words of Joseph Smith* (Orem, UT: Grandin, 1991), 341; see alternative versions on 344 and 357.
7. Eldon J. Eisenach, *The Social and Political Thought of American Progressivism* (New York: Hackett, 1993), xiv; see also Glenda Gilmore, *Who Were the Progressives?* (New York: Bedford/St. Martin's, 1992).
8. My discussion of progressivism relies upon several recent secondary syntheses, particularly T. J. Jackson Lears, *Rebirth of a Nation: The Making of Modern America, 1877–1920* (New York: Harper, 2010); Michael McGerr, *A Fierce Discontent: The Rise and Fall of the Progressive Movement in America* (New York: Oxford University Press, 2005); Kevin Mattson, *Creating a Democratic Public: The Struggle for Urban Participatory Democracy during the Progressive Era* (University Park: Penn State University Press, 1997); and Leon Fink, *Progressive Intellectuals and the Dilemmas of Democratic Commitment* (Cambridge: Harvard University Press, 1999). I also draw on my own book *The*

Mormon People: The Making of an American Faith (New York: Random House, 2012), 152–184.

9. Robert A. Woods, *The City Wilderness* (Boston: Houghton Mifflin, 1898), 240.
10. Lester Frank Ward, *Pure Sociology* (New York: Macmillan, 1903), 251.
11. See W. E. B. DuBois, *The Souls of Black Folk* (Chicago: A. C. McClurg, 1903), 88–110. On Tillman, see Stephen Kantrowitz, *Ben Tillman and the Reconstruction of White Supremacy* (Chapel Hill: University of North Carolina Press, 2000), especially 80–110.
12. See Matthew Bowman, "Eternal Progression: Mormonism and American Progressivism," in Randall Balmer and Jana Riess, eds., *Mormonism and American Politics* (New York: Columbia University Press, 2015), 53–70.
13. Susa Young Gates, *History of the Young Ladies' Mutual Improvement Association* (Salt Lake City: Deseret News, 1911), 59.
14. Ibid., 62.
15. Paul Peterson, "Modern Lysistratas: Mormon Women in the International Peace Movement, 1899–1939," *Journal of Mormon History* 15, no. 1 (1989): 59–89.
16. David Hall, "Anxiously Engaged: Amy Brown Lyman and Relief Society Work, 1917–1945," *Journal of Mormon History* 27 (Summer 1994): 73–91; David Hall, "From Home Service to Social Service: Amy Brown Lyman and the Development of Social Work in the LDS Church," *Mormon Historical Studies* 8, no. 2 (Fall 2008): 67–88.
17. *Latter-day Saints Sunday School Treatise* (Salt Lake City: Deseret Sunday School Union, 1898), 13.
18. George B. Reynolds, *Latter-day Saints' Sunday School Treatise* (Salt Lake City, George Q. Cannon & Sons, 1898), 13–14; Alexander, *Mormonism in Transition*, 137.
19. The most important of Dewey's works here is John Dewey, *Democracy and Education* (New York: Macmillan, 1916), and his later *Experience and Education* (New York: Macmillan, 1938). See also Robert Westbrook, *John Dewey and American Democracy* (Ithaca: Cornell University Press, 1991), 150–95; and Heather Warren, "Character, Public Schooling, and Religious Education," *Church History* 7, no. 1 (Winter 1997): 61–80.
20. Reynolds, *Sunday School Treatise*, 15.
21. Roberts's dismissal of Beecher is in *The Gospel*, 3rd ed. (Salt Lake City: Deseret News, 1901), 271. On Beecher's place in liberal theology, see William Hutchison, *The Modernist Impulse in American Protestantism* (Cambridge, MA: Harvard University Press, 1975), 41–76.
22. Malcolm Thorp, "James Talmage and the Tradition of Victorian Lives of Jesus," *Sunstone* 63 (January 1988): 8–13; Bruce R. McConkie, *The Mortal Messiah* (Salt Lake City: Deseret Book, 1990), 1:xviii. See also Philip L. Barlow, *Mormons and the Bible: The Place of the Latter-day Saints in American Religion* (New York: Oxford University Press, 1991), 112–62.
23. B. H. Roberts, *Defense of the Faith and of the Saints* (Salt Lake City: Deseret Book, 1907), 45.
24. For McConkie's scale of scriptural authority, on which the Bible and Mormon scripture shared the top ranking with the writings of Joseph Smith and select other General Authorities, see McConkie, *Doctrinal New Testament Commentary* (Salt Lake City: Bookcraft, 1966), 1:56–59; Philip Barlow, *Mormons and the Bible: The Place of the*

Latter-day Saints in American Religion, rev ed. (New York: Oxford University Press, 2013), 207–16.

25. James E. Talmage to F. C. Williamson, April 22, 1933, James E. Talmage Papers, Church History Library.
26. Robert Perrin, "Hebert Spencer's Four Theories of Social Evolution," *American Journal of Sociology* 81, no. 6 (May 1976): 1339–59; see also Mark Francis, *Herbert Spencer and the Invention of Modern Life* (Ithaca: Cornell University Press, 2007), 247–61.
27. John A. Widtsoe, *A Rational Theology* (Salt Lake City: Deseret Book, 1915), 87. My argument here and throughout shares certain conclusions with Daymon Mickel Smith, "The First Shall Be Last and the Last Shall Be First, Discourse and Mormon History" (PhD dissertation, University of Pennsylvania, 2007), but differs in our method. Both Smith and I agree that correlation imposed a sort of millennial standardization on the LDS Church; Smith, however, argues that the trauma of the end of polygamy forced the church to cling to the abstraction of correlation's standardized discourse. I emphasize much more Mormonism's engagement with American culture in the progressive era, and give more weight to correlation's emphasis on behavior than does Smith.
28. Walter Lippmann, *The Phantom Public* (New York: MacMillan, 2009 [1927]), 87–88.
29. Cited in Alan Brinkley, *The End of Reform: New Deal Liberalism in Depression and War* (New York: Random House, 1995), 22.
30. Bruce Barton, *The Man Nobody Knows: A Discovery of the Real Jesus* (New York: Bobbs-Merrill, 1925).
31. On Lee's consultation, see Peter Wiley, "The Lee Revolution and the Rise of Correlation," *Sunstone* 4 (1984): 18–22.
32. "Correlation Chronology as reflected in the minutes of Correlation Executive Committee Meetings," Church History Library, 3. On the emergence of this new organizational structure, see Kendall O. Price and Kent Lloyd, "New Approaches to Church Executive Leadership," *Dialogue: A Journal of Mormon Thought* 2, no. 4 (Winter 1967): 41–49; and David J. Whittaker, "Mormon Administrative and Organizational History," in Whittaker and Garr, eds., *A Firm Foundation*, 611–95.
33. "Correlation Chronology," 4.
34. D. Michael Quinn, "Plural Marriage and Mormon Fundamentalism," in Martin E. Marty and R. Scott Appleby, eds., *Fundamentalisms and Society* (Chicago: University of Chicago, 1996), 277.
35. Cited in Prince and Wright, *David O. McKay and the Rise of Modern Mormonism*, 158.
36. Frances Menlove, "A Forty Year View: *Dialogue* and the Sober Lessons of History," *Dialogue: A Journal of Mormon Thought* 39, no. 3 (Fall 2006): 79.
37. Nadine Hansen, "The Garden of my Faith," *Sunstone* 133 (July 2004): 24. See also John Charles Duffy and Hugo Oliaz, "Correlated Praise: The Development of the Spanish Hymnal," *Dialogue: A Journal of Mormon Thought* 35, no. 2 (Summer 2002): 87–113; Elbert Peck, "Engaging Students in the Church's Foyer," *Sunstone* 65, no. 5 (May 1988): 5.
38. Robert Bellah et al., *Habits of the Heart: Individualism and Commitment in American Life* (Berkeley: University of California Press, 2008), 221–22.
39. [Hyrum Andrus], "Priesthood Correlation: The Lord's Battle Plan" (Provo: Fourth Stake, 1971), 1–2. Andrus is identified as the author by his student, Jerry A. Rose,

"The Correlation Program of the Church of Jesus Christ of Latter-day Saints" (M.A. thesis, Brigham Young University, 1972), 106.

40. Andrus, "Lord's Battle Plan," 2.
41. Ibid., 3.
42. *Deseret News* (December 11, 1971), 3. Cited in Rose, "Correlation Program," 2.
43. Rose, "Correlation Program," 3.
44. Dale Mouritsen, "The Historical and Prophetic Significance of Priesthood Correlation," (M.A. thesis, Brigham Young University, 1967), 8, 3.
45. Theodore Tuttle, "A New Emphasis on Priesthood," in *BYU Speeches of the Year* (Provo, UT: Brigham Young University Press, 1973), 42.
46. Harold B. Lee, "Search Diligently, Pray Always, and Be Believing," *Report of the 134th Semi-Annual Conference of the Church of Jesus Christ of Latter-day Saints*, October 1964, 137.
47. Marion G. Romney, "What Is Correlation?," in Antone Romney, "Selective Quotes of the Brethren Relative to Curriculum and Correlation," Church History Library, 2.
48. Mouritsen, "Historical and Prophetic Significance," 7.
49. Rose, "Correlation Program," 46.
50. K. Wayne Scott and Ann Scott, "How Church Programs Help Build Our Family," *Ensign* (February 1976): 39, 41, 43.
51. Harold B. Lee, "Uniting to Save Souls," *Improvement Era* (January 1968): 146.
52. James A. Cullimore, "Home Teachers: Watchmen over the Church," *Ensign* (January 1973): 124–25.
53. Bruce R. McConkie, *The Ten Commandments of Priesthood Correlation* (Salt Lake City: Deseret Book, 1976), 10.
54. "Correlation Chronology," 8.
55. Rose, "Correlation Program," 46
56. Mouritsen, "Historical and Prophetic Significance," 11–12. The basic statement of this millennialism is Joseph Fielding Smith, *Signs of the Times* (Salt Lake City: Deseret Book, 1945).
57. S. Dilworth Young, "When Thou Art Converted," *Ensign* (June 1971): 40.
58. Spencer W. Kimball, "Home Training: The Cure for Evil," Conference Report, April 1965, 60.
59. Andrus, "Lord's Battle Plan," 2.
60. Romney, "What Is Correlation?," 3.
61. "Report of the Correlation–Social Advisory Committee," 3.
62. On progressive education, see David Setran, "Morality and the Democracy of God: George Albert Coe and the Liberal Protestant Critique of American Character Education, 1917–1940," *Religion and American Culture* 15, no. 1 (Winter 2005): 112–14; and Warren, "Character, Public Schooling, and Religious Education," 61–80.
63. "Correlation Chronology," 12.
64. Ibid., 20.
65. Antone Romney, "Principles, Goals, and Functions of Priesthood Correlation," in Romney, "Selective Quotes of the Brethren," 11.
66. *Home Teaching Handbook* (Salt Lake City: Church of Jesus Christ of Latter-day Saints, 1963), 1.

67. On visitation, see Charles Cashdollar, *A Spiritual Home: Life in British and American Reformed Congregation* (University Park: Pennsylvania State University Press, 2000), 131–36. The practice also reflects the "case work" method that developed in American sociology in the early twentieth century, in which social workers would visit the homes of those they studied. See Elizabeth Agnew, *From Charity to Social Work: Mary Richmond and the Creation of an American Profession* (Urbana: University of Illinois, 2004); and Julia Rauch, "Women in Social Work: Friendly Visitors in Philadelphia, 1880," *Social Service Review* 49, no. 2 (June 1975): 241–59.
68. Correlation Executive Committee of the Church, in "Selective Quotes of the Brethren," 36.
69. "Correlation Chronology," 2.
70. Ibid., 7.
71. Ibid., 5.
72. Andrus, "Lord's Battle Plan," 22, 43.
73. "Correlation Chronology," 16.

Chapter 2 | Mormon Ethnicity as Reality and Metaphor

Jan Shipps

Concepts, theories, variables, analyses, and interpretations are held in common by sociology and history. In their calculations, sociologists use cross tabulations, single and multiple regressions, and other forms of statistical analyses, which historians (especially since the coming of computers and digitized data) have borrowed liberally. Adding religion to the mix introduces variables such as levels of belief that are hard to characterize. Furthermore, accounts of spiritual experiences are difficult to quantify, and can only be described in discursive frameworks like "being born again," "gaining a testimony," and "speaking in tongues." Oftentimes such experiences are depicted using analogies—being literally "lifted up" (as Saint Teresa "flew about the kitchen"), hearing sweet sounds, or seeing nature entirely anew.

Occasionally we see books that utilize simultaneously the methods, data, and theories of a sociologist with the sensitivity toward metaphor and spiritual experience more common to the historian and religious studies scholar. One such book is Armand Mauss's *The Angel and the Beehive*. His theoretical scaffolding was the ideal type sect-to-church movement first proposed by Max Weber and later explicated by Ernst Troeltsch. He made effective use of long-established sociological methods, including polls and surveys he and other sociologists conducted. Cross tabulations are his most often used analytical technique. His reading of what they tell us provides the experimental accuracy that Mauss uses to portray the movement from the Mormon "beehive" characteristic of the 1960s toward the LDS "angel" characteristic of Mormonism in the 1980s.[1] The beehive not only symbolizes hard work and busyness, but also nectar brought from many different places "infecting" the honey of life with a great elemental variety leading perhaps inevitably to cultural assimilation. The angel stands for religious and cultural integrity. In this instance, a state of accommodating to the world is opposed to keeping the religious and social world order in its pure unadulterated LDS state.

The process that generates movement away from the beehive Mauss calls "retrenchment," by which he means (1) efforts made by "presiding authorities to reassert the charismatic and prophetic element[s]" that created Mormonism and gave its distinctive character to the faith; (2) efforts made by Latter-day Saints at the folk level "to identify and promote certain values and norms of behavior as uniquely Mormon"; and (3) a "concentrated effort on the parts of Mormon academics and intellectuals to seek out, illuminate, and celebrate their unique historical and cultural identity."[2] Although Mauss's interpretation rests on statistical analyses, in reality his reading of what happened is also profoundly autobiographical.[3] As a faithful, yet liberal Latter-day Saint, this author had to deal with retrenchment for the better part of his scholarly life. For that reason, *The Angel and the Beehive* is a source of information about Mormonism in the 1960s through 1980s that is exceedingly valuable to non-Mormon historians like me.

In the first chapter of *The Angel and the Beehive*, titled "Metaphor and Theory," Mauss describes Mormonism as a new religious movement (NRM) of the kind that has attracted a great deal of sociological attention since the 1960s. He differentiates between the schismatic tendencies of sects versus the more spontaneous origins of cults (using the term technically rather than in a derogatory sense). In line with other sociologists such as Rodney Stark and William Bainbridge, Mauss notes that sects and cults alike generally move toward general assimilation with their host cultures.[4] As a result of this similar process, Mauss—like many sociologists—does not make a real distinction between sects and cults, emphasizing instead what he sees as the larger problem of assimilation that so often endangers the survival of new religious movements.

In placing Mormonism in this sect-to-church trajectory, Mauss downplays the notion of Mormon ethnicity that other scholars have emphasized in their characterization of the movement.[5] He interprets Mormon ethnicity only as an "emergent" state, a condition that was at best temporary in the nineteenth century, as twentieth-century LDS identity moved ever more toward assimilation as Americans and toward an explicitly Christian identity in the face of LDS internationalization, on the one hand, and charges that Mormons are not Christian on the other. I agree with Mauss's reading about Mormon ethnicity as a phase in the Mormon past. But as a historian and religious studies scholar, my understanding of Mormon identity has also been shaped by the work of Werner Sollors's edited volume *The Invention of Ethnicity*.[6] Once invented, ethnicity becomes a memory for descendants and an inheritance that can be embraced by converts in the same way that the Apostle Paul's gentile converts became as much a part of the Jesus movement as were the Jewish followers of the Apostles Peter, James, and John.

Mormonism may technically no longer be an ethnicity, but Mormons share a pioneer story and treasure a homeland that was once a "kingdom in the tops of the mountains." Even if it is now a metaphor, Mormon ethnicity or peoplehood is both a memory and an inheritance that enriches LDS church membership and identity. In what follows here, I will take a cursory look at LDS history starting in 1896 and moving forward across the first half of the twentieth century. This will allow me to describe a period in which I think the Mormons were an ethnic group that was, at the same time, being assimilated into American culture as were other ethnic groups like the East European Jews, as well as the Irish and Italians.[7]

Before looking back at the Mormon past, however, I need to pause and make it clear that unlike many sociologists, anthropologists, and ethnographers who make little distinction between cults and sects because their goal is describing the tension between NRMs and the larger environment within which they came into being, I make an unequivocal distinction between the two. Sects are the result of schisms (sometimes bitter and sometimes not) in which schismatics leave larger groups because of disagreements over doctrine, liturgy and ritual, or even scriptures. More often than not, those who leave become sectarians because they see themselves as "saving remnants" since they believe the larger group has "assimilated" to the world and thus become corrupted. Cults—again, in the technical sense—are never the direct result of schism. They are generally led by a charismatic leader who is the source of a new set of religious claims. If the charismatic leader is a prophet, one who speaks for God, those who gather around him or her hold as their first article of faith that the prophet speaks for God.

The Protestant Reformation generated sectarian factions that became major religious institutions (e.g., Lutheranism and Calvinism), as well as smaller sectarian movements such as the Anabaptists and Mennonites.[8] A variety of cults appealed to young people, especially in the United States in the 1960s. But a better illustration in this instance is Christianity or Islam, both of which were led by charismatic leaders. Though they naturally emerged from their host cultures and were influenced by extant religious institutions and ideologies, their emergence was sufficiently distinctive that they resulted in qualitatively new religious expressions rather than mere schisms.

Sects and cults are both new religious movements and both usually maintain a high level of tension between the group and the host human environment. Nevertheless, if they survive and mature, the outcome is truly dissimilar. When a sect "grows up," it becomes a church, an institution whose membership is made up of persons who make conscious decisions to join, or, in the case of birthright members, whose parents make decisions that youngsters should become members. To the contrary, a cult becomes a culture, one that usually contains within itself an institutional manifestation, but is much more than an institution since, in addition to those who become members through conversion, it is made up of a population whose right to belong is ascribed, or in other words, determined by birth and kinship rather than formal membership. Those who are members of an institution may become a part of the institution's authority structure or they may be disciplined by institutional authority and even disfellowshipped or excommunicated. Members of a culture can be shunned, and their membership in formal institutions can be taken away, but their ascribed identity cannot be stripped. Thus the dissimilarity between sects and cults is substantial and significant.

With the exception of the period of the Utah War, Mormons in the second half of the nineteenth century used the Fourth of July and other appropriate occasions to celebrate their understanding of themselves as Americans. The coming of statehood in 1896 and the subsequent Spanish-American War provided even more particular reasons for the patriotic parades that were captured in photographs found in many Utah-Mormon collections of pictures from the late nineteenth and early twentieth centuries. The shift from the People's Party (the political outlet for nineteenth-century Latter-day Saints) to a division between the Democratic and Republican political parties led to attempts to demonstrate each party's patriotism, while the creation of public school systems around the turn of the century also meant public expressions of loyalty to the nation.[9] At the same time, life in the Great Basin and its environs (the LDS culture region) was thoroughly Mormon. Divided up into wards and stakes whose members reported to "file leaders" above them, the Latter-day Saints and all the inhabitants of the Great Basin lived in an LDS world. In order to capture the nature of that world within what amounted to, at the time, the larger American universe, it is useful to think of Mormonism as a rapidly evolving culture. This culture was populated by Latter-day Saints who shared a history of courageous endeavors and extraordinary triumphs, as well as persecution of the cruelest kind. They shared kinship as persons through whose veins coursed the blood of Abraham that was metaphorical in the beginning, but by the third and fourth generations had taken on a reality that was hard to deny not only because of the inclusion of the importance of the restoration of Israel in sermons, but also because of intermarriage and the tangled skeins of kinship ties that resulted from several generations of plural marriage.

Moreover, this populace shared both a formal and lay authority structure that made no distinction between the birthright statuses of leaders and led (with the significant exceptions of those under the constraints of race and gender). The families of pioneers who traveled across the plains and mountains in the 1840s and 1850s were held in high regard, but there was no aristocratic or clerical status that set one group of believers apart from another. The presence of non-Mormons (gentiles) among them simply made their identity as Mormons more potent. General Authorities were respected and often, but not always, listened to when they asked church members to do this or that. Civic leaders were likewise respected, but not any more than elsewhere in the United States.

Church leadership in the first half of the twentieth century was such that its head was rarely referred to as "the Prophet," but rather as "President Smith" or "President Grant." The church itself struggled to end the practice of plural marriage, even as the aftermath of "the Principle" was met in everyday life because the children of plural marriages were very much in evidence as young religious or civic leaders. The political situation was such that the General Authorities were mostly Republican, but the people were as likely to be Democrats as Republicans, meaning that the political culture in the early twentieth century Mormon world was far less monolithic than it is today. Gathering in the Great Basin did not entirely cease. But it slowed down to such an extent that the Latter-day Saints encircled by the mountains grew mainly by natural increase.[10] This furthered the consciousness of the area's inhabitants of being a part of an aggregate, a collective—that is, of being Mormon.

Whether or not they were intimately involved in the activities of the LDS Church, most of the populace in the Mormon culture region either were Latter-day Saints who had lived in the kingdom in the tops of the mountains or were the first, second, third, or even fourth generation of descendants of those who had done so. They shared a land that continued to call for prodigious efforts to make it blossom as a rose and support its residents. Moreover, as children they learned they had blood ties with other Mormons since the patriarch Abraham was their common ancestor. All this meant that the world in the Great Basin did, in fact, take on an ethnic character—not because everyone looked alike, but because the religious and social connections between the people within Utah and the rest of the Mormon culture region were so intense. Additionally, the very presence of "gentiles" in their homeland made the Mormons more aware of their LDS ethnicity.

That the Mormon cult of the nineteenth century had become an ethnic culture first became truly evident to those outside the Mountain West during the Great Depression. Like other farming areas in the plains and far western states, Utah had suffered an agricultural depression for almost a decade before the stock market crashed and brought the rest of the nation's economy down with it. This meant that the Latter-day Saints were in so much economic trouble that they were forced to turn to the U.S. government for help. As a result, politics appeared to challenge the Mormon religion in at least two ways.

On the day before the U.S. presidential election in 1936, the LDS prophet and president Heber J. Grant used the front page of the church newspaper, the *Deseret News*, to direct church members to vote for Republican Alfred M. Landon rather than Democrat Franklin D. Roosevelt. By a huge margin, they did not do so, thus siding with the nation rather than their prophet. Besides that direct refusal to "follow the Brethren," another repudiation of directions issued by the church's First Presidency came about when the church's General Authorities approved the formation of a Church Welfare Plan. The church president and his colleagues urged the members to seek help from this LDS agency rather than the government. For whatever reason, however, ten times as many members continued to ask for assistance from the government rather than the church.[11]

During World War II, ethnic and racial groups all over the nation turned their hyphenated names roundabout, emphasizing the latter descriptor as they thought about and described themselves. American Protestants became Protestant Americans; American Catholics became Catholic Americans; and the same was true of Jewish Americans, Italian Americans, and virtually all other U.S. citizens who thought of themselves in hyphenated terms. For a time, "American" was the descriptive category in the way American Mormons described and thought of themselves. But this was only temporary. By the time Latter-day Saint servicemen (and the few LDS servicewomen) returned home from World War II, they thought of themselves as Mormon Americans.[12]

After Utah became a state in 1896 and after the Smoot hearings finished in 1908, the nation's perception of the Mormons and Mormonism gradually changed from negative to positive.[13] In the early 1950s, however, this steadily more affirmative view of Latter-day Saints was interrupted by a flood of negative news stories—many of them accompanied with all sorts of unattractive pictures—about a 1952 combined Arizona and Utah law enforcement raid on the Mormons in Short Creek, Arizona, who were continuing to practice polygamy. Reviving the nation's concern about plural marriage that had saturated news accounts of Mormons in the latter part of the nineteenth century, this unwelcome attention was answered by the LDS Public Affairs Department with releases filled with pleasant stories about Mormons that generated positive news and feature stories about LDS members in the middle of the twentieth century. Perhaps the most upbeat of all these affirmations that the Mormons were exceptionally righteous folk was an article called "Those Amazing Mormons" published in 1952 in *Coronet*, a *Reader's Digest* clone.[14] The author described the Latter-day Saints as a tithing people who had all the Boy (and Girl) Scout virtues, did not smoke or drink (either alcohol or hot or cold caffeinated beverages), and who "took care of their own." This depiction would become a narrative logo, a new brand that the church's public relations people could and did use as a means of covering up nineteenth-century Mormonism's most distinctive religious feature, plural marriage.

LDS missionaries who concentrated in suburban neighborhoods in the United States in 1952 and the following decades would certainly have made potential American converts aware of the "Amazing Mormons" concept, as well as relying on a new systematic program for teaching the LDS doctrinal belief structure, introduced that same year. "How much do you know about the Mormons? Would you like to know more?" is the way missionaries approached people who would listen. Queried in precisely the same fashion, using these same words (although in many different languages), these two brief questions were used thousands—perhaps tens or even hundreds of thousands—of times as young missionaries knocked on doors and approached prospective converts to Mormonism during the second half of the twentieth century. Called Mormonism's "Golden Question," this was a standardized tactic for starting a conversation that helped spark the conversion of the nearly ten million people who became members of the Church of Jesus Christ of Latter-day Saints between the end of World War II and the year 2000.[15] The fact that this "GQ" approach, as missionaries often called it, was so practically uniform is a sign of the standardization of the whole missionary message that was spread across the globe.

Determining whether it was that consistency, the zeal of the young elders and "sister missionaries," the promise of upward mobility, the appeal of the message, or, as sociologist Rodney Stark argued, the "fellowshipping in" of potential church members that made the biggest difference in Mormon growth is difficult. But what is of consequence here is that in the 1950s it was not only the full-time missionaries but also active members (and ex-members) who were anxious to tell the world about themselves and their faith. Their new president, David O. McKay, called all church members to be missionaries, and in the heady excitement of rapid church growth they all seemed anxious for people to know more. Gaining more converts was by no means the only purpose of this wholesale sharing of the Mormon story, although this was certainly in the minds of most. Beyond (or as a precursor to) conversion, Latter-day Saints also wanted the world to "know more" about them, their church, and to some extent their culture because it was a way of legitimating themselves and their faith and finding a secure place for Mormonism in the American religious mosaic.

As LDS church growth accelerated so that there were nearly three million members in 1970, a movement designed to reveal negative information especially about Mormon history and LDS doctrine emerged. Led by ex-Mormons and Southern Baptists, these opponents of the church created a book and a movie, both named *The Godmakers*, which were designed to convince the members of the growing evangelical movement and the world in general about the false faith of the Latter-day Saints. Points made in this book and film described LDS theology in such a crude fashion that it is a reminder of the early days of Christendom when Christians were accused of being cannibals because they consumed "the body and the blood" of Christ. Still, the film was shown over and over again in evangelical and fundamentalist Protestant churches.

Critics of the LDS Church also sold Modern Microfilm Co. publications put out in Salt Lake City by ex-Mormons Jerald and Sandra Tanner. This disparaging movement called Mormonism a cult (in the popular, derogatory sense) and accused Latter-day Saints of not being Christians. While by no means entirely responsible for the LDS Church's renewed emphasis on its claim to be the restored Church of Jesus Christ, the prominence of *The Godmakers* and similar evangelical anti-Mormon materials probably figured in the decision made by the institution's leaders to stress the importance of Mormonism's Christian-ness.

In addition to the LDS Church's exceptional full-time missionary program in which persons in their late teens or early twenties spent eighteen to twenty-four months serving as missionaries in the United States or in countries around the world, as well as its "every member a missionary" program, the LDS Church's extraordinary Public Affairs Department was charged with combating negative information about Mormonism and communicating positive information about the church and its members to the outside world. This public relations effort was begun in the 1880s when the Latter-day Saints were making a sustained effort to get Utah recognized as a state rather than a territory of the United States. It was formally established as a department of the church soon after World War I, much earlier than most other religious institutions had public relations departments and before "PR" became a permanent fixture in the American landscape. As was true of public relations in religious institutions generally, in the years after World War II the LDS Public Affairs Department became a more prominent part of the church. As indicated, it had a prominent role in depicting the Latter-day Saints as "Those Amazing Mormons." The work of the department did not stop there. In ads that appeared in *Reader's Digest* as soon as that publication started to accept advertisements, the Mormons were pictured in its pages as people with strong family values. Late-night television ads that asked parents whether they knew where their children were subtly made the point that Mormons certainly did know where their children were.

With some justification, a few observers complained that the Public Affairs Department was so visible that Mormonism had become "religion by news release." No doubt Public Affairs played a major role in the decades following World War II, and was largely responsible for trumpeting the ever-increasing growth statistics of the church worldwide, to the point that for many Mormons growth and truth were conflated. In general, however, the LDS Public Affairs Department was no more or less protective of the institution they served than public relations divisions of the Roman Catholic Church or those of large Protestant denominations. It was not Public Affairs, but the General Authorities—the church's real ecclesiastical leadership—who in the late 1970s and the 1980s kept charging the members of the church to retain and pass on to the next generation LDS cultural patterns as well as the church's doctrinal structure.

In the 1950s and especially in the 1960s, the first decade when more converts were added to the church through conversion rather than by natural increase, and as LDS stakes and wards were organized all across the United States and in other parts of the world, Mormonism, not unexpectedly, appeared to be accommodating to the larger culture.[16] It is the exhortations against allowing this accommodation to occur unchecked—delivered in the church's annual and semiannual conferences, in regional conferences and stake priesthood meetings, and in magazines published by the church—that Armand Mauss describes as retrenchment. For converts, however, these urgings were not so much retrenchment as reminders that in addition to affirming the beliefs they had accepted upon conversion and baptism, they must continue to tithe, to exhibit and pass on the Scouting virtues, to keep the "Word of Wisdom," and to care for their fellow members in need. In short, they must continue to be "Amazing Mormons."

Whether all the General Authorities were fully aware that all their public messages were reaching a double audience, internal and external, is not clear. But an obvious alteration in the nature of many of the messages delivered since the 1980s worked to increase communication to their double audience. This change was the adoption of more stories from the Bible into Mormon doctrinal rhetoric. The pages of the *Ensign*, which had been inaugurated as the church magazine for adults in 1973, were filled during its first decade with stories and attractive color pictures of Mormonism's heroes and heroines, for example. But from the 1980s forward, the featured stories and pictures were of biblical and Book of Mormon figures. Because they were essentially new to Mormon culture, the material in the church magazines and General Authority messages communicated almost equally to converts and to those who had been members all their lives.

The expansion of the LDS Church in the United States, with organized stakes, wards, and branches in every state, and in more than 150 countries around the world has turned Mormon ethnicity into a metaphor that may be adopted or ignored by church members. This is even true in the Mormon culture region. Yet Mormons everywhere continue to incorporate the concept of peoplehood as they create Mormon cultures in a multiplicity of geographic areas. Additionally, now that there are more Mormon converts than children born into the LDS covenant, the members who inhabit these cultures—even when the numbers of members born in the covenant is very limited—can embrace the reality of being Mormon. As they do so, they gradually discover that the ethnicity metaphor works when they go to meeting and especially when they worship in Mormon temples. If they retain their acceptance of Mormon doctrine and stay active in the church throughout their lives, Mormon ethnicity will be an inheritance they can pass on to the next generation.

Notes

1. Armand L. Mauss, *The Angel and the Beehive: The Mormon Struggle with Assimilation* (Urbana: University of Illinois Press, 1994).
2. Ibid., 78–79.
3. Armand L. Mauss, *Shifting Borders and a Tattered Passport: Intellectual Journeys of a Mormon Academic* (Salt Lake City: University of Utah Press, 2012).
4. Ibid., 7.
5. See Dean L. May, "Mormons," in *Harvard Encyclopedia of American Ethnic Groups*, ed. Stephan Thernstrom, Ann Orlov, and Oscar Handlin (Cambridge, MA: Belknap Press of Harvard University Press, 1980), 720–31; Patricia Nelson Limerick, "Peace Initiative: Using the Mormons to Rethink Culture and Ethnicity in American History," *Journal of Mormon History* 21 (Fall 1995): 1–29.
6. Werner Sollors, ed., *The Invention of Ethnicity* (New York: Oxford University Press, 1989).
7. See David J. Bodenhamer, "Narrating Space and Place," in *Deep Maps and Spatial Narratives*, ed. David J. Bodenhamer, John Corrigan, and Trevor M. Harris (Bloomington: Indiana University Press, 2015).
8. Since politics involving royalty and family power was at the heart of the Anglican breakaway from Roman Catholicism, it would be a mistake to describe Anglicans as sectarians, although it is clear that Scottish Presbyterianism was a sectarian move away from Anglicanism.
9. Charles S. Peterson, *Utah: A History* (New York: W. W. Norton & Co., 1977).
10. This changed in 1960. In that year (and in all the years since), Mormonism grew more by conversion than natural increase.
11. John F. Bluth and Wayne K. Hinton, "The Great Depression," in Richard Poll et al., *Utah's History* (Provo, UT: Brigham Young University Press, 1978), especially 486–89.
12. Jan Shipps, "The Scattering of the Gathered and the Gathering of the Scattered: The Mid-twentieth Century Mormon Diaspora," in *Sojourner in the Promised Land* (Urbana: University of Illinois Press, 2000), 258–78.
13. Jan Shipps, "From Satyr to Saint: American Perceptions of the Mormons, 1860–1960," in *Sojourner in the Promised Land*, see especially the graph on page 70.
14. Andrew Hamilton, "Those Amazing Mormons," *Coronet* 31 (April 1952): 26–30. A copy of the manuscript of this article was sent to Sterling McMurrin, the dean of the Graduate School at the University of Utah, with a request that he read it and give his opinion of the piece to the *Coronet* editors. A copy of the letter containing McMurrin's recommendation that the article not be published because it was "full of lies" is found in his chronologically arranged letters in the Special Collections Department in the University of Utah's J. Willard Marriott Library.
15. This number includes children of record as well as converts. Every year between 1960 and the present, more converts than children of record were added to the church's rolls.
16. Without a professional clergy to lead them, so many wards across the South were almost entirely made up of Saints who had been Baptists and Methodists that a Protestantized form of Mormonism appeared to be developing. The same was true in certain parts of

the East and Midwest. When General Authorities recognized the danger, they drafted members from the Mormon culture region who had taken advantage of the G.I. Bill to go to college and graduate school or to establish businesses in these areas to serve as leaders in wards filled with converts, thus preserving an "orthodox" and differentiated religious culture.

Part II | American Church or World Religion?

Chapter 3 | Monks, Nationalists, and the Emperor

The Mormon Struggle in Japan, 1901–1924

Shinji Takagi

Introduction

The Japan Mission of the Church of Jesus Christ of Latter-day Saints operated from August 1901 to July 1924, claiming no more than 174 converts during the twenty-three years of its existence.[1] It thus comes as no surprise that the Mormon proselytizing effort in Japan before World War II is generally considered by the LDS Church's informed membership to have been a total failure. Heber J. Grant, upon returning home as the mission's inaugural president, stated at the October 1903 General Conference: "I regret I am not able to tell you that we have done something wonderful over in Japan."[2] Gordon B. Hinckley, writing in 1964, characterized it as "a work of devotion and disappointment probably without parallel in the history of the missions of the Church." He then noted: "In a single month in 1963 there came into the Church as many as the total baptized from 1901 to 1924."[3]

This does not mean that Christianity failed to make inroads into prewar Japan. Historian Reid Neilson notes that the Mormon achievement in early twentieth-century Japan was lackluster when compared to the experience of American Protestants during "the heyday" of their missionary enterprise, which coincided with the Japan Mission. He then ascribes the Protestants' relative success to their emphasis on education, which was more adapted to Japanese society, while the Mormons "merely imposed or translated their message" and relied almost exclusively on personal contacting.[4] It may be overly simplistic to attribute a large part of the Mormons' apparent lack of success to their failure to establish educational institutions. Even so, it is true that Protestantism gained tens of thousands of Japanese converts during the prewar period, though the height of its success came in the 1880s.

This essay seeks to address some fundamental questions about the LDS Japan Mission. Why was the missionaries' work so difficult and unproductive? Why were their fruits so meager, compared to what the Protestants claimed? Was the work doomed to failure, or was it a failure? Was the decision to close the mission in 1924 the right one? This essay's premise is that such seemingly straightforward questions cannot be adequately addressed unless we understand the religious, intellectual, and sociopolitical climate of Japan during the early twentieth century. By approaching the experience of the Japan Mission from the "demand" side, so to speak, this study departs from the existing literature on missiology, and Mormon foreign missions in particular, where focus has too often been placed on the American missionaries and their message. While such "supply-side" analysis is useful, it is only half the story of how American religious ideas are received in various settings around the globe.

Over the past two centuries, LDS missionaries have carried roughly the same message, cultural packaging, and leadership style with them throughout the world. Why have some mission fields been more productive than others, and why does a particular locale wax and wane in productivity? Is it simply the mysterious workings of the Holy Spirit as it moves upon a people, or are there more terrestrial considerations at play? These are the types of questions that will challenge the next wave of scholars of international Mormonism, particularly those studying the role of the extensive Mormon missionary effort in facilitating the LDS Church's global expansion. This essay is a modest attempt to explore this largely untrodden territory, by analyzing the religious, intellectual, and sociopolitical context in which the prewar Japan Mission operated.

Historical Setting

The decades leading up to World War II were a turbulent period in Japanese history. It began with the opening up of the country to the West in the late 1850s, following about 220 years of self-imposed national seclusion. The country subsequently experienced a revolution in 1868, by which the Tokugawa family's right to rule was abrogated and restored to the emperor (posthumously named Meiji); major wars with China (1894–1895) and Russia (1904–1905), in which Japan defeated both; an annexation by force of Korea in 1910; and the transformation of a feudal, agrarian society into an industrial and military power capable of waging a sustained war with the United States. During this period of modernization, Japan was suddenly exposed to a cascade of new ideas from the outside world. The confluence of indigenous and transplanted thoughts never seemed to find equilibrium.

As to the religious climate, by the time Japan entered the modern era, the public had largely discredited Buddhism while holding a deep-seated fear of Christianity. When in the early seventeenth century the head of the Tokugawa family began to rule from Edo (present-day Tokyo) as the military general (*shōgun*) for the emperor, Roman Catholicism claimed perhaps as many as 750,000 adherents or 4 percent of the population.[5] Suspicious of the political ambitions of Christian nations, especially as Protestant nations had also advanced to Asia around the turn of the seventeenth century, the

Tokugawa shogunate banned Christianity and declared a policy of national seclusion, permitting few foreigners to enter and no Japanese to leave the country. To eradicate any residue of Christianity, the shogunate turned to Buddhism, requiring all Japanese to register at a Buddhist temple and submit to an annual scrutiny of religious beliefs by Buddhist monks.[6]

The eradication of Christianity was meant to be total. Not even a reference to it was permitted in books, and its very name might have been lost were it not written so prominently on the public proclamation boards of every town: "The evil sect of Christianity is strictly prohibited."[7] Those found practicing Christianity, as well as their families and close relatives, were tortured, imprisoned, and in some cases put to death. In time, separate registries for former Christians were created, in order to trace those with any previous ties to Christianity. When they died, their corpses were examined by an official before they could be buried (in a separate location). They were subjected to religious persecution and prejudice that would last more than two centuries. Fear of Christianity was thus implanted in the deepest conscience of the public.[8]

The fear of being labeled as a Christian was so strong that Buddhist monks had enormous leverage over the people, especially those on the Christian registries. The system thus became a hotbed of corruption. Monks, for example, would charge an exorbitant fee for a funeral or solicit funds for the building of a new worship hall. Local monks could be engaged in outright acts of extortion by demanding monetary or sexual favors. Buddhist priesthood, with its social status and a lavish lifestyle, became an attractive occupation for aspiring men with no religious inclinations. As a standard template for religious registries cemented every person to his temple, he had no freedom to choose his own temple regardless of what he actually believed; at birth the place of his funeral was known with virtual certainty.[9]

The corruption of Buddhism, evident from as early as the 1660s, gave rise to the systematic development of anti-Buddhist ideology among Confucian scholars. Buddhism, having become an instrument of state control, lost its ideological influence, and Shinto, the supposed native religion of Japan, came under the greater influence of Confucianism. Under the temple registration system, Shinto priests and their families were also required to be parishioners of a Buddhist temple, preserving the subjugation of Shinto to Buddhism under a Shinto-Buddhist syncretism (*shinbutsu shūgō*) that had developed in the eighth or ninth century and subsequently engulfed the whole nation.[10] Under the new framework of Confucianism, however, Shinto-Confucian syncretism emerged. Subsequently called *bushidō*, it appealed first to the *samurai* class, but the influence then spread to other segments of society.[11]

A sustained period of relative peace encouraged scholarly learning, especially studies of the Japanese classics, broadly known as National Learning (*kokugaku*). The Mito school, based on meticulous historical research, proved that there had been a time when the emperor ruled personally. The end result was to undermine the legitimacy of the shogunate and to create a nostalgic feeling in favor of returning to the days of direct imperial rule. In a nativist reaction to the Confucian domination of national thought, a new school of thought emerged called *Fukkō* Shinto, which emphasized the importance of ancestor worship and claimed the moral and racial superiority of the Japanese. *Fukkō* Shinto turned into a nativist sociopolitical movement towards the end of the Edo period (1603–1868). The slogan *sonnō* (revere the emperor) typified their emphasis on the emperor, while the term *kokutai* (national structure) expressed the uniqueness of their concept of the state.[12]

The opening of Japan in the 1850s, conceded under threat of force, created a vehement anti-Tokugawa reaction, especially among the powerful feudal vassals (*daimyō*) of western Japan. Rallying around the slogan *sonnō jōi*, or "revere the emperor, expel the barbarians," this nativist movement sought to overthrow the shogunate and reestablish the authority of the emperor, who had remained in Kyoto as the symbol of residual sovereignty but without political power. With a decisive victory over the Tokugawa forces in early 1868, rebel clans restored the emperor to political power, moved his residence from Kyoto to Edo (renamed Tokyo), and called the new period of his reign Meiji (enlightened rule). This ended the long historical separation of reigning sovereign and ruling authority that had existed for over seven centuries.

Once established, the new Meiji government sought to consolidate the imperial throne's authority by appealing to the Shinto concept of national structure. In 1868, it proclaimed the unity of religion and politics, restored the ancient office of chief national priest, and placed it over the civil bureaucracy. Over the coming years, it issued a series of ordinances to establish Shinto as the state religion and to remove Buddhist influences from it. From 1871 to 1872, the government confiscated land from Buddhist temples, abrogated the right of self-rule, and abolished the temple registration system. These and other related measures terminated, at the stroke of a pen, the Shinto-Buddhist syncretism that had been part of Japan's religious scene for more than a millennium.[13] Invigorated, Shinto devotees took to the streets, destroying Buddhist temples and removing or burning religious artifacts, in an outburst of frustration over their centuries-long subjugation to Buddhism.[14]

A new system of religion was in the making, dressed in Shinto's clothing. The government centralized authority over all shrines in a hierarchical structure, abolishing a number of minor ones of dubious character, and elevating deities and shrines connected with the imperial court. It ordered magic and other superstitious practices to be removed. The Shinto of Meiji Japan needed to be a modern national religion capable of stacking up against the Christianity of the West. A brief attempt to establish a state religion through a "Great Promulgation Campaign" (*taikyō senpu undō*) ultimately failed, however, proving the futility of prescribing people's religious beliefs by fiat.[15] Instead, the government separated Shinto ceremonial rites from religion. By 1884, Sect Shinto (denominational branches of Shinto) and Buddhism were free of state control, whereas Shrine Shinto, including the ceremonies at the court and the communal Shinto cult, remained under state control as a civic institution.[16]

A New Era of Christian Evangelization

In July 1859, the commercial treaties signed with foreign powers (collectively known as *Ansei* treaties) came into force, giving their nationals the right to freely exercise their religion, as well as the right to build churches, within the restricted foreign settlements. Although the ban on Christianity remained in place for the Japanese public, the first missionaries arrived in quick succession, taking up residence in Nagasaki and Yokohama.[17] In the early 1860s, there were thus missionaries in Japan from the Roman Catholic Church (represented by the Society of Foreign Missions of Paris) and the Russian Orthodox Church, as well as the Episcopal, Congregational, Presbyterian, and Dutch Reformed churches on the Protestant side.

In early 1865, following the construction of a Catholic edifice on a prominent hill in the foreign settlement of Nagasaki, a group of women came forward from the nearby village of Urakami, identifying themselves as Christians. By the middle of the year, Catholic missionaries had learned of such communities of "hidden" Christians in twenty or more places.[18] When the new Meiji government took power in 1868, however, it reaffirmed the Tokugawa ban and posted anew signboards prohibiting Christianity. In fact, the elevation of Shinto was meant in part as a guard against the potential threat of Christianity, which had now become real.[19] The government not only refused to release those seized by the Tokugawa authorities, but in early 1870 deported and incarcerated over three thousand of them across some thirty provinces.[20] The work of Catholic missionaries, however, proceeded in remote areas of Nagasaki Prefecture in search of hidden Christians.[21]

Protestantism was for the most part represented by American missionaries. They brought a particular kind of evangelicalism that emphasized personal conversion, Biblicism, moral rigor, and a sense of mission.[22] From the start, they saw teaching English as a way of getting around the restrictions on proselytizing activities. Some established small schools, often in their homes. Given the absence of Japanese-language literature, the missionaries initially relied on Chinese books, which educated Japanese were able to read; the Chinese translation of William Alexander Parsons Martin's *Evidences of Christianity* (1855) was especially popular. Buddhist monks were occasional students, eager to expose what they thought was an evil religion. In 1868 they published an anti-Christian exposé entitled *Tales of Nagasaki: The Story of the Evil Doctrine*.[23]

Some Japanese were drawn to the Christian message because they considered Christianity, and Protestantism in particular, as the spiritual basis of the great Western powers. It was from among these typically well-educated people that Protestantism claimed their first fruits. The first recorded baptism occurred in Yokohama in 1864, and the second took place in Nagasaki in 1866; there would be an estimated eight more Protestant baptisms through early 1872.[24] These were brave men who embraced a foreign religion in defiance of the law. Especially after the Meiji government started to persecute the Urakami Christians, they fully knew what might befall them if their conversion were made known. In March 1870 the persecution of Protestantism began, involving the arrest of converts and those who assisted the missionaries, though not always in a consistent manner.[25]

In the meantime, the Urakami Incident developed into a serious diplomatic issue. From December 1871 to September 1873, the Japanese government dispatched a high-level delegation to conduct an exploratory renegotiation with the foreign powers for a possible removal of extraterritoriality (giving foreign nationals the right to a consular trial) from the *Ansei* treaties. At each stop, the Japanese diplomats received protest and reproach over the treatment of the Urakami Christians. They were told in no uncertain terms that a revision of the treaty would not be possible as long as Christians were not allowed to practice their religion freely.[26] This diplomatic pressure, once communicated home, started the process toward effectively ending the ban on Christianity. Over the following years, the imprisoned Urakami Christians were released and repatriated, and notice boards against Christianity were removed from public view. Though sporadic harassment continued on a local level, by 1876 the Japanese people felt safe to embrace Christianity and the foreign missionaries likewise spread their message openly.

As the Catholic Church focused almost all of its attention to claiming the hidden Christians in the villages of Nagasaki, the task of evangelizing the Japanese nation fell upon the shoulders of the Protestant missionaries.[27] Because the *Ansei* treaties did not allow foreigners to travel freely in the interior, the Christian message was first preached by missionaries and laymen who were employed by public schools. Enterprising young people gathered about them to study secular subjects mixed with Christianity. The authorities' attitude was equivocal. They were never friendly, but they knew the diplomatic repercussions of mistreatment. Not infrequently local government officials would openly oppose Christian undertakings, though sometimes they were overruled by Tokyo.[28]

While all this was happening, the Meiji government had set out to build modern institutions, including legal codes and a constitution, which would qualify Japan as a civilized nation worthy of equality with the Western powers. From around 1883, it embarked upon an aggressive policy of Westernization. Starting with the court circles, prominent persons began to wear Western clothes and to adopt the Western style of living. Western culture, especially in arts, music, drama, and literature, was readily adopted; indeed, a whole new vocabulary was coming into the Japanese language. The word "freedom" was flooding the country, adopted as the names of public bathhouses, restaurants, and consumer goods.[29] In 1885, some 99,000 English-language books were imported into Japan; in 1886, the number increased to 204,000.[30]

The wave of Westernization was a great boost to the Protestant cause. Christian churches were crowded even with those who cared little for religion, and became a sort of fashionable place where the enlightened men and women would meet.[31] From 1882 to 1889 the adult membership in the Protestant churches increased from a little over 4,000 to nearly 30,000.[32] From 1859 to 1873, only six Protestant denominations had come to Japan; from 1873 to 1879, nineteen additional ones arrived.[33] In 1882, there were nine Christian schools for men with 454 students and fifteen schools for women with 566 students. In 1888, there were fifteen men's schools with 2,709 students and thirty-nine women's schools with 3,663 students.[34] During the same year, nearly 7,000 people were baptized.[35]

Importantly, the success of Protestantism in the 1880s was a self-sustaining process, led by Japanese Christian leaders. Most of the one thousand or so Japanese who had become Protestants during the 1870s were highly educated intellectuals of the *samurai* class, many of whom had been on the losing side of the revolution.[36] By learning about the West from the foreigners they hoped to improve their station, and also to work out the spiritual resurrection of the nation.[37] During the 1880s, missionary work also spread among the rural population. Those who embraced the religion were neither the large landlords who were closely connected with the established religious order nor the peasants whose sustenance was dependent on their communities. Many of the Christian farmers became pioneers in introducing new crops, and some succeeded as agri-business owners.[38]

The Nationalist Reaction

Then, the pendulum swung back. The Westernization of the 1880s had awoken the sense of Japanese identity. Nationalistic undercurrents, which had temporarily lain dormant, gradually came to the surface and fought back against the seeming onslaught of Christianity. Non-Christian and anti-Christian thoughts had also come to Japan: John Stuart Mill was followed by Herbert Spencer and Charles Darwin, causing the people to realize that not all modern civilization was Christian. A division appeared within the Christian movement itself, with the arrival of missionaries from liberal denominations and missionary societies that held a relativistic and evolutionary view of religion.[39] As the Christian cause began to suffer, the number of adult baptisms, which in 1888 had been about seven thousand, would decline to less than three thousand toward the end of the 1890s.[40]

In 1888, leading nationalist reactionaries at the Imperial University began publishing what would become an influential periodical called *Nipponjin* (The Japanese). Buddhists and Shintoists saw in the rise of nationalism an opportunity to assert their positions. Buddhists launched a movement to promote Buddhism under the rubric of "revering the Emperor and protecting the nation" (*sonnō gokoku*). This marked the comeback on the national scene of Buddhism, which had been badly damaged by the anti-Buddhist movement of the 1870s. The persecution had transformed Buddhism into a supporter of the political and military policies of the Meiji state.[41] The 1880s saw a proliferation of books written by Buddhist monks attacking Christianity, some based on Western philosophy. The conclusion that many Christian doctrines contradicted scientific truth while Buddhism's truth was confirmed by science heartened Japanese Buddhists, who had been troubled by the cultural association of Christianity with modernity.[42] The blow to Christianity was effective and many dubious converts renounced their faith.[43]

The policy of Westernization formally ended with the promulgation in 1889 of the Constitution of the Empire of Japan. With it, the fluid period of nation building was over, and reversion to things Japanese began.[44] Christians welcomed the constitution wholeheartedly, as it guaranteed the freedom of religion, but little did they understand that the freedom was a qualified one. Article 28 stated: "Japanese subjects shall, within limits not prejudicial to peace and order, and not antagonistic to their duties as subjects, enjoy freedom of religious belief." As imperial subjects, they were bound to accept the fundamental premise of the constitution, namely: "The Empire of Japan shall be reigned over and governed by a line of Emperors unbroken for ages eternal" (Article 1); and "The Emperor is sacred and inviolable" (Article 3). How to reconcile faith in the Christian God with acceptance of the divinity of the emperor would haunt Japanese Christians during the rest of the prewar period.

Advancing the nationalist cause was the Imperial Rescript on Education, proclaimed by the emperor on October 30, 1890. Stipulating what the imperial subjects should believe, and thus defining the limits of the religious freedom guaranteed by the constitution, the 315-character text upheld Japan's unique national structure and exhorted all subjects to work "courageously" towards maintaining the prosperity of the imperial throne. The Ministry of Education distributed a certified copy to every school in Japan. In July 1891, the ministry issued an order requiring students to assemble on national holidays to read the Rescript and to bow before the portrait of the emperor (and often the empress). The certified copy of the Rescript and the portrait were to be housed in a secure building, and students were expected to bow as they walked past the building each morning and afternoon, in addition to studying and memorizing the text. In this manner, a form of emperor worship was to become a daily activity.

It did not take State Shinto very long to claim its first Christian victim. On January 9, 1891, just two months after the Rescript was proclaimed, a special commemorative meeting was called at Tokyo's prestigious First Higher School to celebrate the receipt of a certified copy. As requested, Uchimura Kanzō, a leading Christian thinker educated at the Sapporo Agricultural College and Amherst, went before the Rescript but failed to bow deeply. Uchimura's action was a target of immediate criticism by the faculty and students. As the incident was reported prominently in the press, there was an outburst of public outcry, leading eventually to Uchimura's resignation from the most prestigious of the nine national higher schools.[45]

The Uchimura Incident gave ammunition to the nationalist critics of Christianity. Inoue Tetsujirō, among them, highlighted the fundamental inconsistency of Christianity with the foundational principles of nationalism in the Meiji Constitution. Christians and their advocates on their part defended Christianity, with Takahashi Gorō providing the harshest rebuttal. A public debate ensued, with leading intellectuals on each side. Whatever the outcome, it was evident that nationalism had defeated Christianity. Even Uchimura, in defending his conduct in the March 1893 issue of the *Kyōiku Jiron*, accepted the Imperial Rescript and argued that the emperor would be more pleased with obeisance in practice than obeisance in ceremony.[46] Christians too became nationalists.

In this environment, the enrollment in Christian schools declined drastically, and harassment of Christian students at public schools became more frequent. In 1892, the governor of Kumamoto Prefecture ordered a Christian school to dismiss a teacher who was reported in the press to have described the mission of the school as teaching cosmopolitanism (as opposed to nationalism). Elsewhere in the same prefecture, encouraged by the governor's anti-Christian stance, the principal of a school expelled a student for reading the Bible.[47] These incidents indicate how the Imperial Rescript excited local political and educational officials to attack Christianity in the 1890s.

The Christian cause suffered another setback in August 1899, when the government issued an order prohibiting religious ceremonies and education in accredited schools. With the strong urging of foreign missions, most Christian schools continued to offer religious education at the risk of being downgraded to nonregular status, which carried the penalty that their students would not enjoy exemption from conscription and graduates eligibility for academic advancement. Some established Christian academies, however, chose to become secular institutions. Compulsory primary education could not be offered by nonaccredited schools, so some Christian schools were forced to close. The intent of the Religious Education Order was to elevate the status of State

Shinto, as embodied in the Imperial Rescript, by removing from the public domain of education any religious elements alien to it.[48]

Such was the world that received the first Mormon missionaries. Christianity had flourished briefly, but its fortunes were now in decline. State Shinto had been established, with the Imperial Rescript on Education serving as the tool of national indoctrination. The nationalist-Buddhist alliance had succeeded in portraying Christianity as unpatriotic and incompatible with the national structure. Buddhism, which had earlier been discredited as a corrupt religion, was proving its usefulness to the country's spiritual aspirations. From a religious and intellectual standpoint, therefore, the Latter-day Saints appear to have arrived in Japan at the worst possible moment. Further handicapped initially by lack of preparation in language and culture, the Mormon missionaries were to struggle against the hostility of the soil.

The Era of the Japan Mission

During the twenty-three-year period of the Japan Mission's existence, a total of 88 American missionaries, including mission presidents and their wives, labored in Japan. This number includes two—Joseph H. Stimpson and Lloyd O. Ivie—who first served as single men and then returned as married mission presidents. These missionaries collectively gave approximately 3,465 months of service, equivalent to what 158 missionaries would provide if each spent 22 months in the field. The average tenure in

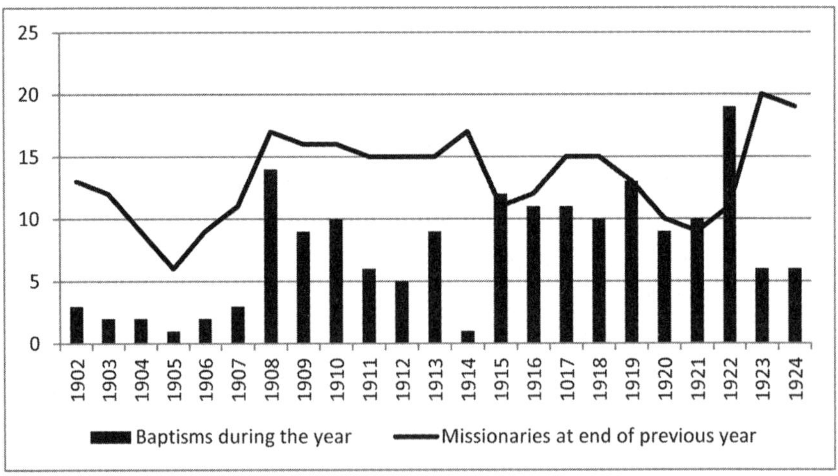

Figure 3.1. Yearly Numbers of Baptisms and Missionaries in the Japan Mission, 1902–1924. Source: Author's estimates based on information in Andrew Jenson, "History of the Japan Mission."

Japan was 39.4 months, with nine missionaries (including Stimpson and Ivie) spending more than five years each. With 174 converts (of which 112 were males and 62 females) spread over twenty-three years, the average annual productivity was 0.58 converts per missionary, with a total of 7.6 converts being produced by 13.3 missionaries per year (calculated from year-end figures).

For all the efforts made by the missionaries, the Mormon evangelization of Japan seems half-hearted. For a country of 45 to 55 million people, the number of missionaries (based on month-end figures) averaged 12.5, including the childbearing wives of missionaries. At no time did the number exceed 20; there were occasional stretches of time when the number languished in single-digits (figure 3.1). The small workforce permitted the mission to proselytize in only a handful of locations; the missionaries stayed long enough to produce one or more baptisms in only seven cities (figure 3.2). Generally, the church had only enough resources to maintain four areas of missionary activity at a given time. From May 1912 (when the structure became more or less stable) to its close, the mission consisted of four conferences: Tokyo, Sapporo, Osaka, and Kofu (which in 1922 was replaced by Sendai).

Except for the capital city of Tokyo, there was little logic in the geographical allocation of missionaries. Population size or in some cases access did not seem to be determining considerations. In April 1903, the first areas in the interior opened for missionary work included Nagano and Naoetsu, neither of which was a major city by

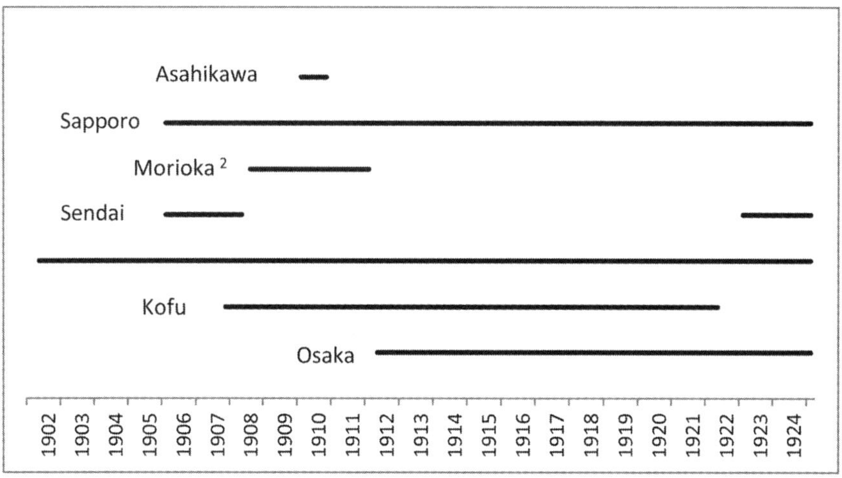

FIGURE 3.2. Proselytizing areas in the Japan Mission, 1902–1924. Includes only those areas where at least one convert was made; excludes several months of proselytizing work in Morioka that resumed between 1922 and 1923. Source: Author's estimates based on information in Andrew Jenson, "History of the Japan Mission."

any stretch of the imagination. These were selected likely because Heber J. Grant had visited them during his nine-day trip to the interior in September 1901 as a companion to a traveling American businessman.[49] In September 1903, missionaries were assigned to labor in Hojo, a small fishing village across Tokyo bay. Clean air and rustic life must have been the reason.[50]

In July 1905, missionaries were sent to Sapporo on the northern island of Hokkaido, although several metropolitan cities of the Pacific coast remained untouched. Though Sapporo was the prefectural capital, it was only the third-largest city. In terms of transportation access, it was far surpassed by the gateway city of Hakodate whose population was not only larger but also more rapidly growing. In March 1907, the small provincial city of Kofu was opened, more than four years ahead of the opening of Osaka, Japan's second-largest city, in September 1911. Comparing annual average baptisms, however, we find no evidence that the average number was any lower in Sapporo or Kofu than in Tokyo or Osaka. Likely, the workforce was too small to experience diminishing marginal returns in any area (table 3.1).

There is no absolute yardstick of success. The number of baptisms—174 over twenty-three years—must be put in perspective, given the limited resources deployed. Certainly there would have been more convert baptisms if the church had made more missionaries available. The annual average productivity of 0.58 converts per missionary, a measure independent of scale, may be more relevant, but this too requires a reference point. This was lower than the productivity of many other LDS missions at the time,[51] but still the number is not unusually low to observers of the LDS Church in contemporary Japan, where the number of baptisms per missionary is likely much less than one per year.[52] One thing we can state with confidence is that Mormonism arrived too late in Japan to benefit from the religious and intellectual climate of the 1880s that favored the spread of Protestantism.

In the tumultuous environment of Meiji Japan, a mere decade or two made a significant difference in terms of the public's receptivity to foreign ideas.[53] The contest of ideas during the prewar period played out over several decades. Initial resistance to foreign ideas was followed by a more accommodating attitude; when the accommodation was carried to the extreme, suppressed indigenous ideas erupted to the surface. The rise of nationalism has been noted by previous LDS authors. Gordon B. Hinckley, for example, explained that Japan, having defeated China and Russia, "was caught up in a wave of ultra-nationalism [which] found expression in feelings against the West and a return to ancestral religions."[54] Such a view is only partially correct. The rise of nationalism was a reaction to the influx of foreign ideas; Mormonism's fortunes were shackled by a new state-sponsored ideology centered on the emperor, not ancestral religions.

TABLE 3.1 Proselytizing Areas and Convert Baptisms in the Japan Mission, 1901–1924

Areas (*principal areas)	Population (1,000s), 1908	Population (1,000s), 1918	Duration of proselytizing work (months)	Number of convert baptisms	Average annual convert baptisms
Tokyo*	2,186	2,347	October 1901–June 1924 (271 months)	57	2.5
Sapporo*	70	95	July 1905–June 1924 (203 months)	42	2.5
Sendai	98	123	July 1905–November 1907; July 1922–June 1924 (51 months)	2	0.5
Kofu*	50	58	February 1907–January 1922 (179 months)	37	2.5
Morioka (2)	36	48	November 1907–August 1911 (45 months)	1	0.3
Asahikawa	40	69	July 1909–July 1910 (12 months)	1	1.0
Osaka*	1,227	1,642	September 1911–June 1924 (153 months)	34	2.7

Note that only areas where at least one convert was made are included. The listing for Morioka excludes several months of proselytizing that resumed between 1922 and 1923. Source: Author's estimates based on Jenson, "History of the Japan Mission"; Japanese government, Nihon Teikoku Jinkō Tōkei, 1908 and 1918.

Nationalism per se did not pose the problem, but rather it was the idea, successfully marketed by the nationalist-Buddhist alliance, that being a Christian was somehow incompatible with the duties as an imperial subject. That such a view permeated Japanese society is evident from the following entry in the missionary journal of Alma O. Taylor about Japanese member Mori Hachirō:

> Yesterday a letter came from him. He requested to have his name taken off the Church records. The reason for such a request is that . . . he has fallen into error on doctrine getting the strange thought that no one can be a Christian and still be loyal to Japan. This letter . . . came as a thunder bolt from a clear sky for all during the past year, Bro. Mori has written very fine spirited letters and paid his tithes regularly and honestly.[55]

In an attempt to dispel such a notion, the national Protestant leaders had earlier given patriotic support during the Sino-Japanese War. Protestant churches nationwide dispatched five chaplains to Manchuria, engaged in relief efforts, and provided assistance to the families of the war dead. A decade later, this was repeated on a larger scale during the Russo-Japanese War.[56]

Japanese Christians were proving that they could be loyal subjects, just as Japanese Buddhists had earlier attempted to prove their usefulness by offering to defend the country from the ideological onslaught of Christianity.[57] Just as the persecution of the 1870s had caused Buddhism to become nationalistic, Christianity was made nationalistic through the process of "Japanization" that followed the traumatic experience of the early 1890s. Christianity's successful rebranding as a nationalistic religion led to a resurgence of Christian proselytizing in the 1900s. Further aiding the Christian cause were the liberalizing forces of industrialization, with its wave of associated societal changes including urbanization and growing labor and social movements. As Christians became involved in social causes, the public began to associate Christianity with works of mercy, and Buddhists eased their attacks.[58]

In order to understand the prewar Mormon experience properly, one must understand this fundamental duality of Japan's religious and intellectual climate. On the one hand, the national campaign of indoctrination in State Shinto had begun, while the anti-Christian campaign of the nationalist-Buddhist alliance had successfully run its course. This exerted an increasingly binding influence on the public's conscience and defined the outer parameters of what Mormonism could achieve. On the other hand, there was a new societal tendency toward openness and pluralism, brought on by the liberalizing forces of industrialization. Coupled with Christianity's successful rebranding, this led to its wider social acceptance and a promotion of broader religious ecumenism.

This duality is the key to reconciling the apparent contradiction between the scanty fruits the LDS Church claimed and the general acceptance of the missionaries by the public. Although few Japanese had the intellectual and spiritual fortitude to embrace the message, along with all that it entailed, the Mormon missionaries had no lack of listeners or friends. The first public meeting in Tokyo, arranged through the assistance of a Buddhist monk in April 1903, drew an audience of some three hundred persons. Likewise, the first Sunday schools in Tokyo (November 1903), Sendai (August 1905), and Morioka (January 1908) had the attendance of eighty-nine, fifty-eight, and twenty-six persons, respectively.[59] Upon returning home in 1910, Alma O. Taylor remained upbeat, stating that the "work in Japan has been, is, and . . . will be fruitful," and that, given "the power and blessing and support of heaven" clearly manifested, it would be "almost an insult to our Father to think . . . that the missionaries in Japan are accomplishing nothing."[60]

The Japan Mission during the Time of Taisho Democracy

The societal trend toward openness and pluralism became progressively strong, stretching out the space within which Mormonism could possibly thrive. The pace accelerated following the 1912 death of Emperor Meiji, which bestowed the throne on his sickly son (posthumously named Taisho). Freed from the oppression of a charismatic leader, Japanese society experienced a rise of individualism and academic freedom, and a remarkable pluralism emerged in politics and thought. For example, there was a view, originally advanced by Minobe Tatsukichi in 1911, that the emperor was an "organ of the state," which effectively denied his divinity and inviolability. The idea of *minponshugi* (literally, "government for the people"), advocated in 1916 by Christian Yoshino Sakuzō as a form of democracy in which sovereignty rested with the emperor, received a large following.[61]

Taisho Democracy, in the narrow sense, refers to the period of 1918–1932, during which party cabinets elected by the people (as opposed to those selected by the oligarchs) ran the government. In a broader sense, it is a symbolic designation for the new currents of cosmopolitanism, discontent, and reform that found expression in the years during and after World War I. Japan was more open to the world. Foreign culture and practices were easily imported. Japanese had ready access to inexpensive editions of translations of virtually all of the major works of European philosophy.[62] Unlike the Westernization of the 1880s, however, Japanese society did not simply import outward ideas; it now had the maturity to absorb contemporaneous thoughts with all their contexts.[63]

"Culture" was the buzzword of the era.[64] During this period, popular culture developed, with weekly magazines, movies and cartoons, and restaurants and cafes appearing on the scene. Between 1918 and 1932, the number of journals registered under the Newspaper Law rose from 3,123 to 11,118. Farmers in rural areas began to drink beer and soda. High-rise buildings in urban centers offered a great display of domestic and imported goods; urban pleasures multiplied and diversified; private railroads connected suburban areas and carried their inhabitants to places of employment and shopping. By 1930, Japan had thirty universities with a total enrollment of about forty thousand students; almost 90 percent of adult Japanese had at least six years of elementary education.[65]

Japanese society's new cosmopolitanism also engendered greater tolerance of Christianity. From the 1910s through the mid-1920s, the government regularly invited representatives of Christianity, along with those from Buddhism and Sect Shinto, for consultation, thus recognizing Christianity as one of the country's three principal religions.[66] In September 1912, Christian representatives were invited to attend the Shinto funeral rites for Emperor Meiji; in October 1915, fifteen Christians were decorated with imperial honors in connection with the coronation of Emperor Taisho. On this occasion, Japanese Christians throughout the country showed no hesitation in displaying their patriotism.[67]

Japan was an urbanized, industrial society. It was no longer a country that could be dominated by a small handful of influential individuals in high office. With the appearance of new professions and occupations, the spread of literacy through public education, new group interests found expression. The public's demand for political participation and social reforms sometimes went wild; there were increasingly violent student, labor, and socialist movements. By and large, however, the party leaders in government steered a moderate course in domestic and international affairs. Throughout the 1920s, they cautiously accommodated the demands of antiestablishment groups, while placing Japan squarely in the prevailing international currents of cooperation, pacifism, and disarmament.

Reflecting these societal changes, especially the national mood of religious tolerance and pluralism, the Taisho period saw a marked increase in the productivity of the LDS Japan Mission. While the annual number of baptisms per missionary averaged 0.37 during 1902–1912, the number rose to 0.79 during 1913–1924.[68] When we smooth out the year-to-year volatility in baptisms by taking a three-year moving average, the increasing productivity of the Japan Mission during the Taisho period, especially from 1915 to 1922, becomes evident (figure 3.3). In fact, the average productivity of 1.02 observed during 1915–1922 exceeded what would be the productivity of LDS missionary work in Japan in the early twenty-first century.

This rather positive assessment of Taisho Japan is corroborated by the repeated pleas of Japan Mission leaders for more missionaries during this period. Frustrated with the lack of missionaries, for example, mission president Joseph H. Stimpson wrote to Mormon apostle David O. McKay in March 1920: "We have so few missionaries here . . . that the devil has to look elsewhere for a workshop."[69] In response, McKay was assigned by the First Presidency to tour the mission from late 1920 to early 1921. Stimpson observed that the visiting authority appeared "well pleased with the people" and was told that "the work ought to be pushed." The shortage of manpower relative to the mission's potential was compared by McKay to "trying to run a sixty horsepower machine with a one horsepower motor."[70] Subsequently, additional missionaries were sent to Japan, but the number, which reached the all-time peak of twenty by the end of 1922, was not sustained.

Taisho Democracy culminated in the passage in 1925 of the Universal Manhood Suffrage Law, which granted suffrage to all males over the age of twenty-five. Although universal suffrage was not achieved at this time, the law more than quadrupled the electorate, from roughly 3 million to 13 million.[71] But this came with a price: the simultaneous enactment of the Peace Preservation Law, which would later become the basis of police repression.[72] As each attempt to reform the Meiji state on democratic principles failed, the public began to doubt that a foreign idea such as democracy would

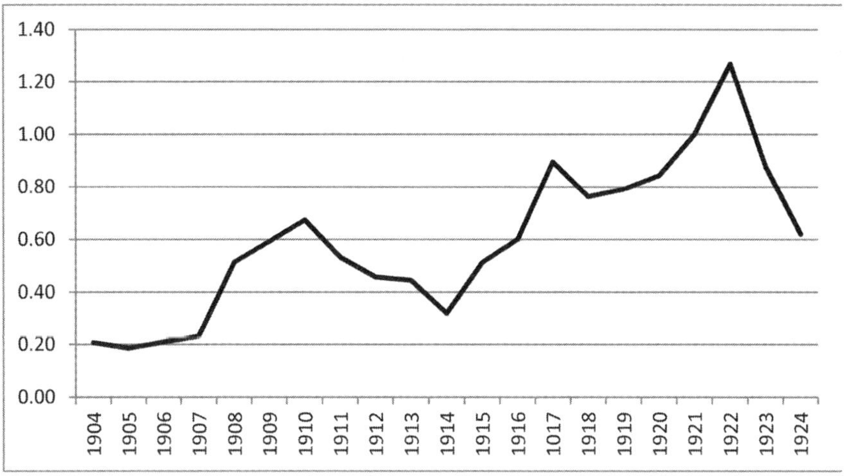

FIGURE 3.3. Latter-day Saint baptisms in Japan per missionary per year (three-year moving average), 1904–1924. Source: Author's estimates based on information in Andrew Jenson, "History of the Japan Mission."

ever take root in Japan. According to intellectual historians Kuno Osamu and Tsurumi Shunsuke, it was this suspicion that led to the rise of militarism in the 1930s.[73] In yet another nationalistic reaction to the increasing encroachment of foreign ideas, the fanatics appealed to the emperor as the nativist symbol, and sought to eliminate the "corrupt" political elites who stood between him and the people.

Conclusion

This essay has discussed how, during the pre–World War II era, the Japanese public's receptivity to a foreign religious idea was influenced by the interplay of indigenous and transplanted ideas within Japan's national consciousness and, within this context, reassessed the experience of the short-lived Japan Mission of the Church of Jesus Christ of Latter-day Saints. That the religious and intellectual climate of a country affects the acceptance of a foreign religion may sound obvious, but few have applied this approach to Latter-day Saint history, especially as it relates to prewar Japan. The essay has argued that, by the turn of the twentieth century, Christianity's fortunes were in decline, Buddhists had succeeded in conspiring with nationalists to attack Christianity as an unpatriotic religion, and Japanese were returning to things Japanese, now that the building of a modern state was complete.

From this standpoint, Mormonism arrived too late to benefit from the Westernization currents that had favored the spread of Protestantism in the 1880s. From the legal standpoint, however, the Mormons could not have come much earlier. The Meiji Constitution guaranteeing religious freedom had come into force only in 1890. Likewise, the revised treaties with the Western powers established in 1899 the freedom of foreign nationals to move freely in the interior. Though the government had unilaterally lifted most travel restrictions in the mid-1890s when the revisions were signed, it would have been difficult for LDS missionaries to proselytize outside the foreign settlements had they come earlier. The timing was thus virtually forced upon them if an evangelization of Japan was to be attempted during the prewar period.

But the Mormon cause was not entirely doomed to failure. The liberalizing forces of industrialization were being unleashed to counter the suffocating grips of State Shinto. Nationalistic undercurrents remained alive in the national consciousness, but there was a tendency toward intellectual tolerance and pluralism, which strengthened after the death of Emperor Meiji in 1912. The productivity of Mormon missionary work was significantly higher during the Taisho period and, during 1915–1922, surpassed the productivity observed in the early twenty-first century. With a more proactive engagement—for example, by addressing the exaggerated dichotomy between Christian belief and patriotism, as the Protestants had done earlier through their successful rebranding efforts, or by increasing the size of the missionary workforce considerably—the LDS Church could have won many more converts than it did in practice.

Unfortunately, the perception of the Japan Mission as a total failure persists. History has also been rewritten, ascribing the closing of the mission in 1924 to the church leaders' prophetic insight concerning what would befall U.S.-Japan relations in the future.[74] Let it be stated clearly that events could have turned either way going forward from 1924. Even if the Pacific War was destined to commence in 1941, there was no reason to close the mission seventeen years ahead of the event on that account. More likely, church authorities closed the Japan Mission because they correctly perceived it to be less productive than the church's other missions. It was their prerogative to do so, given the scarce resources at their disposal, especially during the agricultural and mining difficulties of the 1920s in Utah. But Japan's better days with America were yet to come.[75] Had the mission remained open, it would have continued to claim the converts commensurate with the number of missionaries. While the monks and the nationalists slumbered, the Japan Mission would have hung on for another ten to fifteen years, albeit under an insidiously encroaching shadow of hostility.

Notes

The author thanks Wade Fillmore, Van Gessel, Armand Mauss, Patrick Mason, and Naomi Takagi for their useful comments on an earlier draft. However, he remains solely responsible for the opinions expressed therein as well as for any remaining errors.

1. Andrew Jenson, comp., "History of the Japan Mission," 1934, Japanese Mission Historical Records and Minutes, LR 41872, Archives of the Church of Jesus Christ of Latter-day Saints (hereafter LDS Church Archives), Salt Lake City, Utah. Some previous authors have cited 166 as the total number of baptisms. Not only does Jenson have an entry for each of the 174 baptisms, but church membership records provide the name and birthdate of each person baptized, as well as the names of those who officiated in the ordinances of baptism and confirmation.
2. Church of Jesus Christ of Latter-day Saints, Conference Report, October 1903.
3. Gordon B. Hinckley, "The Church in the Orient," *Improvement Era* 67 (March 1963): 167–70.
4. Reid L. Neilson, *Early Mormon Missionary Activities in Japan, 1901–1924* (Salt Lake City: University of Utah Press, 2010), 84.
5. Otis Cary, *A History of Christianity in Japan*, vol. 1, *Roman Catholic and Orthodox Missions* (New York: Fleming H. Revell, 1909), 83, 91–92; Masaharu Anesaki, *History of Japanese Religion* (London: Kegan Paul, Trench, Trubner & Co., 1930), 244. Other estimates place the number lower. The New Advent Encyclopedia (a Catholic publication) says there were approximately three hundred thousand Roman Catholics in Japan around the year 1600. See "Japan," online at http://www.newadvent.org/cathen/08297a.htm.
6. Fumio Tamamuro, *Sōshiki to Danka* (Tokyo: Yoshikawa-Kōbunsha, 1999), 60–66, 130–62.
7. Cary, *A History of Christianity in Japan*, 1:241.
8. Fumio Tamamuro, "Bakuhan Taisei to Bukkyō," in *Ronshū Nihon Bukkyōshi*, ed. F. Tamamura (Tokyo: Yūzankaku, 1986), 7:28–35; Tamamuro, *Sōshiki to Danka*, 130–68.
9. Tamamuro, "Bakuhan Taisei to Bukkyō," 38–40; Tamamuro, *Sōshiki to Danka*, 72–98, 195–223; Fumio Tamamuro and Junko Oguri, "Bakuhan Taiseika no Bukkyō," in *Edo Bukkyō*, ed. H. Nakamura, K. Kasahara, and H. Kaneoka (Tokyo: Kōsei Shuppansha, 1972), 26.
10. Masao Takatori, *Shintō no Seiritsu* (Tokyo: Heibonsha, 1993), 154, 244, 305; Minoru Sonoda, ed., *Shintō: Nihon no Minzoku Shūkyō* (Tokyo: Kōbunsha, 1988), 3–4; Robert N. Bellah, *Tokugawa Religion* (Glencoe, IL: Free Press, 1957), 64–66.
11. Takeo Yamamoto, "Jinja eno Minzoku Shinkō," in Nakamura, Kasahara, and Kaneoka, *Edo Bukkyō*, 232–35.
12. Hiroto Saegusa and Hiroo Torii, *Nihon Shūkyō Shisō Shi* (Tokyo: Mikasa Shobō, 1938), 235; Helen Hardacre, *Shinto and the State 1868–1988* (Princeton: Princeton University Press, 1989), 16–17.
13. Yoshio Yasumaru, "Tennōseika no Minshū to Shūkyō," *Nihon Rekishi* 16 (Tokyo: Iwanami Shoten, 1976), 325–27; Yoshio Yasumaru, *Kamigami no Meiji Ishin* (Tokyo: Iwanami Shoten, 1979), 51–52; Sonoda, *Shintō: Nihon no Minzoku Shūkyō*, 34–35; Shigeyoshi Murakami, *Nihon Hyakunen no Shūkyō* (Tokyo: Kōdansha, 1968), 37–38; Eishun Ikeda, "Kindaiteki Kaimei Shisō to Bukkyō," in *Ronshū Nihon Bukkyōshi*, ed. E. Ikeda (Yūzankan Shuppan, 1987), 8:11.
14. The physical and psychological damage to Buddhism was substantial. From 1871 to 1876, the number of Buddhist temples declined from an estimated 465,049 to 71,962 and

the number of monks from 75,925 in 1872 to 19,490 in 1876. Winston Davis, *Japanese Religion and Society: Paradigms of Structure and Change* (Albany: State University of New York Press, 1992), 160–61; Yasumaru, *Kamigami no Meiji Ishin*, 117.

15. Yasumaru, "Tennōseika no Minshū to Shūkyō," 334; Hardacre, *Shinto and the State*, 4.
16. Anesaki, *History of Japanese Religion*, 336.
17. Cary, *A History of Christianity in Japan*, 1:274–79; and vol. 2, *Protestant Missions*, 45–50.
18. In 1892 the Vicar Apostolic of Southern Japan estimated that about fifty thousand descendants of the ancient Christians had been discovered and that about a half of them had formally joined the Catholic Church. Cary, *A History of Christianity in Japan*, 1:281–93.
19. Yasumaru, *Kamigami no Meiji Ishin*, 69.
20. Of these, around six hundred died in captivity. Marius B. Jansen, *The Making of Modern Japan* (Cambridge, MA: The Belknap Press of Harvard University Press, 2000), 463.
21. During 1871–1872, nearly 700 children and 1,600 adults were baptized; by the time the persecution ended, the Catholic missionaries had established ties with 15,000 people, and knew that there were many thousands more who had inherited the faith of the ancient Christians. Cary, *A History of Christianity in Japan*, 1:332–34.
22. John F. Howes, "Japanese Christians and American Missionaries," in *Changing Japanese Attitudes Toward Modernization*, ed. Marius B. Jansen (Princeton: Princeton University Press, 1965), 340–45.
23. Hamish Ion, *American Missionaries, Christian Oyatoi, and Japan, 1859–73* (Vancouver: University of British Columbia Press, 2009), 26–27.
24. Ibid., 3, 47; Cary, *A History of Christianity in Japan*, 2:55–56; Charles W. Iglehart, *A Century of Protestant Christianity in Japan* (Rutland, VT: Charles E. Tuttle, 1959), 41.
25. Masashi Sakurai, *Meiji Shūkyō Undō Shi* (Tokyo: Moriyama Shoten, 1932), 84–86.
26. For an English translation of a portion of the official mission records, see Kunitake Kume, *Japan Rising: The Iwakura Embassy to the USA and Europe 1871–1873* (New York: Cambridge University Press, 2009).
27. In 1909, there were 62,694 Catholics in Japan, of which 44,931 were in Nagasaki. See Cary, *A History of Christianity in Japan*, 1:371.
28. Iglehart, *A Century of Protestant Christianity in Japan*, 48–49, 60, 91.
29. Tōru Miyagawa and Kazuo Hijikata, *Jiyū Minken Shisō to Nihon no Roman Shugi* (Tokyo: Aoki Shoten, 1971), 106–9.
30. Masashi Sakurai, *Kinsei Nihon Shūkyō Shisō Shi* (Fukuoka: Tonshindō, 1944), 237.
31. Anesaki, *History of Japanese Religion*, 356.
32. Ion, *American Missionaries*, 300.
33. Hideteru Yamamoto, ed., *Nihon Kirisuto Kyōkai Shi* (Tokyo: Nihon Kirisuto Kyōkai, 1928), 174.
34. Because the government gave limited educational opportunities to women, Christian education was a significant part of women's education. Women constituted more than two-thirds of foreign missionaries during the Meiji period. Misako Kunihara and Rui Kohiyama, "Nihon Joshi Kirisutokyō Kyōikukai no Sōsetsu to Katsudō," *Kirisutokyō Gakkō Kyōiku Dōmei Hyakunenshi Kiyō*, no. 7 (June 2009): 19–20.
35. Sakurai, *Kinsei Nihon Shūkyō Shisō Shi*, 237.

36. In 1877, there were about seven hundred Protestants in Japan. Murakami, *Nihon Hyakunen no Shūkyō*, 62–63.
37. Howes, "Japanese Christians and American Missionaries," 346–47; Anesaki, *History of Japanese Religion*, 337–38; Hiroaki Matsuzawa, "Kirisutokyō to Chishikijin," *Nihon Rekishi* 16 (Tokyo: Iwanami Shoten, 1976), 288.
38. Eiichi Kudō, *Meijiki no Kirisutokyō* (Tokyo: Kyōbunkan, 1979), 45–49.
39. The General Evangelical Protestant Missionary Society, which came to Japan in 1885, represented the liberal Protestantism of Switzerland and Germany, which accepted higher criticism and a more tolerant view of non-Christian religions. The Unitarians, who arrived in 1887, disavowed any missionary activity and defined their aim only as fraternization with the non Christian world; they received broad acceptance among the educated class, including Buddhist scholars. Norihisa Suzuki, *Meiji Shūkyō Shichō no Kenkyū* (Tokyo: Tokyo Daigaku Shuppankai, 1979), 25–70.
40. Iglehart, *A Century of Protestant Christianity in Japan*, 91–93.
41. Davis, *Japanese Religion and Society*, 158.
42. Inoue Enryō, a Jōdo Shinshū monk educated at the anti-Christian Imperial University, was the most prominent critic of Christianity during the 1880s. Yoshio Yasumaru, "Rekishi no nakadeno Kattō to Mosaku," in *Kindaika to Dentō*, ed. Yoshio Yasumaru (Tokyo: Shūjunsha, 1986), 52–56; Hiromichi Serikawa, *Kindaika no Bukkyō Shisō* (Tokyo: Daitō Shuppansha, 1989), 34–66; Yoshiro Tamura, *Japanese Buddhism: A Cultural History* (Tokyo: Kōsei Publishing, 2000), 162–63.
43. Hideo Kishimoto, ed., *Meiji Bunka Shi* (Tokyo: Hara Shobō, 1979), 6:351; Anesaki, *History of Japanese Religion*, 360–61; Tamura, *Japanese Buddhism*, 162.
44. Miyagawa and Hijikata, *Jiyū Minken Shisō to Nihon no Roman Shugi*, 111–12.
45. Kishimoto, *Meiji Bunka Shi*, 6:354–55.
46. Hideo Satō, ed., *Kyōiku: Goshinei to Kyōiku Chokugo* (Tokyo: Misuzu Shobō, 1994), 1:165–69; Kishimoto, *Meiji Bunka Shi*, 6:356–59.
47. Through the intervention of national Christian leaders, the student was eventually allowed to return to school. Akio Dohi, "Kindai Tennōsei to Kirisutokyō," in *Kindai Tennōsei no Keisei to Kirisutokyō*, ed. Tomisaka Kirisutokyō Sentā (Tokyo: Shinkyō Shuppansha, 1996), 239–45, 304–14.
48. Kazuo Ishida, "Shūkyō Kyōiku Kinshi no Shirei nitsuite," *Seisen Joshi Daigaku Kiyō* 8 (1961): 41–43, 66–68.
49. Heber J. Grant, "A Japanese Journal," undated, Americana Collection, Harold B. Lee Library, Brigham Young University, Provo, Utah.
50. Apparently, one of the missionaries was suffering from depression. See Jenson, "History of the Japan Mission," entry for December 21, 1904.
51. Neilson, *Early Mormon Missionary Activities in Japan*, 116.
52. Official LDS Church data do not provide a breakdown of converts and missionaries by country. According to the 2011 Church Almanac, church membership in Japan increased by 637 from end-2010 to end-2011, including births, deaths, and net move-ins. At the time of the Great East Japan Earthquake in 2011, the church announced that 638 missionaries were serving in Japan at the time ("LDS Church to Move Japan Missionaries out of Tsunami Area," March 15, 2011, www.kls.com/?nid=148&sid=14743094).

53. A similar experience was seen in the immediate post–World War II period. How the initial enthusiastic reaction to the Mormon message was quickly followed by widespread apathy is documented by Shinji Takagi, "Riding on the Eagle's Wings: The Japanese Mission under American Occupation, 1948–52," *Journal of Mormon History* 29 (Spring 2003): 200–32.
54. Hinckley, "The Church in the Orient," 169.
55. Alma O. Taylor, Journals, January 5, 1909, Special Collections, Harold B. Lee Library, Brigham Young University.
56. Dohi, "Kindai Tennōsei to Kirisutokyō," 319–30.
57. Iglehart, *A Century of Protestant Christianity in Japan*, 133.
58. Ibid., 95–97, 106–7; Murakami, *Nihon Hyakunen no Shūkyō*, 77–79; Sakurai, *Kinsei Nihon Shūkyō Shisō Shi*, 305–7.
59. Jenson, "History of the Japan Mission."
60. Alma O. Taylor, "Japan, the Ideal Mission Field," *Improvement Era* 13 (July 1910): 781, 783.
61. Osamu Kuno and Shunsuke Tsurumi, *Gendai Nihon no Shisō* (Tokyo: Iwanami Shoten, 1956), 151–60; Jansen, *The Making of Modern Japan*, 537.
62. Jansen, *The Making of Modern Japan*, 537, 550, 574.
63. Keizō Ikimatsu, *Taishōki no Shisō to Bunka* (Tokyo: Aoki Shoten, 1971), 14.
64. Miyagawa and Hijikata, *Jiyū Minken Shisō to Nihon no Roman Shugi*, 109–10.
65. Jansen, *The Making of Modern Japan*, 541, 570–73.
66. Iglehart, *A Century of Protestant Christianity in Japan*, 185–86; Dohi, "Kindai Tennōsei to Kirisutokyō," 297–301.
67. Dohi, "Kindai Tennōsei to Kirisutokyō," 303–4; Katsuhito Kurahashi, "Taishō Demokurashī to Kagawa Toyohiko," in *Taishō Demokurashī, Tennōsei, Kirisutokyō*, ed. Tomisaka Kirisutokyō Sentā (Tokyo: Shinkyō Shuppansha, 2001), 262.
68. The difference is statistically significant at the 5 percent level.
69. As quoted in Murray L. Nichols, "History of the Japan Mission of the LDS Church 1901–1924" (M.A. thesis, Brigham Young University, 1957), 69.
70. As quoted in Neilson, *Early Mormon Missionary Activities in Japan*, 130–32.
71. The tax qualifications for voting rights at the outset of parliamentary government meant an electorate of about half a million males. Tax qualifications for the vote had been lowered in 1900 (from fifteen yen to ten) and again in 1919 (to three yen), but rural landowners were disproportionately advantaged relative to unpropertied urban workers. Jansen, *The Making of Modern Japan*, 508.
72. Ikimatsu, *Taishōki no Shisō to Bunka*, 34–35; Jansen, *The Making of Modern Japan*, 506–7.
73. Kuno and Tsurumi, *Gendai Nihon no Shisō*, 123–25.
74. It appears that this view stems at least in part from the account contributed in July 1949 by Ernest B. Woodward to the Mission Historical Record of the postwar Japanese Mission. Woodward described the anti-American sentiment he had encountered as a missionary in Japan in the aftermath of the passage on May 26, 1924, of the U.S. Immigration (or Johnson-Reed) Act of 1924, which denied Japanese the right to immigrate to the United States. He also recalled the greeting he and other returning missionaries received from Mormon President Heber J. Grant on August 25, 1924, upon arrival in

Salt Lake City: "Thank God you are home because I know what is in store for the people of that land." Japanese Mission Historical Record, January–August 1924, LDS Church Archives. The passage of a U.S. law in May could not have been a reason for the decision to close the mission less than a month later, and any anti-American sentiment was isolated and temporary.

75. In subsequent years, a number of American companies would form joint ventures with Japanese counterparts (e.g., Westinghouse, 1924; Carrier, 1930; Associated Oil, 1931) or build production facilities in Japan (e.g., Ford, 1925; General Motors, 1927; Victor, 1927); and American things would flood the Japanese market through the 1930s (e.g., the Tarzan and King Kong movies). Baseball became a popular pastime for Japanese, who were thrilled to watch Major League all-star teams that included Lou Gehrig (in 1931) and Babe Ruth (in 1934) play against Japanese all-stars. For the Japanese economy of the Meiji and Taisho periods, see Takafusa Nakamura, *Meiji-Taishō-ki no Keizai* (Tokyo: Tokyo Daigaku Shuppankai, 1985).

Chapter 4 | Church Unity and the Challenge of Cultural Diversity

A View from across the Sahara

Walter E. A. van Beek

We are all Africans.

—from a sign welcoming tourists in Ghana

The Church and Cultural Variation

Culture—defined anthropologically as a way of life and thinking that varies over times and places—does not sit easily with the LDS Church, for two reasons. First, the church defines itself as an undivided whole based upon one dominant blueprint for organization, irrespective of where the particular branch, ward, or stake is grounded. Unitary organization is considered as one of the major hallmarks of LDS Mormonism, operating under the assumption that this blueprint is applicable to any kind of cultural background, a one-size-fits-all model. This organization is more than a solution of practical administrative problems: it is considered to be the result of revelation. In Mormonism the restoration of the gospel immediately implied a restoration of the pristine organization of Christ's original church; the two, message and organization, can hardly be separated.[1] Mormon ecclesiastical discourse is replete with notions of unity intimately associated with a unitary organization. From hierarchical priesthood structures to meetinghouse plans, and from priesthood ordinances to Sunday School lessons, unity shines through, but always in the form of uniformity. Even grooming is standardized, as is the male "uniform."[2] The idea is that anyone visiting a ward other than her own will feel immediately at home, recognizing the basic church architecture and layout as well as all pictures in the corridor—taken from a relatively limited range of official options—and attending a lesson that will be taught on the same day (give or take) with the same curricular materials everywhere in the church. This standardization holds true even more with the church's temples, as local temple presidencies have no say at all even in the most minute details of decoration, let alone aspects of the ritual.[3]

The second reason is that the Latter-day Saints' culture in its Deseret setting traditionally tends to be rather homogeneous. The church began in America and has remained a dominantly American cultural institution throughout its history; the many early converts from Europe hailed from North Atlantic countries culturally closest to, and thus readily assimilable into, nineteenth-century America. The church did not tap heavily into the major Irish, Italian, and eastern European immigrations to America of the nineteenth century. Outreach to African Americans has been extremely limited due to the church's former racial restrictions, and LDS growth among Hispanics is a relatively recent phenomenon. So for the first century of its existence the church had limited experiences with significant cultural diversity. Converts from the South Pacific formed an exception, but they developed a presence of their own either in Polynesia or in isolated communities in the American West. The relative homogeneity of the LDS population, and the strong assimilative tendencies that minimized what diversity did exist, has allowed scholars to refer to "the Mormon people" in the singular, not plural.[4]

Only after World War II did cultural diversity become a major issue in the church. First it appeared in the 1960s in Relief Society manuals, where culture meant refreshments and recipes, as well as cute traditional dresses, to be savored, tasted, or shown. Then roadshows in the then-MIA (youth organization) zoomed in on the fountain of forms that cultural diversity offers, allowing and stimulating expression of slightly divergent forms of the general Mormon paradigm. In 1978 a BYU publication defined Mormonism as "A Faith for All Cultures," in which cultural diversity was hailed as a human endowment, all the while stressing that the gospel as such fit comfortably into all of the cultures present on earth.[5] One probable factor for this greater recognition of cultural diversity in the church was that America itself became an increasingly and self-consciously multicultural society in the second half of the twentieth century. Toward the end of the century, scholars studying Mormonism outside the United States showed that certain aspects of the organization were not at all culture-free, and that the notion of a culture-free gospel had no meaning at all.[6]

The aim of this essay is to argue that culture does matter, and that a church as globally present as the LDS one should acknowledge culture's importance and thus come to terms with variation, both for the well-being of its members and for the future expansion of the church. My vantage point is Africa, as I have a long and intimate knowledge and relationship with that continent, and because African cultures differ significantly from the Deseret culture. In this essay I will frequently use the shorthand "African culture," which in no way that should be construed as one synthetic entity, just as a theme with variations. Viewing the enormous expanse of the continent and its ancient inhabitation, one can expect to find most types of cultural construction in Africa, and that is just the case. Africa harbors the whole range from foraging societies

(Bushmen, pygmies), herding societies, various types of horticultural and agricultural societies, as well as fully industrialized complexes, and the major cultural themes covary with each of these ecotypes.

As an opening example of how culture can impinge on organization, let us look at job rotation within the church. This is an integral part of church administration and has been shown to fit well into an American culture, with its role segregation: the individual in American culture stands relatively loose from his job and his position, even more so now when individuals frequently change not only jobs but also careers. If a man becomes bishop, that means a calling with a lot of work, but not a change of personality—he does not become someone else. So when he is released he will fit himself into another role, without necessarily feeling truncated in his existence. In other cultures this is different. Job rotation does not at all fit in the cultural definitions of power in Africa. In this part of the world the idea that a powerful position is for a limited time only is hard to swallow. People called to a position of power or authority integrate the position into their personality, as part of their view of self, and so do the people around them. So a release implies partial loss of personhood, which adds significantly to the cognitive and emotional costs of membership.[7] As Jennifer Basquiat remarked on Haitian Latter-day Saints (mostly of African descent): "I still have to see the first active ex-branch president."[8] Furthermore, none of the original leaders of the Nigerian independent Mormon Church made the transition to the regular LDS Church[9]—nor, for that matter, did those in Zaire. For many of them it meant that through loss of power they lost income as well, illustrating the intimate combination of symbolic and economic capital in Africa.[10]

Whereas in Deseret job rotation builds a large body of experienced administrators in the side benches of the meeting hall, ready to be used for many purposes, in Africa and the Caribbean job rotation creates a large group of inactive members with formerly high-profile positions, a situation I call "bleeding at the top." This, in turn, potentially affects the morale of those who stay and diminishes prospects for building cultural capital in local areas. African cultures see power not as an incidental attribute but as a personality characteristic, not so much as a top-down delegated power or a bottom-up delegation of trust, but rather as personal property that is an inalienable part of one's lasting identity.[11] Loss of power thus means loss of face, even loss of identity. Of course, Deseret Mormons will maintain that this is not a question of power, just a temporary stewardship, but that notion is even more alien to Africans. As I heard one Senegalese official say (upon being pressured to resign a high-profile position), "Africans do not resign, Europeans do."

Africa forms a patchwork of many different cultures, of course, and power is defined in various ways. After all, the continent that hosts its share of dictators also brought us Nelson Mandela, who did step down after one term—which added to his unique international status. I am concerned here with key commonalities throughout African cultural variety, and within these variations culture informs individual agency, especially in fields where social relations are dominant, such as power. Thus, the six cultural models for power in Africa that I have previously identified share as a common denominator the close relation between person and power.[12]

Culture

So culture matters, but it is a difficult concept. The hallmark of culture is variation. In classic anthropological thinking "universals," i.e., cross-cultural human commonalities, stem from nature while culture is the varied response different groups have on their being in the natural world. Present thinking is less rigid, stressing coevolution of human nature and culture, while still considering any substantial divergence to be cultural.[13] *Homo sapiens* is genetically extremely homogeneous. Biologically the single-species genus could well be considered one species within a larger genus, encompassing also chimpanzees and bonobos; *Homo sapiens* is the sole survivor of a long, branching, and often pruned line of hominids. We might say that while our genetic hardware is surprisingly identical, the cultural software varies to a great degree.

When speaking about culture, we immediately go into the plural—cultures—the divergent strains of social heredity, to use Ralph Linton's classic definition. Anthropologists long thought they were able to delineate separate cultures, especially in Africa where the so-called tribal people invited the construction of separate, distinct, and coherent tribal cultures. We have now learned that this could only be done at a rather high level of construction, and that the drive to define tribes came from colonials for whom the division into separate units was administratively expedient. On closer inspection and with a critical reading of history, cultural boundaries become vague, the content less integrated and much more amenable to change. Now anthropologists speak about cultures as emergent realities more than as pre-existing blueprints. That means that the notion of culture has accrued vagueness, even if the pervasiveness of culture is recognized. What remain important, however, are cultural differences; even if cultures cannot be defined unambiguously, the differences between cultures are real.

Culture can be discerned at two levels. The deep level is that of broad guidelines for living, not in the form of precise customs but as general value orientations, say, models *for* behavior. The surface level is the customary solutions to recurrent challenges, or the models *of* behavior. The latter includes customs, organizational and behavioral forms, like etiquette. Each of them solves a puzzle—for instance, funerary customs deal with how to dispose of the dead—as they offer a framework for how to coordinate human action and to smooth out the wrinkles in daily interaction. Some of these challenges are essential, like educational systems; others are epiphenomenal, like the use of proper address forms.

Let us have a short look at the models *for* behavior, the basic orientations that underlie cultural variation. Following Geert Hofstede's research, one can see the cultural variation along four axes: power distance, individualism, uncertainty avoidance, and masculinity.[14] *Power distance* is the extent to which the less powerful members of institutions and organizations within a country expect differences in power and accept their situation, or in Gramsci's term the measure in which power tends toward hegemony. *Individualism* pertains to societies in which the ties between individuals are loose: everyone is expected to look after himself or herself and his or her immediate family. Collectivism as its opposite defines societies in which people from birth onward are integrated into strong and cohesive in-groups. A society is called *masculine*, according to Hofstede, when emotional gender roles are clearly distinct and fixed: men are supposed to be assertive, tough, and focused on material success, whereas women are supposed to be more modest, tender, and concerned with the quality of life. A society is *feminine* if this role division is less fixed or reversed. *Uncertainty avoidance* is the extent to which the members of a culture feel threatened by ambiguous or unknown situations. The crucial aspect is that each of these axes is value-free; no position is "good," "bad," or "better," even if they are not completely independent; also, they are not dichotomies but scales with many intermediate positions.

Let us apply these axes to three cultures: Deseret, Dutch, and "African." "Deseret" I define as the intermountain strand of North American culture, heavily informed by Mormons and Mormonism. In addition to its distinctively Mormon characteristics, Deseret culture includes aspects of the cultures of the American West and North.[15] Thus we see in Deseret the high individualism of American culture moderated into a pioneer ethos: not fully individualist as cooperation is important, but the level of cooperation among group members ultimately depends on the individual. Power distance is large, as people are wont to live in a hegemonic national system, a tendency reinforced by explicit patriotism, which is a national ideology for power distance. The allegiance is to the idea of America, not the actual government, as Deseret culture, fully in tune with the American ethos in general, does not trust its government. Uncertainty avoidance is very high, as neither ambiguities nor open-ended questions are tolerated; in Deseret culture the answers come before the questions. Masculinity is lower than the surrounding U.S. culture, as male emotional responsibility is stressed, more than achievement orientation. This trend is mitigated by the gender hegemony in the power structure, which results in the paradox of masculine management of feminine values.

Dutch culture is less individualist, and Dutch citizens have a network of loyalties to a variety of groups and associations, including families, friends, clubs, neighborhood

FIGURE 4.1. One major coping strategy for Africans is having large families. Here is a picture of my "older brother" Dogolu Saye with some of his sixty grandchildren. Photograph by the author.

and civic associations to schools, political parties (a lot!), and religious denominations. Volunteerism is an important value. A very low power distance characterizes Dutch culture, as social and especially economic differences between people are hardly accepted. Also patriotism is very low, one of the lowest in the world, but paradoxically trust in the government is quite robust, part of a general trust in society. An ideology of collective and emotional unity is only present at ceremonial high times, and these are few and far between. Pledging allegiance to the flag would be simply ridiculous in Dutch culture. Roles are not fixed, and Hofstede considers Dutch culture as very feminine, with the notion of a caring society flying high. Social uncertainty is to be avoided at considerable cost—the system of social security is well built and appreciated—but in existential questions considerable ambivalence is tolerated.

African culture—and again here I am speaking of commonalities in an array of cultures—is highly collectivist, with the individual always relating to family first, fully accepting the obligations that come from group membership. Power distance is huge, as people easily accommodate large differences in power and wealth. It is not the nation that commands respect, but rather the smaller group—ethnic, village, and family. Patriotism usually is very low, simply because nations are new, states are weak, and government is mostly absent—and if present at all surely cannot be trusted. Social unity only exists on the lower echelons, actually little beyond the village and family level. Ambivalence and uncertainty are facts of life in Africa, and people have developed intricate coping mechanisms with unforeseen and unforeseeable situations.

So people think and thus feel and behave differently in various cultures, and evidently this informs church behavior as well, both in organizational and spiritual matters, and in the choices people make. Models *for* behavior result in groups solving practical problems in particular ways, and thus inform the models *of* behavior, or the accepted and cherished ways to arrange life.

Gospel Culture?

From an initial acceptation of culture in its innocuous forms, the LDS Church leadership has moved toward culture as a hindrance. "We do not do culture here," was an expression heard at church headquarters in the 1990s, and in correlated material little is found on cultural diversity. But of course, not only does everybody "do" culture, we "are," to a large measure, our culture, in most of what we collectively do, speak, and think. In an address to the African church leadership in November 2010, Dallin Oaks tried to sidestep the quandaries of cultural diversity with the notion of "gospel culture," which he defined as "a distinctive way of life, a set of values and expectations and practices common to all members. This gospel culture comes from the plan of salvation, the commandments of God, and the teachings of the living prophets." What it entails is not specified at all, other than the Proclamation on the Family, but surely that is but one sector of culture among many, and as far as culture is concerned, just underscores traditional gender relations. As for African culture, Oaks lauded the strong African family as well as modesty, and then zoomed in on what he called "negative cultural traditions," with special attention to the practice of *lobola*, or bride price. His problem with bride price was simple: it delays marriage for returned missionaries and as such presents a moral hazard. He went on to warn against excessive debt incurred by weddings and funerals.

This notion of gospel culture amounts to a cultural critique more than to the definition of a culture, and from Elder Oaks's ecclesiastical standpoint the critique is all-too-easy: all activities that impinge on the present Deseret model of membership are condemned. What seems to be at the core of this model is for young people to go on missions and then marry and raise children while active in the church. This is a quite restricted view of culture, limited only to the dutiful performance of certain church commandments and expectations.

Gospel culture is presented as an ideal culture, but the point is that it has no content. The notion would imply that "the gospel" provides meaningful directives in all social customs and manners, and at least hints at solutions for all of life's everyday quandaries: how to bury one's dead, how to marry, how to define power, how to vote, what side of the street to drive on. That, evidently, is not the case. In fact, Mormons worldwide follow local customs simply because they are part and parcel of their host cultures on the one hand, but on the other hand because a gospel culture does not really exist. The notion of gospel culture is not well considered, and can be seen as a way to avoid cultural issues in a church bent on uniformity—in fact as an excuse to deny that culture matters.

It is not by chance that Elder Oaks brought up culture in an address to members in Africa, as the cultural challenges for the LDS Church in that continent are substantial. The remainder of this essay considers what this all might mean for the forages of Mormonism into the "Dark Continent."

The African Adventure

Africa is the last continent the Church of Jesus Christ of Latter-day Saints ventured into in its drive to spread the restored gospel and to grow into a global player, and a difficult continent it is. Historically, the black priesthood ban shut down most of Africa for LDS evangelization, limiting membership and church presence to the few places, such as South Africa, where a white presence had enough critical mass to establish some LDS foothold.[16] Since 1978, however, the church has aligned itself with the other Christian denominations in affirming equal rights for people of all colors and has resultantly opened up missions on the black continent. Hesitantly at first, limiting its thrust to English-speaking countries, the church gradually branched out into some francophone areas as well, such as Congo and Cameroon (the latter country is officially bilingual). The reasons for these choices have been varied, and often depended upon the chance presence of trusted people in Deseret who happened to have links with these countries. The first LDS missionaries were confronted with that very African phenomenon, the Independent Church. Indeed, the LDS Church was not immune to this grassroots phenomenon that has confronted every other Christian denomination working in Africa. The story of the Nigerian independent Latter-day Saint Church is fairly well-known in Mormon circles.[17] Sometimes it is used as a faith-promoting story about the appeal of Joseph Smith's scriptures, at other times as a warning that without the official leadership members will do the strangest things. The simple truth is that independent churches are bread and butter in Africa and that all foreign religious organizations, especially all colonial churches, have been used as models for endogenous African forms of Christianity.

Africa still is a daunting place for the members as well as the leadership of the LDS Church. Long ago I pleaded with a church official to include Cameroon in the

FIGURE 4.2. A young Kapsiki in an independent African church. Photograph by the author.

missionary project of the church. We also spoke about the way that expatriates live in Africa. I described to him my lasting relationship with Africa, both in Cameroon and Mali where I have a compound in a village far out in the bush, and the way anthropologists such as myself live with and between the people. He remarked that his Africa was quite different, as he had been residing in the best hotels, air-conditioned mansions, and official government offices, and that the only contact with "ordinary" Africans was limited to hotel personnel and taxi drivers. This is not very surprising as that situation is shared by most tourists visiting the continent, and for short visits such as his, is hard to avoid. In anthropology this is called the "bubble," the world created for visitors to travel in those infrastructural arrangements that permit the professional reception of guests—such as hotels, lodges, personnel, and transportation, all part of an intermediary organizational layer protecting the visitor from the unfortunate features of the destination.[18]

For most people in the Western world, Africa is "the Other Continent," a notion heavily influenced by media. Films, documentaries, and brochures depict two Africas, one romantic and the other harsh and unforgiving. In the first, Africa is the prima donna of "nature." Here the "West" goes to find its adventures in the splendor of the African game parks: the vast herds of wildebeest thundering through the immense plains of untouched wilderness, the elusive "big five" every traveler must have spotted and photographed. This Africa is also the continent of colorful, strange cultures, picturesque people, thatched huts in savannah surroundings, where one can encounter a truly "other" culture. That is the romantic neocolonial mix that dominates African iconography: elephants and Bushmen, lions and Maasai, camels and Tuareg. Africa is the continent before the coming of man, or before the coming of "civilization." For some Americans it is the continent of their roots (i.e., for African Americans), but for most it is the "ultimate elsewhere."

The media also show Africa in another way, through the news channels and documentaries, as a continent of suffering and crisis, with hunger and war reducing people to recipients of much-needed charitable donations. Africa has to be helped; the African people have to be kept alive by the rich north. This, too, is not without its reasons, as a number of African countries certainly have their problems. This is the Africa of the journalists.

In between those two Africas there is a third one, the Africa of the people, living in villages, towns, and cities, trying to make ends meet, marrying, trying to remain healthy, and being religious. Quite religious even, for secularism is not a significant presence yet on this continent. This third Africa is also the one of the African Latter-day Saints, who never see a lion, and most of whom never witness a war or experience a famine. It is this Africa where culture rules. The ancient human history in Africa, combined with the loss of political agency in the colonization experience, has resulted in a huge array of small groups with persistent cultural differences, as variations on several general cultural themes. In the following I will touch upon some of those general themes.

Africa, Colonization, and LDS History

Our cultural distance to Africa is somewhat surprising as the continent is the cradle of humanity, where our earliest ancestors carved out the conditions of our existence and laid the foundations for our phenomenal success as a species. As human beings we are more at home in Africa than anywhere else on the planet, or at least we should be. The savannas are our earliest playground, where our species grew up in constant interaction with almost the same animals that we now consider as a parallel universe on television. This notion of origin, by the way, is well engrained in present African thought, and the role of the continent in the origin of mankind is never to be doubted or slighted in their presence. This provides a slight quandary for a church with an America-oriented mythic history, with members who are not always as comfortable with the notion of human evolution as they should be.

The recent history of Africa is shot through with colonization processes in various phases. European expansion brought Africa south of the Sahara within reach beginning in the fifteenth century, but actual colonization came late, in the second half of the nineteenth century. The LDS Church, as young as it is, is still older than most African written history. When Joseph Smith founded his church, the majority of Africa, particularly the interior, was completely unknown and colonization still had yet to take off. At the time of the foundation of Nauvoo, David Livingstone made his first journeys into the depth of the continent along the Zambezi. During the struggle of the church with the United States on the issue of polygamy, Europeans just started to explore the African interior, while Utah gained statehood only a few years after major European colonial powers divided up the continent at the Berlin Conference (1884–1885), known in retrospect as the "Rape of Africa." It was during the administration of the LDS Church's sixth president, Joseph F. Smith, that the first European arrived in the Cameroonian village where I worked; only after World War I did slave raiding stop in that area. The *pax colonialis* was gradually established only after World War II, and I witnessed myself the last attack by one village on another, in 1972. Meanwhile by 1960, during the administration of church president David O. McKay, most countries in Africa had gained their independence in a massive wave of decolonization. Africa shows the contrast of a deep history of biological humanity, with a very late inclusion in officially recorded history, a combination of old cultures in a very young political setting. In the last half century change in Africa has occurred with lightning speed.

In 1973 I refereed the first football match between two villages that formerly had been at war with each other; now, a generation later, all walk with their mobile phones. And, of course, everyone plays football.

The missionaries of the various churches and mission societies were part and parcel of the European colonization effort; thus, white presence and missionary presence on the continent go hand in hand. The LDS Church came late, for several reasons, one of them because they primarily limited their early missionary work to other Christians. Still today, the message of the LDS missionary endeavor is not directed at those who adhere to the traditional religions or Islam. The LDS Church seemingly has little to say to non-Christians, typical of a church born out of dissent with mainstream Christendom and lacking a clear missiology.[19] Yet, Africa is considered a missionary success, judging from the quick growth in membership and the building of temples in Nigeria and Ghana. The fact that LDS presence is postcolonial fits in with the LDS self-understanding as a postcolonial church. However, one has to consider that all churches are a success in Africa, and the LDS Church is not among the spectacularly successful ones, not by far.[20] That has everything to do with cultural differences and the attempts of the church to negate these.

Africa and Cultural Critique

Africa offers the most poignant example of why cultural issues do matter, simply because African cultures are more different than the ones encountered so far in the LDS evangelization of other continents. For a poignant example, we may take a closer look at bride price, one of the issues raised by Elder Oaks in his talk to the African Latter-day Saints. In many local cultures in Africa the groom has to provide a substantial gift to the father of his bride in order to marry her. The term "price" suggests a purchase—and that is the word Oaks uses in his talk—but that is not the case, and "bridewealth" is more used by anthropologists. In my research on the Kapsiki in Cameroon I found a marriage system dominated by bridewealth, as in Southern Africa. Among both the Kapsiki and the cultures of South Africa, marriage clearly is a gift exchange between the family of the bride and the family of the groom: the first party gives a bride, and the groom's family reciprocates this with the gift of the bridewealth. Thus the bride's family is compensated for the loss of her work and her children. The bridewealth is a substantial gift of capital, literally capital meaning heads of stock, cattle, camels, goats, and sheep, with a host of symbolic items thrown in; nowadays money takes an ever-larger place. The expression goes, "the bridewealth is where the bride is not." This marriage exchange is not a purchase but a relationship; for instance, there is no refund in case of disappointment, nor any selling back or selling onward. For us from the North it looks like monetization of the women, in which women are exchanged for cattle, and as such an affront to women's rights and dignity. Western feminism has had its problems with the custom, but was confronted with a massive African female response that Western values should not be imposed and that African women were perfectly capable of deciding on their own what was important in their culture and what was not. And they surely are, as in Africa women always have had an important say in social life.

In fact, bridewealth should be seen as an expression of the female value and the supreme importance of the family. The value of a woman is nowhere higher than in Africa, but in a specific manner: the bridewealth is exchanged for her fertility, her work, and her sexuality, values which resonate with the general pronatality of Africa, as well as with the importance of the family. Polygyny is part of this picture, as it creates a marriage scene where any woman can always find a husband, so always is of worth in reproduction and productive work. Thus family, bridewealth, marriage-*cum*-polygyny, and fertility form a closely knit conglomerate in Africa, a total institution that cannot be dealt with in its constituent parts. Simply put, it does not make sense to laud the strong African family and condemn the *lobola*.

This does not preclude excesses, though. Modern developments in bridewealth payments have followed several lines. In some societies the bridewealth has inflated, leading to high sums being handed over, and indeed the old wealthy men may dominate the marriage market, part of a general gerontocracy that pervades African culture (as well as LDS Church leadership). In most cases, however, the amount of the bridewealth has remained relatively stable, sometimes even decreasing to a symbolic amount handed over just before the wedding. In these latter cases the wedding celebration itself may mushroom. Young men may complain about bridewealth obligations, but they have done so in the past as well, and in the end they conform to the custom: the general age of marriage in modern Africa is declining, not rising. In some East African herding communities in the past, the obligations led to considerable age difference between groom and bride, with the groom much older than the bride, a tendency reinforced by polygyny (a condition well known in nineteenth-century Utah and still present among many Mormon offshoot groups).[21] Sometimes this age difference was regulated by defining age groups for the boys, which led them through several stages in life like herdsman and warrior until they eventually were allowed to marry. Today this age difference is shrinking fast, the grooms becoming younger and the brides more mature, while still bridewealth is paid.

So a blanket condemnation of bridewealth is culturally uninformed, especially when coupled with admiration for the African family and the modesty that indeed comes with all this. In a larger cultural framework this major institution fits in with the other customs mentioned by Oaks, the high-expense weddings and funerals. Funerals

FIGURE 4.3. Our cook, Joseph Zra Mpa, brings a flock of sheep, part of his bridewealth, to his future father-in-law. Photograph by the author.

always are major events in Africa, for nowhere is the farewell for the dead more exuberantly celebrated than on this continent. As the famous anthropologist Claude Lévi-Strauss remarked, in Asian cultures one could write a book on a birth, in Africa on a death. In the continent where we came about as *Homo sapiens*, human life always has been precarious, its increase celebrated, new unions cherished and deaths bewailed. So, also in modern times in Africa the rites of transition are elaborated, feasted with a great gusto, a love of life that is captivating for visitors, bystanders, and even church officials.

Africa "does culture" because Africa "does life." In Africa life means the conquest of death plus the celebration of togetherness and communitas.[22] And here the expensive rituals come in. Births are not overly celebrated in Africa. In traditional Africa a child was a precarious good, only to be celebrated after the first hazardous years of its life. The Kapsiki traditionally had only thirty percent of their children reach the age of five. Weddings are feasted, but not always. Among the Dogon of Mali, marriage is a very gradual process, in which a couple seamlessly moves toward living together and raising children, with the full consent of the community, but without any specific markers or ritualized feasts. This gentle definition of marriage does not give rise to

FIGURE 4.4. Pronatality African style. A Dogon statue indicating the wish to have children. Photograph by the author.

rituals, precisely because there are no major transactions or transitions to be effectuated. Yet marriage in this society is very stable.

Death is the ultimate celebration of African life, and if anything death rituals are a way to show the collective values of the community. They are exuberant, with much drumming, dancing, and singing that emanate the thrilling African gist for life; the funeral is a feast that recharges the positive, creative, and especially fertile forces of the society. In Africa a funeral is considered the best day in one's life, for two reasons. First, in Africa the dead are part of life, as they are all around, never far away from the living. So a funeral is part of one's life, just as it is very much part of the community's life. Second, unless it is an untimely death—of which there are many—at the moment of one's death one can look back at the accomplishments of a lifetime, a moment to be savored. Let us have a look at one particular African death feast.

In Kapsiki culture in North Cameroon, the scene of my first research in Africa, the body of the deceased is meticulously clothed, and then adorned with a host of symbols that indicate all the deeds he or she has performed in life: marriages come first, then children, work, and if relevant heroism in war. After a long morning of decoration, the blacksmiths, who are the funeral directors in this culture, take the dead person on their shoulders and engage in a vigorous dance with the whole village. All relatives of the deceased dance with their dead kinsman, each dancer indicating by specific symbols how he or she relates to the one from whom they take their fond farewell. They dance for the whole afternoon, and the same will happen the next two days; the corpse will be buried in the late afternoon of the third day. It is a beautiful and captivating spectacle, and as for basic LDS gospel values it fits like a glove: life as an accomplishment, the importance of the family, a lasting relation between dead and living, with the ritual as a constant mixture of farewell and the expectation of a later reunion. Perfect!

So let us transfer this to an LDS setting, in an admittedly tongue-in-cheek description of a "Mormon funeral in Africa": An old brother has died, and his funeral dance is under way. I see the branch president of the small Mogode branch (in the village I worked in, there is no LDS presence as yet) dancing towards the corpse with his "triple combination" in hand, his elders quorum holding the sacrament trays, surrounded by Relief Society sisters all clothed in similar cotton prints, on which a portrait of the prophet Joseph Smith swings on their dancing hips. In their hands they hold the calabashes they always serve the refreshments in (in Kapsiki, one cannot dance well without something in hand). A visiting authority, splendidly attired in a deep blue "grand boubou," the beautiful robe of urban Cameroonian culture, with slow and dignified movements dances in honor of the deceased, brandishing his General Handbook of Instructions. Just after him, the children of Primary dance with pictures of Jesus, adding the notion of resurrection that the traditional religion lacks, while of course someone from the branch carries a picture of the current church president (the notion of a prophet comes easily to Africans).

Wonderful! But why do I have some difficulty visualizing this ever happening? Because in the current LDS arrangement, gospel culture, whatever Oaks intends it to mean, will never be allowed to stray too far from the Deseret patterns, and this example is quite different in cultural form. The fact is that no cultural variety in worship is allowed at all. African LDS wards are not allowed to play drums, may not dance and clap, and may not even sing the typical African exchange songs between men and women.[23] The LDS choice for the organ and piano has nothing to do with any gospel principle—the Bible is full of other and very interesting musical instruments—but everything to do with the puritan heritage of the Restoration.[24] If anything, scripture points at trumpets, not pianos, and highlights shofars, not organs. For Africans the lack of song and movement is a definite minus in LDS worship; using drums would be so much easier—and they would be played so much better! But instructions seem to be clear: "No more dancing, no more clapping, since our brothers in America don't do it."[25] As most African converts stem from other Christian denominations, they are used to this lacuna (although most other colonial churches now allow drums and dancing).

This cultural prescript is particularly problematic at major functions such as weddings and funerals, the proper performance of which is often deeply embedded in a particular culture. Regular LDS meetings follow strict liturgies that block cultural intrusions,[26] but the large functions, which are the high times in African culture, are barely scripted at all. For instance, the LDS Church hardly has any specific way of burying the dead, with the exception of dressing the body of endowed members and offering a dedication on the grave. Nor is there a generally accepted format for wedding celebrations beyond the formal temple sealing. These areas seem rife with possibilities for cultural inclusion, or as it has been called elsewhere enculturation, but to my knowledge a diversity of local forms has not emerged.

Cost is one argument. Africa is a continent of relations, of lasting links between human beings, kinsmen, friends, and group members. The exuberant rituals bind people together and show off the celebrated individual in the best possible light, cementing and generating relations that will position the feast givers solidly within their community and culture. Costly they can be, these feasts, but not always and not inevitably so. Traditional funerals, the ones belonging to the indigenous religions like I sketched above for the Kapsiki, are community affairs, where one just has to feed one's guests, bearing no other costs (American funerals, using professional mortuary services, are in fact much more expensive). And even then, hosting guests will eventually be reciprocated, so the feast is more an investment than an expenditure. In a relational society, feasting brings in dividends: social relations, reciprocal obligations, a solid status in the community, and a nodal point in a network of relations that will be of utmost importance in the future. In the terms of the French anthropologist Pierre Bourdieu, celebrations generate social capital, as they solidify a network of relations via an investment of financial capital.[27] This in due time can be converted into symbolic capital as well, meaning status in society and well-being in religion. In Africa these three forms of capital—economic, social, and symbolic—are very closely related and easily convert into one another.[28]

As a socially approved form of investment, the institution of the bridewealth can be compared to American higher education. Americans spend large sums on college education. Parents go into deep debt for their children's education, even taking another mortgage on their house, or the students themselves take on expensive loans. Of course scholarships and grants are possible to cover the cost, but these are not for everyone. During times of economic growth the investment of an expensive education will pay off, but in times of recession this is not at all sure. These debts can surely be a major burden on individuals and families, but I have yet to hear the first critique of the practice from the LDS Church leadership, let alone under the rubric of "gospel culture." Indeed, church leaders' frequent warnings against debt typically exempt study loans, perhaps because the leaders themselves—many of whom went to expensive post-secondary professional or graduate schools—or their children have participated in this system and experienced the evident benefits of the investment.

Clearly, the African cultural equation runs differently than the North Atlantic one, which is based upon individualism, achievement, and the separation of the three forms of capital (economic, social, and symbolic). In the Euro-American system the family is a nurturing base for the individual, a springboard from which one makes it in society. In Africa the family is the ultimate value; the measure of the individual is his contribution to the well-being of his family, not to society. And, it should be noted, the definition of family is much larger and more complex in Africa than in the Western world. In the United States and Europe the insistence is on the nuclear family first; attention for the wider circle of kinship is secondary, and even then this wider circle rarely transcends the borders of aunts, uncles, and first cousins. In Africa extensive lineages and second cousins are routinely considered part of the larger family unit. Africa has an intense discourse on the family, and its idiom is used in many sectors of life; the family is more or less the model for society. "We are all brothers" is a common expression, though that does not always preclude these brothers from harming one another.

The LDS Church cherishes and promotes family values, but of a type that makes sense only in a specific cultural setting. Here the church's monocultural heritage shines through, as if everybody knows and agrees what "family" is. In fact, the notion of family is highly cultural. In Dutch we have two terms for family, *familie* and *gezin*, the latter being the nuclear family only. *Familie* is the general term, but mainly indicates what anthropologists call "kindred," the bilateral group of relatives around a person, up to the level of first cousins, nephews and nieces, grandparents, and grandchildren. Second cousins are considered too distant to be really implied, and usually are not known, a definition not too different from other northwest European kinship systems. Thus, translation of the English term "family" into Dutch always involves a quandary: what is meant, the nuclear family or the kindred? In the Proclamation on the Family it is translated with *gezin*, nuclear family. This makes sense, and probably aligns with the authors' intent, but it renders the proclamation a little void, for two reasons. First, strictly speaking, in a theological argument this unit never can be eternal, since children get married and form their own nuclear families. Second, if the proclamation is simply meant to sanctify the nuclear family, it is hardly needed at all, as in no society and in no historical era has *Homo sapiens* ever managed to sustain itself without some type of nuclear family. The nuclear family as such is nowhere under threat. Some traditional distribution of roles within the nuclear family might be changing, such as who provides and who nurtures, but comparison with other cultures shows that a functioning nuclear family does not depend on role definition. What might be under pressure is which and how many parties might define a nuclear family, and the proper way to start such a nuclear family—hence the LDS insistence on chastity. Also up for debate is the role and importance of the wider circle of kin, in whatever definition, as a factor in society. The notion of kinship has important connotations for broader social and political discourses, as a measure of how people take values of caring and nurturing as crucial and apt roles for society in general.

The notion of family values remains undefined in LDS Church publications, as it does in American and European politics. "Family values," when used as a political buzzword, are seldom spelled out, which makes them unassailable, beyond discussion, and exempt from criticism. Who can have anything against "family values"? Well, Africans can. In African politics family values are never mentioned, as people know how essential and inevitable families are, and how ambivalent the relations within these families can be: they really know about families. The notion of the "great African family" is a powerful model for harmonious human relations, with all members of the large group knowing their place and making decisions after long deliberations and common consent. That is the ideology, but reality can be very different. A large family is an arena too, where battles are fought between brothers, feuds exist between family sides, skirmishes are engaged between generations, and where under the cover of harmony co-wives try to elbow each other out of favor. That contrast between ideology and the actual functioning of the African family is seldom discussed, though, as the ideology is strong, especially in the face of the social fragmentation of Western society.

African Culture and Church Messages

Besides the bridewealth and the expensive feasts, what elements in African culture would impinge on the gospel life of Africans—that is, on the actual message, not the Deseret cultural forms? The first issue, of course, is polygamy—technically, polygyny. In Africa polygyny, the marriage of one husband with more than one wife, is completely normal. Though in all polygamous societies the majority of the marital unions are actually monogamous due to simple demographics,[29] all African countries allow polygamous unions as well, and in no country is monogamy enforced. As Africa is the continent of polygamy,[30] and as Mormonism for the outside world is the religion of polygamy, one would expect a happy match here. The stern antipolygamy stance of the present church comes as a surprise for many Africans, as they see little reason why the church is trying to out-monogamy all the other colonial churches. Polygamy is thus a Deseret (and broadly Euro-American) hang-up, not an African one. Africans are used to the fact that colonial mission churches are against polygamy, so for them Mormonism is just another colonial church, hardly distinguishing itself from the other "official" Christian churches. As Philip Jenkins noted correctly, "In an African context . . . Mormonism looks absolutely mainstream."[31]

Shortly after the 1978 priesthood revelation opened the way for widespread proselytizing in Africa, I raised the polygamy question with the late Jacob de Jager, then our Dutch anchor among the Seventies. He surmised that the church would simply follow the law of each country, a view seemingly supported by the Doctrine and Covenants.[32] Others at the time argued that if the church legitimated polygamy in Africa it would stimulate a massive emigration from America to Africa, and that would be the main reason that the church would not opt for it. I was surprised at this argument, as I could not see how a large number of Americans would dare to migrate to Africa. Also, I wonder whether the church would object strongly to fundamentalist groups moving out of Utah. In the end it boils down to the Mormon perception of unity as a uniformity in rules. The LDS Church would never jeopardize its hard-won respectability as a monogamous church for such an African adventure. But the end result is ironic, to say the least: a formerly polygamous church limiting its recruitment to strictly monogamous converts, on a continent where an option for polygamy would mean a solution of social problems instead of a quandary.

Another minor point of tension between African culture and "gospel culture" is the notion of descent. The gentle streak of lineage reasoning that runs through the LDS Church via patriarchal blessings—declaring which of the twelve tribes of Israel a person is a member of, usually Ephraim—is problematic in Africa. One reason is that people correctly state that they already have a tribe, and thus have a clear lineage adherence and inheritance. The LDS Ephraim story started from a European obsession, whereas the underlying British Israelite ideology of this lineage allotment is absolutely absent in Africa.[33] This illustrates that in the North Atlantic region the myth of Ephraimite lineage is a romantic play with a colorful mythical past, a constructed deep history that reflects a particular Old Testament form of Christianity; it is a mythopoeia of salvation history more than actual or even probable history. In Africa, on the other hand, the tribes have nothing romantic about them, just a self-evident daily identity. Ultimately this is a minor point of friction, since Ephraimite discourse is hardly stressed anymore, appearing chiefly as a remnant in patriarchal blessings and largely disappearing from official LDS teaching.[34]

An American Eden is an evident problem for Africa, as Africans usually are quite proud of their deep human history and the global recognition of their continent as mankind's cradle. But then, the notion of American exceptionalism is gradually disappearing from LDS discourse (though of course many American Mormons, including among the leadership, still harbor substantial exceptionalist views). On the official church website the American location of the Garden of Eden is not mentioned under "Basic Doctrine," and is in fact hard to find at all. The notion of America's chosenness has disappeared from the missionary lessons. It is, in fact, characteristic of doctrinal development inside Mormonism that such notions deemed untenable or no longer useful simply fade out and no longer are openly discussed, usually without ever being formally repudiated.[35]

Africans are used to colonial churches and their claims to exclusive truth and/or authority, and here Mormonism comes in as no surprise. One standard African response is simply to accumulate religions. In the North Atlantic region, one's religious denomination is part and parcel of one's identity; someone is Roman Catholic, Reformed, Mormon, or Jehovah's Witness, one's denomination serving as a crucial part of identity. In Africa identity is primarily wrapped up in the family and ethnic group; the tribal function of religion is absent. A common reaction by families to religious diversity is to diversify and accumulate religions within their own ranks, in two ways. The first is collective religious diversity within the family. Some family members will keep at least part of their traditional religion alive, often in the form of a personal shrine on which small sacrifices are offered, candles burned, and pictures posed. Others, often some of the younger males, have to be Muslim in order to keep the family in good rapport with Allah, while the women are expected to become Christians in the mission churches. In a large family some of them will join an independent church as well, while in Southern Africa an educated member may have his or her own independent congregation.

The second strategy is to accumulate religions at an individual level and develop a switching mechanism, a kind of intellectual spiritual gymnastics that seems quite typical for Africa. I encountered an evident example of this religious strategy in Mali, among the Dogon elite. One sergeant in the Malian army dined with me in the capital Bamako and explained his religion. He said:

> In Bamako where everybody is more or less Muslim, I pray and I memorize and recite the Quran. On Friday I attend mosque with all my other brothers. But in two weeks it will be Christmas, and of course I will attend Mass at Christmas day as most of my brothers and sisters do. The same at Easter, and when I visit in the South near Sikasso, where my sister lives who is a Christian, I am Christian with her. But then, at the New Year I will go to the Dogon country, my village Sangha, and the first thing I do is a visit to the Hogon—the village priest. He will take his bracelet and purify me and then I sacrifice a chicken on the altar of our lineage.

He did distinguish between two kinds of Christianity: "Mon Père" and "Hallelujah," or Roman Catholic and Protestant. Mormons are completely unknown, but would surely be classified as "Hallelujah," as they are not part of the Roman Catholic Church. This kind of multiple religious affiliation has been reported in many other instances.[36] In Africa the LDS Church should expect to be included in such a layering of religions, though of course it is not at all what the missionaries or the leaders aim for, and may even be defined as apostasy.

Africans are used to a multiplex religious scene, where colonial churches superimpose themselves over remnants of tribal religion; the new religion claims to replace the old one, but in fact never does so completely. Various functions of the traditional religions are not covered by the colonial mission churches. For instance, divination is a continuous presence in African life, a road map for one's course through life which helps to gain a modicum of confidence in the future.[37] The many techniques by which people divine are not so much part of the traditional religions, but do feed into the ritual complexes that form the core of African religions, indicating what kind of sacrifices or offerings should be made to appease the problems of the past. Divination is the "ritual of rituals," but not for the colonial churches. Some other remnants will remain as well. Most Africans continue to believe in witchcraft, a deeply entrenched discourse in Africa life.[38] Though all colonial churches have reacted against this belief, it has proven very difficult to eradicate, and in case of serious misfortune immediately resurfaces from the substratum of the old ways.

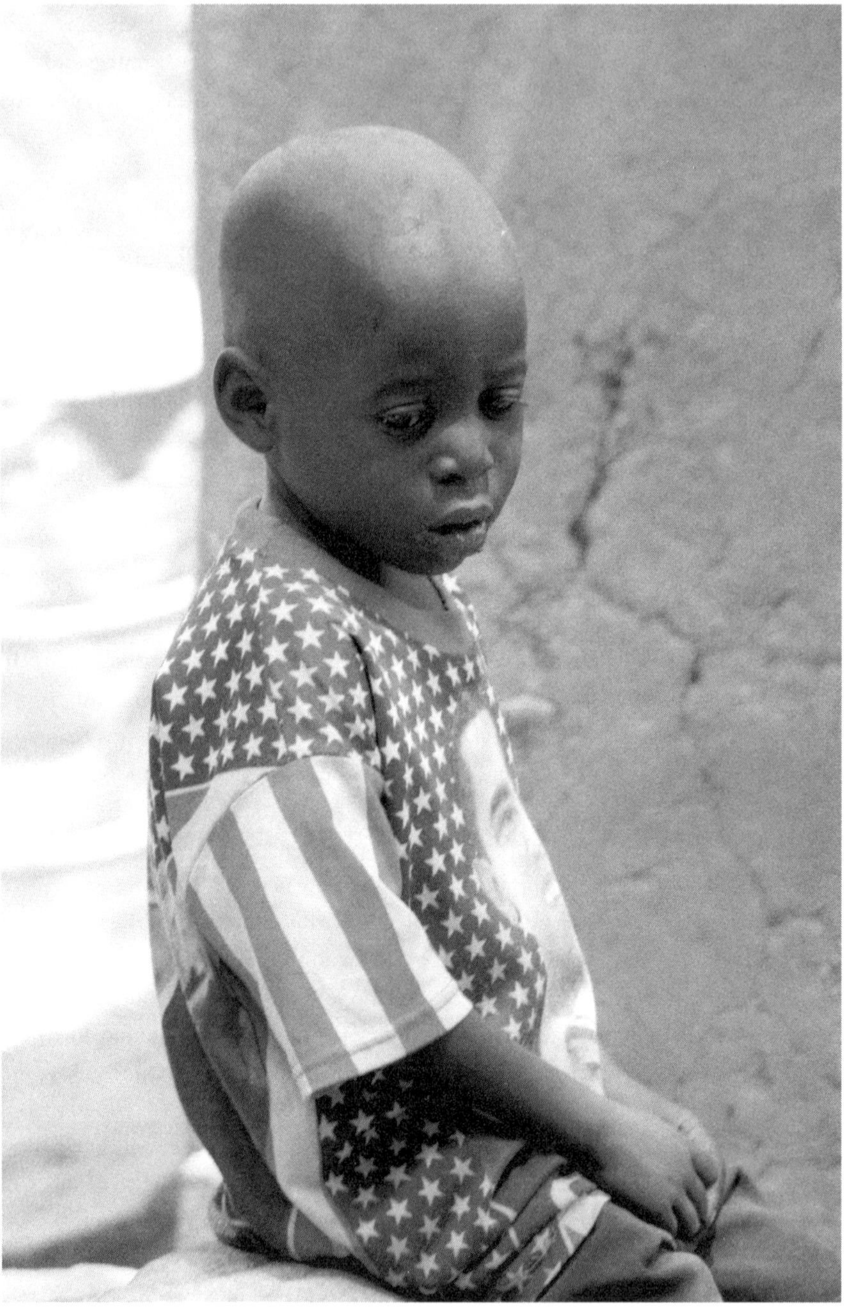

FIGURE 4.5. Being African with an American touch. Photograph by the author.

Conclusion: The Challenge of Culture

We have seen that much of the cultural misunderstanding between Deseret and African culture is based upon the African celebration of life, in its abundance and its fragility, as shown in its rites of passage. But these rituals of transition are not very elaborated in the LDS Church, at least not nearly in the same intensity and passion. The "ordinances"—read "rituals"—of the Mormon Church are not geared at the actual celebrations of life: birth, marriage, and death receive very little ritual attention. The manifold rituals of restoration are mainly directed at the individual and his or her relationship with the divine: the sacrament, ordination, baptism, endowment. Even the temple marriage, which often follows an existing civil marriage, is less concerned with creating a union in this life than with sealing an existing union for the eternities.[39] We might say that the LDS Church does not "do life," it "does eternity"—which would help explain why it does not "do culture."

Thus, African cultural differences highlight a cultural vacuum in the heart of church life. Few societies can exist without functioning rituals of passage, i.e., without customs by which transitions in life can be given form and structure. Of course, life in the LDS Church is quite full of rituals, many of which are age-specific and others which recognize a progression of spiritual (and social) maturity and honor. For a church stemming from Puritan roots, the number of rituals in the LDS Church is surprisingly large, in fact.[40] Most of these rituals are performed under priesthood authority, which means they are governed by exact instructions prescribed in the General Handbook of Instructions. My point here is that the manuals tend to decrease the ritual content of many significant events, at least the social aspect of the ritual: no farewell or welcome services for missionaries, no collective celebration of someone's first endowment, etc. Rituals in the church are defined as individual events, between the person and the divine, with a mortal mediator. What happens in wards and branches is that cultural content is invented and added: open houses for a missionary's farewell or return, baby showers for a birth, a gift party at the baptism of an eight-year-old, wedding services for marriage, and burial services at death.[41] The major function of ritual—to collectivize individual experiences—is done through the inventiveness of the local congregations and members, which in fact means that the host culture of the country dominates. It simply has to. So local and national cultures are not only present but needed in the church—including in Africa—and thus the conundrum of cultural variation is brought into the church by default.

From an organizational point of view cultural differences are daunting. The challenge for the LDS Church is to define what is core and what is periphery—in its doctrine, ritual, and life in the ecclesia. But then the equation between unity and uniformity has to be relinquished, a sort of anticorrelation movement that will demand a lot of courage and much faith in the members. The question is whether the negation of culture as exemplified by the notion of "gospel culture" is a question of awkwardness or a deliberate choice. One major issue is central control, an ecclesiastical priority that easily tops the recognition of individuality. But with the LDS Church increasingly moving into areas with notably different cultures, central control in the end will hurt church expansion, and in fact it already does, as the monocultural approach limits the acceptance of the restored gospel in Africa.

LDS doctrines fit Africa like a glove, or to quote Jenkins, "Mormonism should be at home in Africa as a fish in the water."[42] Compared to other denominations, in Africa the LDS Church is falling back, doing moderately well at best, where other denominations can boast much more spectacular results. Even with Mormonism's belated start, others are gaining ground much faster and the proportion of LDS among African Christians is going down, not increasing. As a whole LDS Church growth is plateauing, and it might well be that for any type of second harvest—or first in the African case—local cultures will have to be allowed in. If the church is ever to evolve from its present situation as an internationalizing church, into a fully international church or even a world church (both of which are still far off), cultural forms as a way to muster local agency have to be given their proper place. If not, the growth plateau will remain much lower. But then, finally, the much-quoted dictum of Joseph Smith Jr. has to be implemented at long last: "I teach my people correct principles and let them govern themselves." Putting that into practice would be new indeed.

Notes

1. D. Michael Quinn, *The Mormon Hierarchy: Extensions of Power* (Salt Lake City: Signature Books, 1997).
2. M. E. Nielsen and D. Whyte, "Men's Grooming in the Latter-day Saints Church: A Qualitative Study of Norm Violation," *Mental Health, Religion and Culture* 11, no. 8 (2008): 807–25.
3. John-Charles Duffy, "Concealing the Body, Concealing the Sacred: The Decline of Ritual Nudity in Mormon Temples," *Journal of Ritual Studies* 21, no. 1 (2007): 1–21; Walter E. A. van Beek, "The Temple and the Sacred: Dutch Temple Experiences," *Dialogue* 45, no. 4 (2013): 27–54.
4. Matthew Bowman, *The Mormon People: The Making of an American Faith* (New York: Random House, 2012); Terryl Givens, *People of Paradox: A History of Mormon Culture* (New York, Oxford University Press, 2007).
5. F. L. M. Tullis, ed., *Mormonism: A Faith for All Cultures* (Provo: Brigham Young University Press, 1978).
6. David C. Knowlton, "Mormonism in Latin-America: Towards the Twenty-First Century," *Dialogue: A Journal of Mormon Thought* 29, no. 1 (1996): 159–76; T. W. Murphy, "Reinventing Mormonism: Guatemala as Harbinger of the Future," *Dialogue: A Journal of Mormon Thought* 29, no. 1 (1996): 177–92. Walter E. A. van Beek, "Mormon Europeans or European Mormons? An Afro-European Look at Religious Colonization," *Dialogue: A Journal of Mormon Thought* 38, no. 4 (2005): 3–36.

7. In Europe job rotation is also less evident than in the United States. See for Belgium: Wilfried Decoo, "Feeding the Fleeing Flock: Reflections on the Struggle to Retain Church Members in Europe," *Dialogue: A Journal of Mormon Thought* 29, no. 1 (1996): 97–118; for the Netherlands: Walter E. A. van Beek, "Ethnisation and Accommodation: Dutch Mormons in Twenty-first Century Europe," *Dialogue: A Journal of Mormon Thought* 29, no. 1 (1996): 119–38; and for Europe in general: Armand L. Mauss, "Can There Be a Second Harvest? Controlling the Costs of Latter-day Saint Membership in Europe," *International Journal of Mormon Studies* 1 (2008): 1–59.
8. Jennifer H. Basquiat, "Embodied Mormonism: Performance, Vodou and the LDS Faith in Haiti," *Dialogue: A Journal of Mormon Thought* 37, no. 4 (2004): 26.
9. Rendell N. Mabey and Gordon T. Allred, *Brother to Brother: The Story of the Latter-day Saint Missionaries who Took the Gospel to Black Africa* (Salt Lake City: Bookcraft, 1984).
10. These notions stem from Pierre Bourdieu, *Outline of a Theory of Practice* (Cambridge: Cambridge University Press, 1990).
11. Walter E. A. van Beek, "Cultural Models of Power in Africa," in *Land, Law and Politics in Africa, Mediating Conflict and Reshaping the State*, ed. Jan Abbink and Mirjam de Bruijn, (Leiden: Brill, 2011), 25–48.
12. Van Beek, "Cultural Models."
13. Timothy Taylor, *The Artificial Ape: How Technology Changed the Course of Human Evolution* (New York: Palgrave Macmillan, 2010).
14. Geert Hofstede and Geert J. Hofstede, *Cultures and Organizations: Software of the Mind* (New York: McGraw Hill, 2005).
15. Steven Pinker asserts that in relation to certain cultural phenomena such as violence, "The United States is not a country, it's three countries," meaning the North + East, South, and West. Steven Pinker, *The Better Angels of Our Nature: Why Violence Has Declined* (New York: Viking Penguin Group, 2011), 93–94.
16. See Lester E. Bush, "Writing 'Mormonism's Negro Doctrine: An Historical Overview's Context and Reflections," *Journal of Mormon History* 25, no. 1 (1999): 229–71.
17. See Mabey and Allred, *Brother to Brother*.
18. Walter E. A. van Beek and Annette Schmidt, "African Dynamics of Cultural Tourism," in *African Hosts and Their Guests: Dynamics of Cultural Tourism in Africa*, ed. Walter E. A. van Beek and Annette Schmidt (Oxford: James Currey, 2012), 1–33.
19. For a thorough comparison of Mormonism with fellow Christian denominations, see Douglas J. Davies, *The Mormon Culture of Salvation: Force, Grace and Glory* (Aldershot: Ashgate, 2000); and Douglas J. Davies, *An Introduction to Mormonism* (Oxford: Oxford University Press, 2003).
20. Philip Jenkins, "Letting Go: Understand Mormon Growth in Africa," *Journal of Mormon History* 35, no. 2 (2009): 11.
21. Irwin Altman and Joseph Ginat, *Polygamous Families in Contemporary Society* (Cambridge: Cambridge University Press, 1996).
22. Ronald L. Grimes, *Deeply into the Bones: Re-inventing Rites of Passage* (Berkeley: University of California Press, 2000); Roy A. Rappaport, *Ritual and Religion in the Making of Humanity* (Cambridge: Cambridge University Press, 1999).
23. This concerns the much broader notion of inculturation, as it is called in the Roman Catholic Church, an issue that all mission churches have wrestled with. See Harry

Leijten, *From Idol to Art: African "Objects of Power": A Challenge for Missionaries, Anthropologists and Museum Curators* (Leiden: African Studies Center, 2015).

24. Rex E. Cooper, *Promises Made to the Fathers: Mormon Covenant Organization* (Salt Lake City: University of Utah Press, 1990); Marvin S. Hill, *Quest for Refuge: The Mormon Flight from American Pluralism* (Salt Lake City: Signature Books, 1989).
25. LeBaron, cited in Jenkins, "Letting Go," 23.
26. Jenkins "Letting Go," 22.
27. Bourdieu, *Outline of a Theory.*
28. Van Beek, "Cultural Models."
29. The same holds for Mormon polygyny in historical Deseret.
30. Miriam Koktvedgaard Zeitzen, *Polygamy: A Cross-Cultural Analysis* (Oxford: Berg Publishers, 2008).
31. Jenkins, "Letting Go," 11.
32. See Doctrine and Covenants 134; Official Declaration 1.
33. Armand L. Mauss, "In Search of Ephraim: Traditional Mormon Conceptions of Lineage and Race," *Journal of Mormon History* 25, no. 1 (1999): 131–73; Armand L. Mauss, *The Angel and the Beehive: The Mormon Struggle with Assimilation* (Urbana: University of Illinois Press, 1994).
34. Armand L. Mauss, *All Abraham's Children: Changing Mormon Conceptions of Race and Lineage* (Urbana: University of Illinois Press, 2003).
35. Walter E. A. van Beek, "The Infallibility Trap: The Sanctification of Religious Authority," *International Journal of Mormon Studies* 4 (2011): 14–44.
36. John Kirby, "Cultural Change and Religious Conversion in West Africa," in *Religion in Africa: Experience and Expression*, ed. Thomas D. Blakely, Walter E. A. van Beek, and Dennis L. Thomson (Oxford: Currey/Heineman, 1994), 56–71. Philip Jenkins calls this "denominational border-crossing"; see Jenkins "Letting Go," 7.
37. Walter E. A. van Beek and Philip M. Peek, *Reviewing Reality: Dynamics of African Divination* (Berlin: LIT Verlag, 2013).
38. Walter E. A. van Beek, "The Escalation of Witchcraft Accusations," in *Imagining Evil: Witchcraft Beliefs and Accusations in Contemporary Africa*, ed. G. ter Haar (Trenton, NJ: Africa World Press, 2007), 293–316.
39. See Grimes, *Deeply into the Bones*; Walter E. A. van Beek, "Meaning and Authority in Mormon Ritual," *International Journal of Mormon Studies* 3 (2010): 17–40; David Buerger, *The Mysteries of Godliness: A History of Mormon Temple Worship* (San Francisco: Smith Associates, 1994).
40. For a concise overview, see John Sorenson, "Ritual as Theology," *Sunstone* (May–June 1981): 11–14.
41. These nonofficial rituals are quite important in LDS culture; see Sorenson "Ritual as Theology."
42. Jenkins, "Letting Go," 11. See also Dennis L. Thomson, "African Religion & Mormon Doctrine: Comparisons & Commonalities," in Blakely, van Beek, and Thomson, *Religion in Africa*, 89–99.

Chapter 5 | Expanding Research for the Expanding International Church

Wilfried Decoo

One of the directions that Mormon studies must take in the twenty-first century is a richer engagement with Mormonism "abroad," by which I mean anything outside the United States. To speak of "the international church" is to deal with a vast range of topics, encompassing as much depth and even greater diversity than we have seen in the scholarly study of American Mormonism. In this essay I highlight areas of potential research that could help us better understand Mormonism in its non-American contexts. My aim here is to be suggestive more than exhaustive, and so I will move quickly from issue to issue and rely on occasional anecdotes rather than detailed analysis to illustrate various aspects. My focus will be on the Church of Jesus Christ of Latter-day Saints, excluding other forms of Mormonism.

American Church or World Religion?

World Religion?

The American origins of Mormonism are well documented. At this stage in its development, is Mormonism best understood as an American church (or denomination), a global religion, or a world religion? If we define "world religion" as a religion with adherents in nearly all countries in the world, then Mormonism is a world religion. However, Mormonism is still a small entity compared to major religions and the tempo of its future growth is uncertain, even gloomy in economically stable countries.[1] True, quantity is relative, since Judaism has similar numbers. But in terms of genesis, age, impact on the world's history, and cultural prestige, Mormonism is not comparable. Rick Phillips, judging from census data from around the world, argues that "Mormonism is a North American church with tendrils in other continents, and that calling Mormonism a 'world religion' is premature."[2] Similarly, Matthew Bowman remarks that "while Mormonism may be a global religion" because of its presence on every continent, "it is not yet a world religion, one that, like Islam or Catholicism, has found a way to adapt its forms to share its meaning in a panoply of cultures."[3] That statement implies cultural adaptations to be a world religion. I will come back to that issue.

A world religion is usually not identified as an individual church, but as an entity or a tradition around a common core, such as Christianity, Islam, Hinduism, or Buddhism. These religions consist of many churches or tendencies, often related to national identities that ensure cultural and social cohesion. Mormonism is far from having reached that point, even when one includes its smaller branches like the Community of Christ.

If Christianity is a world religion, it raises the common question: to what extent is Mormonism part of Christianity? If it is part of Christianity, then it is part of a world religion. However, the fact that Mormon baptism is not recognized by other Christian churches and the Mormon Church does not recognize any other baptisms suggests that Mormonism is bound to remain an outsider to the family of Christian churches. Some have called Mormonism the fourth Abrahamic religion, next to Judaism, Christianity, and Islam. But then such an appellation would also apply to other new religious movements with a Christian basis but removed from the Nicene Creed, such as Jehovah's Witnesses and Christian Scientists. Thus, a taxonomy of Christendom is hardly a straightforward matter.

A related study topic is Mormonism's evolving relations with other religions. Inasmuch as Mormon leaders seem to want their counterparts in other religions to recognize Mormonism as an equal, how much can and will this impact Mormon doctrine and practice? Armand Mauss has stated that the development of religious movements depends on "their ability to make local adaptations of doctrine, policy, and cultural traditions." For Mormonism, he noted "the apparent correlation across time between changes in doctrine (at least conventional, if not canon doctrine), and changes in the outcomes of the proselyting and public relations efforts of the church."[4] We see this in the way church leaders now speak about the great apostasy, or de-emphasize the First Vision statement that "all their creeds were an abomination in His sight." To what extent are changes in the church's doctrinal emphasis and in its policies and profiling meant to match an alleged model of world religion? To what extent is the church trying to find a balance between ideological trends in Christianity, such as left-leaning social justice and right-leaning conservatism? What strains will be encountered between a largely white conservative American membership and the remainder, both in the United States and abroad?

Mormon Church leaders stress that the church is not an American church, but a universal one. One of the goals of the correlation process since the 1970s has been to make the church look "less American" by removing from its publications American lifestyle items and by stressing the core message of the gospel. However, the church keeps strong American components. I would identify four: historical location, authority, ideology, and behavior.[5] The question is how members abroad react to each of these components. To what extent do they experience the church as "American" and view "Americanness" as an attracting or a repelling factor? The question is interesting for studies of attitudes and behavior, and thus of Mormon identity, among church members in different parts of the world.

Historical Location

The Mormon Church is obviously American in its historical location. Founded in the United States by an American, its core history is there. Mormons abroad learn about Palmyra, New York; Kirtland, Ohio; Jackson County, Missouri; Nauvoo, Illinois; Winter Quarters, Nebraska; Martin's Cove, Wyoming; and Salt Lake City, Utah. The experience of that history is now offered as Mormon tourism in America, with a sense of pilgrimage. The physical restoration of Mormon historical locations in the United States for commemoration and pageants contributes to a spatial religious consciousness for members worldwide. Converts abroad take the countercultural step of joining a unique, homegrown American religion. They accept the Book of Mormon and its hailing of America as "a land which is choice above all other lands."[6] The Tenth Article of Faith affirms that "Zion will be built upon the American continent."

Location extends to the present. Salt Lake City is Mormonism's capital, home of the Mormon Church's First Presidency and Quorum of Twelve Apostles, and offers a grandiose setting for the church semiannual General Conferences. There is an American flag at the center of Temple Square—in contrast to the Vatican, an independent state that does not fly the Italian flag. Utah remains, for the rest of the world, the Mormon state. The bulk of independent Mormon intellectual life occurs in the United States: publishers, associations, conferences, meetings, etc. The vast majority of the scholarship in Mormon studies deals with aspects situated in the United States. Also noteworthy is that many Mormons abroad, especially multigenerational members and at leadership levels, have family connections in Utah because for decades Brigham Young University has been a magnet for Mormon students from abroad, many of whom remain in the United States, which in turn triggers further immigration of family members. It would be interesting to have data on the dynamics and the extent of those connections. Significantly, the media abroad, when presenting anything Mormon, almost always stress the American connection.[7]

How do members abroad experience these American aspects? Studies in France and Belgium confirm that they accept them heartily as part of their faith and their religious identity.[8] Former church president Gordon B. Hinckley said that the historic sites were just as relevant for members in the Philippines as in Provo, and that members abroad "are proud of their Church and they are proud of the roots of that Church."[9] Documenting the extent of this appreciation for the American basis for Mormonism in the expanding church would require more research.

Note that this appreciation does not necessarily equate "America" with "the United States." Members in Canada and Latin America can stress "America" as a chosen continent. Furthermore, the history of tensions between the Mormon Church and the U.S. government in the nineteenth century offers a helpful narrative for members in other continents who are less comfortable with the idea of the United States as a chosen nation. To perceive Mormons historically as a separate people on the American soil seems more harmonious with these members' appreciation of the gospel.

However, in 2012, Mitt Romney's candidacy for the U.S. presidency confronted many members abroad with media reports that stressed the relationship between Mormonism and the United States.[10] The media paid special attention to Romney's Americentrism and strong sense of American exceptionalism, including promises to "restore America's greatness" and reaffirm the nation's global leadership. Many reports amplified the awareness of the strong Republican preference of U.S. Mormons. In contrast, surveys showed that 81 percent of people outside the United States would have voted for Obama if they could.[11] Also of interest is the question of how church members abroad react to the disclosure of the political affiliation of most members of the First Presidency and the Quorum of the Twelve as Republicans, considering the rather unfavorable image of that party in the rest of the world.[12] In her assessment of the Mormon moment abroad, Laurie Maffly-Kipp remarked on how much the "Americanness of the Mormon faith" has been negatively reinforced by Republican Mormons and their U.S. patriotism.[13] The whole phenomenon seems research-worthy: to what extent does the strong pro-U.S. stance of many American Mormons, and the strong public identification of Mormonism with America, affect Mormons abroad?

Authority

The top church leaders are nearly all American. Of course, these leaders fully focus on the worldwide expansion of the church. Outreach to all nations is very much their concern. It is also certain they are on the lookout to add non-Americans to the ranks of General Authorities, but the process is slow. For non-Americans to be considered, they must typically be fluent in English, with impeccable credentials of decades-long religious compliance, and, it seems, conform—by personality, professional background, and dress—to the American corporate style of leadership. Anecdotally, upon Dieter Uchtdorf's selection as Second Counselor to President Thomas S. Monson, a European church member was asked if he was not proud that a German was now in the First Presidency. The member answered, "We like President Uchtdorf, but actually, he is

American." Apart from the visible top authorities, there is also the extensive church administration managed largely by Americans, including in the various regional headquarters around the world. It puts an American stamp on anything that is happening.

It seems most members abroad accept the general American leadership as a natural extension of church history filled with American figures. The veneration given to the prophet and the apostles reinforces this acceptance. It may well be that members abroad have more confidence in seasoned American leaders, usually of pioneer stock, with typical Anglo-Saxon names, who embody the traditional Mormon history and experience, rather than in someone with a non-English-sounding name or even someone from their own ranks. Surveys measuring prejudice could map some of those feelings.

However, there are also critical voices who express concern about condescension and colonizing practices from church headquarters, which, it is felt, controls stakes and missions abroad in terms of boundaries, leaders' callings, building program, finances, temple, websites, and every other aspect.[14] Such perceptions could also be surveyed. There is also the recurrent problem that American authorities sometimes give talks from an American outlook, based on American situations, without always realizing the implications elsewhere. For example, to counsel early marriage or to criticize postponement of marriage can be detrimental in countries where underage marriage is already a problem.[15] To decry the "cultural emasculation of males" in young adult males who remain noncommittal and to call for more fortitude and leadership among men may be misunderstood in another society where males already dominate.[16] To reject the African cultural tradition of the bride price does not take into account its possible positive effects on the valuation of women, on in-law families' bonding, and on economical balancing, or its latent merit as a divorce disincentive.[17]

Devyn Smith studied the discrepancy between the predominantly white Mormon leadership and the considerable ethnic diversity in the church membership.[18] An update of this study would show whether the ratio has improved or deteriorated. But the question remains whether the calling of more non-Americans to higher leadership positions would effectively impact diversity in approaches, as these leaders may be chosen partly in recognition of their adherence to American norms and values.

Ideology

Modern Mormonism reflects an American ideology of optimism, assertiveness, and personal achievement. This approach is well visible in church magazines and talks, with stories about how individuals, from various countries, against all odds and through faith and perseverance, achieved success in educational degrees, in their careers, or in sports. Rarely do church publications offer counterparts to Mother Theresa or Gandhi as heroes exemplifying abnegation and contempt for material feats. The pursuit of individual success as part of the American dream is deeply ingrained in modern Mormonism. Young Mormon missionaries from any country are groomed into that mentality of goals, achievement, and praise. The achievement rhetoric may also be partly political, reflecting American superiority and exceptionalism, with the backdrop of America's messianic role in the world.

For members abroad, the ideology of success and achievement could be beneficial if constructively framed. Since the church is established mostly in urban areas and prefers consolidation around centers of strength, that should in theory promote upward mobility. On the other hand, many urban areas deteriorate through unemployment and poverty and the church attracts many converts with such needs. We have few data on education, employment, and prosperity among Mormons around the world. Census data from Mexico, Brazil, Chile, and the Philippines show that the educational attainment and employment of Mormons is somewhat higher than in the rest of the country, but that may be due to the urban locations where they mostly live.[19] The only exception is Chile, where Mormons have less college education and less employment than in the rest of the country. But we lack the data on the extent to which this pertains to converts or to multigenerational members, so we need more research on how much Mormonism's ideology of success may contribute to achievement.

Behavior

Some time ago, an American mission president asked me to recommend a local brother for a calling within the mission. I recommended Eugene, a convert from Congo. The interview with the mission president lasted less than one minute. Eugene came out a little confused as to why the interview was so short and without content. Later the mission president told me that the "spirit of discernment" had immediately convinced him not to call Eugene: "There is a problem when someone avoids eye contact and gives a weak handshake." He failed to realize that in Congo, as in many cultures around the world, such behavior is a sign of deference and meekness, rather than personal weakness or a lack of social or spiritual capacity.

Socialization is important in Mormon life.[20] It carries a number of characteristics that seem part of an outward Mormon identity: intense personal contact, greeting each other by name, often the first name, shaking hands firmly and somewhat longer, with a smile and eye contact; the way to hug another adult; the facial demonstration of assertiveness and commitment; the easiness of social contact between different genders and different ages; a certain looseness in conducting meetings, with moments of humor and a casual speaking style from the pulpit; the use of superlatives, extolling others as "wonderful" and "great," praising each child or youngster as "special." These behavioral patterns may seem trivial to Americans because they have them ingrained. But in other cultures, some of these patterns stand out as different and often as "American." They spread abroad for simple reasons: American missionaries have always been the initiators of church life elsewhere. Converts are often those most amenable to America and American culture, thus facilitating the transmission and modeling of normative behavior. At present, thousands of Mormon American expatriates, as well as scores of older missionary couples, infuse local units with their behavioral patterns. Non-American missionaries are immersed in a mission organization in which behavioral patterns and expectations are shaped by Americans. Mission presidents and visiting authorities, American or Americanized, disseminate through their function as role models the same behavioral patterns. There also is the homogenizing effect of dress and grooming standards on behavior. In the 2007 General Conference Julie Beck praised Mormon mothers who "bring daughters in clean and ironed dresses with hair brushed to perfection; their sons wear white shirts and ties and have missionary haircuts."[21] All this is material for cross-cultural studies.

Does this behavior benefit the members? Normally, the open and warm socialization that characterizes Mormon communities should be beneficial. However, if local patterns of interaction are quite different from American patterns, converts will need to make adjustments to avoid tensions and misunderstandings. There is a higher risk for unease and disengagement. As Marie Cornwall expressed it: "Effective socialization occurs to the extent that one's subjective reality mirrors the objective reality of the group. It is therefore logical to assume that introduction to alternative realities via conversations with significant others whose subjective reality does not mirror the reality of the group will negatively influence the adoption of the group reality."[22]

Occasionally we hear members abroad complain that the church is "too American." That pertains mostly to a corporate, managerial style of doing things—using quantitative goals, charts, report forms, etc.—which does not square with their understanding of religion as an affective and spiritual realm. Moreover, to strengthen this impression, there is the tendency to call as stake and regional leaders, and hire as church employees, members who seem most fit, by personality, profession, and dress, to blend in the American corporate style. Anecdotally, when the first Flemish stake was organized, one of the newly called high priests mentioned to me, with some naïve delight, that he had bought a new suit matching the style and color of the suits worn by General Authorities.

So, even if there are sometimes complaints about the American corporate style of doing things, it may well be that many Mormons abroad appreciate this homogeneous and efficient business approach. It may well be that male members abroad find particular satisfaction in dressing like American white collar professionals or as General

Authorities, as this denotes status and upward mobility in their local environment. In some situations we may underestimate the very American attraction of the Mormon Church, while in other situations the "American ways" are considered distasteful.

Of course, these daily behavioral patterns, such as greeting or forms of social contact, belong to a surface level, in contrast to more profound cultural traits such as language, dating and marriage traditions, hierarchical relations, national or regional festivities, and so on, which I will address later in the essay.

The four components touched upon illustrate the "Americanness" of Mormonism. Church statements that deflect the characterization of Mormonism as an American religion are understandable in order to avoid the political halo or the derogatory connotation tied to the term "American" and to stress the universality of the gospel message. But the church cannot easily shake off its American aura, a predicament that becomes palpable in contrast to other churches that also originated in America, such as Adventists or Jehovah's Witnesses. Around the world, these movements are hardly identified as American anymore. It seems that, overall, most active members of the Mormon Church abroad accept and integrate the various American components of the church, though this remains a field for more refined and systematic study. Conversely, one could study to what extent the dislike of what is sensed as "American" in the church is a factor in dissatisfaction among members and possible disengagement, as well as an obstacle for potential converts.

Profiles of Mormons Abroad
The Need for Data

Every year the Church Almanac releases the exact number of members in every country in the world. Those figures include all recorded baptisms. Not revealed are the few other demographic data that the church has access to—age averages, gender ratios, activity rates, and marriage and birth rates. The church does not seem to collect data (at least not on a regular basis) on race and ethnicity, education levels, professional profiles, income, the employment of women, teen pregnancy and abortion rates, political preferences, and more. In the United States such data are provided by independent polling that include religious affiliation as a variable. It allows scholars to draw statistical profiles of Mormons in the United States.[23] Only a few other countries conduct national censuses that include Mormon affiliation as a variable: Mexico, Brazil, Chile, and the Philippines. Tim Heaton and Cardell Jacobson have included those figures in their entry in the *Oxford Handbook of Mormonism*, which yields some telling perspectives.[24] One result of these censuses abroad is the discrepancy between the membership figures the church publishes and the number of people who identify themselves as Mormons.[25]

For most other countries such national or international surveys are insufficient to study Mormonism due to the insignificant number of Mormons or because religious affiliation is not identified. Without church permission it is almost impossible to organize a national survey among Mormons, such as Euvrard was able to do for France.[26] Former data on member profiles in the U.K. are now outdated as a result of the massive influx of non-European converts since the 1990s.[27] Many if not most studies about Mormonism outside the United States are more historical, chronicling the establishment of the church through the achievements of American missionaries abroad, with global data on growth, but little or no attention to the members themselves. Only a limited number of these profiles of international church membership have been undertaken by scholars.[28] Even the European Mormon Studies Association and the Brazilian Mormon Studies Association (Associação Brasileira de Estudos Mórmons) seem to struggle to organize valid surveys.

The Costs of Membership

One of the reasons why activity rates are higher in the United States than abroad could be explained by a difference in "costs." Of course, not all areas in the United States are similar: the Mormon Intermountain West probably helps push up the American activity averages. The church, it seems, wants to keep an optimal tension between the demands of membership and the norms of the host society, but uses identical rules to do so all over the world. However, situations differ greatly from one country to another, or even from one individual to another, so that tensions play out differently. Armand Mauss has identified the costs of church membership in Europe and showed how these are much higher than on average in the United States: more severe familial breaches over conversion, more conflicts within part-member families, cultural tensions over Sunday observance, greater distances to travel to church and other church functions, more callings to fulfill, and often paying nondeductible tithing on already tax-laden family budgets.[29] As more members drop out, those who remain must care for a growing ratio of inactives, multiplying the burden. One could add the strain of functioning in immature units, sometimes plagued by discord, or the pressure to participate in missionary work when one struggles with one's own membership. In some countries, all of these challenges must moreover be seen in the framework of legal discrimination and stigmatization in the media of belonging to a cult. Still, many members thrive in this setting to form the core of the stalwarts, but many others struggle and give up. Inactivity rates abroad hover around 80 percent. In that respect surveys on religious satisfaction among members abroad would be valuable, as is done in the United States.[30] Data on subjective well-being and correlations with variables such as service involvement, years of membership, convert or not, family support, and more, would help better understand the conditions surrounding Mormon identity.

Factors in Constructing Mormon Identity

Instead of categorizing Mormons as an ethnic group, as some scholars had argued for, Armand Mauss proposed to ask the question differently: how do individual Mormons and leaders "assure themselves of their own distinctive Mormon identity"?[31] Mauss has done groundbreaking work in this area and asks: "What sorts of boundaries define today's Mormons? Just how 'American' can a Mormon be without appearing to be just like all the other Americans (and without undermining the identity that he or she presumably shares with the world's three [now closer to eight] million non-American Mormons)?"[32]

Is there a common identity shared by all Mormons worldwide? Are there also different national or ethnic Mormon identities? The following potential factors in determining Mormon identity, in the United States and abroad, could be part of the research driven by these questions.[33]

Uniformity

Church leaders are anxious about unity, which has been a central concern since the founding and a source of major challenges in early church history. As the church expands worldwide, the leadership has experienced how ethnic and cultural diversity increases the risks of balkanization, for example with Maoris, Tongan and Samoan branches, the Mexican Third Convention, and in African independent Mormon churches.[34] The issue of other-language units in certain regions has been a frequent source of tensions and shifting decisions, namely the choice between integration in solid native-speaking wards or separate lingual wards with a higher risk of deviations.[35]

To maintain unity, uniformity is considered a prime condition. This is not new, as the principle of establishing "a house of order" was present in Joseph Smith's earliest revelations. Since the 1960s, as the church has expanded across the world, the movement generally identified as "correlation" has reinforced streamlining and standardization, as well as financial control of the local units in a tight top-down structure.

Correlation also engendered a "restyling" of the message, with at least two characteristics. First, de-Americanization: in a well-meant effort to make church material acceptable worldwide, correlation set out to delete typical American items from lessons, articles, and conference talks, namely references to the U.S. political system, affluent living style, dating patterns, sports, food, and so on. This trend has been furthered by recent changes in the curriculum for Mormon youth. Second, simplification: the cognitive fortification of gospel understanding, well established in previous decades, was reduced in favor of more literalism and a focus on Christ and moral living. The reasons for these changes are manifold—see Matthew Bowman's chapter in this volume—but among them would be the practical demands of preaching a message in dozens of languages through willing but inexperienced and relatively untrained young missionaries.

The topic of uniformity raises several questions for further research: To what extent is actual unity achieved through external uniformity and compliance? To what extent does uniformity contribute to a worldwide Mormon identity? To what extent does the obligation of uniformity stifle vitality and creativity? To what extent does de-Americanization and simplification of the message reinforce our consciousness of the essence or, instead, limit our understanding to generic Christian statements?[36] To what extent do older members, who grew up with some different traditions, feel they have lost some of their Mormon identity because of correlation and simplification, apparently because the worldwide uniform church could not accommodate those traditions?

Community

I view community as the typical Mormon ward or branch, the social unit where Mormons interact through worship, meetings, lessons, interviews, and activities. Even home and visiting teaching visits are an immediate extension of ward life. The relation between this socioreligious network and identity building is well documented, but complex.[37] Quite a few scholars have studied the social function of the Mormon ward in creating identity.[38]

One of the paradoxical virtues of a geographically based ward system is that it often makes for diverse congregations, especially in multicultural settings; this is less true, of course, where the overall population is relatively homogeneous and/or where high concentrations of members make for geographically small wards. For instance, in our Dutch-speaking ward in Antwerp, as of January 2013, the elders quorum was composed of about twenty-five adults: nearly half were Dutch-speaking Belgians in age range from nineteen to eighty-one; there were three Spanish-speaking men from Latin America; one Armenian who only spoke Armenian; the rest, about ten, were from African countries, some English and some French speaking, four of them being nonmember visitors and the six others recent converts.

We need more detailed descriptions of life in Mormon wards abroad, such as have been done in U.S. wards. It would help identify issues of interest. As many wards abroad (and also in the United States outside Utah) have become melting pots of nationalities and of social cases due to the kinds of converts missionaries bring in, how does a ward cope with such diversity—cultural, social, lingual? How do members abroad cope with frequent ward transformations, such as the splitting or consolidation of wards, changes in callings, the influx of often unprepared converts, or the restructuring of groups? What kinds of member groups can be discerned and how do they interact?

For instance, how do the experiences of pioneering European converts in the 1960s and 1970s differ from recent converts, or from that of their own children and grandchildren whom they raised in the church?[39] What is the effect on members in the choice between separate language wards or their integration into native-speaking wards? What is the nature and extent of Mormon identity among the younger generation, especially those who remain active? Correspondingly, what is the influence of this younger generation on their wards and branches, particularly in the cases of those who learn English and Americanize through various church institutions (missions, BYU, or Especially for Youth camps)? What do expatriates (Americans or otherwise) experience when they move to a ward in a new country? To what extent do they recognize an identical church versus one with a variant identity? One thinks here of studies of the meaning of church membership which may differ from place to place, and from individual to individual.[40]

"Gospel Culture" versus the Others

At a symposium on the international church at BYU in 1976, the term "gospel culture" entered into Mormon parlance as a worldwide identity marker, though precise definitions and interpretations differed widely.[41] Years later Elder Dallin H. Oaks defined gospel culture as "a set of values and expectations and practices common to all members of The Church of Jesus Christ of Latter-day Saints." Converts thus "become part of the worldwide gospel culture of commandments and covenants and ordinances and blessings."[42]

These definitions place the emphasis on the boundaries of personal behavior. At various points church leaders have taken at least four different approaches to the relationship between "gospel culture" and the surrounding culture.[43] These discourses or modes are not mutually exclusive, and often overlap or manifest themselves in the church simultaneously. An *antagonistic* approach is dualistic, with good located in the Mormon community and evil in the outside world. The Mormon Zion appears here as both exceptionalist and exemplary, whereas the undifferentiated remainder of "Babylon" is dark and threatening. A second approach is *appreciation* of others. This was typical within Mormonism for much of the first half of the twentieth century and seems to be recurring in this new century. In this mode overtures are made to the outside world, and a spirit of conciliation with other religions becomes a prominent theme in Mormon discourse. A third, related perspective is one of seeing gospel culture as an *addition* to the good found in the prevailing culture, as George Albert Smith phrased it: "Keep all the glorious truths that you have acquired in your churches. . . . Then let us sit down and share with you some of the things that have not yet come into your lives."[44] That same invitation has been repeated many times by church leaders. How well converts are able to identify and then integrate those cherished elements of their past with more typical Mormon traditions varies from case to case. A parallel mode, which we might call *subtractive*, is to invite people to adopt the gospel in full and then to erase from their original backgrounds what is incompatible. The net effect is probably the same as with addition, but the approach requires members to actively assess what they must cut from their local cultures.[45]

These four approaches proceed from the same underlying principle, namely that the gospel shapes a desirable identity. The differentiating criterion is the way that desirable identity is perceived in relation to its surroundings. Each approach senses the "outside" from a different angle, and therefore as a distinct variety. It means that in their adherence to one of these constructs, church members oscillate on a scale between insularity and more openness. They must construct not only identities as Mormons within the Mormon realm, but also identities in relation to their non-Mormon environment.

Media

I consider media here in the broadest sense: anything that conveys information to the public—news, articles, documentaries, films, and books, including fiction. My assumption from years of observation is that the Mormon image which the media convey impacts the identity of at least some of our members.

First, we would need more analysis to assess the overall media image of Mormonism for each country (and perhaps regionally within countries), perhaps following the model developed by Sherry Baker and Joel Campbell.[46] Pending such analysis for situations in various foreign countries, it is safe to assert that the media convey a rather negative impression of Mormonism, at least in many parts of the world. I surveyed media reports for a dozen European countries in connection with the media attention given to Mormonism during the 2012 U.S. presidential election. Mormonism was usually depicted as tied to polygamy, racism, wealth, and temple secrecy—mostly in the context of cults.[47] Even if a media piece does not emphasize such disturbing items, the attention always goes to the "peculiar" to capture the attention of the public. Mormons are depicted as extreme conservative Christians, with interdictions and obligations in the forefront: no alcohol, no smoking, no coffee, no tea, no sexual relations outside marriage, three-hour church services, a dress code, and more. In some countries, the image of Mormonism is also determined by official or private organizations that function as watchdogs against cults. Some are virulently anti-Mormon.

Next comes the actual question of the impact on members themselves. Positive representation fosters pride and confidence. Negative representation triggers a retrenchment reaction, such as defensiveness and more isolation from a hostile world, which could lead to the fear of acknowledging one is Mormon—a phenomenon I have observed among Mormon schoolchildren in Belgium. It can lead to deep discouragement when, after decades of intense missionary work and public relations efforts, Mormons must concede no progress has been made. Anecdotally, recently a national radio program producer in Belgium called me to ask if I would please participate in a live radio debate on polygamy so I could explain how we as Mormons practice it.

What about the Mormon Church's media efforts to counter negative reporting? Outside the United States, it seems those efforts amount to very little, and may even be counterproductive. For instance, in October 2012, in Salt Lake City, a French television crew called on me for an interview about Mormonism. I referred them to the church's Public Affairs Department, but the journalists were not interested in dealing with them "because they are like state guides in Moscow in the 1960s—only hailing the perfection of their system." I have experienced similar reservations expressed by Belgian journalists. Even with some local PR successes, then, and the church's heavy investment in the "I'm a Mormon" campaign, the question remains to what extent national media continue to determine the prevailing image of Mormonism in most countries around the world.

Language

The Mormon Church's operating language is English, but Spanish could soon become the most widely spoken language by members. The church disseminates its materials in dozens of languages, in an astonishing effort to provide almost instantaneous translations of all lesson materials, conference talks, and magazine articles. Members worldwide can receive the same texts in their own languages all at practically the same time. The church also uses the Internet to make the most current materials immediately available. One would expect this to strengthen a worldwide Mormon identity, but it also prompts a number of research questions.

What is the effect of knowing English on Mormon identity? Knowing English gives access to a much wider array of Mormon sources than what the church offers in translation. Such extra sources can include material published by the church but not available in translation, the numerous publications from Deseret Book, and broadening material from the Maxwell Institute, FAIR, other Mormon publishers, independent Mormon journals, and the lively world of Mormon blogs.

What is the effect of the choice of scriptural language on identity? The tension between a conservative and a more modern approach is well illustrated by one's position on the King James Version, and the debate is similar in other languages.[48] This raises further questions: How is the choice made of the official Bible version in other languages?[49] What discussions were involved in each case? As to the other Mormon scriptures, what is the effect of a growing discrepancy between the versions in English and those in the rest of the world? Indeed, in other languages these scriptures have been regularly revised and modernized, thus providing a different feel. What is the effect of the KJV and KJV-language in church publications and media productions for nonnative English speakers to whom the gospel is being taught in English?[50] This is an issue particularly in African nations, but also for thousands of immigrants in other countries with a limited mastery of English. What is the effect of learning and experiencing Mormonism in one's own language or in a (hardly understood) foreign tongue? In general, to what extent does the use of scriptural language, either ancient or modern, entail a certain way of experiencing the gospel? All of these issues take on a special dimension in the case of the immigrant convert who hardly understood the missionaries and is now a member of a ward where only minimal communication is possible—a situation increasingly common in many parts of Europe and elsewhere.

Translation of Mormon texts is a rich field for linguistic research, which quickly becomes theological.[51] To translate a simple sentence such as "Adam fell that men might be; and men are, that they might have joy" (2 Nephi 2:25) can raise a host of semantic and syntactic problems in certain languages—the first challenge being to understand the semantic value of each English word correctly. The rendering in other languages of concepts such as atonement, redemption, sacrament, or sacrifice calls for scores of considerations. Thomas Murphy devoted a study to the translation problem of the Word of Wisdom's "hot drinks" in Guatemalan culture.[52] Reed Haslam detailed issues of translating the Book of Mormon in Thai, where even concrete concepts such as "church" or "prophet" pose major challenges.[53]

Temples

The Mormon Church's vast temple-building program around the world and the highlighting of temple attendance demonstrate how church leaders see this aspect as an important part of Mormon life, and thus of Mormon identity. Holding a temple recommend and doing temple work seems to reinforce, almost by definition, one's Mormon sense of self-recognition, not only as a devoted church member, but as a well-initiated one. How this conviction is prompted, and to what extent it is nourished and lasts over time, could be a topic for study. In his study of the Dutch temple, Walter van Beek analyzed how the building of a local temple triggered a temporary boost, but then led to diminished temple participation, mainly because of routinization in contrast to the excitement of travel and community experience when members went in groups to faraway temples and derived part of their identity from such a pilgrimage.[54] The degree to which temple participation creates an "elite" class within the Mormon community is yet to be studied adequately.

The Local Culture

When discussing possible American components in the worldwide church, I pointed to the ideology of achievement and to socializing behavior. But what about the impact of the local culture on Mormon identity? This is a vast and complex area, where the danger of stereotyping and generalizations looms. This is not the domain of surface differences, such as in food or dress, but of ways of experiencing values: individualism versus collectivism, gender roles, hierarchical relations, dating traditions, social obligations, and so on. It would be interesting to have the responses of Mormons abroad on surveys such as Geert Hofstede's cultural dimensions.[55] These are known to be practical tools for intercultural management and hence the results may help church leaders become more sensitive in cross-cultural communication.

To what extent are Mormons abroad a mix of Mormon identity and their local cultural identity—and which one prevails? Walter van Beek once phrased it through the question "Mormon Europeans or European Mormons?" He then clarified: "Are they first and foremost in their own self-definitions 'Mormon,' and secondly 'European,' be it Dutch, English, French or Portuguese? Or are they 'Mormon Europeans,' for whom their national (and by extension European) identity comes first, sharing the values and norms of their society before those of the Mormon Church?"[56]

For the Dutch, van Beek concluded the latter—that they are "Mormon Europeans"—citing as examples attitudes toward ecology, social justice, pacifism, marriage, sexuality, and euthanasia. For France, Christian Euvrard surveyed attitudes of members on similar topics.[57] The tendency of French Mormons is not so outspokenly liberal as in Holland; Euvrard found that in terms of ethical questions members closely match the more conservative attitudes of French Protestants. But in political choices they vote across the whole spectrum, with the bulk in the center. Euvrard concludes that French Mormons find a pragmatic balance between Mormon exigencies and their own cultural identity. David Knowlton observed that in Bolivia the "vibrant, active, syncretic Mormonism generally passes unseen before the apparent uniformity of standardized chapels, routine meetings, and white shirts."[58] Thomas Murphy confirmed the same for Guatemala.[59] It raises the question to what extent Mormons abroad are sometimes playing a role when American authorities are present, then quietly doing at least some things "their own way."

It must be underscored that Mormons abroad are as (if not more) diverse as Mormons across the United States. Studies of international Mormon identity will have to probe how diverse they are—e.g., on a scale from religiously orthodox to liberal, or politically right leaning to left leaning—and what those categories even mean in local contexts.

A "Core" with Cultural "Adaptations" around the World?

In connection with the correlation movement, as James Allen has noted, "a constant theme in the 1960s and 1970s was that the essence of the gospel transcended national and cultural boundaries."[60] In 1973 John Sorenson stated that the "core of Mormonism in its most basic expression" is found in the higher levels of ideology, values and knowledge—a common "world view"—but should be allowed to diversify into local cultural forms on the lower levels of physical realization, thus adapting "living the gospel" to other patterns and customs than those in America's West.[61] The solution for a globalizing church was to multiculturalize Mormonism by determining a common, essential core and then allowing regional, national, or ethnic Mormonisms—Japanese, Dutch, Siberian, or Tongan—to develop around that core. Even one General Authority, Elder Ronald Poelman, opted for that direction in a famous 1984 General Conference talk by stressing the difference between the church and the gospel, the latter being the essence. Poelman stated that we should "accommodate a broad spectrum of individual uniqueness and cultural diversity." By so doing "we become less dependent on church programs. Our lives become gospel centered." Elder Poelman was asked to redo his conference talk so as to not seemingly minimize the importance of the church, which created a stir at the time.[62]

To show respect toward other cultures is certainly considerate, but the issue raises more questions than answers.

How to Define Local Culture?

In a 1971 talk about missionary work in Korea, Elder Bruce R. McConkie stated: "Whatever is appropriate and good we want to preserve. It ought to be one of the aims of the Korean people to preserve their culture, to keep their own dances and their own dress and their own mores and ways of life alive, as long as they are not inharmonious with gospel principles."[63]

To start out with dances and dress as typical for a foreign culture betrays a touristic and paternalistic view of foreign cultures. Folklore, indeed, is harmless and may even confirm some backwardness. This attitude is also present in church magazines which portray members in other countries in a stereotyped idyllic environment. It is also evident in the so-called "cultural evening" that local stakes are asked to produce preceding a temple dedication or some other major event. Members respond to the expectation by "performing native folklore," mainly for the visiting American authorities. Some countries and some members may enjoy it more than others, but what is missing is an affirmation of cultural equality with, for example, an homage to achievements in literature, music, art, or science, or the highlighting of modern aspects wherein the country or region excels. Culture, indeed, is much more than a superficial layer which, moreover, is often obsolete and mainly kept alive as a tourist attraction.

Beyond superficialities, each culture contains a range of values and traditions that could remain part of Mormon local life but could also raise questions as to appropriateness, hence creating tensions. Local culture can be shared by a group or a whole nation, but it can also be an individual choice. For example, Chieko Okazaki wrote about how she honored Japanese local traditions for the sake of family unity and peace. She mentioned how the "principle of prayer" allowed her to pray with her mother at the Buddhist household shrine, or how the principle of family unity allowed her and her husband to participate in fun Sunday afternoon activities with her extended non-Mormon family. She concluded: "Before you dismiss any cultural practice, think about the principle behind it, decide if this principle is one you also believe, and see if you can find a way to participate in it in a way that honors that principle."[64] Okazaki constructed an identity where principles permitted the inclusion of activities that other Mormons may consider borderline or prohibited.

Challenges Associated with "Core" and "Adaptations"

The establishment of a "core" with "cultural adaptations" entails a number of intriguing questions. What would be the common, essential core and how would it be defined? As to cultural adaptations, what would be "typical" Japanese, Brazilian, or Dutch Mormonism? Are we not projecting such identities out of stereotypes? Take Dutch: the Netherlands are a small country, but just as much divided into different zones, from Northern Friesland to Southern Brabant, with their own respective characteristics. Even in this limited geographic area one finds a range of religious and ideological positions, including staunch Calvinists, a dozen Protestant tendencies, both traditional and independent Catholics, and of course more liberal and secular tendencies. What kinds of discussions would the creation of a "national Dutch Mormonism" involve? Would it be possible to have even a single "American Mormonism" with its own cultural identity? Mormons from California or New York may not completely identify with Mormon culture in parts of Utah; and of course not all Mormons in Utah are alike. Would assorted forms of Mormonism not open a Pandora's box as to who is more or less orthodox, who has remained the purest to the core, who deserves not to be called Mormon anymore? One can readily see how this dynamic has played out in other world religions such as Islam and Christianity.

How national or regional or ethnic can Mormonism be? Are localized, even balkanized, variations desirable? In many places around the world, including in the United States, Mormon wards and branches have become multicultural units. Through conversions among immigrants, the church in many countries is already a melting pot. Since the 1990s a major characteristic in Western Europe has been the conversion of non-Europeans—refugees, temporary workers, and international students, in particular from Africa and Asia. At present about two-thirds of new converts in Europe were not born in the country of baptism.[65] It makes most local church units in Western Europe multilingual and multicultural. In fact it is in those units that a nonnationalistic, worldwide Mormon identity may be emerging within the framework of uniformity. The slogan that "the Church is the same all over the world" can be a potent reassurance of unity and strength. With increasing mobility for many people in the world, the assurance of finding a Mormon meetinghouse where things are familiar, where the same hymns are sung, where one feels at home, certainly has value.

Therefore, correlation, control, and conformity are perhaps not that objectionable for a church that is still awfully young and inexperienced in many parts of the world. It is interesting to note that the Mormon Church has been extremely careful, even reluctant, to enter some African countries where the probability of independent diversifications is high in view of the ease with which breakaway preachers can start their own versions of a church. The church is moving slowly in such areas. In that respect it seems the church is pursuing a worldwide movement of consolidating fragmentary pieces into centers of strength, such as has been done in parts of Latin America.

What Would be Feasible/Acceptable as Adaptations?

The general statement that everything can be kept that is "not incompatible with the gospel" leaves much room for interpretation. What about "good" religious or semireligious customs that differ from Mormon customs (many of which are products of a Western American context)? There are meaningful traditions that, depending on the criteria chosen, may not be contrary to gospel principles, but would raise eyebrows if followed by Mormons. Can a convert from Catholicism keep a statue of Mary and light a daily candle? Can converts from Judaism continue to have the Seder ceremonial evening meal at Passover? Many of these customs will simply be observed within the privacy of the home, often alongside non-Mormon family members.

Things become more sensitive when we move to church grounds. Can Latino members celebrate a *quinceañera*—a girl's festive fifteenth birthday—with an appropriate church service in the chapel (to approximate the special Catholic Mass at this occasion)? Can Congolese members conduct the funeral procession to the graveyard with jazz accompaniment and dancing—a communal expression in the face of death? Can Spanish members, many of whom are converts from Catholicism who may long after the delight of the Midnight Mass, organize a Mormon variant on Christmas Eve in the chapel? Research could survey to what extent such cultural incursions into Mormon territory are allowed or refused, and on what grounds. Surveys could also identify how members and leaders feel about such adaptations and how much leniency or retrenchment informs behavior.

Researchers have studied at least one case of cultural mixture with a substantial Mormon population over a longer period of time: the Mormon Maoris, who, according to Grant Underwood, can be called an "authentic hybrid."[66]

Reasons for Leniency in Adaptations?

There may be reasons to be more lenient and to establish helping criteria, but this requires more research to assess their value. A number of traditions belong to a cultural heritage that shapes identity within the local community. When such traditions are uplifting, joyful, reassuring, and have nothing detrimental in relation to the gospel, proscribing them could create voids that the church cannot fill. Among these traditions are national or local festive events, historical remembrance dates, peculiar recipe days (when families eat the same distinctive food), and so forth. Activities on annual "children's days," which are celebrated in many countries in various forms and on divergent dates, connect the individual child with the community (as participating in a Pioneer Parade on July twenty-fourth connects a Mormon child in Utah). Sometimes such festivities have a religious origin (e.g., Sinterklaas in Holland, la Befana in Italy). To what extent can prohibiting Mormon children from participation in such cultural traditions encourage an outlook of rejection toward society?

The conversion of a family member to a "foreign" religion is, in many countries, sensed by the rest of the family as a betrayal of the deepest cultural heritage. Researchers can track the ways in which converts keep certain traditions alive and strive to maintain harmony with their family members who have not joined them in their journey to Mormonism. Similarly, one could track the ways in which Mormon branches, wards, and stakes engage (or not) with their local neighborhoods and cultural organizations, thus contributing to images of either isolation or involvement. Studies could survey to what extent communal involvement happens and assess its effect. The matter is important for the image of the church, as cult investigations consider as one of the cult criteria the extent of severance from family and society traditions.

Missionary Work Abroad

As David Golding has explained, missiology and Mormon mission theory can deepen and broaden our understanding of many aspects of the massive Mormon missionary endeavor.[67] I limit myself here to a few issues that I find particularly interesting for more research.

Profiles of Missionaries

Young Mormon missionaries are a unique brand in the world of Christian missions. Researchers have much to learn in profiling these tens of thousands of missionaries who leave home each year, many for a foreign land—aspects such as maturity level, conviction level, reasons for going, preparedness, social aptitudes, expectations, task understanding, context insight, awareness of conversion consequences, acculturation upon entry and deculturation upon return. One approach could entail discourse analysis of missionary blogs that are now widely available. These blogs contain revealing raw material, written in moments of emotion and pressure. One could compare discourse in these blogs across time, starting soon after the mission and then for an extended period thereafter—even decades later.

Missionaries and Local Members

Studies have borne out that missionary work is most effective among those who have been referred to missionaries by their Mormon friends or family members.[68] The question is why so few members are willing to identify potential investigators and collaborate with the missionaries, in spite of the repeated requests to do so. Surveys could answer that. Potential reasons are easy to imagine, but it would be interesting to know their differential weights in various countries. Such reasons could include:

- Respect for the identity of others, particularly in countries where religious belonging is an intrinsic part of the national or the familial culture, and where trying to convert someone is simply "not done."
- Concern by some members that bringing people into Mormonism will not make them happy in the long run because these members' own happiness is not optimal; for they are staying in the church not so much because of their own happiness as out of conviction, loyalty, or social image.
- Consciousness that the costs of Mormon membership are high and that there is a 50 to 70 percent chance that converts will leave the church—which then might undermine relationships with those who introduced them to the church as they depart.
- Fear that the missionaries will be pushy, rushing people to baptism, exacerbating all the above reasons for resisting the call by leaders for member missionary work.

In an ethnographic case study of a Mormon ward in New Jersey, Rick Phillips analyzed missionary strategies and the tensions they created with the members. His conclusion—that the "Church and its missionary program have an organizational structure that hinders church vitality," rather than promoting it—is a statement that invites more research.[69]

Conversion Process

In my home ward in Antwerp, the missionaries wanted to baptize an African refugee couple and their ten-year-old boy. The parents only spoke their own language and could not communicate with the local members. Missionaries taught the parents through translation by the ten-year-old who was going to a local school and had picked up sufficient Dutch for elementary communication. The bishop opposed the baptism because, in his opinion, the candidates were not properly prepared. The missionaries accused him of racism.

Modern Mormon proselytizing strategies, featuring a very short time wherein converts are deemed ready for baptism by eager missionaries, begs for more research. The instructions in the church missionary handbook *Preach My Gospel* project a very constrained definition of conversion—something akin to evangelical Protestants' simple acceptance of Jesus Christ as Savior. It is sufficient for investigators to take four short lessons, attend a few sacrament meetings, answer positively to a few general questions on faith and repentance, and commit to chastity, tithing, the Word of Wisdom, and Sabbath observance. It may be true that "conversion is what a group says it is,"[70] but reality is more complex.

Research could study what determinant role the social factor plays in conversion in various countries, not least the experience of receiving attention from missionaries and members and feeling at home in a welcoming group. In his case studies of conversions, Craig Harline noted that in conversions "relationships come before doctrine."[71]

The study of conversion processes has a long academic tradition in Christian circles, in particular in the fields of process theories, pastoral psychology, social networking, and intercultural analysis. Conversion studies are enjoying a revival with new methods and paradigms.[72] More applications to the study of Mormon conversions, especially abroad, would be welcome.[73] Also important to consider are period and location: to what extent can a conversion to Mormonism in nineteenth-century England be compared to one in twenty-first-century Japan, Nigeria, or Utah? Finally, while conversion to the *gospel* (as a set of abstract beliefs and principles) may be seen as an abrupt change in one's life, the more significant social and cultural conversion is probably a longer process—namely the "Mormonization" of the new convert, as he or she will be encircled by all that the *church* expects. How does conversion to the gospel relate to conversion to the church? Are there cases where the opposite occurs, namely affiliation with the church without a profound commitment to its core doctrines?

Retention

The church uses the positive term "retention" to discuss the continuing adherence of new converts, while the topic is actually "defection." Armand Mauss is one of the few scholars who have studied this phenomenon in a Mormon context, identifying the intellectual, social, and emotional dimensions of religious defection.[74]

The past few decades have seen a vast expansion of research on disengagement, disaffiliation, or defection, as mainline Christian churches have seen massive losses in participation, while new religious movements have been able to grow. To what extent is the problem of defection in the Mormon Church similar to, or different from, that which occurs in older or newer religious movements?[75] To what extent is retention tied to the way people are brought into the church? How and why do various types of defection occur? What are the factors that influence quick departure or slow erosion? Michael Cope studied the process for Utah Mormons, drawing on Albert Hirschman's concepts of *exit*, *voice*, and *loyalty*.[76] One finding was that most members who turn "inactive" do so not because of transgression; furthermore, many continue to consider themselves Mormon or at least retain good memories of their Mormon passage. Other scholars have confirmed the same for Latin America, the Netherlands, and Belgium.[77]

A related aspect is how questioning members can best voice their concerns, while remaining "active," as Mauss put the issue in his famous article "Alternate Voices," which includes his valuable "Decalogue for dissenters."[78] The history of American alternate voices is well documented. But what about those in other countries—including both tragic and heroic cases that also deserve to be understood and remembered? How do local church authorities abroad cope with dissenters? How have those alternate voices fared and how do they fare now, in many cases probably in loneliness? If they know English, to what extent do they seek support and understanding from American kindred spirits?

Collateral Damage

In the 1950s a young Flemish couple joined the Mormon Church. The wife turned inactive after a few years, bitterly disappointed by some incidents, but the husband continued for the rest of his life serving in numerous church capacities and paying tithing. Their married life was one of constant quarrels over his absences and their lack of money. Now a widow, living on a meager pension, she curses the day she had let the missionaries in.

One difficult topic that has hardly been studied is the devastation Mormon missionaries often cause within families and society in general. It is a topic church members would rather avoid for it reflects negatively on missionary work (and the church by extension) and could dissuade prospective missionaries from serving. But the topic of missionary damage is well known in missiology research.

The church acclaims conversion as the path to happiness. The claim is true in thousands of cases every year. For many, however, the path also involves major turmoil—with oneself, family, friends, or the social and cultural environment. Turmoil is an anticipated part of the process because a demanding religion is expected to require sacrifice. But precisely because turmoil belongs to the nature of the process, it is useful to better identify its facets, causes, and consequences and try to develop a multidimensional model for it. The church itself has an interest in forthrightly studying the topic: doing so could lead to better insights and thus help to develop strategies and rules to channel and reduce turmoil, as well as better prepare missionaries to understand the challenges they and their investigators face.

The United States is used to religious diversity and interchurch mobility. Even there, though, conversion to Mormonism can create serious conflicts with families and acquaintances.[79] In cultures without such mobility and with longstanding religious traditions, proselytism will mostly be viewed as a threatening factor of destabilization. Many countries have reached their ideological balance only after decades or even centuries of bloody conflicts or persecutions. Hence the critical attention given to proselyting cults by state security agencies. Missionary work can also be considered as insulting to traditional religious communities because it bespeaks their inadequacy. The Greek judge Valticos called proselytism "the rape of the beliefs of others."[80] Conversion itself is often considered a form of treason, especially if one enters into a foreign church that is maligned in the media as a cult, whose requirements, moreover, upset familial customs and peace. In his poignant book *Conversions*, Craig Harline details the horrid conflicts, sometimes lasting a lifetime, that tear families and friends apart when individuals join another religion.[81]

What about "freedom of religion," guaranteed by various international declarations to which most countries adhere? In some places this freedom means only the right to profess one's religion among its own members, not the freedom to "steal the soul" of one's neighbor. Cole Durham, arguing from an explicitly Mormon perspective, defends the thesis that "normal efforts to engage in religious persuasion" should always be protected as part of religious freedom.[82] But he does not define "normal," nor does he consider the potentially harrowing consequences of even "normal" proselytism on individuals and families in some societies.[83] As issues of "respect" for existing religions enter litigation more and more, missionary work could come to be considered disparagement or vilification of those religions. Thus far, some Mormon legal experts have argued that the principle of freedom must ignore collateral damage.[84]

When Mormon converts are drawn from ethnic or national religions, proselytism creates dramatic conflicts. To deal with such concerns the Mormon Church has pledged not to proselytize in Israel or in Muslim-majority countries, and is extremely careful about approaching Muslims anywhere. But in other countries, missionaries are not taught to be sensitive to collateral damage. To what extent are Mormon missionaries prepared to handle the possibly negative consequences of their conversion efforts? The missionary handbook *Preach My Gospel* briefly mentions the topic three times, with only the vague advice that elders should "rely on the Spirit to help you know how to help [investigators] resolve their concerns." The issue is thus trivialized, and the cause of the concern is solely imputed to a lack of faith or a refusal to make a commitment on the part of the investigator.[85]

Conclusion: Expanding Research

I realize this chapter has been a long listing of items for possible research. Who can do it? How can it be done?

Not many scholars of Mormon studies in the United States are working on aspects of Mormonism abroad. It makes me all the more grateful for the handful that do. That in itself would be a topic to research: how to alter this academic Americentrism. At this time, there are not enough trained scholars in non-American countries with an interest in Mormonism to conduct much of the research suggested, and so we will continue to rely on U.S.-based scholars to initiate many of the requisite studies.

However, there is a way to expand research. Each country has universities with departments in sociology, anthropology, psychology, and history. Past and current experience shows that these can be involved in Mormon studies. In Belgium, for example, non-Mormon students have done valuable research for their theses on Mormon topics at the University of Louvain, the University of Ghent, and the Free University of Brussels.[86] The latter university organized a conference on Mormonism in May 2013. In the U.K., we have analyses of Mormon student religiosity and higher education and of the experience of Mormon children in English school-based religious education.[87] A central figure for Mormon studies in the U.K. has been non-Mormon professor Douglas Davies with his "Study of Religion" research group at the University of Durham. A few academic centers in France are active in Mormon research, mostly within the framework of sociological study of new religious movements. They organize conferences on Mormon topics. Besides master's theses, their interest has led to two doctoral dissertations on Mormonism, and more are being prepared.[88] A central figure there is Bernadette Rigal-Cellard who has been publishing about Mormonism for more than thirty years and in 2012 organized an international conference on Mormonism at the University of Bordeaux, in which Mormon scholars from the United States participated. In Italy, there is CESNUR with Massimo Introvigne, who has also published numerous items on Mormonism. These are only examples of a few European countries. There is more going on across the world.

I am convinced much more research on Mormonism could be stimulated by contacting individual scholars and academic departments that are already working on facets of new religious movements. First, we need a constantly updated overview of what is going on in terms of Mormon studies in the non-Mormon academic world. The Global Mormonism Project at BYU keeps track of the publications on the church abroad, but it limits its scope too much to what Mormon scholars are doing in the usual venues. That project should survey the work at universities across the world, making use of national and international databases that also list theses and dissertations. Next, through networking, more contacts could be established between Mormon scholars and such departments and centers, to suggest and stimulate research projects, as is already being done on a limited scale. The combination of personal experience with Mormonism and the independent look from outsiders, with perhaps other methods and different paradigms, can produce fruitful encounters, as I have experienced in my working with various non-Mormon students and their mentors at Belgian universities. Most of these departments are not aware of the research topics I have listed in this chapter, but suggesting appropriate ones in their realms of specialization, with the necessary background, can lead to a gradual expansion of useful Mormon studies abroad.

Notes

1. Ryan T. Cragun and Ronald Lawson, "The Secular Transition: The Worldwide Growth of Mormons, Jehovah's Witnesses, and Seventh-day Adventists," *Sociology of Religion* 71, no. 3 (2010): 349–73.
2. Rick Phillips, "Rethinking the International Expansion of Mormonism," *Nova Religio* 10, no. 1 (2006): 52.
3. Matthew Bowman, *The Mormon People: The Making of an American Faith* (New York: Random House, 2012), 221–22.
4. Armand L. Mauss, "Mormonism's Worldwide Aspirations and Its Changing Conceptions of Race and Lineage," *Dialogue: A Journal of Mormon Thought* 34, no. 3–4 (2001): 104–5.
5. Wilfried Decoo, "Europe," in *The Oxford Handbook of Mormonism*, ed. Terryl L. Givens and Philip Barlow (New York: Oxford University Press, 2015).
6. This is a common phrase in the Book of Mormon; see, for instance, 2 Nephi 1:5 and Ether 2:7.
7. See, for example, Kim B. Östman, "A Finnish Mormon Temple or America in Karakallio? The Activation of a Stereotype at an Encounter of Cultures," *International Journal of Mormon Studies* 1, no. 1 (2008): 137–53.
8. Christian Euvrard, "Socio-Histoire du mormonisme en France" (PhD diss., École Pratique des Hautes Études, Paris, 2008), 519–25; Bernadette Rigal-Cellard, "Être Français dans une Église d'origine américaine: les Mormons de France," in *Les mutations transatlantiques des religions*, ed. Christian Lerat and Bernadette Rigal-Cellard (Bordeaux: Presses Universitaires de Bordeaux, 2000), 279–308; Alexina Delvaux, "Contribution à l'étude des Saints des Derniers Jours en Belgique: Perspective historique et approche sociologique" (M.A. thesis, Université Libre de Bruxelles, Faculté de Philosophie et Lettres, 2012).
9. Cited in Sheri L. Dew, *Go Forward with Faith: The Biography of Gordon B. Hinckley* (Salt Lake City, UT: Deseret Book Company, 1996), 592.
10. See references for the following items in Wilfried Decoo, "The Mormon Moment Abroad," *Times and Seasons*, December 13, 2012, http://timesandseasons.org/index.php/2012/12/the-mormon-moment-abroad-thank-you-jim-dabakis/.

11. Sarah Kneezle, "In Online Poll, the World (Except for China) Votes Obama," *Time–NewsFeed*, November 5, 2012, http://newsfeed.time.com/2012/11/05/poll-most-of-the-world-would-vote-for-obama-except-china/.
12. "LDS Church President Thomas S. Monson, his first counselor, Henry B. Eyring, and nine Mormon apostles are registered Republicans." Peg McEntee, "Top Mormon Leaders Should Drop Political Party Labels," *Salt Lake Tribune*, December, 5, 2012, http://www.sltrib.com/sltrib/politics/55409550-90/church-lds-political-leaders.html.csp. See also Marc Bohn, "A Look at the Political Affiliations of Some Prominent Members," *Times and Seasons*, January 10, 2014, http://timesandseasons.org/index.php/2014/01/a-look-at-the-political-affiliations-of-some-prominent-members/.
13. Laurie F. Maffly-Kipp, "The Mormon Moment: International Ramifications," *Patheos*, December 02, 2012, http://www.patheos.com/Mormon/International-Ramifications-Laurie-Maffly-Kipp-12-03-2012.html.
14. D. Michael Quinn, "LDS 'Headquarters Culture' and the Rest of Mormonism: Past and Present," *Dialogue: A Journal of Mormon Thought* 34, nos. 3–4 (2001): 135–64; Walter E. van Beek, "Mormon Europeans or European Mormons? An 'Afro-European' View on Religious Colonization," *Dialogue: A Journal of Mormon Thought* 38, no. 4 (2005): 3–36.
15. Thomas S. Monson, "Priesthood Power," *Ensign* (May 2011): 66–69.
16. D. Todd Christofferson, "Brethren, We Have Work to Do," *Ensign* (November 2012): 47–50.
17. Dallin H. Oaks, "The Gospel Culture," *Ensign* (March 2012): 40–47. See also chapter 4 in this volume.
18. Devyn M. Smith, "The Diverse Sheep of Israel: Should the Shepherds Resemble Their Flock?" *Dialogue: A Journal of Mormon Thought* 38, no. 4 (2005): 56–74.
19. Tim B. Heaton and Cardell K. Jacobson, "The Social Life of Mormons," in Givens and Barlow, *The Oxford Handbook of Mormonism*.
20. Marie Cornwall, "The Determinants of Religious Behavior: A Theoretical Model and Empirical Test," *Social Forces* 68, no. 2 (1989): 572–92.
21. Julie B. Beck, "Mothers Who Know," *Ensign* (November 2007): 76.
22. Cornwall, "The Determinants," 574.
23. For examples, see Tim B. Heaton, Stephen J. Bahr, and Cardell K. Jacobson, *A Statistical Profile of Mormons: Health, Wealth, and Social Life* (Lewiston, NY: Edwin Mellen Press, 2004); Armand L. Mauss, "Mormons as Ethnics: Variable Historical and International Implications of an Appealing Concept," in *The Mormon Presence in Canada*, ed. Brigham Y. Card, Herbert C. Northcott, John E. Foster, Howard Palmer, and George K. Jarvis (Logan: Utah State University Press, 1990), 332–52; Robert D. Putnam and David E. Campbell, *American Grace: How Religion Divides and Unites Us* (New York: Simon & Schuster, 2010); Pew Research, "Mormons in America: Certain of Their Beliefs, Uncertain of Their Place in Society," *Pew Forum on Religion and Public Life*, January 12, 2012, http://www.pewforum.org/2012/01/12/mormons-in-america-executive-summary/.
24. Heaton and Jacobson, "Social Life of Mormons."
25. See also David C. Knowlton, "How Many Members Are There Really? Two Censuses and the Meaning of LDS Membership in Chile and Mexico," *Dialogue: A Journal of Mormon Thought* 38, no. 2 (2005): 53–78.

26. Euvrard, "Socio-Histoire," 419–68.
27. See Robert Buckle, "Mormons in Britain: A Survey," in *A Sociological Yearbook of Religion in Britain*, ed. Michael Hill (London: SCM Press, 1971), 4:160–79; Tim B. Heaton, Stan L. Albrecht, and J. Randall Johnson, "The Making of British Saints in Historical Perspective," *BYU Studies* 27, no. 2 (1987): 119–35.
28. For Australia: Marjorie Newton, *Southern Cross Saints: The Mormons in Australia* (Laie, HI: Institute for Polynesian Studies, Brigham Young University–Hawaii, 1991); for Belgium: Wilfried Decoo, "Mormonism in a European Catholic Country: Contribution to the Social Psychology of LDS Converts," *BYU Studies* 24, no. 1 (1984): 61–77; Wilfried Decoo, "Feeding the Fleeing Flock: Reflections on the Struggle to Retain Church Members in Europe," *Dialogue: A Journal of Mormon Thought* 29, no. 1 (1996): 97–118; for Guatemala: Thomas W. Murphy, "Reinventing Mormonism: Guatemala as Harbinger of the Future?," *Dialogue: A Journal of Mormon Thought* 29, no. 1 (1996), 177–92; Thomas W. Murphy, "Guatemalan Hot/Cold Medicine and Mormon Words of Wisdom: Intercultural Negotiation of Meaning," *Journal for the Scientific Study of Religion* 36, no. 2 (1997): 297–308; for Hong Kong: Caroline Plüss, "Chinese Participation in the Church of Jesus Christ of Latter-day Saints (Mormons) in Hong Kong," *Journal of Contemporary Religion* 14, no. 1 (1999): 63–76; for Japan: John P. Hoffmann, *Japanese Saints: Mormons in the Land of the Rising Sun* (Lanham, MD: Lexington Books, 2007); Jiro Numano, "Perseverance amid Paradox: The Struggle of the LDS Church in Japan Today," *Dialogue: A Journal of Mormon Thought* 39, no. 4 (2006): 138–55; for Mexico: F. LaMond Tullis, *Mormons in Mexico: The Dynamics of Faith and Culture* (Logan: Utah State University Press, 1987); for the Netherlands: Walter E. A. van Beek, "Ethnicization and Accommodation: Dutch Mormons in Twenty-First-Century Europe," *Dialogue: A Journal of Mormon Thought* 29, no. 1 (1996): 119–38; van Beek, "Mormon Europeans"; for New Zealand: Ian G. Barber and David Gilgen, "Between Covenant and Treaty: The LDS Future in New Zealand," *Dialogue: A Journal of Mormon Thought* 29, no. 1 (1996): 207–22; Marjorie Newton, "Mormonism in New Zealand: A Historical Appraisal" (PhD diss., University of Sydney, 1998); Marjorie Newton, *Tiki and Temple: The Mormon Mission in New Zealand, 1854–1958* (Draper, UT: Greg Kofford Books, 2012); for Nicaragua: Henri Gooren, "Latter-day Saints under Siege: The Unique Experience of Nicaraguan Mormons," *Dialogue: A Journal of Mormon Thought* 40, no. 3 (2007): 134–55; for Tonga: Tamar Gordon, "Inventing the Mormon Tongan Family," in *Christianity in Oceania: Ethnographic Perspectives*, ed. J. Barker (Lanham, MD: University Press of America, 1990), 197–219; and for Latin America in general: Mark L. Grover, "The Maturing of the Oak: The Dynamics of LDS Growth in Latin America," *Dialogue: A Journal of Mormon Thought* 38, no. 2 (2005): 79–104; Knowlton, "How Many Members"; David C. Knowlton, "Mormonism in Latin America: Towards the Twenty-First Century," *Dialogue: A Journal of Mormon Thought* 29, no. 1 (1996): 159–76; F. LaMond Tullis, "Three Myths about Mormons in Latin America," *Dialogue: A Journal of Mormon Thought* 7, no. 1 (1972): 79–87.
29. Armand L. Mauss, "Can There Be a 'Second Harvest'?: Controlling the Costs of Latter-day Saint Membership in Europe," *International Journal of Mormon Studies* 1 (2008): 1–59.

30. See Chaeyoon Lim and Robert D. Putnam, "Religion, Social Networks, and Life Satisfaction," *American Sociological Review* 75, no. 6 (2010): 914–33.
31. Armand L. Mauss, "The Mormon Struggle with Identity," *Dialogue: A Journal of Mormon Thought* 27, no. 1 (1994): 141.
32. Armand L. Mauss, "Refuge and Retrenchment: The Mormon Quest for Identity," in *Contemporary Mormonism: Social Science Perspectives*, ed. Marie Cornwall, Tim B. Heaton, and Lawrence A. Young (Chicago: University of Illinois Press, 2001), 25. See also these publications related to Mormon identity by Mauss: *The Angel and the Beehive: The Mormon Struggle with Assimilation* (Urbana: University of Illinois Press, 1994); and the already mentioned "Can There Be a 'Second Harvest'?"; "The Mormon Struggle"; "Mormonism's Worldwide Aspirations"; and "Mormons as Ethnics."
33. See also Wilfried Decoo, "In Search of Mormon Identity: Mormon Culture, Gospel Culture, and an American Worldwide Church," *International Journal of Mormon Studies* 6 (2013): 1–53. I wrote that article after the present chapter, and it is therefore more detailed, but it was published earlier. I acknowledge the reciprocal use of some parts.
34. Barber and Gilgen, "Between Covenant and Treaty"; Newton, *Tiki and Temple*; Ruby Welch, "Ethnicity among Auckland Mormons" (M.A. thesis, University of Auckland, 1989); F. LaMond Tullis, "A Shepherd to Mexico's Saints: Arwell L. Pierce and the Third Convention," *BYU Studies* 37, no. 1 (1997): 125–57; Tullis, *Mormons in Mexico.*
35. Jessie L. Embry, "Ethnic Groups and the LDS Church," *Dialogue: A Journal of Mormon Thought* 25, no. 4 (1992): 81–96.
36. See Betty Ventura, "Cultural Differences and Gospel Unity," in *A Heritage of Faith: Talks Selected from the BYU Women's Conferences*, ed. Mary E. Stovall and Carol Cornwall Madsen (Salt Lake City, UT: Deseret Book Company, 1988), 139–46; Armand L. Mauss, "Feelings, Faith, and Folkways: A Personal Essay on Mormon Popular Culture," in *"Proving Contraries": A Collection of Writings in Honor of Eugene England*, ed. Robert A. Rees (Salt Lake City, UT: Signature Books, 2004), 33.
37. See Lim and Putnam, "Religion"; Daniel V. A. Olson and Paul Perl, "A Friend in Creed: Does the Religious Composition of Geographic Areas Affect the Religious Composition of a Person's Close Friends?," *Journal for the Scientific Study of Religion* 50, no. 3 (2011): 483–502.
38. See Douglas D. Alder, "The Mormon Ward: Congregation or Community?" *Journal of Mormon History* 5 (1978): 61–78; Mario S. De Pillis, "The Persistence of Mormon Community into the 1990s," *Sunstone* (October 1991): 28–49; Jessie L. Embry, *Mormon Wards as Community* (Binghamton, NY: Global Publications, 2001); Jan Shipps, Cheryll L. May, and Dean L. May, "Sugar House Ward: A Latter-day Saint Congregation," in *American Congregations, Volume 1: Portraits of Twelve Religious Communities*, ed. James P. Wind and James W. Lewis (Chicago: University of Chicago Press, 1994), 293–348; Susan Buhler Taber, *Mormon Lives: A Year in the Elkton Ward* (Urbana: University of Illinois Press, 1993).
39. An interesting parallel to this in a U.S. context would be the Outmigration Leadership History Project; see G. Wesley Johnson and Marian Ashby Johnson, "On the Trail of the Twentieth-Century Mormon Outmigration," *BYU Studies* 46, no. 1 (2007): 41–83.

40. Michael R. Cope, "You Don't Know Jack: The Dynamics of Mormon Religious/Ethnic Identity" (M.A. thesis, Brigham Young University, 2009); Henri Gooren, "The Mormons of the World: The Meaning of LDS Membership in Central America," in *Revisiting Thomas F. O'Dea's "The Mormons": Contemporary Perspectives*, ed. Cardell K. Jacobson, John P. Hoffman, and Tim B. Heaton (Salt Lake City: University of Utah Press, 2008), 362–88; Knowlton, "How Many Members"; James A. Toronto, "Challenges to Establishing the Church in the Middle East," in *Global Mormonism in the 21st Century*, ed. Reid L. Neilson (Provo, UT: Religious Studies Center, Brigham Young University, 2008), 134–45; James A. Toronto, "'Strangers in a Strange Land': Assessing the Experience of Latter-day Saint Expatriate Families," *BYU Studies* 45, no. 4 (2006): 25–45.
41. See F. LaMond Tullis, ed., *Mormonism: A Faith for All Cultures* (Provo, UT: Brigham Young University Press, 1978).
42. Dallin H. Oaks, "Give Thanks in All Things," *Ensign* (May 2003): 95–98. See also by Oaks, "Repentance and Change," *Ensign* (November 2003): 37–40; "The Gospel Culture."
43. In Decoo, "In Search of Mormon Identity," I expand this paradigm to six perspectives on an antonymic scale.
44. George Albert Smith, *Sharing the Gospel with Others* (Salt Lake City, UT: Deseret Book Company, 1948), 201. The excerpt comes from a sermon delivered on November 4, 1945.
45. See Oaks, "Give Thanks" and "Repentance and Change." Also: Richard G. Scott, "Removing Barriers to Happiness," *Ensign* (May 1998): 85.
46. Sherry Baker and Joel Campbell, "Mitt Romney's Religion: A Five Factor Model for Analysis of Media Representation of Mormon Identity," *Journal of Media and Religion* 9 (2010): 99–121.
47. Decoo, "The Mormon Moment."
48. See Philip L. Barlow, "Why the King James Version? From the Common to the Official Version of Mormonism," *Dialogue: A Journal of Mormon Thought* 22, no. 2 (1989): 19–42; Mauss, "The Mormon Struggle," 132; Mauss, *The Angel*, 102–8.
49. See van Beek, "Mormon Europeans," 21, on the hassle with the Dutch choice for the Bible, which illustrates the tension between different views on Mormon identity.
50. See Wilfried Decoo, "Thou-Thee-Thy from Other Angles," *Times and Seasons*, May 21, 2009, http://timesandseasons.org/index.php/2009/05/thou-thee-thy-from-other-angles/; Grant Hardy, "The King James Bible and the Future of Missionary Work," *Dialogue: A Journal of Mormon Thought* 45, no. 2 (2012): 1–44.
51. See Van C. Gessel, "Strange Characters and Expressions: Three Japanese Translations of the Book of Mormon," *Journal of Book of Mormon Studies* 14, no. 1 (2005): 32–47, 127–28; Marcellus S. Snow, "The Challenge of Theological Translation: New German Versions of the Standard Works," *Dialogue: A Journal of Mormon Thought* 17, no. 2 (1984): 133–49.
52. Murphy, "Guatemalan Hot/Cold Medicine."
53. Reed B. Haslam, *The Light Breaks on Southeast Asia: A History of the LDS Church in Asia's Ancient Kingdoms* (Sandy, UT: HTown Publishing, 2012), 366–410.
54. Walter E. A. Van Beek, "The Temple and the Sacred: Dutch Temple Experiences," *Dialogue: A Journal of Mormon Thought* 45, no. 4 (2012): 27–52.

55. Geert Hofstede, Gert Jan Hofstede, and Michael Minkov, *Cultures and Organizations: Software of the Mind* (New York: McGraw-Hill, 2010).
56. Van Beek, "Mormon Europeans," 20.
57. Euvrard, "Socio-Histoire," 419–68.
58. David Knowlton, "'Gringo Jeringo': Anglo Mormon Missionary Culture in Bolivia," in *Contemporary Mormonism: Social Science Perspectives*, ed. Marie Cornwall, Tim B. Heaton, and Lawrence A. Young (Urbana: University of Illinois Press, 1994), 221.
59. Murphy, "Guatemalan Hot/Cold Medicine."
60. James B. Allen, "On Becoming a Universal Church: Some Historical Perspectives," *Dialogue: A Journal of Mormon Thought* 25, no. 1 (1992): 15.
61. John L. Sorenson, "Mormon World View and American Culture," *Dialogue: A Journal of Mormon Thought* 8, no. 2 (1973): 17–29.
62. See Peggy Fletcher, "Poelman Revises Conference Speech," *Sunstone* (January 1985): 44–45.
63. Cited in Spencer J. Palmer, ed., *The Expanding Church* (Salt Lake City, UT: Deseret Book Company, 1978), 147.
64. Chieko N. Okazaki, *Disciples* (Salt Lake City, UT: Deseret Book Company, 1998), 149.
65. Information obtained from the Membership and Records Department, prepared by the Management Information Center, mail of October 14, 2011; see also C. Gary Lobb, "Mormon Membership Trends in Europe among People of Color: Present and Future Assessment," *Dialogue: A Journal of Mormon Thought* 33, no. 4 (2000): 59–68.
66. Grant Underwood, "Mormonism, the Maori and Cultural Authenticity," *The Journal of Pacific History* 35, no. 2 (2000): 133–46; see also Ian Barber, "Between Biculturalism and Assimilation: The Changing Place of Maori Culture in the Twentieth-Century New Zealand Mormon Church," *New Zealand Journal of History* 29 (October 1995): 142–69; Peter Lineham, "The Mormon Message in the Context of Maori Culture," *Journal of Mormon History* 17 (1991): 62–93; Newton, *Mormonism in New Zealand*; Newton, *Tiki and Temple*.
67. David Golding, "The Foundations and Early Development of Mormon Mission Theory" (M.A. thesis, Claremont Graduate University, 2010). See his notes for a wealth of further resources for research.
68. See Armand L. Mauss, *Shifting Borders and a Tattered Passport: Intellectual Journeys of a Mormon Academic* (Salt Lake City: University of Utah Press, 2012), 44.
69. Rick Phillips, "'De Facto Congregationalism' and Mormon Missionary Outreach: An Ethnographic Case Study," *Journal for the Scientific Study of Religion* 47, no. 4 (2008): 628–43.
70. Lewis R. Rambo, *Understanding Religious Conversion* (New Haven, CT: Yale University Press, 1993), 7.
71. Craig Harline, *Conversions: Two Family Stories from the Reformation and Modern America* (New Haven, CT: Yale University Press, 2011), 66.
72. Lewis R. Rambo, "Conversion Studies, Pastoral Counseling, and Cultural Studies: Engaging and Embracing a New Paradigm," *Pastoral Psychology* 59, no. 4 (2010): 433–45.
73. See Henri Gooren's research: "Towards a New Model of Conversion Careers: The Impact of Personality and Contingency Factors," *Exchange* 34, no. 2 (2005): 149–66;

"The Religious Market Model and Conversion: Towards a New Approach," *Exchange* 35, no. 1 (2006): 39–60; "Latter-day Saints under Siege"; "The Mormons of the World"; *Religious Conversion and Disaffiliation: Tracing Patterns of Change in Faith Practices* (New York: Palgrave Macmillan, 2010).

74. Armand L. Mauss, "Dimensions of Religious Defection," *Review of Religious Research* 10, no. 3 (1969): 128–35; Armand L. Mauss, "Apostasy and the Management of Spoiled Identity," in *The Politics of Apostasy: The Role of Apostates in the Transformation of Religious Movements*, ed. David G. Bromley (New York: Praeger, 1998), 51–73; Armand L. Mauss, "'Japanese Saints: Mormons in the Land of the Rising Sun' by John P. Hoffmann (Review)," *Social Forces* 87, no. 3 (2009): 1698.

75. See Stan L. Albrecht and Howard M. Bahr, "Patterns of Religious Disaffiliation: A Study of Lifelong Mormons, Mormon Converts, and Former Mormons," *Journal for the Scientific Study of Religion* 22, no. 4 (1983): 366–79; M. Howard Bahr and Stan L. Albrecht, "Strangers Once More: Patterns of Disaffiliation from Mormonism," *Journal for the Scientific Study of Religion* 28, no. 2 (1989): 180–200; Gooren, *Religious Conversion and Disaffiliation.*

76. Cope, "You Don't Know Jack"; Albert O. Hirschman, *Exit, Voice and Loyalty: Responses to Decline in Firms, Organizations, and States* (Cambridge, MA: Harvard University Press, 1970).

77. Grover, "The Maturing of the Oak," 100–101; van Beek, "Mormon Europeans"; Decoo, "Feeding the Fleeing Flock."

78. Armand L. Mauss, "Alternate Voices: The Calling and Its Implications," *Sunstone* (April 1990): 7–10.

79. For a historical example, see Patrick Q. Mason, *The Mormon Menace: Violence and Anti-Mormonism in the Postbellum South* (New York: Oxford University Press, 2011). See also Richard L. Bushman, "Comment on 'Conversion in 19th Century Mormonism: Identities and Associations in the Atlantic World,'" *Dialogue: A Journal of Mormon Thought* 45, no. 3 (2012): 51–55.

80. Cited in Peter G. Danchin and Lisa Forman, "The Evolving Jurisprudence of the European Court of Human Rights and the Protection of Religious Minorities," in *Protecting the Human Rights of Religious Minorities in Eastern Europe*, ed. Peter G. Danchin and Elizabeth A. Cole (New York: Columbia University Press, 2002), 203.

81. Harline, *Conversions.*

82. W. Cole Durham, "The Impact of Secularization on Proselytism in Europe: A Minority Religion Perspective," in *Global Mormonism in the 21st Century*, ed. Reid L. Neilson (Provo, UT: Religious Studies Center, Brigham Young University, 2008), 114–33.

83. For the line between "proper" and "improper proselytism," see Tad Stahnke, "Proselytism and the Freedom to Change Religion in International Human Rights Law," *Brigham Young University Law Review* 1999, no. 1 (1999): 251–350.

84. Paul M. Taylor, "The Questionable Grounds of Objections to Proselytism and Certain Other Forms of Religious Expression," *Brigham Young University Law Review* 2006, no. 3 (2006): 811–36.

85. *Preach My Gospel* (Salt Lake City: Church of Jesus Christ of Latter-day Saints, 2004), 187; see also 113 and 153.

86. Tim Vanhove, "Religieus gemengde huwelijken bij de Mormonen" (M.A. thesis, Katholieke Universiteit Leuven, Faculteit Sociale Wetenschappen, 1999); An Burvenich, "Het ontstaan van de Kerk van Jezus Christus van de Heiligen der Laatste Dagen in België, 1861–1914" (M.A. thesis, Rijksuniversiteit Gent, Departement Geschiedenis, 1999); Delvaux, "Contribution à l'étude."
87. Craig Lithgow Marshall, "Mormon Student Religiosity and Higher Education" (PhD diss., University of Nottingham, 1996); Ronan James Head, "The Experience of Mormon Children in English School-Based Religious Education and Collective Worship," *International Journal of Mormon Studies* 2 (2009): 197–205.
88. Euvrard, "Socio-Histoire"; Sophie-Hélène Trigeaud, "Conversion, éducation, communauté: Une étude socio-anthropologique, transnationale et contemporaine, des pratiques et représentations des 'Saints des Derniers Jours' ou 'Mormons'" (PhD diss., École des Hautes Études en Sciences Sociales, Paris, 2008). Trigeaud's revised dissertation was published in book form as *Devenir mormon: La fabrication communautaire de l'individu* (Rennes: Presses Universitaires de Rennes, 2013).

Part III | The Burden of Race

Chapter 6 | What Jane James Saw

Quincy D. Newell

Introduction: Looking at Jane, Looking with Jane

The story of Mormonism, as it is usually told, begins with Joseph Smith Jr. or, occasionally, with one of his associates.[1] Concerned with the twin tasks of organization building and religion making, the story usually stays focused on Smith and the people he drew to the center of his church, following them from upstate New York, through Smith's death in Illinois, and finally to the "kingdom in the tops of the mountains," in present-day Utah. Comprehensive histories continue with the church's quest to become American even while remaining distinctive, and to become a global church organized around an American narrative. The focus usually remains institutional and elite, with the men, and sometimes the women, who did the most to lead and shape the church taking center stage.

In recent years, scholars have paid increasing attention to those who do not fit neatly into this narrative, excavating the stories of nonwhite Latter-day Saints throughout the history of the church. Building on the scholarship of Lester E. Bush Jr., Newell G. Bringhurst, and others,[2] those who have unearthed the histories of early black Mormons collectively make a straightforward argument: black people have been members of the LDS Church since its beginnings, and their stories ought to be remembered.[3]

As an act of recovery, this thesis is powerful stuff. The evidence is ample, if fragmentary. But recuperating these stories is not enough. The real power of this history for Mormon studies is in its potential to radically reshape our thinking about the history of the LDS Church, American religious history, the intersections of race and religion, and beyond. These stories should not simply add to our given narratives; they should change them in fundamental ways. In this essay, I examine the life of Jane Elizabeth Manning James, a nineteenth-century African American convert to Mormonism. I take my cue from Caroline Walker Bynum's admonition that "we must, at least some of the time, stand *with* those whom we study"[4] and suggest that the story of nineteenth-century Mormonism changes when we look *with* James rather than *at* her.

First, a brief introduction to Jane James is in order.[5] James was born a free black child in Connecticut, probably in the 1810s or 1820s. In the winter of 1842–1843, she heard a Mormon missionary preach and was convinced that she should leave her Congregational church and be baptized as a Latter-day Saint, which she did. Jane appears to have persuaded most of her family to convert, and they all went to Nauvoo, Illinois, where the church was then based, in the fall of 1843. There, Jane worked for Joseph Smith as a servant. She met and married another black convert, Isaac James. After Smith was killed in 1844, Jane, Isaac, and Jane's first son, Sylvester (her child from a previous relationship), joined the majority of Latter-day Saints and followed Brigham Young to Utah. They were among the first companies to arrive in the Salt Lake Valley. Jane remained a faithful Mormon for the rest of her life, and dictated a short autobiography before she died in 1908. She also left a surprisingly robust paper trail in Mormon records—meeting minutes, periodicals, other people's diaries, and other records all contain traces of Jane. Pieced together, these fragments allow us to reconstruct, to a degree, a different perspective on the development of Mormonism than the standard narratives suggest.

As a nineteenth-century African American Mormon woman, Jane James is unusual: we only know about a few people like her, though I would guess that there are many more whose stories are lost to us. Certainly she was not typical—but neither was Joseph Smith or Brigham Young. Looking *with* James, as Bynum suggests, unsettles the standard narrative of Mormon history, which assumes the universality of white male experience. In what follows, I will show that Jane James's story displaces the temple as the primary location of religious experience; disperses spiritual authority, distributing it with little regard for priesthood qualifications; and disputes the legacy of Joseph Smith, revealing the power and persistence of unauthorized memories of the religion's founder. Ultimately, I suggest that by looking at the LDS Church *with* its members of color, we gain a crucial—and otherwise unavailable—perspective on the church's nineteenth-century development.

Locating Religious Experience with Jane James

When Jane James joined the LDS Church, its temple ceremonies were still inchoate. The Latter-day Saints had not completed the temple in Nauvoo; rituals that would later be restricted to the temple were performed instead in spaces improvised for the occasion. Brigham Young recalled that when he received his endowment in the room above Joseph Smith's store in Nauvoo, Smith admitted, "Bro. Brigham this is not arranged right but we have done the best we could under the circumstances in which we are placed." Instructed to "take this matter in hand and organize and systematize all these ceremonies," Young refined the ceremony as the temple took shape, until he felt "we had our ceremonies pretty correct."[6] As Young's recollection illustrates, temple rituals developed over time. This process was far from complete at the end of Joseph Smith's life; in fact, Smith's successors continued to elaborate temple theology and rituals well after his death.[7]

Unlike many of the Latter-day Saints who lived in Nauvoo, James did not receive her endowments in the temple the Mormons constructed there before leaving for the Great Salt Lake Valley in 1846. Jane and Isaac James also were not sealed to each other in the Nauvoo temple, even though many church members were sealed to their spouses before embarking on the westward journey.[8] There is almost no documentary evidence on Jane and Isaac James's life from this time, leaving us to speculate about the reason or reasons for these omissions: perhaps one or both of them felt spiritually unprepared for the rituals at that time; perhaps church leaders discouraged them from seeking their endowments; or perhaps there was another reason. In the latter decades of the nineteenth century, Jane James petitioned church leaders repeatedly for the privilege of receiving her endowments and being sealed in the temple.[9] By that time, church leaders had begun to formulate a coherent policy that excluded people of African descent from any temple rituals beyond baptism for the dead. James was permitted to visit the Logan temple in 1888 and perform baptisms for a number of her deceased family members, but her repeated requests to receive her endowments and to be sealed went unfulfilled.[10]

Nevertheless, James enjoyed a rich religious life that centered on charismatic experiences of the divine. In contrast to the secrecy that surrounded temple rituals, James spoke at length about her encounters with God to anyone who would listen. Supernatural healings were one form in which James interacted with the divine. For example, in 1896, James told a gathering of LDS women about healing herself. The secretary who reported on the gathering put it this way: "Sister Jane James bore a faithful testimony and said she had been terribly afflicted in her head, and she took her consecrated oil and anointed herself and she was healed. Felt that *that* was faith, and praised the Lord for her blessings."[11]

James also received revelations from the Holy Spirit. The most dramatic episode was her experience of doing the Smith family's laundry shortly after being hired as a domestic servant in Nauvoo. "Among the clothes I found brother Josephs Robes," James recalled in her autobiography. "I looked at them and wondered, I had never seen any before, and I pondered over them and thought about them so earnestly that the spirit made manifest to me that they pertained to the new name that is given the saints that the world knows not off [*sic*]. I didnt know when I washed them or when I put them out to dry."[12] The "new name" that James mentioned about was a reference to the temple endowment ritual, suggesting that James received information about temple ceremonies directly from God.[13]

Perhaps the most frequent charismatic experience in James's life was speaking in tongues, a practice that was very familiar to early Mormons. James's first recorded instance of glossolalia was shortly after her conversion. In her autobiography, James recalled, "About three weeks after [baptism] while kneeling at prayer the Gift of Tongues came upon me, and frightened the whole family who were in the next room."[14] Glossolalia was a common occurrence in the early LDS Church. The earliest converts understood it as a sign that would follow true believers, but church leaders soon emphasized the utilitarian value of glossolalia in communicating the restored gospel to those who spoke other languages.[15] Leaders also warned church members against relying on glossolalia for anything beyond its value in comforting and strengthening believers. "If any have a matter to reveal," Joseph Smith told the newly founded Relief Society in 1842, "let it be in your own tongue. Do not indulge too much in the gift of tongues, or the devil will take advantage of the innocent. You may speak in tongues for your own comfort but I lay down for a rule that if any thing is taught by the gift of tongues, it is not to be received for doctrine."[16]

Apart from her first, James's recorded experiences of glossolalia occurred in social settings where their value in encouraging and comforting church members is clear. Most reports come from the minutes of a women's group known as the Retrenchment Society, which had been formed in 1870 to promote plain, faithful living among LDS women and girls. In 1885, for example, the Retrenchment Society secretary reported that in the society's semimonthly meeting, "Sister Jane James spoke powerfully in tongues, and the interpretation was given by Sister Bishop."[17] Similar reports appeared sporadically throughout the remainder of the nineteenth century.[18]

In seeking and valuing charismatic experiences like these, James was very similar to many members of the church she joined in the 1840s. Janet Ellingson has shown that early Mormons experienced spiritual gifts like healing, visions, and speaking in tongues quite regularly. Moreover, Ellingson argues, many people who became Latter-day Saints regularly experienced spiritual gifts *before* their conversion, and they converted to Mormonism because it accepted and valued these experiences.[19] Paired with James's accounts of charismatic experiences, Ellingson's provocative argument suggests a new interpretation of James's conversion narrative. "[W]hen about fourteen years old I joined the Presbyterian Church," James recalled. "Yet I did not feel satisfied it seemed to me there was something more that I was looking for."[20] Scholars have interpreted this statement as a claim about the deficiencies of the Presbyterian Church and as corroboration of LDS claims to have the "fullness of the gospel." Ellingson's argument, however, suggests that the "something more" James sought was a place where her charismatic experiences were recognized and encouraged.

James's ability to construct a rich, satisfying religious life within the LDS Church, along with her persistent campaign, late in life, to receive her endowments and be sealed, highlights the ways religious experience moved, physically, during the church's first century. Jan Shipps argued that the "esoteric restoration" of Mormonism, in which Joseph Smith developed the religion's distinctive cosmology, "placed the ordinances of the temple—most especially the endowment . . . and celestial marriage—at the very core of Mormonism."[21] The performance of these rituals in the temple—for oneself and for the dead—is now a "staple" of LDS worship, an intense expression and experience of LDS spirituality. Richard Bennett has pointed out that this was not always the case: "Even during the Mormon Reformation of 1856," he wrote, "the symbol of recommitment among the Saints was not increased temple worship but rather rebaptism."[22] The LDS Church has thus shaped its members' religious experiences in important ways, moving significant rituals out of public view and discouraging members from discussing them.[23]

James's religious experience highlights the degree to which scholars have interpreted temple ritual as the normative religious experience in Mormonism. Indeed, according to Kathleen Flake, temple ritual is the "privileged source of LDS truth."[24] By this standard, James's religious life was deficient because she was excluded from the temple. This interpretation also lends itself to a view of James's extratemple religious experience as a form of resistance to church leaders.[25] James dictated her autobiography, ostensibly, so that it could be read at her funeral. However, it was also distributed to church leaders during James's lifetime, almost certainly with her permission. When scholars interpret temple ritual as normative, James's recollection of learning from the Holy Spirit that Joseph Smith's temple robes were related to the "new name" that church members received appears to be designed to let those church leaders know that their authority was insufficient to control the secrets of the temple.[26]

An alternate interpretation of James's religious experience that looks *with* James would focus instead on the ubiquity of extratemple religious experience among early Mormons. From this angle, James's lack of temple experience takes a back seat to her charismatic experiences. These episodes allowed her to fit in with other early Mormons and construct a religious identity affirming the proposition that God interacted actively with humans in ways that echoed Joseph Smith's own experiences and confirmed the restoration of ancient spiritual gifts. This perspective moves us away from official LDS doctrine and toward the lived religion of nineteenth-century Mormons, acknowledging their sense that Mormonism accepted and valued their charismatic experiences regardless of whether those experiences occurred in temples.

Reconceptualizing Religious Authority with Jane James

In LDS cosmology, the efficacy of temple ritual depends on priesthood authority. The LDS priesthood originates in the life and teachings of Joseph Smith, and specifically in Smith's concern over authority. Understood quite literally as the authority to act in God's name, the priesthood was what guaranteed the efficacy of temple rituals, blessings, baptisms, and prayers. It was (and is) the prerequisite for holding most leadership positions in the church, and it was a required qualification in the nineteenth century for men considering plural marriage. Men who converted to Mormonism were frequently ordained within days of their baptism. Parley P. Pratt's experience was typical: baptized by Oliver Cowdery, a trusted associate of Joseph Smith, Pratt was confirmed the same evening and then immediately ordained.[27] This sense that the priesthood was available to virtually anyone, that divine authority was widely distributed in the church, has led scholars to see the nineteenth-century church as broadly democratic and as typical of what Nathan Hatch has famously called the "Democratization of American Christianity."[28]

While Hatch's analysis of the democratic impulse in Mormonism was based on the "distinct class bias" he saw in "Smith's overall vision" and in the LDS scriptures, that impulse extended beyond text to church structures, most especially the priesthood.[29] Richard Bushman, for example, has characterized the church as "simultaneously hierarchical and democratic" because it is led by a very small group of men (the First Presidency and the Quorum of the Twelve) and yet authority is dispersed "to millions of individual members in every congregation."[30] Similarly, Paul Johnson pointed out that "rather than create a priestly caste, Smith ordained ordinary men as elders, priests, teachers, and deacons, fitting them into an elaborate, graded hierarchy in which virtually all Mormon men (the operative term was and is 'all worthy males') held spiritual gifts and occupied positions of real authority and responsibility."[31]

Johnson noted, as Hatch did not, the ways in which this democratizing impulse was limited to men. He wrote, "There was a domestic component to that understanding—that Mormonism resurrected and reformulated not only the class systems of the *Book of Mormon*, the Old Testament, and the American eighteenth century but their gender systems as well."[32] As a patriarchal system, Mormonism was premised on the submission of women to righteous male authority, constituted through and signified by the LDS priesthood.

Scholars have recently begun to unpack the ways in which this patriarchal authority was racialized. Both the Book of Mormon and the Pearl of Great Price constructed hierarchies of righteousness that corresponded to gradations in skin color.[33] In addition to associating white skin with righteousness and dark skin with sinfulness, LDS sacred texts developed the already existing stories of Cain and Canaan in ways that sacralized the subordination of black people. In 1880, the church canonized the Book of Moses and the Book of Abraham, two texts that Joseph Smith produced, as part of the Pearl of Great Price. The Book of Moses, part of Smith's inspired translation of Genesis, incorporated a racialized interpretation of the story of Cain into its rendition of the story of Enoch. When God took him up into heaven, Enoch saw "the residue of the people which were the sons of Adam," those who remained on the earth. These people were "a mixture of all the seed of Adam save it was the seed of Cain, for the seed of Cain were black, and had not place among them."[34] This narrative expanded on the Genesis story of Cain in which God placed a mark on Cain. By specifying the color of Cain's descendants, the Book of Moses corroborated existing cultural interpretations of the mark of Cain.[35]

The Book of Abraham, Joseph Smith's inspired translation of Egyptian funerary papyri, elaborated on the curse of Canaan, another narrative in Genesis that white Christians had used to justify the racial hierarchy that subordinated black people. In Genesis, Noah cursed Canaan, his grandson through Ham, to be "the lowest of slaves . . . to his brothers."[36] Europeans and Euro-Americans frequently used this passage to justify slavery, theorizing that Africans were the descendants of Ham.[37] The Book of Abraham extended that theory, explaining that Egyptians had descended from Ham through his daughter Egyptus. "And thus, from Ham, sprang that race which preserved the curse in the land," the text explained, specifying that Egyptians were "cursed . . . as pertaining to the Priesthood."[38] This text thus provided a scriptural foundation upon which to exclude black men from the priesthood. The system of racial hierarchy that these texts reinforced made possible the populist, democratic ethos to which Hatch pointed, but it made that ethos available only to white men.

Despite the explanation that descendants of Ham were "cursed . . . as pertaining to the priesthood," a few African American men were ordained to the priesthood during Joseph Smith's lifetime. However, church leaders reversed this potentially egalitarian policy after Smith's death in 1844. Over the next several decades, Latter-day Saints incorporated the racialized interpretations of scripture that were prevalent in other Christian denominations and worked out the application of these ideas in specifically Mormon contexts like priesthood ordination and temple ritual.[39] As Brigham Young put it in 1849, "The Lord cursed Cain's seed with blackness and prohibited them the priesthood, that Abel and his progeny might yet come forward and have their dominion, place, and blessings in their proper relationship with Cain and his race in the world to come."[40] None of the men to whom Jane James was related were ordained. The ubiquitous, democratic priesthood of Mormonism was thus startlingly distant from Jane James's everyday life. As sociologist O. Kendall White noted, the priesthood restriction rendered black Mormons "dependent upon the white priesthood for their religious needs."[41]

Looking *at* Jane James, it is impossible to miss the ways the structure of LDS authority excluded and subordinated James and her family. Looking *with* James, however, it becomes apparent that the official structure of authority in the LDS Church was less central to James's religious experience than we might expect. In fact, like many of the Mormons who joined the church in its earliest years, James seems to have prioritized the exercise of spiritual gifts like healing as a mark of "moral and religious authority."[42] James downplayed the importance of the priesthood in many of the archival traces she left. As I discussed above, faith healing was commonly accepted in early Mormonism, and its practice was unrestricted: church leaders and ordinary members, men and women, all participated. However, as the century wore on, women's roles in healing became more attenuated, receding before men's expanding priesthood authority. In 1901, an unsigned editorial in the *Deseret News* stated: "The ordinance appointed in the Church for the healing of the sick is to be performed by the Elders. They are to anoint with oil and lay their hands upon them. . . . A Priest, Teacher or Deacon may administer to the sick, and so may a member, male or female, but neither of them can seal the anointing and blessing, because the authority to do that is vested in the Priesthood after the order of Melchisedek [*sic*]."[43] This editorial articulated a policy that had been in place since the previous year, essentially subordinating healing by women to healing by priesthood holders.[44] By 1903, church leaders had decided that the practice of administering to the sick should be "confined to the elders," or male Melchizedek priesthood holders.[45]

In this context of institutional constraints on women's healing, James dictated a short autobiography in which she obliquely critiqued the church hierarchy's restriction of healing authority. James recounted two 1843 healings in which she and her family had participated as they made their way to Nauvoo. In the first episode, James and her traveling companions were the ones who received healing. James recalled her journey from Buffalo, New York, to Nauvoo six decades earlier: "We walked until our shoes were worn out, and our feet became sore and cracked open and bled until you could see the whole print of our feet with blood on the ground. We stopped and united in prayer to the Lord, we asked God the Eternal Father to heal our feet and our prayers were answered and our feet were healed forthwith." The group with whom James traveled included several of her family members as well as a few other African Americans who had also converted to Mormonism. There is no evidence that any of them held the priesthood. James presented this corporate healing simply, so that the dramatic result functioned as a testament to the great faith of the group. James solidified this meaning a few sentences later. Shortly after she recounted this episode, James remarked that despite suffering the cold and frost as they made their way to Nauvoo, "we went on our way rejoicing singing hymns and thanking God for his infinite goodness and mercy to us, in blessing us as he had, protecting us from all harm, answering our prayers and healing our feet."[46]

This testament to the party's faith and God's blessings set up another brief healing episode that followed almost immediately. About thirty miles from their destination, in La Harpe, Illinois, James recalled, "there was a very sick child, we administered to it, and the child was healed I found after the elders had before this given it up as they did not think it could live."[47] This dig at "the elders"—LDS priesthood holders—makes clear James's critique of the policy that limited women's healing practices: the elders, though they held the priesthood, lacked sufficient faith to heal the child, whereas James and her traveling companions, although they lacked the priesthood, had enough faith to perform a miraculous healing.

In her petitions, James made clear her desire for the temple ordinances, rituals that priesthood authority invested with spiritual power and efficacy. However, in everyday life, James recognized spiritual authority as it was expressed in believers' ability to heal and to otherwise channel divine power. At least in some cases, she seems to have viewed these alternative forms of authority as more spiritually efficacious than the official LDS priesthood. From the documents James left, it appears that the LDS priesthood, which scholars have understood as both widespread and democratic, was more distant from James's religious life than those adjectives suggest.

Re-Remembering Joseph Smith with Jane James

In addition to relocating religious experience and redistributing religious authority, looking at Mormon history with Jane James pushes us to reconsider Joseph Smith's legacy and recognize the alternative ways in which Latter-day Saints remembered Smith after his death. James's memories of Smith were clearly important to both her and her community. In her autobiography of approximately 2,500 words, nearly 1,100—close to half—concern James's experience in Nauvoo, where she lived with and worked for Joseph Smith and his family. She began that portion of the autobiography with an exclamation: "We have now arrived to our destined haven of rest, the beautiful Nauvoo!" James was probably eighty years old or more when she dictated that autobiography, yet she spent nearly half of her words on a period of about eight months.[48]

By the time James dictated her autobiography in the early twentieth century, the generation of Latter-day Saints who had known Smith was almost entirely gone. Younger Saints, and even older Saints who converted after Smith's death, faced with the challenges of Mormonism's transition from a radical, fringe faith to a mainstream American religion, actively built this identity by collectively constructing usable memories of their founder.[49] But historical memory is complicated, rarely consistent, and malleable in ways that may threaten the established order.[50] Jane James's version of Joseph Smith matched that of her white coreligionists in some ways, but it simultaneously challenged the authorized memory of Smith that church leaders both created and appealed to.

Like many women who remembered Joseph Smith, James lingered over his physical appearance: "Oh, he was the finest man I ever saw on earth," she reminisced in a 1905 interview printed to commemorate the centennial of Smith's birth.[51] James was not alone in idealizing Smith's body. Bathsheba W. Smith, interviewed for the same issue of the *Young Woman's Journal*, recalled that "the Prophet was a handsome man,—splendid looking, a large man, tall and fair and his hair was light. He had a very nice complexion, his eyes were blue, and his hair a golden brown and very pretty."[52] Other women made similar comments.[53] Taken together, these physical descriptions of Joseph Smith attested to Smith's manhood and established his whiteness—both important tasks for a church struggling to gain acceptance in the American nation.[54]

Latter-day Saints also sought to model their behavior on that of their founder, and to that end they collected and passed down stories about Smith's words and deeds.[55] In this context, James's memories took on a subversive quality. According to James, Joseph Smith treated her as if she was a member of the family. "He'd always smile, always just like he did to his children. He used to be just like I was his child," she recalled in the 1905 interview. That familial love was, perhaps, all the more striking because of the racial difference between James and Smith. In James's telling, Smith did not see racial difference as an obstacle to kinship. She insisted, repeatedly, that Joseph Smith, through his first wife, Emma, offered to adopt Jane as a child.[56] James's assertion that the offer of adoption came from Joseph Smith via Emma Smith was virtually unassailable: both Joseph and Emma had died. Few remained who could contradict James's memories with stories of their own. Scores of Latter-day Saints during this time period sought and received adoption to Joseph Smith; perhaps James believed that her memory of Smith's intent to include her in his eternal family, which signaled the founding prophet's racial inclusiveness, would persuade contemporary church leaders to afford her full inclusion.[57]

This story and the others that James told about Joseph Smith, all of which portrayed Smith as a benevolent, paternalistic figure willing to create interracial family structures, was at odds with the authorized memory of Smith, in which he was the source of the priesthood and temple restrictions that church leaders worked out over the course of the nineteenth century. Church officials used questions surrounding Elijah Abel, an African American man who had been ordained during Joseph Smith's lifetime, as an opportunity to construct the authorized memory of Joseph Smith with regard to African Americans and priesthood in the late 1870s. Zebedee Coltrin asserted in 1879 that when he was a president of the Seventies, "the Prophet [Joseph Smith] directed that Abel be dropped because of his 'lineage.'" Abraham Smoot recalled hearing much the same thing. Joseph F. Smith, the nephew of the founding prophet, disputed these stories, but his was the minority voice. The process of memory construction continued through the turn of the century, concluding with a reversal by Joseph F. Smith, who stated that Abel's "ordination was declared null and void by the Prophet [Joseph Smith] himself."[58] James's alternative perspective—a memory of a racially progressive prophet, willing to create family relationships that breached the color barrier—remained sidelined.

James's focus on Joseph Smith is instructive, not only because it illustrates how important Smith was to ordinary believers, but also because it shows that there was more than one Joseph Smith at work in LDS memory by the turn of the twentieth century. Sociologist Daniele Hervieu-Léger has pointed to the relationship between authorized and alternative memory as a key dynamic in modern religion and a subtle gauge of the distribution of power. "Authorized memory," she wrote, "develops and is passed on in different ways. It legitimates itself differently in accordance with the type of religious sociality proper to the group in question, and in accordance with the type of domination that prevails. . . . But in all instances it is the recognized ability to expound the true memory of the group that constitutes the core of religious power."[59] James contested church leaders' version of Joseph Smith as the "true memory" of the founder, and thus threatened their claim to religious power. Her persistence in this effort was at least partly rewarded: in 1898, the Quorum of the Twelve Apostles authorized a ceremony in the Salt Lake Temple to "attach" James to Smith as a "servitor." Although James was living in Salt Lake at the time, Zina D. H. Young acted as a proxy for her.[60] This ritual innovation did not end James's quest, though: the minutes of a 1902 meeting of the Council of the Twelve Apostles record that "Aunt Jane was not satisfied with this [ritual], and as a mark of her dissatisfaction she applied again after this for sealing blessings, but of course in vain."[61]

While James's version of Joseph Smith did not prevail during her lifetime, more recently the LDS Church has placed greater value on racial inclusiveness and the institution's official depiction of Joseph Smith has changed accordingly. One example is the church's most recent film about Smith, which shows him interacting in sensitive, caring ways with African American characters—including Jane James.[62] James's memories of Smith have become part of the evidentiary base of a new authorized memory of the church's founder that is more in keeping with the twenty-first-century church's imagined future.[63]

Conclusion: Writing the History of Mormonism with Jane James

By examining the development of Mormonism from Jane James's perspective we see that Mormonism is not—and never was—the lily-white church that it appears to be in the American imagination. But neither was it the always-already racially diverse, racially harmonious church that the contemporary LDS Church sometimes imagines itself to be.[64] Instead, looking with James, we see a mostly white church where racial identity has an uncertain, contested meaning. Church leaders and members debated that meaning partly in terms of their memories of the founder, Joseph Smith, pitting authorized and alternative memories against one another as they shaped a usable past for the institution. Those debates alert us to the ongoing work of memory construction in the LDS Church. Further, they suggest that a resurgence in talk about Jane James at the turn of the twenty-first century has a lot to do with the church's need for a usable past in a world that now values racial diversity in a way that was not true at the turn of the last century.[65]

Jane James's experience also illuminates the obvious and subtle ways in which racial identities shape religious experience. Distanced from the priesthood and excluded from temple rituals, Jane James constructed a religious life for herself that de-emphasized these aspects of Mormonism. For James, religious experience took place, by necessity, outside the temple. Narrating these experiences, James claimed a connection with the divine independent of the LDS priesthood and untethered to temple rituals. From James's perspective, the priesthood appears significantly less democratic and inclusive, and much more hierarchical and exclusive. However, for James, the priesthood did not exhaust the possibilities for channeling divine power. While she accepted the leadership of the church hierarchy, James also recognized and privileged other paths for the acquisition and exercise of moral and spiritual authority.

Looking with Jane James provides a fresh angle on Mormonism's nearly two centuries of history and suggests new trajectories for future scholarship. Calls to incorporate the experiences of "ordinary people," of nonwhite people, and of women, are common in the twenty-first century,[66] but these incorporations must do more than simply recover untold stories. As I have shown using Jane James's story, looking *with* those who had different experiences of the LDS Church can and should change our understanding of Mormon history in fundamental ways.

Notes

1. For examples of the former, see Claudia L. Bushman, *Building the Kingdom: A History of Mormons in America* (New York: Oxford University Press, 2001); Richard L. Bushman, *Mormonism: A Very Short Introduction* (New York: Oxford University Press, 2008); and Douglas J. Davies, *An Introduction to Mormonism* (New York: Cambridge University Press, 2003). For an example of the latter, see Matthew Bowman, *The Mormon People: The Making of an American Faith* (New York: Random House, 2012), which focuses initially on Parley P. Pratt.

2. Newell G. Bringhurst, *Saints, Slaves, and Blacks: The Changing Place of Black People within Mormonism* (Westport, CT: Greenwood Press, 1981); Newell G. Bringhurst and Darron T. Smith, eds., *Black and Mormon* (Urbana: University of Illinois Press, 2004); Lester E. Bush, "Mormonism's Negro Doctrine: An Historical Overview," *Dialogue: A Journal of Mormon Thought* 8, no. 1 (1973): 11–68.
3. See, for example, Henry J. Wolfinger, "A Test of Faith: Jane Elizabeth James and the Origins of the Utah Black Community," in *Social Accommodation in Utah*, ed. Clark S. Knowlton, American West Center Occasional Papers (Salt Lake City: University of Utah, 1975), 126–72; Newell G. Bringhurst, "Elijah Abel and the Changing Status of Blacks within Mormonism," *Dialogue: A Journal of Mormon Thought* 12, no. 2 (Summer 1979): 23–36; Connell O'Donovan, "The Mormon Priesthood Ban and Elder Q. Walker Lewis: 'An Example for His More Whiter Brethren to Follow,'" *John Whitmer Historical Association Journal* 26 (2006): 47–99; William Kesler Jackson, *Elijah Abel: The Life and Times of a Black Priesthood Holder* (Springville, UT: CFI, an imprint of Cedar Fort, Inc., 2013); Russell Stevenson, "'A Negro Preacher': The Worlds of Elijah Ables," *Journal of Mormon History* (Spring 2013): 165–254; Russell W. Stevenson, *For the Cause of Righteousness: A Global History of Blacks and Mormonism, 1830–2013, Part I: The History* (Salt Lake City, UT: Greg Kofford Books, 2014).
4. Caroline Walker Bynum, "Women's Stories, Women's Symbols: A Critique of Victor Turner's Theory of Liminality," in *Fragmentation and Redemption: Essays on Gender and the Human Body in Medieval Religion* (New York: Zone Books, 1992), 51.
5. For a more thorough overview of James's life, see Quincy D. Newell, "The Autobiography and Interview of Jane Elizabeth Manning James," *Journal of Africana Religions* 1, no. 2 (2013): 251–91.
6. Diary of L. John Nuttall (Brigham Young's secretary), February 7, 1877, quoted in David J. Buerger, "The Development of the Mormon Temple Endowment Ceremony," *Dialogue: A Journal of Mormon Thought* 20 (Winter 1987): 47.
7. Buerger, "The Development of the Mormon Temple Endowment Ceremony"; Kathleen Flake, "'Not to Be Riten': The Mormon Temple Rite as Oral Canon," *Journal of Ritual Studies* 9, no. 2 (Summer 1995): 5, 9; Devery S. Anderson, ed., *The Development of LDS Temple Worship, 1846–2000: A Documentary History* (Salt Lake City: Signature Books, 2011).
8. Anderson, *Development of LDS Temple Worship*, xxiii.
9. See the letters from Jane James to various church leaders, spanning the years 1884–1903, transcribed in Wolfinger, "A Test of Faith," 148–51.
10. James also performed baptisms for the dead in the Salt Lake City Endowment House, the space Mormons set aside for temple rituals before the Salt Lake Temple was completed. See "Record of Baptisms for the Dead for the Seed of Cain," microfilm (Salt Lake City, Utah, September 3, 1875), Film 255,498, LDS Family History Library.
11. Lydia D. Alder, "Ladies' Semi-Momthly [*sic*] Meeting," *Woman's Exponent*, December 15, 1896.
12. Jane Manning James, "Jane Manning James Autobiography" (Salt Lake City, Utah, n.d.), folio 3r, MS 4425, LDS Church History Library; see Newell, "The Autobiography and Interview of Jane Elizabeth Manning James," 265.

13. For further analysis of this episode in James's autobiography, see Quincy D. Newell, "'Is There No Blessing for Me?' Jane James's Construction of Space in Latter-day Saint History and Practice," in *New Perspectives in Mormon Studies: Creating and Crossing Boundaries*, ed. Quincy D. Newell and Eric F. Mason (Norman: University of Oklahoma Press, 2013), 54–56.
14. James, "Jane Manning James Autobiography," folio 1r; see Newell, "The Autobiography and Interview of Jane Elizabeth Manning James," 263.
15. Lee Copeland, "Speaking in Tongues in the Restoration Churches," *Dialogue: A Journal of Mormon Thought* 24, no. 1 (Spring 1991): 22.
16. Ibid., 23, quoting Andrew F. Ehat and Lyndon W. Cook, eds., *The Words of Joseph Smith: The Contemporary Accounts of the Nauvoo Discourses of the Prophet Joseph Smith* (Provo, UT: Brigham Young University Religious Study Center, 1980), 119.
17. Unsigned, "R.S. and Y.L. Meeting," *Woman's Exponent*, November 1, 1885.
18. James appears speaking in tongues in the following Retrenchment Society reports: Unsigned, "Semi-Monthly Meeting," *Woman's Exponent*, December 1, 1889; Lydia D. Alder, "Ladies' Semi-Monthly Meeting," *Woman's Exponent*, December 1, 1893; Lydia D. Alder, "Ladies' Semi-Monthly Meeting," *Woman's Exponent*, June 1, 1894; Lydia D. Alder, "Ladies' Semi-Monthly Meeting," *Woman's Exponent*, January 1, 1895; Lydia D. Alder, "Ladies' Semi-Monthly Meeting," *Woman's Exponent*, June 1, 1897; J. S. Woolley, "Ladies' Semi-Monthly Meeting," *Woman's Exponent*, July 1, 1899; J. S. Woolley, "Ladies' Semi-Monthly Meeting," *Woman's Exponent*, October 15, 1899.
19. Janet Ellingson, "Becoming a People: The Beliefs and Practices of the Early Mormons, 1830–1845" (PhD diss., University of Utah, 1997), chapter 2, especially 48–53.
20. James, "Jane Manning James Autobiography," folio 1r; see Newell, "The Autobiography and Interview of Jane Elizabeth Manning James," 263.
21. Jan Shipps, *Sojourner in the Promised Land: Forty Years among the Mormons* (Urbana: University of Illinois Press, 2000), 295–96.
22. Richard E. Bennett, "'Line upon Line, Precept upon Precept': Reflections on the 1877 Commencement of the Performance of Endowments and Sealings for the Dead," *BYU Studies* 44, no. 3 (2005): 52.
23. Shipps, *Sojourner in the Promised Land*, 299.
24. Flake, "'Not to Be Riten': The Mormon Temple Rite as Oral Canon," 13.
25. See Max Perry Mueller, "Playing Jane: Re-Presenting Black Mormon Memory through Reenacting the Black Mormon Past," *Journal of Africana Religions* 1, no. 4 (2013): 525–36, especially 525, 529–32; Newell, "'Is There No Blessing for Me?,'" especially 57–58.
26. See Newell, "'Is There No Blessing for Me?,'" 56.
27. See Parley P. Pratt, *The Autobiography of Parley P. Pratt, One of the Twelve Apostles of the Church of Jesus Christ of Latter-day Saints: Embracing His Life, Ministry and Travels: With Extracts in Prose and Verse from His Miscellaneous Writings* (New York: Russell Bros., 1874), 43; Terryl L. Givens and Matthew J. Grow, *Parley P. Pratt: The Apostle Paul of Mormonism* (New York: Oxford University Press, 2011), 33.
28. Nathan O. Hatch, *The Democratization of American Christianity* (New Haven, CT: Yale University Press, 1989).
29. Ibid., 120, 121.

30. Bushman, *Mormonism*, 51.
31. Paul E. Johnson, "Democracy, Patriarchy, and American Revivals, 1780–1830," *Journal of Social History* 24, no. 4 (July 1991): 849.
32. Ibid.
33. For a somewhat contrasting interpretation, see Armand L. Mauss, *All Abraham's Children: Changing Mormon Conceptions of Race and Lineage* (Urbana: University of Illinois Press, 2003), 117–18.
34. Moses 7:22.
35. Sylvester A. Johnson, *The Myth of Ham in Nineteenth-Century American Christianity: Race, Heathens, and the People of God* (New York: Palgrave Macmillan, 2004), 43. Earlier in the Book of Moses (5:16–33), the story of Cain was elaborated as well: Cain made an explicit pact with Satan, and his murder of Abel was a part of that agreement.
36. Genesis 9:25.
37. Johnson, *The Myth of Ham*, 31.
38. Abraham 1:24, 26.
39. Richard L. Bushman, *Joseph Smith: Rough Stone Rolling* (New York: Alfred A. Knopf, 2005), 288.
40. O. Kendall White Jr., "Boundary Maintenance, Blacks, and the Mormon Priesthood," *The Journal of Religious Thought* 37 (Fall–Winter 1980–1981): 41; see also Bush, "Mormonism's Negro Doctrine," 25.
41. White Jr., "Boundary Maintenance," 44.
42. Ellingson, "Becoming a People," 60.
43. Editor, "Who May Rebuke Disease?" *Deseret Evening News*, April 8, 1901, 4, quoted in Jonathan A. Stapley and Kristine Wright, "Female Ritual Healing in Mormonism," *Journal of Mormon History* 37, no. 1 (Winter 2011): 45.
44. Ibid., 46.
45. Meeting Minutes of the First Presidency and Twelve, Journal History, February 18, 1903, 4, quoted in ibid., 51.
46. James, "Jane Manning James Autobiography," folio 1v; see Newell, "The Autobiography and Interview of Jane Elizabeth Manning James," 264.
47. James, "Jane Manning James Autobiography," folio 2r; see Newell, "The Autobiography and Interview of Jane Elizabeth Manning James," 264.
48. James, "Jane Manning James Autobiography," folios 2r–3v; see Newell, "The Autobiography and Interview of Jane Elizabeth Manning James," 264–66.
49. Kathleen Flake, "Re-Placing Memory: Latter-day Saint Use of Historical Monuments and Narrative in the Early Twentieth Century," *Religion and American Culture: A Journal of Interpretation* 13, no. 1 (Winter 2003): 69–109.
50. The literature on collective memory is vast. The foundational work is Maurice Halbwachs, *On Collective Memory* (Chicago: University of Chicago Press, 1992).
51. Susa Young Gates, ed., "Joseph Smith, the Prophet," *Young Woman's Journal* 16, no. 12 (December 1905): 551.
52. Ibid., 548.
53. See the collection of interviews published in ibid., 548–58.

54. Sarah Barringer Gordon, *The Mormon Question: Polygamy and Constitutional Conflict in Nineteenth-Century America* (Chapel Hill: University of North Carolina Press, 2002); Kathleen Flake, *The Politics of American Religious Identity: The Seating of Senator Reed Smoot, Mormon Apostle* (Chapel Hill: University of North Carolina Press, 2004); W. Paul Reeve, *Religion of a Different Color: Race and the Mormon Struggle for Whiteness* (New York: Oxford University Press, 2015). See also Paul Reeve's essay in this volume.
55. Grant Underwood, "The Prophetic Legacy in Islam and Mormonism: Some Comparative Observations," in *New Perspectives in Mormon Studies: Creating and Crossing Boundaries*, 109–13.
56. See Jane E. James to President John Taylor, Salt Lake City, December 27, 1884; Jane E. James to Apostle Joseph F. Smith, Salt Lake City, February 7, 1890; Zina D. H. Young to Apostle Joseph F. Smith, Salt Lake City, January 15, 1894, all reprinted in Wolfinger, "A Test of Faith," 148, 149, 150. On the temple ritual of adoption, see Gordon Irving, "The Law of Adoption: One Phase of the Development of the Mormon Concept of Salvation, 1830–1900," *Brigham Young University Studies* 14 (Spring 1974): 291–314.
57. Irving, "The Law of Adoption," 310.
58. Bush, "Mormonism's Negro Doctrine," 31–34. Joseph F. Smith's conclusion is at odds with his own earlier statements and the fact that Abel acted as a priesthood holder to the end of his life, including participating in priesthood quorums in Utah and serving multiple missions for the church.
59. Danièle Hervieu-Léger, *Religion as a Chain of Memory* (New Brunswick, NJ: Rutgers University Press, 2000), 126.
60. Scholars debate whether this ceremony was a "sealing" ceremony or something else, given that the operative verb in the ritual was "attach" rather than "seal." The sources on the ceremony, its participants, and the aftermath are surprisingly varied. The official record of the ritual is Adoption Record, Book A, p. 26, LDS Church History Library. This source is restricted and therefore not available to most researchers. I have examined photographs of this document. At least three other sources provide transcriptions of this record: Confidential Research Files, 1950–1974, David J. Buerger Papers, Special Collections and Archives, Marriott Library, University of Utah; Anderson, *The Development of LDS Temple Worship*, 97–98; and "Connell," "Chronology Pertaining to Blacks and the LDS Church," "Jane M. James sealed as eternal servant to Joseph Smith," http://www.xtimeline.com/evt/view.aspx?id=66094. Unfortunately, each of these transcriptions differs from the original and from each other. While most variations are cosmetic—encompassing details like punctuation and spelling—one is crucial: none of the available transcriptions names Zina D. H. Young as a proxy for Jane James. Only one, "Chronology Pertaining to Blacks and the LDS Church," names a proxy for James, but this version names Bathsheba W. Smith. Another, Anderson's *The Development of LDS Temple Worship*, claims that "in 1895, Church leaders revoked Manning's [*sic*] sealing"; that the sealing "was restored in 1902"; and that the 1902 ceremony was performed "with Bathsheba Smith acting as proxy" for Jane James (97n51). Anderson cites no source to support these claims.
61. Minutes of a meeting of the Council of the Twelve Apostles, January 2, 1902, in "Excerpts from the Weekly Council Meetings of the Quorum of the Twelve Apostles, Dealing

with the Rights of Negroes in the Church, 1849–1940," George Albert Smith Papers, University of Utah, transcribed in Wolfinger, "A Test of Faith," 151.

62. See *Joseph Smith: The Prophet of the Restoration* (Intellectual Reserve, 2011), http://www.mormonchannel.org/joseph. This version of the film is significantly changed from the original released in 2005, but still contains scenes with Jane James and her traveling companions. On the revisions, see "Mormon Newsroom: Film about Joseph Smith Now Available Online," http://www.mormonnewsroom.org/article/film-about-joseph-smith-now-available-online.
63. I develop this argument at length in "Remembering Joseph by Remembering Jane: Constructing a History of Racial Diversity for the Twenty-First Century LDS Church," paper delivered at "Race and Religion in American History," March 8, 2014, Princeton University, Princeton, New Jersey. See also the LDS Church's recently posted essay "Race and the Priesthood," which selectively describes Joseph Smith's thought on racial issues, thus depicting him as progressive (if not radical). The same essay also includes mention of Jane James as an example of an early black Mormon. The Church of Jesus Christ of Latter-day Saints, "Race and the Priesthood," https://www.lds.org/topics/race-and-the-priesthood?lang=eng.
64. The LDS Church's recent "I'm a Mormon" marketing campaign appears to include a disproportionate number of Americans of color. See http://www.mormon.org/people.
65. For examples of this explosion in discourse, see "Erin," "LDS Women's History: Jane Manning James," *LDS Women's History*, March 3, 2008, http://ldswomenshistory.blogspot.com/2008/03/jane-manning-james.html; Pioneer Chapter of the National Society of the Sons of Utah Pioneers, "Days of '47 Sunrise Service Program" (Salt Lake City, Utah, July 25, 2005), in which Jane Manning James is named an "Exemplar of Virtue and Faith"; Margaret Blair Young and Darius Aidan Gray, *One More River to Cross*, vol. 1 in *Standing on the Promises* (Salt Lake City: Bookcraft, 2000); Margaret Blair Young and Darius Aidan Gray, *Bound for Canaan*, vol. 2 in *Standing on the Promises* (Salt Lake City, Utah: Bookcraft, 2002); Margaret Blair Young and Darius Aidan Gray, *The Last Mile of the Way*, vol. 3 in *Standing on the Promises* (Salt Lake City: Bookcraft/Deseret Book Co., 2003); Scott Young Freebairn and Hey You Pictures, *Jane Manning James: Your Sister in the Gospel* (Layton, UT: Hey You Pictures, 2005); and the repeated performances of Margaret Blair Young's stage play "I Am Jane" and Jerri Harwell's one-woman performance of Jane James's autobiography. The latter is analyzed in Mueller, "Playing Jane."
66. See, for examples, the essays included in "What We Will Do Now That New Mormon History Is Old: A Roundtable," *Journal of Mormon History* 35, no. 3 (Summer 2009): 190–233, especially Rachel Cope, "The Unexplored Drama within the Drama," 195–200; Megan Sanborn Jones, "Performing Mormon History," 204–8; Lisa Olsen Tait, "Mormon Cultural Studies," 218–23; W. Paul Reeve, "Post New Mormon History: A Manifesto," 223–25; Amy Harris, "Converting Mormon History," 226–29; Patrick A. Polk, "History That Reveals Itself," 230–33.

Chapter 7 | All "Mormon Elder-Berry's" Children

Race, Whiteness, and the Attack on Mormon "Anglo-Saxon Triumphalism"

W. Paul Reeve

On April 28, 1904, less than two months after then-president of the Church of Jesus Christ of Latter-day Saints, Joseph F. Smith, spent a withering six days as a witness before a United States Senate committee, *Life* magazine published a political cartoon which offered a profound pictorial vision of what its cartoonist, C. J. Rudd, imagined Mormonism to look like at the dawn of the twentieth century. Rudd's cartoon was simply labeled "Mormon Elder-Berry—out with his six-year-olds, who take after their mothers" (figure 7.1). There was no text or story to accompany the cartoon, only Rudd's short caption and the picture itself. This was fairly typical of general-interest magazines such as *Life*; the picture was the text.[1]

From a twenty-first-century perspective, the image seems incongruous with what one might expect a Mormon family to look like in 1904. Apart from the blatant attack on polygamy explicit in the image, if the cartoon appeared in 2015 the LDS Church's Public Affairs Department might well embrace Elder-Berry's racially and ethnically diverse family. It might even recruit several of Elder-Berry's children to be featured in its "I'm a Mormon" media campaign, an effort to promote a heterogeneous and globally diverse identity for Mormonism in the twenty-first century.[2]

In 1904, however, the cartoon was certainly not meant as a compliment, nor was it intended as a celebration of Mormon diversity. In fact, Elder-Berry's imagined family stood as a lingering critique, a holdover from the nineteenth century when politicians, Protestant ministers, journalists, news editors, overland migrants, dime novelists, graphic artists, and others all contributed in various ways to the construction of mythic mixed-race Mormon families similar to that of Mormon Elder-Berry's. The timing of *Life*'s publication was crucial. It came at the very moment in which Mormon leaders were attempting to orchestrate a new image for the faith, to transition away from a polygamous and racially suspect past toward a monogamist and racially pure future. Joseph F. Smith, in fact, returned to Salt Lake City following his testimony before the United States Senate and issued what historians refer to as the "Second Manifesto." On April 6,

FIGURE 7.1. C. J. Rudd, "Mormon Elder-Berry—out with his six-year-olds, who take after their mothers." Reprinted from *Life*, April 28, 1904, 404.

1904, less than a month before *Life* published its cartoon, Smith put teeth into Wilford Woodruff's Manifesto issued almost fourteen years earlier. Woodruff as church president had promised to use his influence to ensure Mormon compliance with the laws of the land and to end Mormon polygamy. Now Smith said that he would keep that earlier promise and actually begin to enforce it. Any Mormon who engaged in future plural marriages would be subject to excommunication, the church's most severe punishment.[3]

It was a profound moment of transition for Mormonism and it played out on a national stage with intense media scrutiny. The Senate hearings in Washington, D.C., at which Smith testified, generated curiosity and at times appealed to the nation's prurient interests. The hearings dragged on for three years as the U.S. Senate decided if it would allow Reed Smoot, a sitting LDS apostle, a monogamist, and a Republican, to retain his seat. The hearings constituted an effort by the nation to come to terms with Mormonism, to situate this uniquely American-born faith within a broader American religious landscape, and to decide if it belonged.[4] The Utah state legislature elected Smoot in 1903—the direct popular election of senators under the Seventeenth Amendment would not come about for another decade—but reports of continuing plural marriage among the Mormons, church interference in politics, and lingering questions over Mormon loyalty to the nation, prompted the Senate investigation. Historians have long viewed the Reed Smoot hearings as the culmination of an Americanization process that began with the Woodruff Manifesto in 1890 and continued through Utah statehood in 1896. That process was solidified with the Senate's vote in 1907 to allow Smoot to retain his seat.[5]

It is a compelling argument and an important way in which to think about Mormonism's transition from the nineteenth to the twentieth century, from polygamy to monogamy, from outsider to insider, from communalism to capitalism, from isolation to integration, and perhaps even the beginning of a transformation from insular to global. Those transformations were slow and left lingering vestiges of the old mixed with the new. Nonetheless, Mormonism was in fact "in transition" and the Smoot hearings served as an important harbinger of change.[6] This chapter posits that one of those transitions was racial, an upward move for Mormons on the American racial ladder, from not securely white in the nineteenth century, to too-white by 2012.

When considering questions of race in Mormonism, it is difficult to overestimate the importance of Armand Mauss's seminal work on the subject, *All Abraham's Children*. It is a book that established a much-needed framework for understanding Mormon racialism and racism. It is a foundational text, a place to begin one's scholarly approach to Mormon racial visions of the world. Mauss, along with Lester Bush and Newell Bringhurst, mark the founding generation of scholars on Mormonism and race, intellectual giants to whom the future generation of students will be perpetually in debt.[7]

It is fitting, then, that Mauss's work in *All Abraham's Children* will serve as both a touchstone and a point of departure in this essay, a way to suggest new directions as scholars transition beyond the Mitt Romney "Mormon moment" and contemplate the future of scholarship on Mormonism and race. In *All Abraham's Children*, the chapter on "Mormons and Israelite Lineage" chronicles the ways in which nineteenth-century Mormons tapped into then-current notions of "British Israelism" and "Anglo-Saxon Triumphalism." As Mauss puts it, Mormons came to "identify the favored Ephraimite (or Israelite) 'blood' primarily with Anglo-Saxon ancestry."[8] The fact that the bulk of Mormon missionary success came from England and the "Nordic" or Scandinavian nations of Europe tended to reinforce the notion of "believing blood" inherent in a convert's (northern European) ancestry. In 1851 there were more Mormons in the United Kingdom and Ireland than there were in Utah Territory. An estimated thirty-two thousand British and Irish Latter-day Saints immigrated to the Great Basin between 1847 and 1869. Thus the Mormon missionary harvest was a matter of reclaiming lost descendants of ancient Israel who hailed from the "white" nations of the United States, Canada, the United Kingdom, and Scandinavia. One of Joseph Smith's earliest revelations concerning missionary work—that "the field is white already to harvest"—thus took on new meaning, even if the prophecy was not read through a racial lens at the time.[9] The white conversions that followed only added certainty to the ways in which Mormons constructed a triumphal Anglo-Saxon identity for themselves.[10]

Yet, to date, scholarly approaches to Mormonism and race have largely focused upon the ways in which Mormons themselves constructed race over time, not the ways in which outsiders attempted to situate Mormons within a shifting national racial context. British Israelism and Anglo-Saxon triumphalism help to account for the ways in which Mormons constructed a racial identity for themselves vis-à-vis Native Americans ("Lamanites"), Jews, and blacks. Yet, how does the Mormon racial story change when scholars interrogate the constructed racial identities that outsiders imagined for Mormons and use whiteness as a theoretical lens? Using Mormon whiteness as a contested variable rather than an assumed fact dramatically alters the Mormon racial story and opens new vistas for scholarly inquiry.

Mormonism's founding decades coincided with a period in American history wherein whiteness itself came under question. Between the 1840s and 1920s, America underwent a dramatic industrial transformation which in turn produced what whiteness scholar Matthew Frye Jacobson calls a "voracious appetite for cheap labor." Immigrants swarmed to America to meet that demand. Corresponding nativist backlashes also permeated the same period, especially as older Americans perceived the new influx of immigrants as threats to a smooth-functioning republic. As a result "a fracturing of monolithic whiteness" occurred, shored up by "scientific doctrines of race" which blended with "political concerns over the newcomers' fitness for self-government." These forces all combined to produce an emerging hierarchy of whiteness, with Anglo-Saxons on top and other undesirable less-white "races" situated at various lower rungs on the racial ladder.[11]

As Jacobson suggests, due to an influx of "massive waves of Irish immigrants in the 1840s, whiteness itself" became problematic and began to "lose its monolithic character." The Irish "Famine Migration announced a new era in the meaning of whiteness in the United States, an era greeted by many as a full-blown political crisis." The "monolithic quality of whiteness" gave way to "fragmentation *within* the 'white race.'" Irish immigrants were singled out for their "physical traits, their moral character and their peculiar customs." Their "wild look and manner, mud cabins and funeral howlings" all conjured "the memory of a barbarous age" in the mind of one observer. Another decried the Irish as so many "thousands of barbarians in our midst, every whit as ferocious in their instincts as the Minnesota savages."[12]

Outsiders described Mormons in similar terms, a discourse that borrowed from the racialization of the Irish and other groups but also manifested its own distinctive characteristics. Rather than an undesirable immigrant group struggling to claim whiteness for itself in the face of hostile nativist backlashes, Mormons were already American insiders, first-generation converts from American stock or European converts predominantly from Ireland, the United Kingdom, and the Scandinavian countries of northern and western Europe. Yet outsiders consistently called the whiteness of Mormons into question and marked them as racially incapable of self-rule. Mormonism was born into an era of fracturing monolithic whiteness in America and did not escape its consequences. In this light, Mormon efforts at asserting British Israelism and Anglo-Saxon triumphalism might profitably be reconsidered as an effort among Mormons to claim whiteness for themselves, to position themselves at the top of America's racial ladder at the same time that outsiders consistently attempted to decenter their whiteness and push them several rungs down that very same ladder. Indeed, Mormon Elder-Berry's imagined 1904 family both illustrates and invites an exploration into that attack on Mormon Anglo-Saxon triumphalism and the corresponding struggle for whiteness.

Before doing so, it is important to understand a few basic ideas regarding race and whiteness in the nineteenth century.[13] As the historian David R. Roediger contends, "In the United States of a century ago people did not talk about race in the way we do."[14] And, as Bruce Dain reminds us, "Race itself was a monster if ever Americans conceived one, but a monster hidden in their minds, not, as many of them came to think, in the reality of nature behind the appearances. That reality," Dain argues, "was obscure, shifting, and complex." Much of the discourse about race in the early American republic was centered upon blacks and whites in general and more specifically upon "whether slaves and ex-slaves were capable of citizenship," a question that politicians and nineteenth-century intellectuals asked of Mormons as well.[15] Yet, the bulk of whiteness scholarship has focused primarily upon the immigrant experience and upon labor, class, race, and an economic transition from not securely white to white. Whiteness studies are only beginning to explore religion as a complicating factor and have not yet fully considered the ways in which Americans racialized Mormons, the nation's quintessential homegrown religion. In neglecting Mormons, scholars of race and whiteness miss the important lessons that Mormonism teaches about race and its power in American culture.[16]

Notions of race in the nineteenth century were far from clear-cut—or even black-and-white. How does one classify a black albino, or a light mulatto, the offspring of perhaps several generations of interracial liaisons, who by appearance could easily pass for white? In order to shore up racial notions of superiority and to support racial segregation, some Americans invented racial stereotypes that went far beyond what the eye could observe to suggest that race was woven into the biological fiber of the human body regardless of the color of the skin that covered that body. As the historian Mark Smith explains, "The apologists for slavery attempted to expand the definition of blackness beyond the eye. Blackness was not just seen—it could be smelled, heard, and felt." Race, in other words, became what Smith calls "a visually unstable category" in the nineteenth century and as such "ended up encouraging an emotional, visceral, and febrile understanding of racial identity." As with those who racialized Mormons, it was an understanding that was both "immune to logic" and "impervious to thought," but that nonetheless held profound implications for the group being racialized.[17] For the Mormons, outsiders became obsessed with *seeing* a physical difference despite Mormon whiteness in an effort to shore up and empiricize the boundaries that they constructed. The preservation of American morals and ultimately of American democracy were at stake. The creation of a distinct Mormon otherness can only be understood within this broader, slippery, shifting, and illogical racial context. In fact, the very absurdity of the arguments about racialized Mormon bodies has perhaps prevented historians from recovering the rightful prominence of those arguments in the creation of a distinct physical otherness and its impact upon keeping Utah and the Mormons well outside of prevailing notions of citizenship in the nineteenth century.[18] The Mormons, like Irish and other immigrants, were constructed as "in-between peoples," somewhere between "hard racism and full inclusion," "neither securely white nor nonwhite."[19]

Mormon Elder-Berry's family thus represents a culmination and amalgamation—or miscegenation if you will—of ways in which outsiders constructed Mormons as racially suspect. Even the northern and western European children in Elder-Berry's family, the children who one might logically believe were white and acceptable—or in Book of Mormon terms, "white and delightsome"[20]—did not escape scrutiny. The Scottish boy, the wild Irish girl, the two British street urchins who were seemingly straight out of Oliver Twist, the Dutch girl, and the spinster in the making, were all white, children who should have easily assimilated and drawn no special attention. As we shall see, such was not the case.

In 1856 a reporter for the *New York Times* visited Castle Garden to survey for his readers a new shipload of Mormon immigrants from Liverpool. The reporter counted 454 Mormons who had recently arrived on "the packet-ship *Caravan*." As he described it, "They came from England, Wales, Scotland, Ireland and Denmark," but then noted that to the credit of Denmark there were "only two Danish families amongst them" and to the "credit of Ireland, there [was] only one Irishman." Even though the Mormon immigrants originated in desirable parts of Europe, they were not deemed desirable. As the *Times* put it, "Our reporter saw these people, conversed with them, and estimated them, intellectually and otherwise. They all belong to the lower, almost to the lowest classes of society." Even within each society from which they came, the Mormons somehow located the lowest strata. A typical "Welsh peasant is notably clean," the *Times* declared, whereas the Mormon "Welsh peasants were dirty." Typical Welsh girls were distinguished by their "very ruddy" complexions, "very wholesome" appearance, and "very staid and chaste . . . manners." In contrast, the Welsh girls who converted to

Mormonism "were neither ruddy, wholesome nor staid." "Some of them," the *Times* predicted, "will perhaps be added to Brigham Young's harem" within a few months.

The English and Scottish Mormons were no different. "Their countenances were imbruted with ignorance and dirt—not the material dirt of a sea voyage, but the moral dirt of a life of imbecility and indolence. The Apostles of Joe Smith and Brigham Young found them an easy prey." In total, the *Times* declared that "among the whole four hundred and fifty, there was scarcely one face that showed that its possessor was greatly elevated above the animal. Dissipation had done its work with many." All of this left the *Times* to predict, "If Salt Lake City is wholly peopled by individuals of the average of intellect possessed by the newly-arrived emigrants, we should, following the law of depreciation, expect that in a century it would be merely a congregation of apes with tails."[21]

Other such racializing efforts continued over the ensuing decades. By the 1880s the arrival of Mormon immigrants at New York had grown into a cultural discourse readily expressed in pictorial form. As typically depicted the European converts were all women who were unwittingly snared into a system of "white slavery" against their will. Mormon men were caricatured as lecherous patriarchs who preyed upon the unsuspecting females with promises of freedom in America but who in reality only desired to add them to their growing harems in Utah.

The term "white slave" grew out of a much larger antebellum context in which wage laborers sometimes described themselves as white slaves in efforts to emphasize their sometimes deplorable conditions. As early as the 1830s, however, workers themselves began to reject the metaphor in part because it "detract[ed] from the dignity of the laborer." Northern workers especially rebuffed the term "white slave" when deployed by Southerners to attack northern wage labor. As historian David R. Roediger explained, "To be a slave, even a white slave, was to be associated with degradation." Factory women in the North recognized this when they spurned the term, especially as slavery implied sexual exploitation and a "connection with blackness."[22] In fact, Republican advocates of free white labor argued in 1857 that in deploying the term "white slave" Southerners in essence degraded free white labor to nothing "but the counterpart of the negro." It put "the white pioneer in Kansas" on par with a black slave in the plantation South, a conflation that Northerners disdained before the Civil War but one that they and others turned with zeal on the Mormons after the war.[23]

To be sure, "white slave" was a term fraught with paradox simply because on the surface it seemed to reify the whiteness of the person so labeled. In its application, however, it implied that a white slave was not free and therefore not fully white, a way to decenter whiteness without ever defining what the white slave actually was. As deployed against Mormon immigrant women, the rhetoric of white slavery also highlights the

HARPER'S WEEKLY.

PURE WHITE "MORMON IMMIGRATION" ON THE ATLANTIC COAST.

FIGURE 7.2. Thomas Nast, "Pure White 'Mormon Immigration' on the Atlantic Coast. More *cheap* 'help-mates' for Mr. Polygamist." Reprinted from *Harper's Weekly*, March 25, 1882, 191. Courtesy of the Library of Congress.

ways in which nineteenth-century Americans viewed race as a performance. As outsiders imagined it, Mormon immigrants entered polygamy and in the process sacrificed their liberty, something that no true white person would ever do. As white slaves, Mormon women performed blackness and in the process abandoned their racial heritage.

Political cartoons in the 1880s were rife with such messages. *Harper's Weekly* published a picture in 1882 that poked fun at the "Pure White 'Mormon Immigration' on the Atlantic Coast" (figure 7.2). Rather than immigrating to enjoy a life of freedom as

FIGURE 7.3. "'The Twin Relic of Barbarism.'—The Wolves and the Lambs—Arrival of Scandinavian Converts, in Charge of Mormon Missionaries, at Castle Garden, en route for Salt Lake City." Reprinted from *Frank Leslie's Illustrated Newspaper*, December 15, 1883, 264–65.

Anglo-Saxon heritage would suggest, these women immigrated as "cheap 'help-mates' for Mr. Polygamist." In joining Mormonism, these European converts lost their individual and their racial identities and became nothing more than exploited laborers: cooks, chambermaids, laundresses, and waitresses. In 1883, Frank Leslie added a more sexual and sinister nature to the Mormon immigration, calling it the "twin relic of barbarism" and depicting the anxious male patriarchs as lecherous wolves waiting to sexually devour the latest flock of innocent lambs (figure 7.3).[24]

A cover image from *Frank Leslie's Illustrated Newspaper* for March 1882 offers a more detailed visual depiction of how outsiders sometimes imagined the Mormon system to work (figure 7.4). First the Mormon "agent" lured unsuspecting females into his bait by offering them the "promise of a happy home out west." But the "happy home" was only a trap with sharp metal claws that would capture the female immigrants and funnel them into polygamy and ultimate degradation. Once they arrived in Utah they would be employed as slave labor, held captive to the ball and chain of ignorance and by their sealing to an indolent patriarch. That patriarch employed the

FIGURE 7.4. "Woman's Bondage in Utah. The Mormon Solution of the 'Cheap Labor' Question." Reprinted from *Frank Leslie's Illustrated Newspaper*, March 11, 1882, 1. Courtesy of Church History Library, The Church of Jesus Christ of Latter-day Saints, Salt Lake City, Utah.

whip of intimidation to keep his wives under control and only cared about his financial bottom line. The account sheet he held pleased him as he contemplated the amount of money he had saved in farmhands by importing "cheap" foreign labor in the form of wives. According to this cartoon, black slavery was not as degraded as the white slavery practiced in Utah. The black man in the cartoon looks on with the Emancipation Proclamation tucked securely under his arm. Even he is racially superior and more free than white women among the Mormons. The women, in contrast, bear the marks of degradation and sorrow on their faces, with one in the foreground wearing wooden Dutch shoes to remind readers of her foreignness. Mormon immigrants in this depiction, even if coming from England and northern Europe, did not perform whiteness.[25]

Other cartoons of the era echoed similar themes. In February 1882, Frank Leslie's newspaper again depicted Mormon immigrants in ways that called their whiteness into question (figure 7.5). In converting to Mormonism and immigrating to Utah, they performed race. Rather than the triumphal march of western civilization toward an ever-expanding freedom and the blessings of self-rule, ideals that racial thinkers taught were the special preserves of the Anglo-Saxon "race," Mormon polygamy marked civilization's racial decay. Most of the women in this depiction were marked with the word "sealed," an indication that they were already married into polygamy even before their arrival. Their entrance into the "cave of despair" only guaranteed their fate. One woman's bag is marked "Norway," another "England," while a third wears Dutch wooden shoes. Clearly it is a western European immigrant group, but in converting to Mormonism they marked themselves racially, not just as religiously inferior. In converting to Mormonism they performed an act of racial regression. If Anglo-Saxons were racially ordained the keepers of freedom, then those who entered the cave of despair signaled the forfeiture of their racial heritage. They abandoned their independence and love of liberty to the waiting tyrannical patriarchs, men who presided over a despotic kingdom littered with the bones of the Mountain Meadows Massacre. Polygamy and despotism were sure signs of civilization's decay, a backward evolutionary descent into barbarism and ultimate savagery.[26]

The Wasp, a San Francisco newspaper, also picked up the theme of immigration as one facet of the Mormon problem. In November 1886 its cover image featured its vision of what "Mormon Fishing in Foreign Lands" looked like (figure 7.6). The Mormon patriarch flew over Europe riding upon the back of an eagle as he snared a harvest of female converts from across the continent. Women from Russia, Italy, Spain, France, Holland, Austria, Switzerland, Sweden, and Turkey were all lured in by his bait. The ratio of women to men in the illustration was thirty-six to one, a visual depiction meant to heighten alarm over Mormon polygamy and in this case to emphasize the decidedly foreign nature of the women swept up in its snare.[27]

FIGURE 7.5. "Mormonism in Utah—The Cave of Despair." Reprinted from *Frank Leslie's Illustrated Newspaper*, February 4, 1882, 1. Courtesy of Utah State Historical Society, Salt Lake City, Utah.

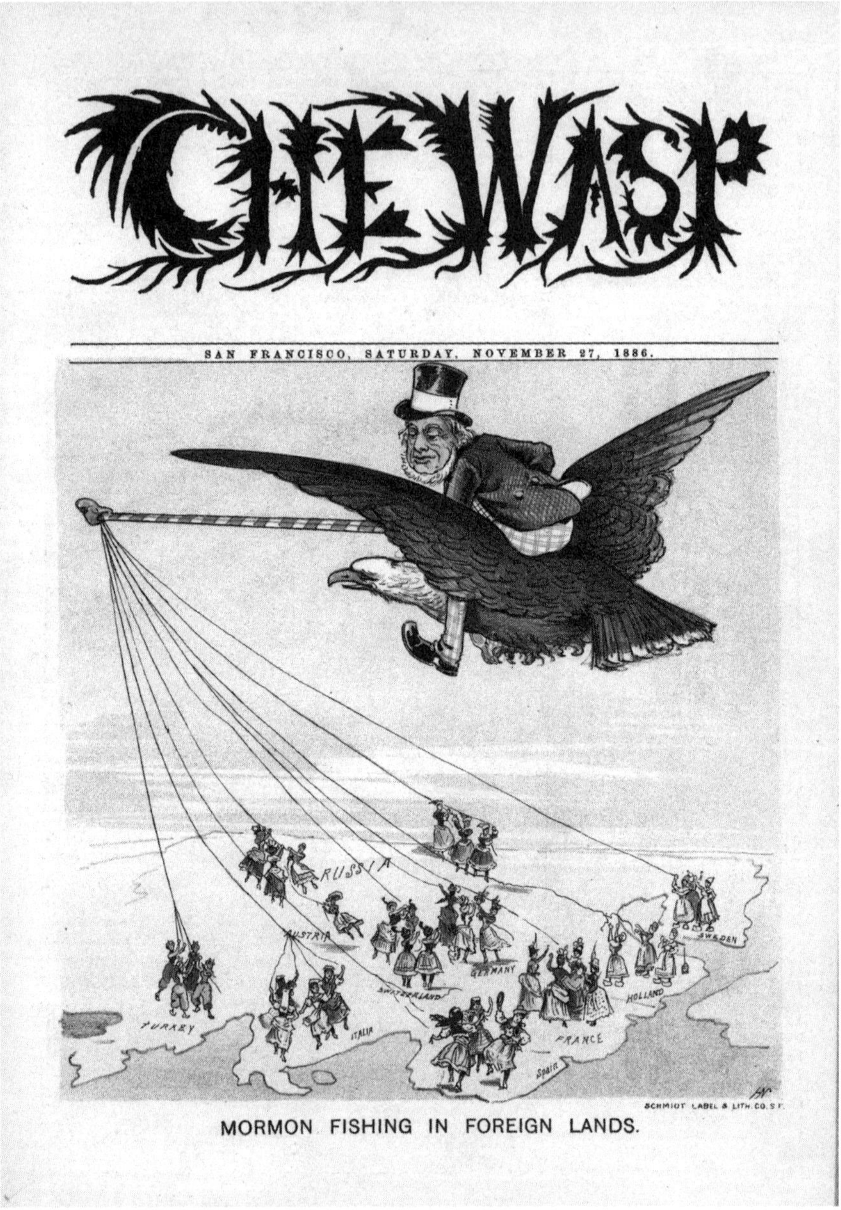

FIGURE 7.6. "Mormon Fishing in Foreign Lands." Reprinted from *The Wasp*, November 27, 1886. Courtesy of the Bancroft Library, University of California, Berkeley.

FIGURE 7.7. Walter, "America—The World's Dumping Ground. Uncle Sam. Neither party prevents; both seek to profit from this garbage." Reprinted from *The Wasp*, June 11, 1887. Courtesy of the Bancroft Library, University of California, Berkeley.

A two-page illustration in *The Wasp* the following year emphasized a similar point, but this time situated Mormon immigrants alongside a variety of other undesirable groups and lamented the fact that America had become the "World's Dumping Ground" (figure 7.7). In this picture Uncle Sam stands aghast as he witnesses "Irish paupers," "French criminals," "Spanish paupers," "Italian immigration," "Russian immigration," "Chinese slave importation," "German paupers," and "Mormon proselytes," all being dumped into a filthy cesspool of "cheap labor." The snake of "socialism" slithers through the pool while the ugly faces of "anarchism" and "demagogism" look on. Republican and Democratic party leaders, rather than attempting to thwart the dumping of such filth, wallow in it, a fact which prompted Uncle Sam to complain that "neither party prevents" the influx of undesirables, but "both seek to profit from this garbage."

Interestingly, of all the groups depicted the "Mormon proselytes" were the only people who did not derive their identity from a foreign nation-state. It was a construction that placed Mormons alongside "paupers" and other undesirable immigrants as one facet of the nation's immigration and cheap labor problem, but it did so with a twist. Mormons were religious adherents from a church headquartered in the United

States, a community of believers who apparently warranted their own separate identity juxtaposed against the various nation-based immigrants. In this construction Mormon foreignness was essentialized, a depiction that turned Mormons into an alien group on par with Irish, Italian, French, Spanish, Russian, Chinese, and German immigrants, all contributors to the nation's slithering socialist menace. Mormonism was not merely a religious threat but a racialized immigrant threat, foreign and dangerous at its core.[28]

Even though these cartoons were all published in the 1880s at the height of the federal crackdown on Mormon polygamy, the ideas they conjured were in circulation in American political and racial thought from at least the 1850s onward. Francis Lieber, a German-born political philosopher and professor of history and political science at South Carolina College and later at Columbia, raised such concerns in an article he wrote for *Putnam's Monthly* in 1855. Lieber's article anticipated that the Mormons in Utah Territory would soon apply for statehood, an application Lieber urged Congress to deny. As he saw it, Utah would introduce a "foreign and disturbing element" into the sisterhood of states, an element that violated "sound morality" and republican government. Monogamy and republicanism were both racial to him, the preserves of European civilization. "Monogamy goes beyond our religion," he wrote. "It is 'a law written in the heart' of our race," the special domain of the "western Caucasian." As Lieber saw it, monogamy was "one of the pre-existing conditions of our existence as civilized white men" and "together with the endeavor to establish political liberty" it constituted two of "the main distinctions between Asiatic and European mankind."[29] It was a common and frequent way in which outsiders called Mormon whiteness into question. It offered a fitting introduction to another member of Mormon Elder-Berry's family, the Asian child.

Benjamin Morgan Palmer pastored the First Presbyterian Church in Columbia, South Carolina, in January 1853, when he delivered a lecture simply titled "Mormonism" to the Mercantile Library Association in Charleston. Palmer is best remembered as a southern fire-eater, an outspoken defender of slavery, and a supporter of secession in the years leading up to the Civil War. In 1853, however, his focus was upon the trouble he perceived brewing in the American West, not the South. "We cannot cast our gaze beyond the Rocky Mountains, and scrutinize the face of society collecting upon our extreme western coast, without a measure of anxiety for the unfolding future," he announced. "Our country is certainly entering upon one of the grandest experiments it has ever been called to undertake, and is passing through the severest crisis it has ever been made to know."[30]

The crisis was not slavery, or the sectional rift then starting to pull at the threads of union, it was instead Asiatic—specifically, the Mormons and the Chinese. As Palmer saw it, Mormonism represented "a bold attempt . . . by Anglo-Saxons themselves to reproduce the old civilization of Asia." And if that were not bad enough, "a strong and copious tide of really Asiatic population has been pouring into our California territory." He estimated that seventeen thousand Chinese arrived on the west coast within a three-month period during the prior year. It was an alarming number, especially when considered in light of the growing Mormon presence in the Rocky Mountains. The Chinese and Mormons were two Asiatic groups who were in Palmer's mind destined to combine. "What is to be the issue of this commingling of races on this continent?" he wondered, with clear intent to heighten alarm.[31]

As the tide of Chinese immigration grew from the 1850s to the 1880s, American fears of an Asiatic invasion seemed to grow with it. Mormons, with their Asiatic "sensualism" and subjection to authoritarian regimes were natural allies for the Chinese—at least in the imaginations of some Americans.[32] The conflation of the two groups occurred against a backdrop of growing American consternation over what was frequently described as the "yellow peril" of Asian immigration. It was a sentiment that permeated nineteenth-century American culture and politics. It also infused the landmark 1879 U.S. Supreme Court decision, *Reynolds v. United States*. George Reynolds, a secretary to Brigham Young and a polygamist, agreed to offer himself up for a legal test case. Mormons long insisted that the Morrill Anti-Bigamy Bill of 1862, which made polygamy a federal crime, was an unconstitutional violation of the free exercise of their religion. Plural marriage, they argued, was a sacrament to them, a religious requirement to reach the highest degree of the LDS heaven. Any law against plural marriage was therefore a violation of their religious freedom.[33]

In the *Reynolds* decision, the Supreme Court unanimously disagreed. In doing so, it relied in part upon racial arguments commonly in circulation in America at least since Francis Lieber had argued that polygamy was a mark of a group's racial inferiority and therefore incapacity for self-rule. Charles Sinclair, a federally appointed district judge for Utah Territory, made a similar argument in 1858. He noted that in ancient Greece polygamy was regarded "as the practice of barbarians" and asserted that it was "exclusively the feature of Asiatic manners, and of half civilized life." Chief Justice Morrison Waite wrote the Supreme Court's opinion in *Reynolds* and referenced these earlier ideas, even citing Lieber by name in doing so. "Polygamy has always been odious among the northern and western nations of Europe," Waite contended, "and, until the establishment of the Mormon Church, was almost exclusively a feature of the life of Asiatic and of African people." Drawing upon Lieber, Waite further argued that polygamy was grounded in "the patriarchal principle," a system that fettered "people in stationary despotism."[34] Religious liberty had its limits, Waite concluded, and Asiatic polygamy on American soil was one of them.

Outsiders also turned to two of America's most despised inside racial groups, Indians and blacks, to further question Mormon whiteness. Of all of the children in Mormon Elder-Berry's mythic family, it was only the Indian child whom Mormons were sometimes actually encouraged to marry. Nevertheless, the ways in which outsiders imagined the practice versus its implementation on the inside were frequently starkly different. When Mark Twain wrote *Roughing It*, a book about his tales of adventure in the American West, he included a story about Indian marriage and racial decline in Brigham Young's own family. Twain's account began with a woman showing up at Young's home one day with a child in tow. The little boy had "a curious lifeless sort of complexion" similar to his mother's. The woman informed Young that the child was his and that she was Young's wife. She told Young that she had married him some time ago but that she had forgotten which number wife she was. No matter, Young could not recall her name anyway. The woman then drew Young's attention to the child, a boy whom she declared looked like him. It was a fact that Young could not dispute. Young dutifully placed the child in his nursery and the woman departed. To Young's later astonishment, "When they came to wash the paint off that child it was an Injun!"[35]

The story was clearly calculated to poke fun at polygamy on several levels. Young was the husband of so many wives and the father of so many children that in Twain's story Young could not recall a wife to whom he was married or a child whom he allegedly fathered. No matter, Young readily admitted that the child looked like him and that was enough. He welcomed the boy into his nursery only to discover later that he had fathered an "Injun." The story implied that Young was a parent to racial decline and by implication to civilization's backward descent into savagery. Twain may or may not have known about the actual (if limited) practice of Mormon intermarriage with Indians, but he tapped into a broader cultural critique, present since the 1830s, that in their fraternization with the continent's natives Mormons transgressed the boundaries between red and white, savagery and civilization, theocracy and democracy, wickedness and righteousness, morality and depravity, monogamy and polygamy, and ultimately between racial purity and racial filth.

Outsiders simultaneously fabricated another, even more racially charged identity for the Latter-day Saints, an identity that turned overwhelmingly white Mormons into interracial families and placed them at the nexus of America's fears of racial deterioration. In these depictions, polygamy did not merely destroy the traditional family, it destroyed the white race.

Brigham Young's family was racialized, for example, following Young's arrest on charges of "lascivious cohabitation" in the fall of 1871. The case dragged on through the spring of 1872 and was eventually dismissed, but not before it provided fodder for the national press. *Frank Leslie's Budget of Fun*, a pictorial magazine published in New York City, capitalized on the story to imagine what the scene must have looked like when federal marshals hauled Young off to court (figure 7.8). Young's "interesting little family" is noticeably distraught over the removal of their husband and father, but it is the degraded and interracial nature of Young's family that most dramatically catches the eye. The lead wife who reaches toward Young with partially outstretched arms is a stereotypical black mammy from the South, a character who was nonexistent in reality but promoted in caricature by southern whites. Southerners encouraged the black mammy stereotype in an effort to counter northern charges that slavery was inherently brutal and that it frequently gave cover to interracial rape. For Southerners the black mammy was living, albeit fictionalized, evidence that slaveholders cared for their slaves and welcomed them into their families. The black mammy stereotype was a fat, happy, contented woman who was so well cared for and devoted to her owners and to their children that she had no desire for freedom. She was also so overweight and ugly that no white man could possibly desire her sexually.[36]

When the black mammy was integrated into Brigham Young's family, however, the messages were reversed. Polygamy was so corrupt that Brigham Young was willing to do what no self-respecting Southerner would do, that is have sex with a black mammy *and* marry her. The third wife to the left of Young is also black, although the view is from behind as she wipes tears from her eyes with a handkerchief. The children too were interracial, with at least two black girls among them, evidence of the "hybrid" and darkened offspring of polygamy.

Even some of the white children and women were racialized. The second wife to the left of Young and several of the children are more apelike than human, sharing several key markings of racial deterioration. It was a common caricature in the nineteenth century to depict Irish-born immigrants with simian or apelike features, a way to mark them as primitive and beastly, a construction aimed at the Mormons in this cartoon. The heavy brow and forehead, the flat nose and angle of the upper face were all key elements meant to evoke primate characteristics. The message was clear: polygamy despoiled the white race and marked a racial regression, a backward evolutionary descent into blackness and species decline.[37]

Given that *Life* magazine's publication of the Mormon Elder-Berry cartoon came within two months of Joseph F. Smith's testimony in the Smoot hearings, it is hardly a stretch of the imagination to suggest that Elder-Berry was an intended Joseph F. Smith look-alike. In that vein, then, Elder-Berry's mythical multiracial Mormon family stood in for all Mormon families, a family portrait of the ways in which Mormons were racialized across the course of the nineteenth century. In essence, it was a summarizing attack on Mormon Anglo-Saxon triumphalism, a jeer of disapproval over Mormon polygamy, and a concluding commentary on Mormonism as a system of racial decline.

Affecting parting of Brigham Young from his interesting little family.

FIGURE 7.8. "Affecting parting of Brigham Young from his interesting little family." Reprinted from *Frank Leslie's Budget of Fun*, January 1872, 16. Courtesy of Library of Congress.

Elder-Berry's family offers an intriguing juxtaposition against which scholars might evaluate the "Mormon moment" of the early twenty-first century, culminating in Mitt Romney's Republican nomination for the presidency in 2012. The Reed Smoot Mormon moment suggested racial deterioration through interracial mixing, something outsiders suggested was inherent in Mormon polygamy. In response, nineteenth-century Mormons clamored for acceptance and respectability; they persistently attempted to parry the attacks on their whiteness in part through their adoption of Anglo-Saxon triumphalism. In contrast, the Mitt Romney Mormon moment suggested a racial profile of Mormonism that was the near polar opposite of a century earlier. The twenty-first-century perception was typified by what one culture critic called "the whitest white man to run for president in recent memory."[38] Now Mormons were *too* white for an increasingly multiracial culture, and this time the Mormon response was not designed to shore up that perceived whiteness, but instead to give it a bit of color. At least four mixed-race couples were included in the LDS Church's representation of the twenty-first-century faces of Mormonism. This included Mia Love, the mayor of Saratoga Springs, Utah, and 2012 Republican candidate for Congress, who as a woman of Haitian descent was featured in an "I'm a Mormon" ad with her white husband and mixed heritage children.[39] In this regard, Mormon Elder-Berry's family was a century ahead of its time.

What does all of this mean for twenty-first-century scholarship on Mormonism and race? One path forward is to situate "changing Mormon conceptions of race and lineage" on the inside within broader national and international conceptions of race on the outside. As Mormon Elder-Berry's family suggests, scholars might profitably interrogate Mormon whiteness, especially from the 1840s to the 1920s, an era in which waves of foreign immigration fractured the nation's monolithic whiteness and simultaneously called Mormon whiteness into question. The Mormon racial story should not take Mormon whiteness for granted, in other words, and future scholarship should consider ways in which whiteness as a contested variable impacted the Mormon racial story across time and space. And what of the children absent from Elder-Berry's family but integral to the growing international Mormon family, especially those from Latin America, the Pacific islands, the Philippines, and West Africa, all hotbeds of Mormon growth in the twentieth and twenty-first centuries? Recent scholarship has addressed Mormon racialization of Hawaiians, but much more needs to be done.[40] Here, too, whiteness as a variable is crucial to the various stories awaiting scholarly treatment.

Whiteness studies scholars and scholars of national and transnational racialization and multiculturalism would also do well to take note of the Mormon example. Certainly Mormonism forces the story of whiteness to expand its scope beyond labor and immigration to consider the ways in which race intersected with religion across time and space. And, as Mormonism continues its international outreach, the field is no longer "white already to harvest" but multicultural and transnational—rich and inviting prospects for future research.

In short, scholars should not neglect to situate Mormon views on race from the inside looking out alongside views from the outside looking in. In this regard scholars might well imagine what the resulting family reunion might look like if they introduced *All Abraham's Children* to all Elder-Berry's children. It would no doubt be a reunion to remember, one that might offer new insights into the ever-changing Mormon family, especially as it evolved from not-white-enough in the nineteenth century to too-white by the twenty-first.

Notes

The bulk of this chapter is drawn from W. Paul Reeve, *Religion of a Different Color: Race and the Mormon Struggle for Whiteness* (New York: Oxford University Press, 2015), and is used by permission from Oxford University Press.

1. "Mormon Elder-Berry—out with his six-year-olds, who take after their mothers," *Life*, April 28, 1904, 404; Michael Harold Paulos, "Under the Gun at the Smoot Hearings: Joseph F. Smith's Testimony," *Journal of Mormon History* 34 (Fall 2008): 181–225; Michael Harold Paulos, ed., *The Mormon Church on Trial: Transcripts of the Reed Smoot Hearings* (Salt Lake City, UT: Signature Books, 2008), 19–142, 177–84.
2. For the "I'm a Mormon" campaign, see mormon.org; and Eric Marrapodi, "With 'I'm a Mormon' campaign, church counters lily-white image," CNN Belief Blog, http://religion.blogs.cnn.com/2011/11/02/with-im-a-mormon-campaign-church-counters-lily-white-image.
3. Thomas G. Alexander, "The Odyssey of a Latter-day Prophet: Wilford Woodruff and the Manifesto of 1890," *Journal of Mormon History* 17 (1991): 169–206; *LDS Conference Reports, Seventy-Fourth Annual Conference of the Church of Jesus Christ of Latter-day Saints, Held in the Tabernacle, Salt Lake City, April 3rd, 4th and 6th, 1904, with a full Report of the Discourses* (Salt Lake City, UT: Deseret News, 1904), 75.
4. Kathleen Flake, *The Politics of American Religious Identity: The Seating of Senator Reed Smoot, Mormon Apostle* (Chapel Hill: University of North Carolina Press, 2004); Walter Kirn, "Mormons Rock!" *Newsweek*, June 5, 2011, www.thedailybeast.com/newsweek/2011/06/05/mormons-rock.html; Michael H. Paulos, "Political Cartooning and the Reed Smoot Hearings," *Sunstone*, Issue 144 (December 2006): 36–40.
5. Flake, *The Politics of American Religious Identity*, 1–33; Harvard S. Heath, "Reed Smoot: First Modern Mormon," (PhD diss., Brigham Young University, 1990), 84–197; Milton R. Merrill, *Reed Smoot: Apostle in Politics* (Logan: Utah State University Press, 1990); Gustive O. Larson, *The "Americanization" of Utah for Statehood* (San Marino, CA: Huntington Library, 1971).
6. Thomas Alexander, *Mormonism in Transition: A History of the Latter-day Saints, 1890–1930* (Urbana: University of Illinois Press, 1986).
7. Armand L. Mauss, *All Abraham's Children: Changing Mormon Conceptions of Race and Lineage* (Urbana: University of Illinois Press, 2003); Newell G. Bringhurst, *Saints,*

Slaves, and Blacks: The Changing Place of Black People Within Mormonism (Westport, CT: Greenwood Press, 1981), 84, 97; Lester E. Bush Jr., "Mormonism's Negro Doctrine: An Historical Overview," *Dialogue: A Journal of Mormon Thought* 8 (Spring 1973): 11–68.

8. Mauss, *All Abraham's Children*, 23.
9. *Doctrine and Covenants of the Church of Jesus Christ of Latter-day Saints* (Salt Lake City, UT: The Church of Jesus Christ of Latter-day Saints, 1981), 4:4.
10. Bryan J. Grant, "The Church in British Isles," in *Encyclopedia of Mormonism*, ed. Daniel H. Ludlow, 5 vols. (New York: Macmillan, 1992), 1:227–32.
11. Matthew Frye Jacobson, *Whiteness of a Different Color: European Immigrants and the Alchemy of Race* (Cambridge, MA: Harvard University Press, 1998), 41.
12. Jacobson, *Whiteness of a Different Color*, 37–38.
13. It is on this count that I turn to whiteness studies for inspiration. My thinking is informed by scholarship such as Matthew Frye Jacobson, *Whiteness of a Different Color*; and *Barbarian Virtues: The United States Encounters Foreign Peoples at Home and Abroad, 1876–1917* (New York: Hill and Wang, 2000); David R. Roediger, *Working Toward Whiteness: How America's Immigrants Became White* (New York: Basic Books, 2005); and *The Wages of Whiteness: Race and the Making of the American Working Class* (New York: Verso, 1991; reprint, 2007); Nell Irvin Painter, *The History of White People* (New York: W. W. Norton & Company, 2010); Eric L. Goldstein, *The Price of Whiteness: Jews, Race, and American Identity* (Princeton, NJ: Princeton University Press, 2006); Mark M. Smith, *How Race Is Made: Slavery, Segregation, and the Senses* (Chapel Hill: University of North Carolina Press, 2006); and Reginal Horsman, *Race and Manifest Destiny: The Origins of American Racial Anglo-Saxonism* (Cambridge, MA: Harvard University Press, 1981).
14. Roediger, *Working Toward Whiteness*, 4–5.
15. Bruce Dain, *A Hideous Monster of the Mind: American Race Theory in the Early Republic* (Cambridge, MA: Harvard University Press, 2002), vii–viii.
16. Two examples of Jewish whiteness studies are Goldstein, *The Price of Whiteness*; and Karen Brodkin, *How the Jews Became White Folks and What That Says about Race in America* (New Brunswick, NJ: Rutgers University Press, 1998). For examples of scholars who have used whiteness to interrogate religion in terms of the ways in which Jesus is represented, see Stephen Prothero, *American Jesus: How the Son of God Became a National Icon* (New York: Farrar, Straus and Giroux, 2003); and Edward J. Blum and Paul Harvey, *The Color of Christ: The Son of God and the Saga of Race in America* (Chapel Hill: University of North Carolina Press, 2014).
17. Smith, *How Race Is Made*, 46–47, 68.
18. Historians have explored physical characterizations of Mormons in the past, but not to the extent of placing Mormons on par with other western groups kept from the Union in the nineteenth century. See Davis Bitton and Gary L. Bunker, "Double Jeopardy: Visual Images of Mormon Women to 1914," *Utah Historical Quarterly* 46 (Spring 1978): 184–202; Gary L. Bunker and Davis Bitton, "Illustrated Periodical Images of Mormons, 1850–1860," *Dialogue: A Journal of Mormon Thought* 10 (Spring 1977): 82–94; Davis Bitton and Gary L. Bunker, "Mischievous Puck and the Mormons," *BYU Studies* 18

(Summer 1978): 504–19; Gary Bunker and Davis Bitton, *The Mormon Graphic Image, 1834–1914: Cartoons, Caricatures, and Illustrations* (Salt Lake City: University of Utah Press, 1983); Davis Bitton and Gary L. Bunker, "Phrenology Among the Mormons," *Dialogue: A Journal of Mormon Thought* 9 (Spring 1974): 42–61; Gary L. Bunker and Davis Bitton, "Polygamous Eyes: A Note on Mormon Physiognomy," *Dialogue: A Journal of Mormon Thought* 12 (Autumn 1979): 114–19; Terryl Givens, "Caricature as Containment: Orientalism, Bondage, and the Construction of Mormon Ethnicity in Nineteenth-Century American Popular Fiction," *Nineteenth-Century Contexts* 18, no. 4 (1995): 385–403.

19. Roediger, *Working Toward Whiteness*, 12.
20. 2 Nephi 30:6, 1830 edition of Book of Mormon. In the 1840 edition the phrase was changed to "pure and delightsome," which is how it reads in the current (1981) edition.
21. "Our Reporter Visits the Mormons," *New York Times*, March 29, 1856, 2.
22. Roediger, *Wages of Whiteness*, 82–87.
23. "The True Dignity of Labor," *The National Era*, May 21, 1857, 84.
24. Thomas Nast, "Pure White 'Mormon Immigration' on the Atlantic Coast," *Harper's Weekly*, March 25, 1882, 191; "The Twin Relic of Barbarism," *Frank Leslie's Illustrated Newspaper*, December 15, 1883, 264–65.
25. "Woman's Bondage in Utah," *Frank Leslie's Illustrated Newspaper*, March 11, 1882, 1.
26. "Mormonism in Utah—The Cave of Despair," *Frank Leslie's Illustrated Newspaper*, February 4, 1882, 1. On the Mountain Meadows Massacre see Ronald W. Walker, Richard E. Turley Jr., and Glen M. Leonard, *Massacre at Mountain Meadows: An American Tragedy* (New York: Oxford University Press, 2008). On barbarism see J. Spencer Fluhman, *"A Peculiar People": Anti-Mormonism and the Making of Religion in Nineteenth-Century America* (Chapel Hill: The University of North Carolina Press, 2012), chapter 4.
27. "Mormon Fishing in Foreign Lands," *The Wasp*, November 27, 1886, 1.
28. "America—The World's Dumping Ground," *The Wasp*, June 11, 1887, 8–9.
29. [Francis Lieber], "The Mormons: Shall Utah Be Admitted to the Union?," *Putnam's Monthly* 5 (March 1855): 228, 234, 235.
30. Benjamin Morgan Palmer, *Mormonism: A Lecture Delivered Before the Mercantile Library Association of Charleston, S.C.* (Columbia, SC: I. C. Morgan, 1853), 33. For Palmer's biographical information, see Christopher M. Duncan, "Benjamin Morgan Palmer: Southern Presbyterian Divine," (PhD diss., Auburn University, 2008); and William Deverell, "Thoughts from the Farther West: Mormons, California, and the Civil War," *Journal of Mormon History* 34 (Spring 2008): 1–19.
31. Palmer, *Mormonism*, 33–34.
32. Ibid., 16–17, 22–23.
33. B. Carmon Hardy, ed., *Doing the Works of Abraham: Mormon Polygamy, Its Origin, Practice, and Demise* (Norman, OK: Arthur H. Clark Company, 2007), 73–80, 111–14, 263–66; Sarah Barringer Gordon, *The Mormon Question: Polygamy and Constitutional Conflict in Nineteenth-Century America* (Chapel Hill: University of North Carolina Press, 2002), 114–16; Nathan B. Oman, "Natural Law and the Rhetoric of Empire: *Reynolds v. United States*, Polygamy, and Imperialism," William & Mary Law School Research Paper No. 09-43 (February 26, 2010).

34. *Reynolds vs. United States* (1879), 98 U.S. 153, 161–68; [Lieber], "The Mormons," 228, 234, 235; "Charge of Hon. Chas. E. Sinclair," *Valley Tan* (Corrine, UT), November 26, 1858, 2; Gordon, *The Mormon Question*, 119–45; Martha M. Ertman, "The Story of *Reynolds v. United States*: Federal 'Hell Hounds' Punishing Mormon Treason," in *Family Law Stories*, ed. Carol Sanger (New York: Foundation Press, 2008).
35. Mark Twain, *Roughing It* (Berkeley: University of California Press, 1993), 103–4.
36. "Affecting parting of Brigham Young from his interesting little family," *Frank Leslie's Budget of Fun*, January 1872, 16. On black mammies see Catherine Clinton, *The Plantation Mistress: Woman's World in the Old South* (New York: Pantheon Books, 1982), 201–2; and Patricia A. Turner, *Ceramic Uncles and Celluloid Mammies: Black Images and Their Influence on Culture* (New York: Anchor Books, 1994), 44. On Young's arrest and eventual dismissal of charges, see Leonard J. Arrington, *Brigham Young American Moses* (Urbana: University of Illinois Press, 1986), 371–74.
37. For evidence of simian depictions of Irish, see L. Perry Curtis Jr., *Apes and Angels: The Irishman in Victorian Caricature*, rev. ed. (Washington, DC: Smithsonian Institution Press, 1997), 29–67. On the Irish struggle for whiteness, see Noel Ignatiev, *How the Irish Became White* (New York: Routledge, 1995).
38. Lee Siegel, "What's Race Got to Do with It?" *New York Times*, January 14, 2012.
39. The ad campaign was featured at www.mormon.org. When Love declared her candidacy, her profile and ad were removed from the website. See also Stephen Clark, "New Mormon Ad Campaign: Seeking to Dispel Myths or PR for Romney '12 Run?" foxnews.com, September 4, 2010, http://www.foxnews.com/politics/2010/09/04mormons-new-ad-campaign-seeking-dispel-myths-pr-romney-run; Marrapodi, "With 'I'm a Mormon' campaign."
40. Matthew Kester, *Remembering Iosepa: History, Place, and Religion in the American West* (New York: Oxford University Press, 2013); Hokulani K. Aikau, *A Chosen People, a Promised Land: Mormonism and Race in Hawaii* (Minneapolis: University of Minnesota Press, 2012).

Part IV | Theoretical Models in the Study of Mormonism

Chapter 8 | Authority in Mormonism
A Rational Choice Analysis

Michael McBride

"So far as I can judge from what I have seen, the organization of the Mormons is the most nearly perfect piece of social mechanism with which I have ever, in any way, come in contact, excepting alone the German army. . . . We have faith, authority, obedience, operating through this marvellous social mechanism, and touching life at all points."

—Richard Ely, *Harper's Monthly Magazine*, 1903

"The [Mormon] church . . . is one of the most centralized, hierarchical, authoritarian churches in America to come out of the era famous for the 'democratization of religion.'"

—Terryl Givens, *People of Paradox: A History of Mormon Culture*, 2007

Introduction

Since its beginning in the early nineteenth century, the Church of Jesus Christ of Latter-day Saints (LDS Church or Mormon Church) has sustained a reputation for authoritarianism.[1] Although individualist strains within Mormonism exist, academics and social commentators associate this authoritarian reputation with the church's hierarchical structure, teachings that emphasize obedience to church leaders' directives, the emphasis on community, official church discipline of dissidents, and the high level of religious commitment among many Mormons.[2] In its earliest years, Mormonism quickly developed a unique ecclesiastical structure, and a claim to unique divine authority was central to that development.[3] Founder Joseph Smith was a prophet who received divine direction for the entire membership of the church on a variety of topics ranging from the drinking of coffee to the building of cities. Subsequent church presidents have also acted as prophet-spokespersons for God, and their proclamations have guided the church and its members through nearly two hundred years of growth and adaptation. Devout Mormons view their own willingness to follow their leaders not as authoritarianism in a pejorative sense but rather a deliberate and active outgrowth of faith; to critics, Mormons' obedience to leaders is ignorance and naiveté at best or the result of coercion and illusion at worst.[4] Yet, both sides agree that authority matters to Mormons.

This paper provides the first examination of authority within Mormonism using a rational choice (or economic) approach. This approach understands authority as a solution to underlying economic problems of coordination faced by a group in undertaking collective action. Authority can be manifest in various forms, including informal social norms that govern dress and communication, or formal leadership structures with well-defined positions and responsibilities, but all authority serves a common function to create commonly shared beliefs about others' actions that are necessary for successful social coordination. After summarizing the basic economic theory of authority, I identify various manifestations of authority within Mormonism and relate them to underlying social coordination problems faced by Mormon communities. I then examine two manifestations of authority in Mormonism, using the economic theory to generate new insights into our understanding of authority within Mormonism.

Rational choice methodology provides an important—even if controversial—paradigm within which to study religion.[5] During recent decades, the rational choice or economics approach to human behavior has been applied to many religious phenomena, from an individual's decision to attend church to national levels of religiosity.[6] However, only recently has there been an attempt to study authority from this paradigm.[7] The primary contribution of this chapter is to use this newly developed rational choice theory of religious authority to study a particular religious group. This approach is not meant as a comprehensive study but rather as an exploration of authority in Mormonism through one set of lenses.

The study of Mormonism has actually played an important role in the development of the rational choice theory of religion. The most prominent sociologists to use ideas from rational choice theory to examine Mormonism are Rodney Stark and Armand Mauss. Stark, one of the founders of the rational choice approach to religion, frequently relied on the Mormon experience to support his arguments.[8] Meanwhile, Mauss, arguably the preeminent sociologist of Mormonism, drew from the rational choice literature but with a sharper focus on Mormonism.[9] Economists, too, have used the rational choice approach in studying Mormonism.[10] My approach here follows on my earlier work that used game theory to study how the LDS Church confronts the free-rider problems inherent in congregational religious production.[11] As in that work, I draw heavily from game theory, but here I focus on how authority functions to solve coordination problems—as distinguished from free-rider problems—in the Mormon Church and communities. Because this particular social scientific approach focuses on fundamental problems of collective action rather than on Mormonism itself, insights gleaned from this study may inform our understanding of other religious groups, a point to which I return in the conclusion.

Other related literatures deserve mention. The first is that which constructs a rational choice theory of leadership and authority. Max Weber provides the classic, sociological treatment of the different kinds of authority.[12] His view of authority was revised in light of developments in rational choice theory by James Coleman[13] and has since been examined in more detail game-theoretically by economists and others.[14] I draw directly from this existing theory and apply it to study Mormonism. Another relevant body of scholarship is the rational choice literature on religious groups, especially those works that examine the production of religious club goods.[15] Finally, I also draw from game-theoretic and rational choice studies of coordination games and culture. The work by Thomas Schelling and David Lewis on coordination games provides many of the ideas applied here.[16] Michael Chwe's work on ritual provides an example of how peculiar features of culture may be understood through the eyes of game theory.[17]

The Economics of Authority

The Economic Approach

Economists understand social phenomena as emerging from many actors allocating scarce resources in social settings. For most economists, this methodological approach combines the rational actor representation of individual choice and the tools of game theory to consider action in social settings. This modern economic approach should be distinguished from Marxian theory which is referred to by some as economic analysis. Both posit economic agents engaged in productive endeavor, though the latter but not the former is associated with dialectical interpretations of history and primary roles for class relations.

The rational choice (or rational actor) representation of individual action dominates economics and decision theory and is common but not dominant in political science and sociology. It assumes that actors (e.g., individuals, organizations, states) behave systematically and consistently. It is an unfortunate and mistaken misconception that equates the rational actor model with the *Homo economicus* caricature of the calculating and selfish sociopath. *Homo economicus* is a particular manifestation of the rational actor model which assumes both selfish and instrumental behavior, but it is merely one manifestation. Neither selfishness nor instrumental motives are necessary aspects of a rational choice approach; selfless, altruistic, vengeful, and still other other-regarding behaviors or motives can also be examined in a rational choice approach, as can the noninstrumental behavior of insects or other nonhuman actors.[18] Indeed, evidence suggests that the behavioral consistency of the rational actor with preferences that balance self-regarding and other-regarding interests was selected by evolutionary processes.[19] For this and other reasons, the rational actor framework dominates the study of actors, be they human or nonhuman, in evolutionary biology. Below, I will describe actors as instrumental (i.e., individuals consciously consider the benefits and costs of their actions and attempt to choose actions that best accomplish their desires) because this interpretation corresponds best to emphasis on common knowledge in which each actor maintains a theory of mind about other actors.

The second element of the economic approach is the use of game theory to study actions in socially interactive settings in which the actions and well-being of an actor depend on the actions of other actors. Classical game theory examines strategic choices in these settings, while evolutionary game theory is used to study the cultural transmission of values and preferences and the emergence of social norms. Both of these bodies of research analyze the behavior of rational actors in well-defined social settings where those actors have choice sets and consistent preferences over outcomes. For my purposes, the value of using game theory to study authority is that it provides clarity and insights into stylized social interaction settings. In this particular paper, it will demonstrate the important role leaders play in generating common expectations among a group of people.

How researchers combine the rational actor model with game theory differs. On the one hand are researchers, typically sociologists, who draw ideas from rational choice analysis (e.g., cost-benefit decision making) but do not rely heavily on mathematical or game-theoretic analysis. Stark and Finke's general treatment of religion and Mauss's examinations of Mormonism are examples.[20] On the other hand are others, typically economists, who place additional emphasis on the game-theoretic elements.[21] This paper falls into the second category.[22]

Coordination Problems and Coordination Devices

The rational choice theory of authority is grounded in economic problems of coordination.[23] In a simple coordination problem, members of a group only succeed in collective action if their actions are appropriately aligned. There are a wide variety of coordination problems, and I here provide a few simple examples that capture the richness of the more complex scenarios. In one class of coordination games, which can be called Focal Action Games, all actors choosing the same action is preferred to any situation in which the actors do not all choose the same action. Such may be the case if Adam and Eve are choosing at which restaurant to meet for lunch. If no coordinated action is preferred to another (e.g., all restaurants are liked equally by both Adam and Eve), then we call it a Pure Coordination Game. The matrix in figure 8.1(a) depicts this Pure Coordination Game scenario. Each actor has two alternatives labeled B and C, which represent the two restaurants under consideration. If both choose restaurant B, then they are in the upper left cell in the matrix, and the payoffs (1,1) inside the cell represent how well that outcome is liked relative to other outcomes. The first number in each cell is Eve's payoff, and the second number in each cell is Adam's payoff. In this case, the payoffs are the same when both choose restaurant C as when both choose restaurant B, but the payoffs are lower (each gets 0) when they miscoordinate such that one chooses B and the other chooses C. Observe how the numbers in the cells of the matrix reflect how the alternatives are ranked, i.e., a lower payoff implies that the associated outcome is preferred less than an outcome with a higher payoff. The scenario in figure 8.1(a) is called a Pure Coordination Game because the actors care only that they both select the same option, and not on which alternative they coordinate.

If coordination on one alternative is preferred by both to coordination on another alternative (e.g., McDonald's is preferred by both to Burger King), then we call it a Hi-Lo Coordination Game, as in figure 8.1(b). The higher payoffs when coordinating on B (2,2) than on C (1,1) implies that both prefer coordinating on B than on C. If each party most prefers a different coordinated action (e.g., Adam prefers McDonald's but Eve prefers Burger King), then we call it an Impure Coordination or Battle-of-the-Sexes Game, as depicted in Figure 8.1(c).

Another class of coordination games, called distributed action games, are ones in which coordination only succeeds if the parties all select different actions. For example, suppose a potluck dinner only succeeds if one actor brings a main course and another brings dessert. If it does not matter who brings what so the scenario is symmetric, then we have a Pure Distributed Action Game. In the Hi-Lo Distributed Action Game, both actors prefer one way of distributing actions (e.g., Adam brings main course and Eve brings dessert). In the Impure Distributed Action Game, actors differ in how they rank different ways of distributing actions.[24]

A key feature of coordination games is that there are multiple ways of coordinating and multiple ways of miscoordinating, and the collective action problem is that actors may not successfully coordinate. A large literature establishes that the key to resolving coordination problems is to create "shared beliefs" (also called "common knowledge" or "common expectations") among the actors about what each other will do.[25] For example, in a Pure Coordination Game, if Adam and Eve both believe each other will choose restaurant B, then each has an incentive to also choose restaurant B, and successful coordination on restaurant B will occur. Technically speaking, common knowledge exists when each actor knows what the other will do, both know that both know what

(a) Pure Coordination (Focal Action)

Eve \ Adam	B	C
B	1,1	0,0
C	0,0	1,1

(b) Hi-Lo Coordination Game

Eve \ Adam	B	C
B	2,2	0,0
C	0,0	1,1

(c) Impure Coordination Game (Battle of Sexes)

Eve \ Adam	B	C
B	2,1	0,0
C	0,0	1,2

FIGURE 8.1. Simple 2×2 Coordination Games.

the other will do, both know that both know that both know what the other will do, and so on. In short, actors must share accurate beliefs about what others will do.

It follows that the important question is how the actors achieve shared beliefs about the joint plan. In scenarios with few people, cheap communication, and closely aligned preferences, then agreement by communication may easily create shared expectations. In scenarios with large numbers of actors, costly communication, a degree of disagreement in tastes, and frequently changing circumstances, actors often resort to social devices for the creation of shared expectations.

There are many kinds of social devices that align expectations, and it is convenient to distinguish these by their level of formality. On one end of the spectrum are informal conventions and social norms that emerge in a community, perhaps even without any apparent purposeful design, possibly enforced by a threat of social sanction. Examples include hairstyles and manners. On another end of the spectrum are institutionally designated leaders and official policies, such as company presidents and enacted legislation. These classifications are useful but not strict. A coordinating device may move from one category to another. An example is a social convention that becomes a formal policy, such as the dress standards at work.

To understand how these devices coordinate, consider a publicly designated leader. If the leader announces that everyone should go to restaurant B and nobody else gets to make an announcement, then a belief that everyone else will follow the leader is enough to convince an actor to follow the leader. Given the presumption that the leader will be followed, the leader's announcement is a salient device that serves to generate shared expectations. Commonly known norms and conventions serve a similar function because their wide acceptance yields shared expectations about behavior.

Authority

Coordinating devices direct action by creating shared expectations about what others will do, i.e., by creating common knowledge. We can thus say that these coordinating devices have authority. Authority is here defined as the right to direct action.[26] Because actions are inalienable (not tradable), an actor cannot give up her ability to act, but she can allow a device to direct (i.e., suggest, propose, instruct) her action. A right is a commonly recognized, social agreement about who is allowed to make a choice.[27] A right might or might not be legal, and there might be disagreement about how the right is used, but the existence of a right implies sufficient consensus about the identity of which actor or device makes the choice. A device has authority when it is recognized by the relevant social actors as having the right to direct action. Leaders are devices in the form of persons with authority to direct certain actions. Norms are devices in which the members of the community have authority to direct action.

These devices have authority because of their ability to coordinate action, yet conflict may still exist. Conflict with respect to rights can exist for two reasons. First, different actors may have different beliefs about what device has the right to direct action. For example, a student might believe she has the right to trample the flowers in front of the school, but the school principal might disagree. Because the right only exists, by definition, when there is sufficient consensus, social actors use various mechanisms to create agreement about rights. Rituals provide one formalized means of creating agreement about who has rights, such as an elected official whose right to act in office is only official upon being sworn in; I return to the role of rituals in Mormonism below. Traditions also create agreement about rights, such as in a family where the grandparents' choice of what to eat for the holiday dinner is never disputed.

The second type of conflict is that, even if actors agree on who has the right, there may exist disagreement regarding how that right is used. For example, I might agree that my neighbor has the right to allow her front yard to fall into disrepair but disagree with her decision to allow it, or we may agree that the social norm is that I not tattoo an expletive on my forehead, even though I may sincerely want such a tattoo. Notice that the device's authority can still be respected even with such disagreement.

If, in figure 8.1(c), Eve acts as leader and publicly announces to Adam that they should go to restaurant B for dinner, then Adam still has the incentive to follow Eve's lead even though he prefers restaurant C, assuming that he believes Eve will go to restaurant B. That is, coordination will work even with disagreement as long as the actors' values are sufficiently aligned.

There are still other aspects of authority that could be considered, but I here restrict my attention to the role of authority in creating shared expectations in Mormonism because, according to the theory, that is the primary function of authority.

Authority Devices in Mormonism

Formal Authority

The authoritarian reputation of the LDS Church is often associated with the church's formal hierarchical structure. Except for the relatively small professional clergy named "General Authorities" located largely at church headquarters in Salt Lake City, Utah, the LDS Church is run entirely by lay members. The worldwide church membership is partitioned geographically into wards and branches (individual congregations) and stakes and districts (collections of five to ten neighboring wards and branches).[28] Wards and stakes (akin to parishes and dioceses in the Roman Catholic Church) constitute the local level in which essentially all church-related activities take place under the direction of local leaders. Each local leader is appointed by the leader one step higher in the organizational hierarchy. In Mormon terminology, an appointment is referred to as a "calling" because the appointee is considered "called by God" to fill the position.[29] This terminology is used for all positions, both leadership and nonleadership, and all members are encouraged to have a position, or a "calling." The positions and the authoritative scope of those positions are defined in the official handbooks that are published and disseminated from headquarters as the official guide for local leaders.[30]

Figure 8.2 presents a network depiction of some of the key leadership callings in a ward. The directed arrows represent the position making the appointment of another position; e.g., the bishop, who is the leader for the entire congregation, appoints ("extends the calling") to all other leaders of the ward. Two exceptions are the high priest group leader and elders quorum president, who are appointed by the stake president upon recommendation by the bishop, depicted by the dotted line. Also depicted by a dotted line is the position of Area Authority which acts as liaison between General Authorities and stake leaders. These arrows also reflect the order of directed action. Each ward leader has particular responsibilities with a degree of flexibility within the bounds of the position's responsibilities (as defined in the Church Handbook of Instructions), but each ward leader regularly reports to, consults, and takes direction from the bishop. Most ward leaders also have officially appointed counselors or

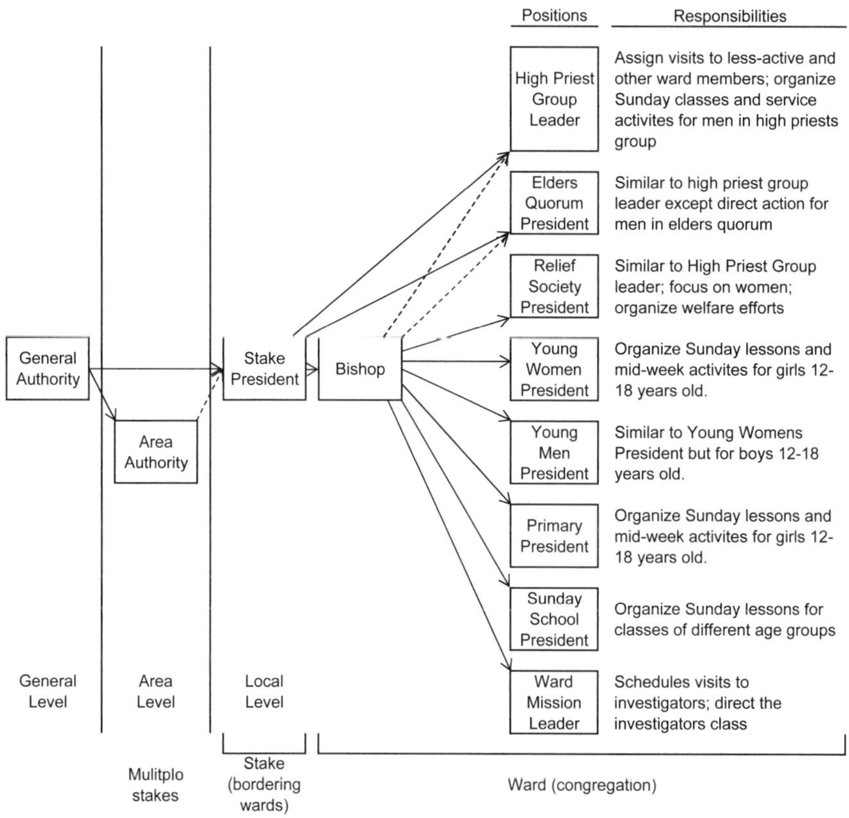

FIGURE 8.2. Ward Leadership Callings. Note that all leaders at the local level except the ward mission leader have two counselors and a secretary to assist. Stake leaders (more than thirty men and women per stake) are not listed here to conserve space.

assistants (not shown in figure) to help in carrying out their responsibilities. Altogether, thirty or more individuals will serve in ward leadership positions in a fully staffed ward. Other ward members may serve in stake leadership positions (also not shown). Furthermore, there are dozens of other nonleadership callings within a ward, most of which involve teaching classes within the various church organizations.

According to the Church Handbook, "The Church of Jesus Christ of Latter-day Saints was organized by God to assist in His work to bring to pass the salvation and exaltation of his children."[31] In wards and stakes, this general commission is broken down into smaller categories: "This work of salvation includes member missionary work, convert retention, activation of less-active members, temple and family history work, and teaching the gospel."[32] Each church member is responsible to help accomplish these tasks, but their efforts are organized by the local leaders. Thus, the church's mission essentially puts into practice a large number of coordination problems, with success in each domain dependent on the successful coordination of many persons' efforts.

A few examples will illustrate the point. Member missionary work involves members sharing church teachings with nonmember friends, inviting them to church events, working with full-time missionaries to teach potential converts, preparing themselves and youth to serve as full-time missionaries, and more. This work is directed by the bishop and ward mission leader.[33] The ward mission leader meets with full-time and ward missionaries, arranges visits with nonmember investigators, organizes special Sunday School classes for investigators, and more. Coordinating these tasks is a type of distributed action problem, where different members are asked to undertake different responsibilities that together create a friendly environment for investigators and a higher chance of conversion. With many possible investigators to choose from, the bishop and ward mission leader must also determine which investigators will receive which sort of personal attention, and this is a kind of focal action problem. Working to increase the participation levels of "less-active" members involves a similar kind of organized effort. Bishops and other ward leaders including Relief Society presidents, elders quorum presidents, and high priest group leaders identify which actions are to be taken (focal action) and then assign different ward members to carry them out (distributed action). This includes assigning ward members to make in-home visits, extending invitations to receive gospel lessons or participate in ward events, and more.

The bishop plays the central role in all of the above and more in a ward. He, in prayerful consultation with counselors, identifies persons to fill different callings (distributed action), plans and organizes weekly church services (distributed action), and identifies and selects what short- and medium-term goals should be pursued by the ward (focal action). Overall, the amount of effort spent undertaking actions directed by a ward leader is tremendous, by one estimate up to six hundred hours of voluntary labor per week in a single ward congregation.[34] The role of leaders is vital in all ward efforts. The Handbook has an entire chapter on basic leadership principles and ward leaders undergo regular training by stake leaders and General Authorities.

Coordination directed by leaders occurs at other levels of the church organization. The leaders of a stake teach and train ward leaders, plan and carry out stake-level activities, appoint stake and certain ward leaders, and meet with ward leaders.[35] In some cases, these responsibilities involve solving stake-level coordination problems, such as the organizing of stake-level social or service activities. In other cases, these activities involve helping the ward leaders become better leaders, thereby improving ward-level coordination. Coordination at the level of the entire church is directed by General

Authorities, including the First Presidency and the Quorum of Twelve Apostles. Committees headed by these and other leaders must solve distributed action problems such as how to distribute tithing donations collected from around the world back to congregations as well as to humanitarian and welfare efforts and how to allocate full-time missionary volunteers (currently numbering some eighty thousand) to various mission locations around the world.

General leaders must also solve focal action problems. For example, by setting official policies, general leaders create uniform expectations about membership, administration, and conditions for group membership, thereby coordinating behavior by members worldwide. The Church Handbook lists a number of official policies (e.g., open flames and lighted candles may not be used in church buildings) and stances (e.g., the King James Version of the Bible should be used) and also clarifies that there is no official stance on some issues (e.g., birth control is neither encouraged nor discouraged).[36] These policies solve focal action problems by creating a uniform expectation about appropriate behavior for leaders, organizing of church services, and more. This coordination, by being directed high up in the church hierarchy, creates a uniform experience for members around the world, thereby increasing a sense of unity and community.

Informal Authority

Though formal authority devices are more readily visible than informal authority devices in Mormon congregations, the informal devices also play fundamental roles in coordinating congregational life. Because these are less visible, they cannot be as systematically reviewed as the formal authority devices despite their ubiquity. Nonetheless, the important role of unofficial yet commonly recognized behavioral codes was acknowledged by Elder Boyd K. Packer of the Quorum of Twelve Apostles, the LDS Church's second-highest governing body. In a well-known sermon, Elder Packer specifically mentioned a number of behaviors that are not written in canonized scripture or handbooks but that constitute the "unwritten order of things."[37] A few of these are: the highest ranking leader at a meeting should sit on the stand; a member should not decline a calling when extended, nor should a member ask to be released from a calling; a person should ask a family member first for a blessing, then a home teacher; and a person should approach a family member first for advice and counsel, then the bishop, but not a General Authority of the church.

Speaking of this unwritten code of conduct, Elder Packer explained: "Although they are very ordinary things, they are nevertheless, very important! . . . [They] are not so rigid that the Church will fall apart if they are not strictly observed all the time. But they do set a tone, a standard, of dignity and order and will improve our meetings and classwork; they will improve the activities." He also referred to passages in the LDS scriptural canon that state the importance of "order." These norms thus establish standards relating to the proper way to conduct church services, the proper way to enlist help from others, and more, to create an orderly experience for church members. Having a set of behaviors identified as proper, even if unwritten, creates a shared expectation about the appropriate way to behave. The unwritten order directs action by coordinating church members' behavior. In other words, as defined in this paper, the unwritten rules have authority.

Packer also acknowledged one of the difficulties with unwritten rules, namely, that the learning of these rules by members is not systematic. Indeed, the very purpose of his talk is to teach those who have not yet learned them through observation: "We somehow assume that everybody knows all the ordinary things already. If you do know them, you must have learned them through observation and experience, for they are not written anywhere and they are not taught in classes. So, as we continue, if you are ones that know it all, please be patient while I teach those who do not." His sermon thus alerted the listeners to the existence of the unwritten norms and, by virtue of the sermon's public nature, created a shared understanding of these norms for the listeners through the spoken word delivered by a leader universally recognized within the church as having great authority. In other words, Packer's sermon was itself given to help create shared expectations about the unwritten order.

"Authority" and "Priesthood"

The key role of shared expectations in the economic view of authority should be distinguished from normal usage of the word "authority" in LDS communities. The entry for "Authority" in the semiofficial *Encyclopedia of Mormonism* identifies multiple usages of the term in common practice but emphasizes that primary usage within the church associates authority with divinely given power and permission to act as an agent for God, called "priesthood."[38] Figure 8.3 charts how the LDS concept of priesthood compares with the social scientific definition of authority used in this paper. Whereas authority as used herein refers to a socially recognized right to direct action, priesthood is understood as a power and right to act for God. Whereas authority can be vested in a variety of devices, both personal and impersonal, priesthood office can only be given to worthy male individuals (generally called priesthood holders). Whereas a device's authority exists with sufficient social consensus about the device's right to direct action, priesthood office is given only through a ritual ordination using laying on of hands. Whereas authority can be downward (the leader acts on behalf of God or another official of higher rank) or upward (the leader acts on behalf of member constituents), priesthood is described as downward (priesthood power is believed to

	Authority (Social Scientific)	LDS Priesthood
Definition	Socially recognized right to direct action	Power of and right to act for God
Type of Device	Individuals, roles, formal rules, unwritten rules	Individuals (Priesthood holders)
Requirements for existence	Social consensus that device directs action	Conferral/ordination by laying on of hands
Agency relationship	Downward or upward	Downward, in chain back to God

FIGURE 8.3. Comparison of social scientific authority and LDS priesthood.

ultimately originate with God, and priesthood authority is divested downward through ever-decreasing-in-scope, partitioned leadership roles).

In many respects, the LDS concept of priesthood could be viewed as one type of social scientifically conceived form of authority in LDS communities, albeit a singularly important one.[39] This view is largely accurate though it misses some subtleties. For example, priesthood power and authority is widely understood by Mormons to be held by God independently of any social agreement among humans about God's right to hold the priesthood. Thus, to a Mormon, God has authority whether or not people allow God to direct action, while the social scientist would say that God does not have authority if God's right to direct action is not commonly recognized.

The Ritual Creation of Authority

As defined, authority exists when there is sufficient consensus that a device has the right to direct action. But with many possible coordinating devices, the selection of a device is itself a second-order coordination problem that, once solved, helps to solve the original, first-order coordination problem. Consider the simple Battle-of-the-Sexes game in figure 8.1(c). If Eve is leader, she will choose her preferred restaurant; if Adam is the leader, he will choose his preferred restaurant. If both try to be leader, then they are back to conflict, and if neither is leader, then they are also back to the original coordination problem. If one person needs to exercise leadership but both cannot simultaneously be leaders, then how is the leader chosen? This problem of leadership selection has actually been studied under the name the Leadership Game, which is represented as an impure, distributed action coordination problem akin to this Battle-of-the-Sexes game.[40]

Drawing from the game-theoretic analysis of coordination games, Michael Chwe argues that public rituals provide one way to create shared expectations, thereby facilitating coordination.[41] That the ritual is public is crucial to his argument because only the *public* ritual can create common knowledge of beliefs. Royal processions are one example in which the king's or queen's identity is made public knowledge, thus cementing his or her position as leader. In other words, a public ritual is used to solve the Leadership Game.

This insight has direct application to the selection and installment of leaders in the LDS Church. The invitation to fill a position is made in downward fashion, as depicted in figure 8.2, with the leader at the next level up privately extending the invitation. However, before the person begins functioning in that position, the person must, according to Mormon scripture and official Handbook policy, be ritually "sustained" via a public vote in front of the entire congregation (or set of congregations for stake leaders, or the entire church for General Authorities). This sustaining vote is not a vote for one candidate over another, as only the proposed and "called" person is presented to the congregation. Rather, it is a public display by the members of the congregation of their willingness to support the person in his or her responsibilities.[42] Congregation members supporting the proposed action first vote to sustain by raising the right hand, and then those who oppose the action can vote in opposition in like manner. A sustaining vote is held for each person newly assigned to each position, whether leadership or not, and leaders with larger responsibilities are also sustained annually at ward and stake conferences.

The public nature of the sustaining vote creates authority by creating multiple layers of shared beliefs and common knowledge, called "common consent" in LDS scripture.[43] The leader's identity is publicly revealed by the announcement, thus resolving the Leadership Game. The public signals of support in the form of the raised hand create a shared belief that others will follow the leader. Everyone's hand can be seen, as well as lack of disapproval if no hand is raised in opposition. A unanimous vote in the affirmative (which almost invariably occurs) implies that the leader's right to direct action is commonly acknowledged, thereby satisfying the conditions necessary for that person to have authority as defined here. Moreover, this creation of authority occurs for every person and every position, not just those positions normally considered leadership positions, so it is accurate to say that every person in a position has some amount of authority. For example, the teacher of a Sunday School class for teenagers has authority to direct action with respect to the associated teaching responsibilities. Although the "leadership" label is used in Mormon congregations to refer to specific positions with larger administrative scope, every person acting in a position is in some sense a leader because he or she directs action in some form or another.

Authority is thus created in the act of sustaining, but this is not how Mormons would understand it. Rather, authority is understood to be bestowed through appropriate priesthood channels via the laying on of hands in a ritual "setting apart," which occurs subsequent to the congregation's sustaining vote.[44] With hands laid on the person's head, the priesthood leader bestows the rights to function in the position and pronounces a blessing of encouragement and support. This ritual bestowing of authority is conducted in private for most positions, but it is sometimes done in public for some callings, such as elders quorum presidency members in front of the elders quorum.

Here we see how the Mormon notion of bestowed authority differs subtly from the social scientific understanding of authority. To a social scientist, authority is created during the sustaining vote because it is then that common knowledge about the person's right to direct action is created and expressed, but in Mormon doctrine the authority is bestowed, normally privately, via laying on of hands. This practice of combining public sustaining with private setting apart thus reflects a balancing of two competing demands: the first is the creation of shared belief in the person's right to direct action which allows for upward authority; the second is the reinforcing of the notion of downward bestowal of rights to act. The former satisfies the social requirements of common knowledge creation, while the latter satisfies the doctrinal position that all authority goes down from God though appropriate leaders in the priesthood hierarchy to the person.

An obvious question is: Why does the church not have as a policy that each setting apart also take place publicly? A public setting apart would further reinforce the authority of the newly appointed person by creating shared knowledge of the bestowal of authority. Whereas Mormon scripture and the Church Handbooks require a public sustaining vote, the procedures for setting apart do not specify that it be done in private or in public.[45] Indeed, there is no official explanation for the practice of private setting apart. Possible reasons could be that a private setting apart is more intimate for the person and his or her family, that it saves scarce time in the congregational meetings, and that the setting apart could be combined with initial instructions in duties not relevant for the entire congregation. Whatever the original intent of the practice, it now constitutes yet another example of the "unwritten order of things" described earlier; it emerged over time and continues to guide action despite not being formally prescribed.

The Stability and Fragility of a Social Norm's Authority

Adherence to many social norms follows a tipping-point logic.[46] An actor adheres to the norm if the number of others adhering to the norm exceeds a threshold. If all people have the same threshold, then the scenario is a many-person, symmetric, focal action coordination game with two stable behavioral patterns: all adhere or none adhere. More generally, there is variation in thresholds across persons; some always adhere, some never adhere, and the rest have varying threshold levels.

The general situation is illustrated in figure 8.4(a). The S-shaped curve identifies the number of people willing to adhere to the behavior given the number of people expected to adhere, and the dotted line is a 45-degree line. That the curve is positively sloped reflects the threshold nature of norm adherence: as the number expected to adhere increases, the number willing to adhere increases. The S-shape reflects the idea that most people have a threshold somewhere in the middle of the population. If the actual number is less than expected (i.e., S-curve below the 45-degree line), then the number expected declines, and the number adhering declines. If the actual is greater than expected (i.e., S-curve above the 45-degree line), then the number expected increases, and the number adhering increases. The arrows in figure 8.4(b) reflect these dynamics and reveal that the system has three equilibrium behavioral outcomes where the curve crosses the 45-degree line. The filled circles labeled *a* and *c* mark the stable behavioral equilibria, where small deviations drive the system back to the equilibrium. The *a* equilibrium has low adherence, while the *c* equilibrium has high adherence. The empty circle labeled *b* is an unstable behavioral equilibrium; a small deviation from circle *b* drives the system away. This unstable point *b* also serves as a critical mass point; if the system can get to the critical mass or just beyond it, then the entire system shifts.

These diagrams illustrate how difficult it can be to switch norms. If the society is at point *a*, then a shift to point *c* requires getting a large mass of people to switch their expectations about how others will behave. If such a shift is able to happen, then a dramatic change in behavior can occur rapidly. However, if there is no centralized actor or device that can create a shared expectation of this shift, then it is difficult to get past the critical point. Such is the case for informal norms that have emerged in communities without any direct hand. A norm that emerged without any explicit direction is not controlled by any particular actor, and thus no single actor is understood as directing the action. In such a case, the norm is very unlikely to switch from a change in expectations alone. A change in the distribution of tipping points is more likely to cause the shift, because the sheer difficulty in creating a shared belief about a switch in the norm is too difficult a hurdle to overcome. Figure 8.4(c) illustrates how a small shift in the distribution from *A* to *A″* leads to a small change from *a* to *a′*, but that a further small shift to *A″* in the distribution leads to a dramatic shift from *a′* to *a″*. The change in behavior can be quite rapid once the critical mass point is reached, yet the changes in the distribution of tipping points may change slowly over time. Thus, the rapid changes may be difficult to predict, but once the tipping point is crossed, the behavior can change rapidly.

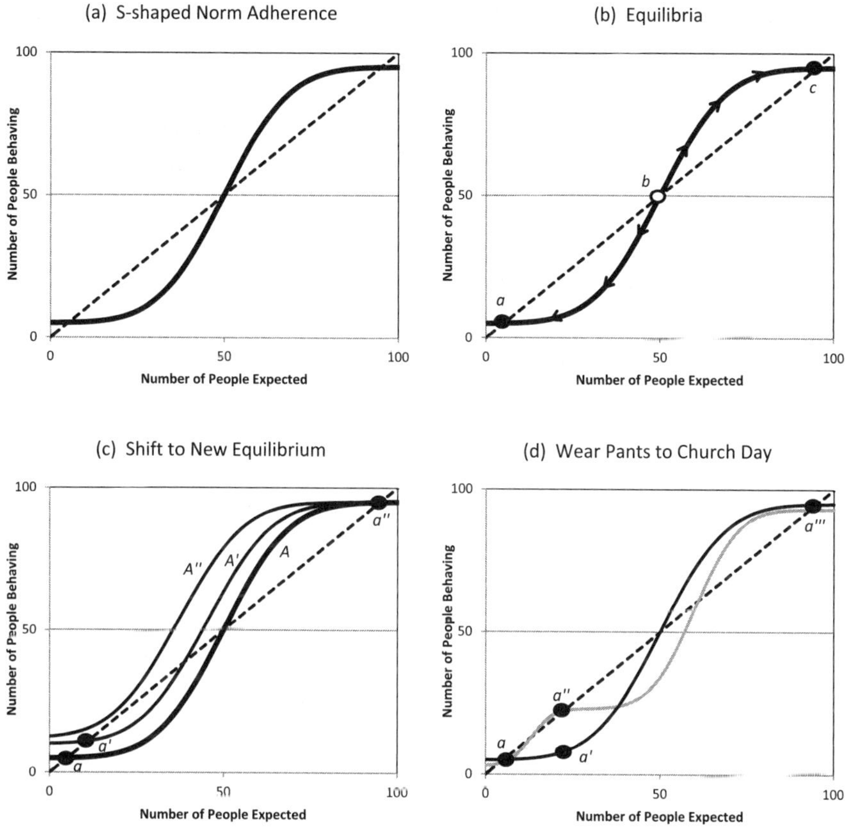

FIGURE 8.4. Social norms and tipping points.

Using this framework, I now examine a norm in Mormonism that recently received national attention when it was publicly challenged—the norm that women wear dresses or skirts instead of pants when attending Mormon Sunday services.[47] A group of Mormon women made a collective effort to violate the norm by wearing pants to Sunday services on December 16, 2012, an event they called "Wear Pants to Church Day."[48] The dress standard being challenged is an informal norm rather than an official policy because the church's official position is that it does not have a position for or against women wearing pants to church services.[49] That some critics of the event sought to enforce the norm by vocally criticizing the participants reveals how widely known the norm is within the community. Wearing a dress or skirt is what emerged over time in the community as the way for a woman to show proper respect for God while at Sunday church services. Because different dress standards could potentially be understood as respectful, for the public display of respect to be adequately conveyed to community members, those community members must agree on what constitutes respectful dress. Coordination is crucial. The organizers of the event proposed that women wear dress pants rather than sweats or jogging pants, which indicates that they were proposing to modify the existing norm rather than get rid of a dress norm altogether.[50]

Another norm challenged by the Wear Pants to Church Day event is the norm against public displays of disapproval with the church. The organizers of the event explained that their purpose was not so much the wearing of pants but rather the public showing of a united front on the matter of gender inequities in the Mormon community. Some opponents of the event criticized the event's participants not for wearing pants but instead for using church services as a venue to advance their own ideal. As one critic said, "I am disappointed that anyone would choose sacrament meeting to carry out a personal agenda (regardless of whether or not they believe it is for the common good). . . . This call for action is an act of contention and has no place in Sacrament meeting."[51] There is no official church policy against such coordinated efforts, so again we have a norm that is enforced by the community.

The event was coordinated via social media (Facebook) and was at the time called "the largest concerted Mormon feminist effort in history" by one participant-observer.[52] The social media provided a unique forum for the organizers to create a shared belief among the participants about the number of other participants in the event, thereby facilitating their coordinated wearing of pants. Though this effort was known by participants and many online observers, it was not, however, known by the entire church community, and many congregations would have no participants. Those that did have participants would have had a few women in pants at most, and if the event was unknown by other congregation members, then the appearance of a few pants-wearing women at church services one Sunday may not disturb the normal course of the church services. It may have been perceived as a norm violation by many, but it still might not cause large waves or be understood as part of a larger movement or as a symbolic statement without prior knowledge of the intent behind the wearing of pants. This lack of full public awareness thus limited the ability of the organizers to reach critical mass for a full switch to a new dress norm, and there is no indication that a fundamental shift in the norm has occurred.[53]

That there has been no shift in the norm can be understood in different ways, two of which are depicted in figure 8.4(d). If the actual distribution of tipping points is the black curve, then the Wear Pants to Church Day event could be understood as a temporary but still unsuccessful shift in behavior, such as a move from *a* to *a′*, only to shift back down to *a*. If the actual distribution is the gray curve, then the Wear Pants to Church Day event achieved an initial critical mass among Mormon feminists, thus moving the equilibrium from *a* to *a″*, but was not sufficient to achieve the full complete critical mass necessary to bring the system to *a‴*.

These diagrams reveal the inherent difficulty of switching to a new norm. Switching from one equilibrium to another requires a critical mass shift in expectations, and by virtue of being an informal norm there is no centralized method of generating this critical mass. Indeed, this is true despite the national media coverage of the event. Social media fostered coordination among the set of Mormon feminist participants but not among the majority of churchgoers who were completely unaware of the event. As explained earlier, even seeing the participants wear pants to church services might not have been interpreted by most churchgoers as a shift toward a new dress standard or a social protest but rather as just unconventional or even disrespectful dress. The critical mass logic of social norms implies that this norm can change rapidly and unexpectedly once the change begins. However, the analysis suggests that, because of the difficulty in reaching a critical mass through communication for such a large body of churchgoers, the norm is more likely to shift from an underlying change in the distribution of tipping points rather than by intentionally coordinated events.

This analysis also reveals a subtle matter about authority in religious communities. Authority is often depicted as something under the control of a few elites or leaders, but recognizing the informal authority of social norms reveals how authority in communities is more complex. Yes, LDS Church leaders direct action on a large scale, but not everything within Mormon communities is under the control of church leaders. Social norms that emerge from the actions of community members rather than the dictates of church leaders govern many aspects of Mormon life. In other words, the authority of LDS Church leaders, though extensive, is not complete. Indeed, regular, churchgoing Mormons have their own share of authority in the community. The Mormon identity is thus only partially controlled by church leaders. Wearing pants to church could very well someday become a widely accepted practice, but if it does, it will likely be through the changing perceptions of appropriate dress by Mormons themselves.

Conclusion

This paper presents the first rational choice analysis of authority in Mormonism. As presented herein, authority functions to coordinate action by creating the shared beliefs among actors necessary for that coordination. I provide examples of many coordination problems in Mormon congregational and community life for which various forms of authority serve to solve. I also use the theory to examine the creation of formal authority via the ritual act of sustaining and the difficulty in shifting social norms about appropriate dress. A contribution of this approach is its actor-level description of how authority devices serve as stabilizing factors in Mormon communities. That the authority devices yield shared expectations and mental constructs also aids in the very creation of a Mormon community because the domain of the authority structures acts as a kind of marker of the community's boundary.

Moreover, the role that these devices play in Mormon communities will, in principle, be similar across many different religious communities. Though the manifestations of the authority structures in Mormonism may be unique (such as a norm that women should not wear pants to Sunday church services), the presence of authority structures is not. It is in this generalizability that we see one of the primary contributions of a social scientific approach to the study of human behavior, i.e., the construction of theories of human action meant to apply across a broad domain of human life experience. This attempt to generalize stands in contrast to much work in the humanities that focuses on the particularities of individual cases, yet it also reveals where the social scientific and the humanistic approaches may complement each other. The humanist's study of the uniqueness of the actor's or community's experience fills in gaps in the social scientist's theory, while the social scientist's theory places the unique experience within the larger social patterns and structures.

In the academic field known as Mormon studies, which has been dominated largely by humanists, this attempt at generalization should be welcome. The methodological approaches of the humanist and the social scientist each have their own advantages and disadvantages. Identifying how they complement one another would result in not only a richer Mormon studies, but also a Mormon studies that gains wider appreciation from those outside the field. The Mormon experience is a part of human experience, and as such should inform our larger understanding of human experience.

Notes

For valuable comments and feedback, I thank Caroline Kline, Patrick Mason, and participants of "Beyond the Mormon Moment: Directions for Mormon Studies in the New Century," a conference held at Claremont Graduate University in March 2013. I also acknowledge financial support from Army Research Office Award No. W911NF-11-1-0332 and Air Force Office of Scientific Research Award No. FA9550-10-1-0569.

1. For general treatments of Mormon history and culture, see Leonard Arrington and Davis Bitton, *The Mormon Experience: A History of the Latter-day Saints* (Urbana: University of Illinois Press, 1992); Richard Ostling and Joan Ostling, *Mormon America: The Power and the Promise* (New York: Harper Collins Publishers, 1999); Claudia Bushman, *Contemporary Mormonism: Latter-day Saints in Modern America* (Westport, CT: Praeger, 2006); and Matthew Bowman, *The Mormon People: The Making of an American Faith* (New York: Random House, 2012).
2. The associations have been made frequently, in numerous contexts, and by a wide range of observers both inside and outside the church. A small sample includes D. Michael

Quinn, "Echoes and Foreshadowings: The Distinctiveness of the Mormon Community," *Sunstone* 3 (1978): 12–17; D. Michael Quinn, "From Sacred Grove to Sacral Power Structure," *Dialogue: A Journal of Mormon Thought* 17 (1984): 9–34; Thomas O'Dea, "Mormonism and the Avoidance of Sectarian Stagnation: A Study of Church, Sect, and Incipient Nationality," *American Journal of Sociology* 60 (1954): 285–93; Thomas O'Dea, *The Mormons* (Chicago: University of Chicago Press, 1957); O. Kendall White and Daryl White, "A Critique of Leone's and Dolgin's Application of Bellah's Evolutionary Model to Mormonism," *Review of Religious Research* 23 (1981): 39–53; Armand L. Mauss, *The Angel and the Beehive: The Mormon Struggle with Assimilation* (Urbana: University of Illinois Press, 1994); and M. Lou Chandler, "Why Do Some Perceive the Church to Be a Cult? Inside and Outside Perceptions versus Reality," *Dialogue: A Journal of Mormon Thought* 28 (1995): 121–33. Janet Dolgin, "Latter-day Sense and Substance," in *Religious Movements in Contemporary America*, ed. Irving Karetsky and Mark Leone (Princeton, NJ: Princeton University Press, 1976), 519, and Mark Leone, "The Economic Basis for the Evolution of the Mormon Religion," in Karetsky and Leone, *Religious Movements in Contemporary America*, 722, suggest Mormonism is less authoritarian than supposed. Chiung Hwang Chen and Ethan Yorgason, "'Those Amazing Mormons': The Media's Construction of Latter-day Saints as a Model Minority," *Dialogue* 32 (1999): 107–28, identify ambiguity in media representations of Mormons. Terryl Givens, *People of Paradox: A History of Mormon Culture* (Oxford: Oxford University Press, 2007), explores the tension within Mormonism between authority and personal freedom. For a review of social-scientific studies of Mormonism, see Armand L. Mauss, "Flowers, Weeds, and Thistles: The State of Social Science Literature on the Mormons," in *Mormon History*, ed. Ronald Walker, David Whittaker, and James Allen (Urbana: University of Illinois Press, 2001).

3. See Mario De Pillis, "The Quest for Religious Authority and the Rise of Mormonism," *Dialogue: A Journal of Mormon Thought* 1 (1966): 68–88.
4. For the Mormons' own view of authority, see the "Authority" entry in Daniel Ludlow, ed., *Encyclopedia of Mormonism* (New York: Macmillan Publishing Company, 1992). For examinations of Mormonism's critics, see J. Spencer Fluhman, *"A Peculiar People": Anti-Mormonism and the Making of Religion in Nineteenth-Century America* (Chapel Hill: University of North Carolina Press, 2012); and Terryl Givens, *The Viper on the Hearth: Mormons, Myth, and the Construction of Heresy* (New York: Oxford University Press, 2013).
5. For arguments of proponents and critics, see, respectively, Lawrence Young, ed., *Rational Choice Theory and Religion: Summary and Assessment* (New York: Routledge, 1997); and Steve Bruce, *Choice and Religion: A Critique of Rational Choice* (New York: Oxford University Press, 1999).
6. Rodney Stark and Roger Finke, *Acts of Faith: Explaining the Human Side of Religion* (Berkeley: University of California Press, 2000), provide a comprehensive depiction of the rational choice approach to religion from their sociological point of view. Laurence Iannaccone, "Introduction to the Economics of Religion," *Journal of Economic Literature* 36 (1998): 1465–96, provides a good introduction to economists' work. R. Stephen Warner, "Work in Progress Toward a New Paradigm for the Sociological Study of Religion in

the United States," *American Journal of Sociology* 98 (1993): 1044–93, labels the rational choice approach a "new paradigm" in the study of religion.

7. The seminal book, Stark and Finke, *Acts of Faith*, does not offer any theory of authority. A recent attempt is Michael McBride, "A Rational Choice Theory of Religious Authority," manuscript in author's possession (2013).
8. Rodney Stark, *The Rise of Mormonism*, ed. Reid Neilson (New York: Columbia University Press Stark, 2005), provides a compilation of his essays on Mormonism, but examples drawn from Mormonism also permeate the more comprehensive treatment in Stark and Finke, *Acts of Faith*.
9. Mauss, *The Angel and the Beehive*, draws heavily from the rational choice literature while simultaneously advancing the theory by developing the notion of optimum tension. Armand L. Mauss, "Mormonism in the Twenty-First Century: Marketing for Miracles," *Dialogue: A Journal of Mormon Thought* 29 (1996): 236–49, and Armand L. Mauss, "Seeking a 'Second Harvest': Controlling the Costs of LDS Membership in Europe," *Dialogue: A Journal of Mormon Thought* 41 (2007): 1–54, provide more recent analyses of Mormonism in the twenty-first century.
10. See Laurence Iannaccone and Carrie Miles, "Dealing with Social Change: The Mormon Church's Response to Change in Women's Roles," *Social Forces* 68 (1990): 1231–50.
11. Michael McBride, "Club Mormon: Free-riders, Monitoring, and Exclusion in the LDS Church," *Rationality and Society* 19 (2007): 395–424.
12. Max Weber, *Economy and Society: An Outline of Interpretive Sociology*, ed. Guenther Roth and Claus Wittich (Berkeley: University of California Press, 1922 [1968]).
13. James Coleman, *Foundations of Social Theory* (Cambridge, MA: Harvard University Press, 1990).
14. See references in Michael McBride, "A Rational Choice Theory of Religious Authority."
15. E.g., Iannaccone, "Introduction to the Economics of Religion," and McBride, "Club Mormon."
16. Thomas Schelling, *The Strategy of Conflict* (Cambridge, MA: Harvard University Press, 1960); Thomas Schelling, *Micromotives and Macrobehavior* (New York: Norton, 1978); David Lewis, *Convention* (Oxford: Blackwell Publishing, 1969).
17. Michael Chwe, *Rational Ritual: Culture, Coordination, and Common Knowledge* (Princeton, NJ: Princeton University Press, 2001).
18. Gerald Gaus, *On Philosophy, Politics, and Economics* (Belmont, MA: Thomson, 2008).
19. Samuel Bowles and Herbert Gintis, *A Cooperative Species: Human Reciprocity and Its Evolution* (Princeton, NJ: Princeton University Press, 2011).
20. Stark and Finke, *Acts of Faith*. Mauss, *The Angel and the Beehive*; Mauss, "Mormonism in the Twenty-First Century"; and Mauss, "Seeking a 'Second Harvest.'"
21. Examples include Laurence Iannaccone, "Sacrifice and Stigma: Reducing Free-riding in Cults, Communes, and Other Collectives," *Journal of Political Economy* 100:2 (1992): 271–291. and Michael McBride, "Religious Pluralism and Religious Participation: A Game-Theoretic Analysis," *American Journal of Sociology* 114 (2008): 77–108.
22. Game theory has also been used to interpret Mormon scripture in Robert Schwartz, "Game Theory, the Prisoner's Dilemma, and the Book of Mormon," *BYU Studies Quarterly* 52 (2013): 67–112.

23. This section summarizes the ideas developed in McBride, "Religious Authority."
24. This distinction between focal action and distributed action games is technically artificial though conceptually useful. The actions in distributed action games could be relabeled in a way to convert the distributed action game into a focal action game, thus implying an analytical equivalence between focal action and distributed action games. See Lewis, *Convention*, for discussion. For example, if plan 1 is "Adam brings main course, Eve brings dessert" and plan 2 is "Adam brings dessert, Eve brings main course," then the distributed action potluck scenario can be framed as a focal action game in which success occurs when they choose the same distributed-action plan.
25. Colin Camerer, *Behavioral Game Theory: Experiments in Strategic Interaction* (New York: Russell Sage Foundation, 2003).
26. Coleman, *Social Theory*.
27. Ibid.
28. Smaller congregations are called branches instead of wards, and if there are not enough individual congregations of sufficient size, then instead of a stake it is called a district.
29. See "Callings" entry in Ludlow, *Encyclopedia of Mormonism*.
30. For a history of the Church Handbook and its development and evolution over time, see Michael Paulos, "'Does Not Purport to Comprehend All Matters of Church Government': The LDS General Handbook of Instructions, 1899–2006," *Journal of Mormon History* 38 (2012): 200–25. The current handbook is divided into two sections. Printed copies of Handbook 2 are distributed to all local leaders and are available to the public online on the church's official website. Handbook 1 is only available to bishoprics and stake presidencies and is not made publicly available. It includes detailed information about managing ward and stake finances including tithing donations, maintaining church membership information, conducting disciplinary councils, and other matters of a more sensitive nature.
31. Handbook 2, Section 2.2.
32. Ibid., Section 5.10. These exact activities are defined differently in different places in Handbook 2 but with only minor differences. In one section, the church is described as providing the means for teaching the gospel of Jesus Christ and providing priesthood authority to administer ordinances of salvation (1.1.5), and in another it identifies our divinely appointed responsibilities to help members live the gospel, do missionary work among nonmembers, care for the poor and needy, and enable salvation for the dead (2.2). These descriptions are largely consistent and overlapping.
33. Ibid., Sections 5.1–5.5.
34. Stark reports this estimate from a paper presented by James T. Duke in chapter 4 of *The Rise of Mormonism*.
35. Handbook 2, Sections 15.1–15.6.
36. Ibid., Section 21.
37. Boyd K. Packer, "The Unwritten Order of Things," BYU Devotional Address, October 15, 1996, available at http://emp.byui.edu/huffr/The%20Unwritten%20Order%20of%20Things%20—%20Boyd%20K.%20Packer.htm.
38. See "Authority" and "Priesthood" entries in Ludlow, *Encyclopedia of Mormonism*. Referring to the *Encyclopedia of Mormonism* as "semiofficial" reflects two features of

the publication. On the one hand, the multivolume work was intended to include professional-level entries and is not considered an official text of the church, a point explicitly stated in the preface. On the other hand, the work was produced in collaboration with the church-owned Brigham Young University.

39. For another important dimension of authority, namely that of church doctrine, see Nathan Oman, "A Defense of the Authority of Church Doctrine," *Dialogue: A Journal of Mormon Thought* 40 (2007): 1–28.

40. For the first game-theoretic treatment of the Leadership Game, see Josep Colomer, "Leadership Games in Collective Action," *Rationality and Society* 7 (1995): 225–46. Others have also used the Leadership Game to develop ideas and theories of leadership, e.g., Andrew King, Dominic Johnson, and Mark Van Vugt, "The Origins and Evolution of Leadership," *Current Biology* 19 (2009): R911–R916.

41. Chwe, *Rational Ritual*. For an introduction to the study of ritual, see Ronald Grimes, *Beginnings in Ritual Studies*, 3rd ed. (Waterloo: Ritual Studies International, 2013). For consideration of religious rituals in the Christian tradition, see Paul Bradshaw and John Mellah, *Foundations in Ritual Studies: A Reader for Students of Christian Worship* (Grand Rapids, MI: Baker Academic, 2007).

42. See "Callings" entry in Ludlow, *Encyclopedia of Mormonism*.

43. See *The Doctrine and Covenants of the Church of Jesus Christ of Latter-day Saints* (Salt Lake City: The Church of Jesus Christ of Latter-day Saints, 1981), 26:2.

44. See "Callings" in Ludlow, *Encyclopedia of Mormonism*. One of the church's thirteen Articles of Faith states, "We believe that a man must be called of God, by prophecy, and by the laying on of hands by those who are in authority, to preach the Gospel and administer in the ordinances thereof."

45. See Doctrine and Covenants 20:65. The Handbooks outline the appropriate public audiences for sustaining various positions.

46. Schelling, *Micromotives and Macrobehavior*.

47. Diana Douglas, "Mormon Women Dare to Wear Pants to Church," National Public Radio, December 14, 2012, http://www.npr.org/2012/12/16/167284923/mormon-women-dare-to-wear-pants-to-church; Timothy Pratt, "Mormon Women Set Out to Take a Stand, in Pants," *New York Times*, December 19, 2012, http://www.nytimes.com/2012/12/20/us/19mormon.html?_r=0.

48. Peggy Fletcher Stack, "Mormon 'Pants Day': Debate Heats up as Women Prepare to Dress Down," *Salt Lake Tribune*, December 13, 2012 (updated December 19, 2012), http://www.sltrib.com/sltrib/lifestyle/55464305-80/church-women-mormon-pants.html.csp.

49. For a broader examination of Mormon women's clothing norms, see Katie Clark Blakesley, "'A Style of Our Own': Modesty and Mormon Women, 1951–2008," *Dialogue: A Journal of Mormon Thought* 42 (2009): 20–53. The LDS Church First Presidency issued a statement in 1971 that clarifies there is no official position on women wearing pants; see Hortense Child, "Q&A: When and Where Is It Acceptable for Young Women to Wear Pants when Involved in Church-related Activities?" *Ensign*, December 1974. This position was reiterated by a church spokesperson around the time of the Wear Pants to Church event, as cited in Stack, "Mormon 'Pants Day.'"

50. All Enlisted, "Wear Pants to Church Day," created December 9, 2012, https://www.facebook.com/WearPantsToChurchDay.
51. Erin McBride, "Pants in Church; A Feminist Movement," *Meridian Magazine*, December 13, 2012, http://ldsmag.com/article/1/11915.
52. Pratt, "Mormon Women Set Out."
53. That the event was repeated in December 2013 is evidence that the organizers saw no fundamental change in dress norms after the first event in December 2012. Information about the second event can be obtained on the organizers' Facebook page https://www.facebook.com/WearPantsToChurchDay.

Chapter 9 | Statistical Content Analysis of Historical Documents

A Case for Social Science Analysis in Mormon Studies

Gary Shepherd and Gordon Shepherd

Most historical research and virtually all biography are conceptually grounded within an idiographic framework of analysis. Idiographically, one seeks to objectively describe and, if possible, explain a specified set of uniquely related actions and events that jointly provide a narrative account of how (and sometimes why) particular human outcomes have occurred in the past. To generate this account, researchers seek to locate and verify as much reliable, factual evidence regarding relevant actions and events as possible. Idiographic research is the particularizing science of historical case studies. Most especially, traditional historiography depends on authenticating and analyzing preserved historical documents deemed to be significant for representing the events and actions under study. Subsequently, historians' personal and professional competence in deciphering or interpreting thematic meanings—and consequently formulating valid conclusions about historical events from the documentary evidence—is always crucial. One standard method for comparing and interpreting a set of relevant documents is to read them all carefully and critically while taking notes on their contents, summarizing what appear to be their modal themes, and consequently excerpting selected passages to validate one's inferences about the reasons for and meanings of particular outcomes.

The social science approach to historical questions typically is grounded in nomothetic research, which is the generalizing science of comparative cases. This nomothetic conceptual framework has a different analytical objective than traditional historiography. Rather than focusing on all of the particulars that constitute a specific explanation for a unique outcome, scholars attempt to generate a general explanation for general categories of outcomes. Nomothetically, one looks for larger patterns that are common across individual or group histories. When such patterns are identified, they may become incorporated into theories that can be applied to explaining general outcomes in a number of particular cases. When dealing with historical questions at the nomothetic level of analysis, one could employ the same documentary analysis techniques used by most historians, famously illustrated, for instance, in the pioneering sociological work of Karl Marx, Max Weber, and Robert Merton.[1] An alternative approach, however, and one arguably more suited to nomothetic objectives, would be to perform a statistical content analysis of relevant documentary materials.

Content analysis is a standard methodology widely used in social science for systematically analyzing a set of documents. A statistical content analysis requires that investigators (1) identify a comprehensive list of key words, phrases, or even designated themes that appear in the documents under study; (2) scan every line of every document; and (3) count the number of times, or frequency, with which key words, phrases, or themes actually occur. Once the relevant frequency counts are made, it is possible to process them so that descriptive and inferential statistics can be calculated to aid researchers' interpretations of the documents.

As with any methodology, content analysis has both strengths and weaknesses. It arguably is a more objective way to evaluate written documents, especially when a relatively large number of them constitute a meaningful set of records—such as the semiannually published LDS Conference Reports or Michael Marquardt's compilations of early Mormon patriarchal blessings[2] (to cite two examples from our own work)—that can be used to infer group norms and changing social trends. Enhanced objectivity in the method used for analyzing documents increases the prospects for replicating research findings and, hence, generating greater consensus among scholars. When content analysis methods are used, different researchers can examine the same set of documents and arrive at the same conclusions concerning which group thematic concerns were most or least salient in particular historical periods.

The methodology of content analysis is not, however, a mechanical hermeneutic device for revealing definitive meanings. Statistical word or theme counts may help identify central group concerns, but they do not speak for themselves, and they do not replace the necessary insights of qualified scholars. They must still be interpreted in cultural and historical context and in conjunction with the knowledge of other relevant documentary sources and the investigators' personal insight shaped through trained experience.

In this essay we argue that, given the abundance of primary documentary sources for the study of both early and modern Mormonism, Mormon studies can benefit in significant ways by utilizing the methodology of statistical content analysis. To illustrate both the value of enhanced objectivity and the heightened potential for broader theoretical insights that content analysis methods make possible, we draw upon examples from our own social science analysis of LDS General Conferences and early patriarchal blessings.

LDS General Conference

Published by the University of Utah Press as A *Kingdom Transformed: Themes in the Development of Mormonism*, our study of leader rhetoric at LDS General Conferences covered the first 150 years of Mormon history, from 1830–1979.[3]

Methodology Considerations

Our primary empirical objectives in *Kingdom Transformed* were to: (1) identify the major thematic categories emphasized by LDS general authorities in their conference addresses over the course of Mormon history up until the time our research had begun, (2) chart changes and constants in thematic emphasis over that period of time, and (3) analyze variations in conference themes as a case study for testing various hypotheses derived from sociological theories of development in new religious movements.

The methodology by which we pursued these objectives was to first obtain a representative sample of all recorded and available LDS General Conference addresses given by general authorities from 1830 through 1979. Our basic sampling strategy was to randomly select four conference addresses for each year: three given by LDS authorities for each year (alternating between annual and semiannual conferences) along with one randomly selected address from the current president of the church for every year. These procedures (a more detailed discussion of which—including technical difficulties and their resolution—can be found in *Kingdom Transformed*, Appendix A) resulted in a final sample size of six hundred conference addresses (including a few appropriate nonconference substitute documents for years with a dearth of recorded addresses) covering 150 years of history.

Our second procedure was to carefully read each of these six hundred selected conference addresses and identify and record all themes determined to be present in each paragraph of each document. Our determination of themes was based on a topical index of 216 general themes (along with approximately 1,000 associated subthemes) that we had previously developed from preliminary readings of the conference addresses. For example, we identified "Kingdom of God" as an important general theme. Subthemes attached to Kingdom of God in our index included: (1) establishment of in last days; (2) sacrifice in building up; (3) spiritual aspects of; (4) submission of nations to; (5) temporal aspects of; and (6) ultimate triumph of. Thus if a passage in a conference address said something like: "God has called upon us in these latter days to endure these trials that have currently come upon us so that his kingdom may take root and finally prosper until it fills the whole world," we would code it as containing subthemes 1, 2, and 3 under the general theme of "Kingdom of God."[4]

Our next step was to convert coded themes from each conference address into numeric indicators of the relative importance accorded to them. We calculated these indicators as the ratio of the number of theme occurrences to the number of paragraphs in a document and called them "salience scores." For instance, if the theme of "obedience" was counted as appearing in five different paragraphs within a document consisting of a total of twenty-five different paragraphs, then the ratio of theme to paragraphs would be 0.25. This ratio then becomes a measure of the relative importance (or salience) of the obedience theme in this particular address. But since we were interested in larger patterns of theme importance, we finally aggregated particular theme saliences into mean scores across all conference addresses for the time period that we decided was most meaningful for our purposes, namely thirty-year intervals, or what we called "generations," these being 1830–1859, 1860–1889, 1890–1919, 1920–1949, and 1950–1979.

Sample General Findings

Consequently, we were able to detect if and how the salience of different themes varied over five generations of Mormon history. For example, to continue with the obedience theme, we found that obedience was more or less constantly emphasized over the entire span of conference history, but that it varied in its relative importance over time: obedience salience scores steadily increased for the first three generations but then dropped in emphasis for the last two generations to almost half of their previous high-water mark by 1950–1979.

Note that our procedures created general information categories that were susceptible to both sociological and nomothetic levels of analysis. That is, we were no longer confined to describing particular actions or events but had measures that could be used to describe larger patterns of change over time with regard to general conceptual categories, such as obedience. These measures could also serve as general variables in relation to other measured variables, which allowed us to test and explore possible connections between them. Thus, besides obedience, we were able to chart salience variation over time for all 216 of our main themes (along with variations in the accompanying subthemes) and subsequently determine which themes were most and least prominent during different historical periods, presumably reflecting prevailing historical forces in conjunction with institutional needs and the corresponding thematic changes that occurred.

Among other things, then, we were able to identify (1) a general cluster of themes that was most prominent in early generations of Mormon history but faded from mention in latter eras, (2) a cluster of themes that emerged as most important only in modern times, and (3) a theme cluster that had remained more or less constantly emphasized throughout all generations of Mormon history. The first, early theme-cluster we labeled "utopian" (including themes of church government, enemies, gentiles, kingdom of God, persecution, plural marriage, and Zion). The second, modern theme-cluster we labeled "family and respectability" (including themes of family, marriage, parenthood, church growth, church reputation, and Word of Wisdom). And the third, constant salient theme-cluster we labeled "authority and legitimacy" (including themes of blessings, church divinity, God's will, the gospel, Jesus Christ, knowledge, Latter-day Saints, missionary work, obedience, priesthood, prophets, and restoration of the church/gospel).

Even though these three theme-clusters were highly significant per se in interpreting the historical development of the LDS Church, examining variation within the clusters also provided important insights. For instance, Joseph Smith and Jesus Christ were both salient themes within our authority and legitimacy cluster, i.e., both were prominently mentioned by LDS authorities over the entire course of General Conference history through 1979. However, when we made *relative* comparisons between the patterns of salience scores for both of these specific themes, we found that Joseph Smith's ascendency as a conference topic dramatically diminished during the 1950–1979 era, while the importance of Jesus Christ as a conference topic during that same time period dramatically escalated. More specifically, from 1830 through 1949, Joseph Smith's salience scores ranged from being one-and-a-half to four times higher than the salience scores accorded to Jesus Christ. But during the generation from 1950–1979, this pattern was reversed, with Jesus Christ becoming the single most prominent subject at General Conference and generating a salience score five times higher than that of Joseph Smith. An interpretation of these patterns, from a social science perspective, seems fairly clear: The further removed from its tumultuous history of conflict with the U.S. government and other religious organizations, the greater the membership growth and corresponding rise in the social and political influence of the LDS Church. In a position of directing this transformative process, modern LDS leadership was anxious to cement their religion's increasing respectability and overcome the aggravating, persistent public perception that Mormonism was an alien, non-Christian cult. Displaying their Christian bona fides by increasingly emphasizing the doctrinal centrality of Jesus Christ in their conference rhetoric became part of an important marketing strategy for reshaping public opinion about the Mormons.

Sample Commitment Findings

Construction of thematic salience scores allowed us to go beyond describing historical development and change in specific LDS institutions. A number of sociologists have pointed out that Mormonism constitutes a prime case study for better understanding the emergence, survival, development and ultimate success of a new religious movement—see particularly the arguments of Rodney Stark in this regard.[5]

We adopted this perspective in *Kingdom Transformed* by examining three different areas of theoretical concern in the sociology of religious movements: (1) development and maintenance of necessary levels of member *commitment* in heretical or socially deviant groups; (2) organizational change and *accommodation* to external pressures exerted by oppositional, established groups and governments and to internal pressures generated by member inequities and dissent; and (3) responses to cultural and social changes occurring in larger, host societies, especially due to large-scale processes of modernization and *secularization*.

Because all three of these theoretical areas of concern involved abstract concepts, we needed to create corresponding variable measurements that reflected these concepts. We were able to do this by combining appropriate salience scores from our theme index into single, new composite variables. To take a well-known social science example, if we wanted to create an indicator of socioeconomic status for members of a designated population, we could merge previously validated measures of their income, amount of education, and level of occupational status. The result would be a total, single-score indicator across these more specific measurements, each one representing one facet of what we would now call socio-economic status.

A more specific example of creating a complex empirical indicator of an abstract concept from our own study involved our examination of LDS commitment patterns. We drew upon Rosabeth Kanter's well-known conceptualization of commitment that identifies six distinctive but related elements: (1) sacrifice, (2) investment, (3) renunciation, (4) communion, (5) mortification, and (6) transcendence.[6] In order to measure the salience of *sacrifice* for LDS conference speakers, we combined scores for such specific themes as "temptations," "Word of Wisdom," "adversity," "poverty," and a number of similar concerns. For *investment*, we combined salience scores for such themes as "blessings," "prosperity," "salvation," "eternal life," and so on. We constructed indicators of Kanter's remaining four commitment categories in the same way, by selecting measured themes from our index that meaningfully corresponded to the conceptual definitions Kanter provides for each commitment category.[7] Once we had calculated these new commitment salience scores we looked at the pattern of salience for each of the six commitment categories over time; we also combined the six commitment category scores into a single, overall salience score for commitment as a general variable.

When we looked at variation in the salience history of each of the six commitment categories, we discovered that different aspects of commitment were differentially emphasized in ways that reflected the unique pressures and corresponding needs of particular historical periods. To take just one example from many possibilities: During the 1880s, when Mormon theocracy and the practice of polygamy were attracting the full punitive wrath of the U.S. federal government, our data show a notable increase in rhetoric related to sacrificial themes along with a significant corresponding drop in conference rhetoric touting the beneficial (or investment) outcomes of the Latter-day Saint faith. However, following the 1890 Woodruff Manifesto that renounced official sanction and practice of polygamous marriages (leading to cessation of draconian government penalties and admission of Utah as a state in the union in 1896), these two rhetorical trends became exactly reversed during the next two decades; i.e., the alleged rewards (or investment potential) of Mormonism surged upward again in conference rhetoric while emphasis on sacrifice plummeted.

Overall, in examining the relative salience history of all six commitment categories, we found that transcendence themes (beliefs in divine guidance or historical destiny that promise comforting protection, meaningful identity, and solutions to collective problems afforded by exclusive group life), consistently ranked highest in salience among all of Kanter's commitment categories across the entire span of LDS General Conference rhetoric. This result, we theorized, may be generalizable to all new religious movements. That is to say, from our case study of Mormonism, we inductively generated the testable hypothesis that appropriate utilization of transcendence mechanisms may be the single most important aspect of maintaining commitment in the successful development of new religious movements generally.

Finally, when we combined salience scores for all six commitment categories, this overall measure of commitment as a single, general variable showed a pattern of high salience from the very beginning of LDS conference history (1830–1859) and escalated to an even higher level during the second generation (1860–1889). Subsequently, however, LDS authorities' conference rhetoric concerning commitment dropped precipitously over each of the next two generations of our study and then leveled off at a moderately high level beginning with the generation of 1950–1979. The LDS Church is still a relatively high-demand denomination that requires higher levels of member commitment and participation than the average religion. But it no longer requires, expects, or needs anywhere near the levels of commitment characteristic of its earlier years as a struggling, persecuted minority faith on the fringes of American society.

Accommodation Example

Sociologists have long been interested in the developmental careers of a wide variety of social movements, whether political, economic, or religious. Thus we were able to draw from a number of theoretical analyses in the social movement literature to shed light on the organizational development of Mormonism as it changed from a small, heretical, socially deviant group—subjected to numerous challenges to its existence from both external and internal sources—into an expanding international church that, although still viewed suspiciously by many outsiders, commands a substantial amount of respect and influence in the modern world. We particularly drew upon the work of Mayer Zald and Roberta Ash because they proposed specific theoretical hypotheses that could be empirically tested by using our content analysis data from LDS General Conferences.[8]

We will summarize just one accommodation example taken from *Kingdom Transformed*, namely the effect of societal pressures on organizational goals. According to Zald and Ash, new, emergent movements that are relatively exclusive (i.e., demand high levels of commitment from their members), and have goals that imply changing (or, especially, actively seek to change) social norms and existing institutions, will receive much greater oppositional pressure from established groups than will movements that are more inclusive (i.e., are less demanding of members) and have goals that focus on only reforming or improving individual member's personal qualities. Zald and Ash call the first type an "outward oriented" movement and the second an "inward oriented movement." The more a relatively small but high commitment movement is outward oriented, the more likely it will be forced to make changes in its goals if it is to survive the inevitable oppositional pressures exerted by powerful external foes.

We already noted the transformation of LDS commitment rhetoric from very high levels in its early history to much more moderate levels in modern times, making the LDS Church a more inclusive organization than previously. Are there also corresponding changes in LDS organizational goals over this same span of history? To empirically answer this question, we created additional composite variables—a measure of "individual reform" and a measure of "social reform" by combining salience scores of rhetorical themes that matched the meaning of these two new categories. For our individual reform measure we merged scores from such conference topics as marital, parental, and family ideals; sin, repentance, and forgiveness; the Word of Wisdom; faith; ethical practices; and a number of additional desirable character traits. For our measure of social reform we combined salience scores taken from such theme categories as the United Order, the Law of Consecration, the gathering, plural marriage, prohibition, election of government officials, political parties, labor unions and welfare, and so on.

Looking at our findings over time we found that, although both measures showed high salience during the beginning generation of conference history (1830–1859), LDS authorities' emphasis on social reform issues was significantly higher than their concern for individual reform. The relative emphasis on social reform continued into the second generation (1860–1889) as well. These results told us that, although the LDS Church was not exclusively an outward oriented movement in its early years, it certainly had strong tendencies in that direction. But during Mormonism's third generation (1890–1919)—following the capitulation of LDS authorities to government demands to abolish polygamy, disentangle direct church involvement in government affairs, and establish a two-party political system in Utah—a dramatic reversal in conference rhetoric emerged: salience scores of individual reform were now three times greater than social reform, and by the 1950–1979 generation they were four times greater. In fact, social reform issues virtually disappeared from conference rhetoric altogether during this latter period. These results led us to conclude that, by the late nineteenth century, Mormon accommodation to the demands of American society were correlated with a transformation of goals such that the LDS Church increasingly became an inward oriented organization in modern times—just as Zald and Ash's formulation predicts. More specifically, the modern LDS Church has largely given up its former goals of societal reconstruction to focus its attention almost entirely on its own institutional programs for the recruitment, participation, development, and self-improvement of its members.

Secularization Examples

In the nineteenth century, the chief Mormon challenge was to build and preserve a theocratic commonwealth at odds with the sectarian orthodoxy and mores of the day, the authority of the federal government, and the master trends of industrial capitalism. Having survived these irresistible pressures by making major concessions, the LDS Church today is principally challenged in the same manner as all organized religion: by the secularization of modern society and culture. For our purposes we adopted Peter Berger's definition of secularization as "the process by which sectors of society and culture are removed from the domination of religious institutions and symbols."[9] Although contemporary thinking about secularization has become more nuanced and much less linear (even Berger has readjusted his views in light of late twentieth- and early twenty-first-century religious developments),[10] we were particularly attracted then to Berger's formulation because he offered very specific hypotheses that we could directly test with our conference data.

Thus, Berger's analysis produces a number of propositions concerning the impact of secularization on the structure and beliefs espoused by modern religious organizations. His propositions concerning beliefs are much more susceptible to direct testing by our conference data, and we will summarize our findings for three of these. Berger emphasizes that secularization is strongly correlated with another powerful characteristic of most modern societies, namely a growing array of available state-tolerated religious organizations and a corresponding freedom for individuals to make religious choices. A pluralistic religious situation is, ipso facto, a market situation, and Berger uses the logic of consumer preference to formulate the following theoretical proposition: In a pluralistic situation, religious organizations must compete with one another for adherents; consequently, the dynamics of consumer preference encourage changeability in doctrines and religious practices.

One proposition resulting from these considerations is that consumer influence on religious belief encourages what Berger refers to as standardization and marginal differentiation of content among competing religious groups. This means that religious beliefs in particular groups will tend to shed much of their original doctrinal distinctiveness and become centered on a core of essential teachings that are quite similar across a number of different groups within the same general religious tradition. At the same time, relatively minor differences in belief or doctrinal emphasis may be highlighted in order to provide a competitive marketing advantage. In the LDS case, we already pointed to the example of greatly increased emphasis on Jesus Christ in modern conference rhetoric and the corresponding downplay of focus on Joseph Smith. Is there additional evidence from our conference theme index regarding Berger's hypothesis?

We created a new composite variable from our data by not only including salience scores for Joseph Smith, but also those that incorporated such distinctive LDS teachings as restoration of the true church and priesthood authority, modern revelation and prophetic leadership, the Latter-day Saints as God's chosen people to carry out his plan in the last days, and a number of other characteristic Mormon beliefs, including pre-earth existence, personal deification and plurality of Gods, temple work, celestial marriage, the Word of Wisdom, and so forth. The results of our analysis were similar to those we reported regarding emphasis on commitment themes: For the first two generations of conference history doctrinal differentiation was very high, with the peak period occurring from 1860–1889. Subsequently, for the next three generations, emphasis on uniquely Mormon beliefs dropped off considerably—although this trend leveled off during the 1950–1979 period of conference history, a fact that Armand Mauss incorporated in his theory of modern LDS retrenchment.[11]

Decreasing conference emphasis on doctrinal points of difference in modern times needs to be interpreted in light of the immutability of certain core Mormon beliefs and the leveling of this decline from 1950–1979. First, we should note that enunciation of distinctive Mormon doctrines has always been frequent, even during modern periods of relative decline compared to the extremely high emphasis of earlier generations. In addition, the modern decline in our doctrinal differentiation measure largely represented the abandonment of the nineteenth-century utopian themes of Zion, theocratic politics and economics envisioned in the Kingdom of God, and plural marriage—not a retreat from such fundamental claims as the LDS Church's supreme truth and authority based on prophetic revelation. Thus we concluded that the modern LDS Church, through the conference proclamations of its leaders, continues to insist that it is importantly different in its authorized possession of irreducible truths, but the latter are increasingly represented within the boundaries of modern, conventional acceptability, not as dangerously radical ideas that might appear unreasonable to contemporary understanding.

In a closely related vein, Berger also says that religious consumers in secular societies, as he defined "secular" in the late 1960s, will tend to prefer religion that is consonant with a secular consciousness.[12] This creates pressure to expunge supernatural or mythological elements from religious theologies or at least to deemphasize supernatural elements while other elements of the faith more congenial to secular consciousness are emphasized. We tested this proposition by constructing two new composite variables from our conference theme index: supernaturalism and eschatology. Supernaturalism consisted of such merged themes as Adam and Eve, angels, spirits, Satan, miracles, prophecies, heaven and hell, resurrection, the atonement, and so on. Eschatology was built from such themes as the second coming of Jesus, the millennium, and several other associated events of the "last days."

Our results for both these measures supported Berger's hypothesis regarding the influence of secular consciousness on the articulation of traditional religious beliefs. First, there was a moderate linear decrease in the salience of supernatural rhetoric in every generation of General Conference up through 1950–1979, by which time the relative emphasis placed on supernatural themes was only half that generated by LDS authorities in the first generation. Second, and even more striking, was the decline of LDS eschatology references: the salience of eschatology reached its peak at a very high level during the generation of 1860–1889 but then drastically fell to a level that was approximately six times lower by the generation of 1950–1979. Thus, even though a millennial scenario of "the last days" is still a central LDS doctrine, it is no longer enunciated by modern conference speakers with anything like the emphatic fervor and immediacy of nineteenth-century leaders.

In summary, our content analysis of the LDS Conference Reports allowed us to both describe and test theoretical propositions concerning a wide variety of issues germane to the historical study of new religions, including problems of member commitment, organizational accommodation, and religious authorities' responses to the challenges of modernity and secularization. To further illustrate the social science possibilities produced through an application of content analysis procedures, we will next summarize the methods we employed and some of the key results obtained in our study of early LDS patriarchal blessings.

Early Patriarchal Blessings

Published by the Pennsylvania State University Press as *Binding Earth and Heaven: Patriarchal Blessings in the Prophetic Development of Early Mormonism*, our study of early LDS patriarchal blessings was much more narrowly focused than *Kingdom*, spanning only a decade of time and spotlighting the religious functions of a singular Mormon practice with doctrinal and commitment implications for understanding the initial development of a fledgling religious movement.[13]

Methodology Considerations

To repeat our earlier observation, content analysis methods are most beneficial for the generalizing goals of social science when they can be applied to sets of organizationally connected records or documents that constitute meaningful units of material produced during specified periods of time. As reviewed above, the LDS Conference Reports are a pertinent case in point. Michael Marquardt's compilation of *Early Patriarchal Blessings of the Church of Jesus Christ of Latter-day Saints* constitutes another pertinent set of documentary records. Marquardt's ample volume is a chronological compilation of over 750 patriarchal blessings dated from December 18, 1833, through September 11, 1845, which Marquardt collected from various sources for over forty years. Among Marquardt's primary sources was Joseph Smith Sr.'s "Book of Patriarchal Blessings." This record book contained copies of Father Smith's blessings from 1834–1839 and subsequently was used for recording additional blessings from 1843–1845 bestowed by Hyrum and William Smith after they succeeded their father in turn to occupy the hereditary office of church patriarch. For the years 1840–1842 in particular, Marquardt had to rely on a variety of other sources for obtaining his collection of blessings.

Thus, Marquardt's compilation is not a complete inventory of official patriarchal blessings given to Latter-day Saints during the first decade and a half of their history (hundreds of blessings are unaccounted for), but it constitutes a substantial proportion of official blessings pronounced upon Mormon converts and their children during the stormy Kirtland, Far West, and Nauvoo chapters of LDS history.[14] It is the single largest collection of early patriarchal blessings available and constitutes an invaluable documentary collection for students of new religions in general and Mormon history in particular. Analogous to collections of an artist's repertoire of works displayed in galleries or museums, Marquardt's compilation makes it possible for us to acquire a much deeper understanding and appreciation of the role played by the institution of patriarchal blessings in the doctrinal development of early Mormonism.

As with our survey of the General Conference reports, we decided to draw a random sample of blessings contained in Marquardt's compilation rather than attempt to code every blessing therein contained. If a sufficient number of documents is randomly selected for inclusion in a sample, the representativeness of the sample is maximized and can be tested for accuracy by employing statistical tests of significance. Our criteria for drawing a sample of blessing documents were: (1) manageable size—a sample large enough to be representative of Marquardt's entire compilation but small enough for careful and reliable coding; (2) an equal number of blessings given by each patriarch; and (3) an equal number of male and female blessings. We met these criteria by randomly selecting fifteen male and fifteen female blessings given by all three Smith patriarchs, for a subtotal of thirty blessings per patriarch and an overall total of ninety patriarchal blessings in our sample for the period 1834–1845. Similar to the way we coded themes in our earlier study of LDS conference rhetoric, we then read through all ninety blessings, systematically identifying and recording key words and phrases which we used to construct an index of the language terms used by the Smith patriarchs in their blessings.

Our resultant theme index consisted of 431 key words and phrases, constituting the linguistic building blocks for the religious and doctrinal themes expressed in early patriarchal blessings. Utilizing this theme index, we rescanned every line of every blessing in our sample to numerically code the various themes expressed in the patriarchs' words to different blessing recipients.

In contrast to the more complex scoring procedures we devised for our study of Conference Reports, in recording word counts for our analysis of patriarchal blessing themes we made the decision to record a word or phrase only once per document (on average, patriarchal blessings are substantially shorter in length than conference addresses). For example, if "inheritance in Zion" was a phrase occurring more than once in a particular blessing, it was only scored once for that blessing. Thus, the maximum frequency count for any single word or phrase in our index was 90 (the number of blessings sampled), indicating that it appeared in every blessing we examined. Simple frequency counts, rather than theme-to-paragraph ratios, gave us a straightforward way to measure the relative salience of particular blessing themes. We inferred that blessing themes with high frequency counts in our sample reflected some of the most important religious concerns and doctrinal teachings for early Latter-day Saints, while blessing themes with relatively low frequency counts were indicative of lesser or even idiosyncratic concerns.

Thus, even though we employed somewhat different scoring procedures than those used for our earlier study of General Conference themes in historical context, we still relied on otherwise similar content analysis methods to produce objective measures of thematic salience in early patriarch blessings that permitted us to make both statistical and theoretical generalizations about those blessings and the part they played in early Mormon history.

Sample General Findings

If they are to survive, let alone eventually flourish, new religious movements must propagate and defend heretical new teachings while sufficiently reinforcing the religious commitment of their convert members to withstand concerted opposition—both legal and extralegal—from powerful religious and secular adversaries. It is precisely these two essential survival concerns in early LDS history that can be inferred from a systematic content analysis of Mormonism's earliest patriarchal blessings.

According to our sample results, the most common blessing themes, in rank order of their frequency from 1834–1845, were: salvation and eternal life; lineage; posterity; Zion; priesthood; faith; spirit; afflictions; husband; material blessings; spiritual blessings; knowledge and understanding; end times; Israel; good name and reputation; power; kingdom; gospel; covenants; and angels. The religious meanings connected with these thematic belief-topics gave us a clear indication of the primary concerns and doctrinal convictions shared by both the patriarchs who bestowed the blessings and LDS converts who received them during this early period of LDS history. Once statistically identified and confirmed in their salience, we proceeded to analyze the importance of these particular core values and beliefs in the birth of Mormonism as a new religion and in the sorely tested commitment of its founding generation.

In this regard we note that, at first glance, most of the blessing themes identified in our sample may simply appear to register fairly standard religious concepts within the Judeo-Christian tradition. But in the context of LDS restorationist beliefs, they take on a decidedly Mormon meaning. As the doctrinal foundation of a new religious movement, the ideology of prophetic restorationism functioned to justify the distinctive development of LDS institutions and practices in directions that immediately stimulated charges that Mormonism was not merely another contentious Christian sect, but an intolerable heresy that necessitated active resistance and suppression. From the perspective of restoration ideology, most of the major blessing themes in our sample were, in fact, recast by Mormon leaders and converts as distinctive LDS teachings. Thus, for example, our sample's most salient blessing theme of salvation and eternal life represents a central soteriological concern that is common in some form or fashion to a great many religious traditions worldwide. The Christian tradition in particular has always emphasized human salvation through the atoning sacrifice and resurrection of Jesus Christ as its cardinal article of faith. For early Latter-day Saint converts, however, the meaning of Christian salvation and eternal life could not be separated from their acceptance of the prophetic restoration proclaimed by Joseph Smith Jr. In their view, it was only through obedience to the *restored* gospel of Jesus Christ as authoritatively taught and administered in the *restored* church that ultimate salvation and eternal life in the presence of God could be assured.

For those early Mormon converts who remained most loyal to Smith's prophetic teachings, adherence to the increasingly esoteric implications of the new salvation theology promulgated in Nauvoo prior to Smith's assassination was justified by their fundamental belief in the restoration of latter-day prophetic guidance and the restored authority of the priesthood to act and officiate in God's name. All of this may seem perfectly obvious in retrospect but, at the time, it was not a foregone conclusion that Mormonism would even survive, let alone flourish worldwide in centuries to come. All successful movements need to develop effective commitment mechanisms for propagating core beliefs and strengthening people's devotion to a cause. The doctrinal themes that our data show were reiterated in early patriarchal blessings demonstrate one important way this was accomplished in early Mormonism through the innovative office of the Church Patriarch.[15]

As was true for most Christians, chief among Latter-day Saints' concerns was the ultimate fate of their immortal souls. For early LDS converts, however, eternal life was not only promised in their patriarchal blessings, it was *sealed* to them (eternally guaranteed) through the restored priesthood authority of the patriarch. Phrasing such as "I seal these blessings," "I seal these promises," "I seal upon your head the gift of eternal life," and the like, was used in virtually every blessing in our sample. For beleaguered religious seekers and believers, such authoritative reassurance of their ultimate salvation was of the utmost, transcendent value. Shared belief in the patriarch's sealing authority clearly functioned as an important institutional mechanism in early Mormonism for reinforcing blessing recipients' commitments and resolve to remain faithful to their heretical religion in spite of the many adversities they consequently had to endure.

In conjunction with salvation and eternal life, our sample of blessings also highlighted other restoration themes such as gospel, priesthood, power, covenants, kingdom, spirit, angels, and assorted events associated with the projected latter-day end times. A systematic exposition of each of these items would reveal an interconnected set of core LDS beliefs that, when considered through the lens of restorationist ideology, constituted a distinctive Mormon version of the fundamentals of Christian soteriology, ecclesiology, and eschatology. While perhaps less obviously Christian in connotation, other salient themes in our blessings sample—such as lineage, posterity, Israel, and Zion—were also intimately connected with the emergence of early Mormon restorationist doctrines and linked converts' identification with ancient Israel and their own divine destiny as a new covenant people in the last days.[16]

At the same time, both men and women were bluntly informed in their blessings that, as converts to the restored church, they would have to suffer sacrificial sorrows and trials to build God's Kingdom; they would be reviled and persecuted for their faith in the restored gospel. Our content analysis showed, in fact, that "afflictions" ranked as the eighth most commonly reiterated theme in our blessing sample. Blessing recipients were repeatedly promised, however, that if they remained faithful, their sacrifices would be richly rewarded in the end with both the material blessings of an abundant life on earth and all the spiritual blessings of eternal life. These contingent, compensatory promises were essential sources of motivation for early LDS converts, many of whom would in fact undergo terrible hardship and suffering for their faith. Eternal life was the authoritative promise offered in patriarchal blessings to those who endured to the end, while those who faltered and lost their faith would forfeit their covenantal inheritance.

Sample Gender Differences

The way that gender distinctions are socially constructed in different religious traditions is fundamentally important for understanding how their adherents define and conduct their lives. When contemplating the research possibilities afforded by Marquardt's compilation of early patriarchal blessings, we immediately recognized the potential of content analysis methods for making systematic gender comparisons in the blessings bestowed on early Latter-day Saint converts.

As a nineteenth-century lay religion that emphasized the restoration of patriarchal priesthood authority, early Mormonism partook of the political and cultural ethos of antebellum American society. To an appreciable extent we might expect to see contemporaneous gender role distinctions reflected in the early LDS institution of patriarchal blessings. In the process of propagating and reinforcing member commitment to Mormonism's most distinctive religious claims, were early patriarchal blessings given to women substantially different from the blessings given men? In particular, did those blessings serve to reinforce women's subservience to male dominance in a patriarchal religious culture? It may be perfectly plausible to assume this was true but, through a statistical content analysis of the pertinent documents in question, we had the methodological means for arriving at factual conclusions.

A summary review of all the statistical findings produced by our content analysis of patriarchal blessings actually led us to a mixed and more nuanced conclusion regarding gender differences in the early LDS Church from 1834 to 1845. On the one hand, during those years of church history, more males received blessings than females; their blessings were longer on average; they were older in age than their female counterparts; and they were more likely than women to receive their blessings independently of a spouse. On the other hand, gender differences based on these measures turned out to be quite modest and even showed clear signs of diminishing over time.

Yet our statistical analysis of major blessing themes and their corresponding subthemes showed several important gender discrepancies in the verbal content of members' blessings that had implications for male authority and subordinate roles for women. For example, references to lineage, inheritance in Zion, priesthood, Israel, power, and preaching the gospel—all items in harmony with taken-for-granted male role prerogatives—were significantly more frequent in male blessings than in female blessings. The only discrepant themes that occurred significantly more often in female blessings were references to blessings in common with husband—providing at least one very clear example of gender bias in our sample—accompanied by blessings of health/long life, and ministering angels. In contrast, references to a man's wife, and corresponding specifications (including "blessings in common with") and admonitions to comfort, obey, or support, were virtually absent in the blessings of male recipients.

In contrast to these several discrepancies, however, our content analysis revealed over a dozen consonant blessing themes that failed to show significant gender differences. Consonant gender themes included important theological and ultimate reward concerns, such as salvation and eternal life, posterity, faith, spirit, afflictions, material blessings, spiritual blessings, knowledge and understanding, end times, good name and reputation, kingdom, and covenants. Thus, while early patriarchal blessings were not perfectly egalitarian in their content, they did not exhibit an extreme male bias, either. To the contrary, our data in fact show a substantial egalitarian tendency in these blessings: consonant themes among both men's and women's patriarchal blessings outnumbered discrepant themes by a ratio of two to one. Consonant blessing themes in our analysis highlighted a shared commitment expectation for both men and women converts to Mormonism's highest theological ideals and to the prophetically restored church of Jesus Christ, under covenantal obligation, to build God's kingdom on earth in the last days. Based on these findings—which were achieved through systematic and objective empirical methods of data definition, classification, retrieval, and analysis rather than conventional qualitative assessment of documents—a perhaps surprising argument can be made that, in comparison to other nineteenth-century Christian women, the religious status and roles of LDS women as active participants in the forging of a new religion on the American frontier were relatively progressive for their time and place.[17]

Conclusion

Statistical data obtained through a systematic content analysis of a compilation of early patriarchal blessings provided strong empirical support for our study's principle theoretical inference—that the supernatural valence attached by both sexes to their blessings made them a unique and powerful commitment mechanism for strengthening their faith, while simultaneously contributing to the promulgation of the emerging doctrines of the Mormon restoration. In like manner, while also focusing on Mormonism as a historical case study, our earlier content analysis of the LDS General Conference addresses provided broad empirical support for testing a number of theoretical propositions concerning the long-term development and growth of new religious movements. Through both of these examples we have made an argument for the value of nomothetic social science analysis and methodology in contemporary Mormon studies, with particular emphasis on the application of content analysis techniques to designated sets of documents. The LDS Church is justifiably well known for its record-keeping proclivities and production of official messages, editorials, periodicals, manuals, and other religious materials that potentially lend themselves to statistical analysis. Aided by quantitative methods in the pursuit of nomothetic objectives, these kinds of documents can and should be much more thoroughly exploited by social science researchers.

Notes

We gratefully acknowledge the intellectual and collegial influence of Armand Mauss on our scholarly writing over the years, especially in the two books that supply the methodological examples for this essay: *A Kingdom Transformed* and *Binding Earth and Heaven* (see below for full citations). Armand was a critical reader of both these works when they were in manuscript form, and we benefited greatly from his critical insights and helpful suggestions.

1. Karl Marx, *Selected Writings in Sociology and Social Philosophy*, trans. and ed. Thomas B. Bottomore (London: McGraw Hill, 1969); Max Weber, *The Protestant Ethic and the Spirit of Capitalism*, trans. Talcott Parsons (New York: Charles Scribner's Sons, 1930); Robert K. Merton, "Science, Technology and Society in Seventeenth Century England," *Osiris* 4 (1938): 360–632.
2. Michael Marquardt, *Early Patriarchal Blessings of the Church of Jesus Christ of Latter-day Saints* (Salt Lake City, UT: Smith-Pettit Foundation, 2007).
3. Gordon Shepherd and Gary Shepherd, *A Kingdom Transformed: Themes in the Development of Mormonism* (Salt Lake City: University of Utah Press, 1984).
4. See *Kingdom Transformed*, Appendix A, 214–17, for details, including reliability validation of coding decisions.
5. Rodney Stark, *The Rise of Mormonism*, ed. Reid Neilson (New York: Columbia University Press, 2005). Also see Rodney Stark, "The Rise of a New Religious Faith," *Review of Religious Research* 26 (1984): 18–38.
6. Rosabeth Kanter, *Commitment and Community* (Cambridge, MA: Harvard University Press, 1972).
7. See *Kingdom Transformed*, 105–28, 133–34.
8. Mayer Zald and Roberta Ash, "Social Movement Growth, Decay, and Change," *Social Forces* 44 (1966): 327–41.
9. Peter Berger, *The Sacred Canopy: Elements of a Sociological Theory of Religion* (New York: Doubleday, 1969).
10. For more recent, diverse, and complex discussions of secularization in modern societies, see Craig Calhoun, Mark Juergensmeyer, and Jonathan VanAntwerpen, eds., *Rethinking Secularism* (New York: Oxford University Press, 2011); Charles Taylor, *A Secular Age* (Cambridge, MA: Harvard University Press, 2007); and David Martin, *On Secularization: Toward a Revised General Theory* (London: Ashgate Publishing Co., 2005). For a contrarian but influential sociological perspective, see Rodney Stark and Roger Finke, "Secularization, R.I.P.," chapter 3 in *Acts of Faith: Explaining the Human Side of Religion*

(Berkeley: University of California Press, 2000). For Berger's own reassessment of his earlier views on secularization, see Peter Berger, Grace Davie, and Effie Fokas, *Religious America, Secular Europe? A Theme and Variations* (Burlington, VT: Ashgate, 2008); and Peter Berger, *The Desecularization of the World: Resurgent Religion and World Politics* (Grand Rapids, MI: Wm. B. Eerdmans Publishing, 1999).

11. Armand L. Mauss, *The Angel and The Beehive: The Mormon Struggle with Assimilation* (Urbana: University of Illinois Press, 1994). In this context, we should mention that we are working on an update of *Kingdom Transformed* that examines General Conference addresses delivered over the thirty years that have passed since our original study. The primary theoretical reference that will frame and be tested by our new analysis is Mauss's recently modified version of his retrenchment theory. See "Rethinking Retrenchment: Course Corrections in the On-going Campaign for Respectability," *Dialogue: A Journal of Mormon Thought* 44 (Winter 2011): 1–42.

12. Notwithstanding current criticisms of classical secularization theory, there remain a number of ways and spheres in which institutional influence has in fact diminished in modern societies, including the United States. At the same time religious belief and activity and personalized religious meanings clearly remain vital and flourishing, if not rising, in other spheres. Thus, it is not possible to point to one overarching, linear trend that would accurately characterize the whole of religion's current status and future outcome in the modern world. It now seems in fact a quite mixed outcome and will undoubtedly remain so for the foreseeable future. What we can say is that a subset of specific hypotheses derived from Berger's older (and admittedly insufficient) overall conceptual view of modern secularization nevertheless accurately predicted empirical results we obtained from our General Conference data up through 1979. We can also report that, in our new analysis of General Conference talks from 1980 through 2009, mentioned above, our measures of "secular consciousness" in contemporary LDS conference addresses continue to conform to Berger's hypotheses.

13. Gary Shepherd and Gordon Shepherd, *Binding Earth and Heaven: Patriarchal Blessings in the Prophetic Development of Early Mormonism* (University Park: Pennsylvania State University Press, 2012).

14. Marquardt has subsequently published a companion volume of sample Mormon patriarchal blessings given throughout the entire span of LDS Church history up through 1995. See Michael Marquardt, *Later Patriarchal Blessings of the Church of Jesus Christ of Latter-day Saints* (Salt Lake City, UT: Signature Books, 2012).

15. For a thorough explanation of the office of the Church Patriarch and an account of its rise and demise, see Irene Bates and Gary Smith, *Lost Legacy: The Mormon Office of Presiding Patriarch* (Urbana: University of Illinois Press, 2003).

16. For a full discussion of the interrelated doctrinal themes expounded in early patriarchal blessings and their corresponding commitment implications, see chapter 5 of *Binding Earth and Heaven*.

17. This argument is also in harmony with sociological theories and findings that women are typically afforded more participation and status opportunities in the early years of new religious movements. See Laura Vance, *Women in New Religions* (New York: New York University Press, 2015).

Chapter 10 | Theory and Interpretation in Mormon Studies

Richard Lyman Bushman

Some years ago while teaching at Claremont Graduate University, I offered a course on Mormonism with Armand Mauss whom I consider to be the preeminent theorist of Mormon history. We intended to approach the subject from our respective disciplinary perspectives, mine history, his sociology. Of course, he knew all the history, but I did not know the sociology. We thought that the friction and tension arising from the combination would be provocative.

Soon after the course began, Mauss posed a question to the seminar that I could not comprehend. He asked, "What is the natural history of a religious movement?" "Natural history?" What could that mean? The relationship of religion to nature—animals and plants in religious history? Perhaps something to do with creation stories? Only gradually did it dawn on me that he meant that religious movements followed a growth pattern like plants and animals, or perhaps like evolving solar systems. Embedded in their natures were particular qualities that directed their growth along a certain path, as DNA directs animal growth. Individuals within a species differ in the details of their appearance and function, but they all follow a similar recognizable pattern. They have a natural history and, said Mauss, so do religions.

Underlying Mauss's question was the work of classification that sociologists have been pursuing since Max Weber made a distinction between a church and a sect.[1] This classification system which was elaborated to include the categories of cult and denomination became over time a description of change as well. Some of the categories were dynamic, evolving from one form to another, e.g., religions that began as a sect then evolved into a church, or started as a cult and became a denomination. Mauss had these various categories and their evolutionary patterns in mind when he asked the seminar about the natural history of a religion. He wanted the class to see that religions in many times and places fell into these various groupings and migrated from one to another form as time went by. Of course he was thinking of the cult-denomination distinction when he spoke of Mormonism.

This theoretical underpinning had been greatly elaborated by the group of sociologists that Mauss studied with at the University of California at Berkeley, often referred to as the Berkeley Circle, headed by Charles Y. Glock, their chief mentor, and featuring such luminaries as Rodney Stark.[2] These scholars, notably Stark, took on another dimension of sociological theory: the prediction, dominant until the 1970s, that religion was doomed to extinction. Eventually secularism would weaken and then crush active religious faith. Secularization was part of the natural history of religion in modern times, so it was thought. Stark and his colleagues contested this view. They noted that in the late twentieth century this was not happening as predicted. Far from dissipating, religion was reasserting itself, albeit in a new form. The old-line religious denominations were faltering, but new religious movements (NRMs) were thriving. A good part of the theoretical work of the Berkeley Circle was to explain how new religions managed to grow in the face of supposedly lethal secular forces.

Mauss entered into this religious ferment because he happened to be at Berkeley for his graduate work and because his Mormon background gave him access to one of the most hardy of the NRMs. Mauss took up the key conception of Stark and company—social tension—and made it work for Mormonism. The Berkeley theorists postulated that successful movements stood apart from society in a state of continuous tension. That was the secret of their success. They were not bland versions of standard orthodoxies, but deviants, distinguished in rather demanding ways from the world around them. Their appeal and their strength came from these strains with the ambient culture. However, if they went too far from social norms, the strain became more than adherents could bear, and the movement declined. Success depended on keeping the strain level at just the right pitch.

Mauss was trying to introduce our students into this line of thinking with his natural history question. The question became more and more interesting the more I heard him talk. Eventually I realized that sociologists think quite differently about society than historians do—or at least the emphasis is different. Mauss could rightly use the term "natural history" because sociologists conceive of society as an organism. Society is actually an organized entity, like a forest or a solar system. Its component parts are all linked together like the cells of a squirrel or the planets whirling around the sun. An investigator can look for regularities in the functions of society just as astronomers find them in the stars or botanists in a forest. Social scientists are scientists not just in the sense of basing conclusions on inquiry, hypothesis, and evidence, but in the sense of looking for the laws of nature—or at least regular patterns.

The historian in me was actually taken aback by this realization even though I probably had known this about sociologists all along. The word that immediately sprang to mind was "reification." It seemed to me the sociologists were calling something real or natural that actually was a human conception or a label. To my mind it was something like the idea of race, a conception that draws together some qualities but does not actually exist in nature. You can't find a fixed set of characteristics that rigorously define race. The term only works because people have agreed on how to use it, not because nature has created races. I use the term society all the time, just as I use words like culture or the American mind, but I don't think society exists out there, a functioning reality like a locomotive or pond, waiting to be investigated. Hence when Mauss started talking about the laws of new religious movements as if they were part of natural history I was stunned.

Historians do employ conceptions to explain what happens in society. They look for overarching ideas that bring together events into a pattern, but they speak of interpretation, something quite different. Kathleen Flake has interpreted the renewed interest in Joseph Smith after 1900—purchasing the birthplace, erecting a monument—as an attempt to reaffirm the foundations of the Mormon Church after polygamy had been abandoned.[3] Matthew Bowman speaks of the influence of the American progressive movement on church welfare programs in the first decades of the twentieth century.[4] Years ago Leonard Arrington interpreted the nineteenth-century emphasis on the Word of Wisdom as Brigham Young's effort to reduce the drain on currency that resulted from importing tobacco into Utah.[5] These are all historical interpretations. They differ from theory in that they are all historically contingent. They depend on circumstances of the moment—the end of polygamy, the rise of progressivism, Brigham Young's drive for economic autonomy. They are not rooted in the nature of society but in conditions of a certain time and place. That is the key difference: theory identifies regularities that occur in society time after time. Interpretation looks for regularities at a given time and place. The two seek different ends. One is trying to understand how society works; the other, how change over time occurred in one segment of history. One seeks to discover the natural order of the social world; the other doubts that one set of laws governs all societies. For historians virtually everything in society is contingent. There are no governing laws. Historians would be embarrassed to imply that some force outside of history caused an event. You are cheating if you give up the hunt for historical causes and rely on a borrowed generality about human behavior. To historicize means to put events into the chain of historical contingencies. Nothing stands outside the all-encompassing historical reality.[6]

You would think that these divergences in underlying conceptions would drive sociology and history apart, but in fact the opposite is true. Historians are forever borrowing from sociologists, not to contribute to the noble dream of a "natural history" of society but to understand the moment. Marx has been immensely useful to historians. The ideas of class and class struggle have been used by all kinds of historians. I grew up in the heyday of Marxist history in the United States and have spent my life resisting its impositions on historical thought. I thought the Marxian idea of the masses a travesty and a slur. I got to know the masses as a Latter-day Saint missionary knocking on doors in Halifax, Nova Scotia, in the 1950s and they were not the faceless, lumpish clay the Marxists made them out to be. I was outraged by the Marxist idea that when laboring people worked for better hours and higher wages rather than an overthrow of capitalism it was a form of false consciousness. It seemed to me the Marxists only wanted to manipulate working people for their own revolutionary ends rather than accepting them as they were.

And yet when I came to write about Joseph Smith I was very aware of his sense of class and of the sorrows of the poor.[7] I was tempted at one point when describing his occasional claims to be the best lawyer and the best doctor in existence to speak of the permanent insult of class. I think Smith labored under the burden of knowing that he and his people were not respectable, they were not educated, they were not polished. Boasting of his own achievements was a way of mocking the professional pretensions of the educated. One of his enduring wishes was to honor plain people—his social class—and give them dignity. When it came down to understanding Joseph I found myself drawing on the Marxism I had learned in my youth.

Or again when I was seeking to understand the mysterious wonders of LDS Church organization I turned to the Max Weber I had read in college. Who can find a better idea for explaining the evolution of church government than Weber's routinization of charisma? The term seems to explain change from the early Joseph Smith through the formation of quorums and on to Brigham Young. Mormons who know anything of church history sense instinctively how well the routinization of charisma applies. Joseph was the man of revelatory gifts, the charismatic figure who spoke from heaven and gathered followers on the basis of his divine gift—a perfect case study of Weber's charismatic leader.[8] As the church evolved, we all know, bureaucracy began to form: priesthood quorums, bishoprics, high councils and First Presidencies, the Quorum of the Twelve. Instead of only one gifted revelator we had a bureaucracy invested with authority like the offices and boards in a corporation or a government. These officials did not have to have a revelation every week to enlist followers. People complied because they knew authority was vested in the office. When Joseph died, and authority was passed along, it went (in the LDS view) to the person with office—the President of the Twelve Apostles. Joseph had effected the routinization of charisma in his own lifetime and what is more, brought the church along with him. When the chips were down, most of the early Latter-day Saints went with Brigham Young, not James J. Strang, the pretender to charismatic power.

Mormons embrace Weber because he works so well in our own history. I have even tried to insert a wrinkle of my own into this Weberian account. I have argued that Joseph's true genius was to combine charisma and bureaucracy. He not only created an apostolic bureaucracy to succeed his own charismatic leadership. He invested this whole bureaucracy with charismatic power. Bishops not only hold the authority of their office; they are believed to receive revelation in administering the powers of that office. Indeed today the entire church organization from the Deacon's Quorum President to the President of the Church is told to seek revelation, infusing the whole bureaucratic structure with charisma.[9]

Social scientists have a double purpose in applying their theories to the analysis of social phenomena. They want to understand the events and people they study and at the same time confirm their theories. They are searching for theoretical models with the widest possible applications, and when a new body of data conforms to their theories, they have doubly succeeded. Most historians (not all) have little interest in creating master theories that apply universally. They want to know what is going on in their particular realm of study. All to the good if their explanations have wider application, but that is not the object of their investigations. The few who do attempt grand theories, while splashy for a moment, tend to fall into disrepute. Arnold Toynbee's grand attempt to explain the rise and fall of the twenty-one civilizations that have inhabited the globe, for example, has been shot full of holes. The specialists in each segment of human history find his generalizations forced and misleading. Toynbee argued that civilizations grew in response to a challenge—social, economic, physical, military, climactic. If they had it too easy, if people did not have to exert themselves, they would be defeated. For instance, Massachusetts, Toynbee suggested, flourished intellectually and culturally more than Virginia because people in Massachusetts had to cope with a cold climate and inhospitable soils, while the Virginians had it much easier with their warm climate and lucrative tobacco crop. Hence Harvard and a vigorous literary culture in Massachusetts compared to a much less ambitious Virginia. In Maine, on the other hand, the cold was too great and people were too hard-pressed to write books and found universities. It therefore bore little cultural fruit. The trouble with the generalization, it came to be seen in time, is that it only represented prejudices about what constituted civilization. Historians found that private libraries in the South equaled anything in the North and the architecture was more elaborate and refined. Rather than finding the sources of civilization, Toynbee was only reinforcing his prejudices about the importance of religion. His theory of civilization has become an artifact of his time rather than a revelation of the governing laws of civilizations.[10]

The criticisms, however, do not vitiate the worth of theory or make it useless to historians. To the contrary, historians call on theories all the time. In my own work, theory has proven invaluable in drawing attention to or even creating evidence. Most of the words and images that pass before one's eyes while searching an archive or interviewing a historical actor go totally unattended. They do not even attain the level of fact. There are no words for them; one cannot see them as an entity without a concept, a theory for perceiving them. The researcher passes by almost all of what she sees or hears as she searches for the bits and pieces that are relevant—the facts that have meaning. Theory serves to turn the blur of sensation into meaningful evidence—the facts that have to be ordered and explained. With the help of general ideas, a trivial item, virtually invisible at first, is seen to fit into a pattern or helps to tell a story. Theory becomes immensely valuable to historians insofar as it helps them with their essential task which is to tell a story. Most theories are a form of story that absorbs details scattered in the record into elements of a dramatic rendition.

I chanced upon a theory recently that lit up certain parts of the early Joseph Smith story for me. I was telling one of my sons about my preliminary thoughts on the meaning of the gold plates and made a comment about their ambiguity. The plates were both mystical and rational, fraudulent and profoundly religious. He had studied literature in college before turning to medicine and observed that my take on the plates reminded him of the Franco-Bulgarian literary theorist Tzvetan Todorov. Todorov is not a social scientist, but he has the same confidence in the regularities of genres in literature as sociologists do in the regularities of society. Literature, Todorov says, is a system.[11] He is persuaded that world literature falls into categories called genres, each with common structural characteristics wherever they occur, much like animals can be grouped into species. Todorov can be thought of as a natural scientist of literature. Another literary theorist in this tradition, Northrop Frye, titled his master work *Anatomy of Criticism*.[12] Literary forms, Frye argued, can be categorized like the parts of the human body. From body to body, people have hearts, lungs, muscles, eyes. Though differing in detail, they all have the same basic structure and perform the same function. Todorov believes, with Frye, that genre can be identified in all literatures that have the same structure and perform the same functions.

Todorov is most famous for his explication of the fantastic, a literary form that flourished in the nineteenth century and still turns up in films and stories today. Some of Ingmar Bergman's films (*The Magician*, 1958) delved into the wonders of the fantastic as did Kevin Spacey in *K-PAX* (2001). I was attracted to Todorov because of the obvious applicability of the fantastic to stories of the gold plates. By the fantastic Todorov does not refer to fairy stories about imaginary creatures with magic powers, or to science fiction where characters armed with fabulous technical powers accomplish impossible feats. On Todorov's account, stories of the fantastic begin in the world readers know and accept, the ordinary world we all live in. Then gradually the stories introduce happenings that suggest the supernatural—events that could not happen in the world as we know it. But in the story, these happenings are made entirely plausible.

The possibility of a natural explanation for the fantastic events is reduced to nearly zero, so much so that the reader hesitates, unsure whether these happenings are real or imaginary. Here is how Todorov puts it:

> In a world which is indeed our world, the one we know, a world without devils, sylphides, or vampires, there occurs an event which cannot be explained by the laws of this same familiar world. The person who experiences the event must opt for one of two possible solutions: either he is the victim of an illusion of the senses, or a product of the imagination—and the laws of the world then remain what they are; or else the event has indeed taken place, it is an integral part of reality—but then this reality is controlled by laws unknown to us.[13]

In the moment of hesitation, the question remains up in the air. For a moment the reader wonders if new laws apply, if unnatural or supernatural things do happen. Usually this uncertainty does not last, and resolution is achieved. The author helps the reader decide if the world is actually different than he or she thought. In one outcome, the fantastic turns out to have a rational explanation and the event assumes the form of the merely uncanny. In this case, familiar natural laws still hold. In the second, the event has no natural explanation and the story takes on the character of the marvelous. New laws are seen to apply, and the world is changed in that the supernatural is shown to exist. The story is fantastic only while it hovers between these alternatives, that is, so long as the reader—and the story's hero—hesitates.

All this made me look again at the reaction of some of the early players in the gold plates story. The plates did not take the form of the fantastic for everyone. Some disbelieved from the beginning while others, like Joseph Smith's family, immediately accepted his visions. But for a few the story caused them to pause: Could it be true? Do other laws apply? Lucy and Martin Harris were two of the hesitants. Though they came down on opposite sides at the moment of resolution, for a time they both were uncertain. When most Palmyrans scoffed at Joseph Smith's tale of the plates, Martin wondered, unsure of what to believe. He took the trouble to interrogate individual members of the Smith family trying to catch them in a contradiction. Would they give themselves away and show they were lying for their brother? The stories proved consistent, and so the suspense continued. For months Martin was unsure, seeking for evidence to either dispel the illusion or to confirm the marvelous. In that time he inhabited the realm of Todorov's fantastic. His expedition to New York City sought a judgment from a learned man about the characters. Were they authentic or not? A year later, he pled to see the plates more passionately than anyone in hopes of resolving the tension. For a long time, he hesitated, remaining unsure, embroiled in the anxiety of the fantastic.

Lucy Harris was enthralled more briefly than her husband, but more eagerly. Lucy Smith said Martin's wife began pressing money on her the moment she heard about the plates. On visiting Joseph Smith, Lucy Harris insisted that "she was determined to assist in the business." But she was frustrated by his refusal to show her the plates. After Joseph and Emma moved to Harmony to translate, Lucy Harris came again. In Lucy Smith's account:

> As soon as she arrived there she informed him that her object in coming, was to see the plates and that she would never leave until she had accomplished it. Accordingly without delay she commenced ransacking every nook and corner about the house—chests, trunks cupboards, &c. . . . Not finding them in the house, she concluded that Joseph had buried them, and the next day she commenced searching out of doors, which she continued to do until about two o clock p.m.[14]

Lucy Harris was no believer, but no skeptic either. She could not decide. She was driven by the anxiety of the fantastic to search the cupboards and hunt for a burial place outside the house. She had to find out, just as any reader of a fantastic story wants to know if supernatural powers are actually at work.

Todorov's theories made me look at the Harrises' reactions in a new light. Facts that I had simply seen as parts of the story began to light up. For a moment the gold plates story was fantastic in the classic sense of Todorov. The Harrises' response could be generalized. It was part of a common set of reactions in a time when traditional religious belief was in question. The fantastic enthralled people who yearned for belief but were uncertain. They loved to be tantalized, dancing about on their own doubts. Although I do not subscribe to the notion of universal literary genres, Todorov's exploration of a universal genre with fixed characteristics helped me to comprehend Lucy and Martin Harris's situation. Like other historians, I am a jackal, living off the big game that literary and social scientists have brought down.

On every hand, people like myself who resist the metaphysics of sociology or of scientific literary criticism benefit from the analysis of those who pursue the generalized knowledge we historians think is impossible to find. Weber combed the world for instances of charisma and routinization, looking into Asia and Africa, as well as Europe, searching for universal regularities. Todorov has done the same for fantastic stories. Historians complain that these regularities are an imposition that does an injustice to the particularities, doing what has been called "cultural violence" to these varied peoples. And yet humphing about as we do, we still use the findings of the social scientists to illuminate our own more confined segments of space and time.

I would go further and say that Mormon studies will make some of its most illuminating advances in the coming years as we let theory inform our research. I am of the opinion that the way forward in Mormon studies is through establishing wider and wider contexts for Mormon events. There is a strong impulse within Mormonism to focus narrowly on the Mormon story. The religion means so much to its adherents that events are meaningful solely for what they tell of Mormonism itself. Every small fact acquires significance as it is attached to the divine story of Restoration—God actively intervening in human affairs once more. Mormons' fascination with their own history resembles the antiquarian impulses of nineteenth-century historians of New England. Every bit of information about the Puritans was valued simply because it was part of the Great Migration narrative. Nothing had to be interpreted or contextualized if it was associated with the Puritan pioneers. Mormons feel the same way about the events surrounding Joseph Smith or the pioneer trek to Utah. Establishing the exact sequence of events or adding a detail to well-known occurrences was in itself worthy scholarship. Mormon culture acts like a black hole sucking everything into its center. Mormon studies is now in the process of escaping that gravitational pull and situating Mormonism in broader American and world contexts. Where does Mormon thought stand among the philosophies and theologies of the Western world? How does Mormon lived religion compare to the experiences of Pentecostals or Sikhs? Mormon studies is becoming broadly comparative, addressing issues posed by religious studies.

Theory has an important part to play in this broadening. The intellectual structure of theory is necessarily comparative and contextual. The point of theory is to discover and understand the regularities in human society and culture. What conceptions account for broad ranges of human experience? Todorov found examples of the fantastic throughout Western culture. In applying his theories to Martin and Lucy Harris, I situate this fragment of Mormon history in a broad movement across European and American literature. Indeed Todorov would likely say the fantastic is inherent in the human imagination. Theory automatically compels Mormon scholars to think of their subject's place in the larger world.

I will never forget my first reading of Mircea Eliade's *Myth of the Eternal Return* on a plane ride from Boston to Salt Lake City.[15] In the regularities of what Eliade called traditional life across the globe I recognized the very essence of the ceremonies through which I worshipped God in Latter-day Saint temples. The idea of a point where heaven touched earth and all creation began added a dignity and resonance to the endowment and the whole temple idea. Since then Eliade has been discredited for the very reasons I have questioned the sociological quest for social regularities—because he crushes the particulars of actual societies in his quest for the overarching principles of the traditional mind. But diminished as he has been, Eliade still helped me to perceive patterns in temple worship I might never have recognized without him. In other words, the search for universal regularities may be beneficial even when wrongheaded. The drive for a natural history of religion compels sociologists to rise to a level of generalization that more earthbound minds never achieve. The results benefit even skeptics like me.

Notes

1. Weber enunciated his classic categories in various places, among them *The Protestant Ethic and the Spirit of Capitalism* which first appeared in 1904–1905 and in various forms after that. The fundamental notion was elaborated by the theologian Ernst Troeltsch in *The Social Teachings of the Christian Churches*, vol. 1 (New York: Macmillan, 1931). For a discussion of the concept's development, see William H. Swatos Jr., "Weber or Troeltsch? Methodology, Syndrome, and the Development of Church-Sect Theory," *Journal for the Scientific Study of Religion* 15 (June 1976): 129–44.
2. Armand L. Mauss, *Shifting Borders and a Tattered Passport: Intellectual Journeys of a Mormon Academic* (Salt Lake City: University of Utah Press, 2012).
3. Kathleen Flake, *The Politics of American Religious Identity: The Seating of Senator Reed Smoot, Mormon Apostle* (Chapel Hill: University of North Carolina Press, 2004).
4. Matthew Bowman, "Eternal Progression: Mormonism and American Progressivism," paper presented at the Mormonism and American Politics conference, Columbia University, February 4, 2012. See also Bowman's chapter in this volume.
5. Leonard Arrington, "An Economic Interpretation of the Word of Wisdom," *BYU Studies* 1 (Winter 1959): 37–49.
6. Historians do dabble in large-scale generalizations. Frederick Jackson Turner's frontier theory of American history has been applied to other parts of the world. Turner, "The Significance of the Frontier in American History," *Proceedings of the State Historical Society of Wisconsin* (1893), and *The Frontier in American History* (1921); Philip Wayne Powell et al., *Essays on Frontiers in World History*, ed. George Wolfskill and Stanley Palmer (College Station: Texas A & M University Press, 1983).
7. Richard Lyman Bushman, with the assistance of Jed Woodworth, *Joseph Smith: Rough Stone Rolling* (New York: Alfred A. Knopf, 2005).
8. Max Weber, *The Theory of Social and Economic Organization*, ed. Talcott Parsons, trans. A. M. Henderson and Talcott Parsons (New York: Free Press, 1947), 324–72.
9. Richard Lyman Bushman, "Joseph Smith and Power," in *A Firm Foundation: Church Organization and Administration*, ed. David J. Whittaker and Arnold K. Garr (Salt Lake City, UT: Deseret Book, 2011), 1–13.
10. Arnold J. Toynbee, *A Study of History*, 12 vol. (London: Oxford University Press, 1934–1961).
11. Tzvetan Todorov, *Genres in Discourse*, trans. Catherine Porter (New York: Cambridge University Press, 1990), 5.
12. Northrup Frye, *Anatomy of Criticism: Four Essays* (Princeton, NJ: Princeton University Press, 2000 [1957]).

13. Tzvetan Todorov, *Fantastic: A Structural Approach to a Literary Genre*, trans. Richard Howard (Ithaca, NY: Cornell University Press, 1975), 25.
14. Lavina Fielding Anderson, ed., *Lucy's Book: A Critical Edition of Lucy Mack Smith's Family Memoir* (Salt Lake City, UT: Signature Books, 2001), 395 (cf. 398), 405.
15. Mircea Eliade, *The Myth of the Eternal Return: or, Cosmos and History*, trans. Willard R. Trask (Princeton, NJ: Princeton University Press, 1971).

Part V | Autobiography and Memoir in Mormon Studies

Chapter 11 | "I Still Think of Myself as a Mormon"

The Autobiography of Wayne Booth— A Bold Experiment in Historiography

Levi S. Peterson

AUTOBIOGRAPHY HAS LONG BEEN A GENRE THAT HAS HELD INTEREST FOR Mormon writers and readers. In recent years we have had the pleasure of reading autobiographies from some of twentieth-century Mormonism's brightest intellectuals, including Leonard Arrington and Armand Mauss.[1] In this essay I will assess another work that I believe should be ranked among that small handful of outstanding Mormon autobiographies. This is the life story of Wayne C. Booth, titled *My Many Selves: The Quest for a Plausible Harmony* and published posthumously in 2006.[2]

I will not attempt to distinguish between autobiography and memoir here. The terms are synonymous in popular usage, and even the lexicographers can't do more than get partial agreement on a distinction between them. Obviously, autobiography is a species of biography, which in turn is a species of historiography. Autobiography can be substantiated as densely as other kinds of historiography by reference to old letters, diaries, newspaper articles, tax bills, interviews, and other sorts of visible documentation.[3] In addition, it relies extensively upon its author's memory, which serves as a kind of implied documentation. I will also remind my reader that history of any sort, including autobiography, while primarily serving to inform, can also please by having aesthetic qualities, particularly in matters of style and organization. As a reader might well expect from a literary critic of Booth's stature, his autobiography is admirable for its literary qualities. For one thing, it is notable for a daring innovation in organizational structure. For another, it is written in a style that is dexterous in sentence construction and word choice.

Born in rural Utah in 1921, Wayne Booth grew up in a zealous Mormon family and served two years in the North Central States Mission. Following a stint in the U.S. Army during World War II, he married Phyllis Barnes and embarked on a long and distinguished career as a professor of English at the University of Chicago.[4] He became internationally famous for his books on rhetoric, particularly for his first, *The Rhetoric of Fiction*, published in 1961.[5] At the time of Booth's death in 2005, his department chairman characterized this book as "the single most important American contribution to narrative theory—a book that continues to be read, taught, and fought about. In person and in print, Wayne Booth demonstrated how significant the act of literary analysis could and should be."[6]

Booth aspired to write a *new* kind of autobiography, one that would earn a place among such world-class works as *The Confessions of St. Augustine*, *The Autobiography of Benjamin Franklin*, and *The Education of Henry Adams*. Accordingly, Booth rejects a conventional chronological structure because, as he says in his preface, his life, "if viewed as a mere chronology, is quite ordinary, uncolorful, undramatic" (ix). Instead, he proposes to concentrate upon his internal conflicts, ambivalences, and self-contradictions. As the title of his book indicates, he names his contending impulses, values, and attitudes as *Selves* or, as he sometimes calls them, *Personae*, *Voices*, or *Splits*. He gives these Selves names, which allows him to move back and forth between first, second, and third person discourse. He speaks of himself as Thinker-Booth or Moral-Booth, connecting the qualifying noun or adjective to his name with a hyphen or, more often, substituting an unhyphenated B for Booth, as in ThinkerB or GullibleB.

Moreover, as his title also indicates, Booth is bent upon reconciling his contending Selves, although his use of the term "plausible" casts some doubt upon the success of his quest for harmony among them. He divides the book into three parts containing a total of seventeen chapters. Predictably, he offers little explanation as to the order of his chapters. I will not attempt to treat all of them, but will delve into enough of them to demonstrate, first, that Booth's work does indeed represent a bold, even audacious literary experiment and, second, that it may justifiably be called a Mormon autobiography.

Chapter 1 is titled "A Devout Mormon Is Challenged by Rival Selves." As it makes clear, Booth emerged from a boyhood spent in rural American Fork, Utah, with Mormon habits and attitudes so indelibly imprinted upon his character that he remained on the rolls of the LDS Church throughout his life and engaged enough in the life of his Chicago ward to know and be known by his bishop and his home teachers. Moreover, at his own behest, he is listed in *Who's Who* as Mormon. "To understand fully my diverse Split-Selves, the Mormon-Split is crucial," Booth writes, going on to declare, "I still think of myself as a Mormon" (4). Obviously, Booth and his wife—who shared his disbelief—pleased their believing relatives by remaining Mormons of record. Booth judges, however, that "perceptive observers—not only those who patted us on the shoulder to feel if the undergarments were there—could detect, in word and deed, that we were hypocrites" (25). Booth is dubious about the usefulness of trying to please his relatives. "Will my assertions here that I still believe in God—according to my definition—lead the stricken ones to forgive me?" he asks (27). Nonetheless, he values his Mormon upraising highly for its ethical influence upon his adult life.

He ends chapter 1 with an unequivocal expression of gratitude—a "daily gratitude," he emphasizes—"for having been indoctrinated into the fact that there are serious moral limits to individualistic code breaking. . . . The Mormon teaching that 'standards are real, not just invented,' though formulated differently in different decades, continues with me now, and I see many moments when, if I had not been indoctrinated from day one, my so-called Thinking might have landed me in disaster" (32).

Chapter 2 of Booth's autobiography consists of a confession of a life-long impulse toward a covert dishonesty—an impulse which, fortunately, he gave in to only rarely after becoming an adult. Titled "A Pious Moralist Confronts a Cheater," chapter 2 alludes to thefts, lies, and evasions of various sorts. At age seven he stole a bag of marbles. At fourteen, he kept part of the fast offerings he collected. At nineteen, he skimmed a part of the proceeds at a hamburger stand where he worked. The dishonesty for which he feels the greatest shame occurred when he and other typists who had been serving in Paris were mobilized during the Battle of the Bulge in December of 1944. Examined by an army doctor, Booth first tried faking poor vision by failing to read a vision chart. When the suspicious doctor asked whether he had some better reason for being exempted, Booth cited his flat feet, for which ironically the U.S. Navy had refused to accept him as a volunteer. Satisfied with this excuse, the doctor exempted Booth from combat. "If I had been a conscientious objector or complete pacifist, escaping combat at that point would not have been shameful," writes Booth. "But I was a passionate anti-Nazi, a total supporter of our army effort. . . . Yet I lied in order to avoid my own probable death at the front. The fact that it was my feet that really saved me doesn't mitigate my vision lie at all" (44).

Chapter 3, titled "The Cheerful Poser Comforts a Griever, or A Would-be Tough Guy Meets Grief and Conceals the Tears," begins with the death of Booth's only son, Richard, at age eighteen in an automobile accident—an event which plunged Booth, his wife, and their two daughters into years of intense mourning. Despite their overwhelming grief, both Booth and his wife maintained a face of composure in public. "And that posing, I would argue, has been useful—in fact, one of our best tools in coping with the grief," Booth writes. "We went on grieving (in a sense, even until today). But we learned that if you can put on the mask of good cheer, the mask sometimes becomes—at least for the moment—the real face. Acting out cheerfulness cheers you up" (55–56).

Having said that, Booth moves on to another major tragedy, the death of his father soon after he had turned six, a loss that had a far-reaching impact. For one thing, his mother had to earn a living by teaching school and she moved with Booth and his little sister Lucille into the house of her widowed father, where farm work and the persecutions of an uncle a little older than Booth made his life miserable. Though he mourned the loss of his father deeply, he later developed a "proud resistance to grieving—even contempt for it" (73), a hypocritical posture that lasted through his teens and beyond. But by middle age he has given up his Would-be Tough Guy stance and mourns his mother's death by "sobbing almost as uncontrollably" (74) as he had at his father's death. Predictably, he concludes this chapter on grief by admitting to anxiety born of the fated vulnerability of all human beings. "There is no conclusion to grief, unless one dies early," he writes. "How will I deal with the next loss? Who knows?" (75)

In the title of chapter 4, "My Many Selves Confront the Man Who Believes in Love," the word Love is cast in larger font to indicate an unusual signification. Love in the sense Booth intends here means doing almost anything for no other reason than the simple pleasure of doing it. This is a topic about which Booth felt so strongly that in 1999 he wrote a book on it, *For the Love of It: Amateuring and Its Rivals*, in which he concentrates upon playing the cello.[7] He took up this activity in 1952 in order to accompany Phyllis, who played the violin and viola with expertise.[8] Fated by a lack of musical talent to something less than a professional mastery of his instrument, Booth nonetheless tried to achieve an amateur's mastery of it for the simple pleasure of doing so. However, doing things for the simple love of it hasn't come easily to him. Booth devotes most of this chapter to a discussion of his proclivity toward ambition and vanity—ambition being the desire "to *be* number one, whether as a teacher, scholar, husband, father, amateur cellist, or autobiographer who really *thinks* about the meaning of life," and vanity being the desire "to be *seen* as moving toward the top, maybe even as number one, whether I've really made it or not" (79).

Unwilling to concede entirely to a desire to excel, Booth continues the theme of doing things for the pleasure of it in chapter 5, which is titled "Ambition vs. Teaching for the Love of It." Booth esteems that he chose and pursued his lifetime vocation, teaching, with little intrusion from ambition and vanity. Having narrated his development as a teacher, he moves on—with relish—to a discussion of his teaching methodology. He insisted on small classes, required student participation, and found himself so caught up in preparing for classes and grading papers that he found little time for his own writing during the academic year. Nonetheless, he managed to publish an astonishing array of articles and books, many of them related to rhetoric and teaching, which he wrote during summers and on sabbatical leaves.

In later chapters, Booth characteristically discounts his actual achievement. Among his contending Selves at the outset of his academic career were a would-be scholar and a would-be novelist. His temperament being what it was, he chose to become what he calls a wandering generalist, on the basis of which he achieved international fame. But his insatiable ambition is such that he pines for more. In chapter 12—titled "A Wandering Generalist Longs to Be a True Scholar"—Booth reveals that in his judgment it is scholars, not prolific authors like himself, who truly excel. "Scholars are those who dig deep in one single cavern—and go on digging until they come to layers no one else has even suspected. . . . Genuine literary scholars pursue single authors or topics for decades—even for a lifetime" (211). Furthermore, in chapter 13, "A Would-be Novelist Mourns behind the Would-be Lover and Would-be Scholar," Booth laments yet another unrealized ambition.

Moving on from where the themes of chapter 5 led us, we find chapter 6 to be titled "The Hypocritical Mormon Missionary Becomes a Skillful Masker, and Discovers 'Hypocrisy-Upward.'" Obviously, this is another confessional chapter. Given that Booth has informed us in chapter 1 that he became a doubter at a precocious age, at least as early as sixteen, we might well ask why he accepted a call to the North Central States Mission in 1941 at the age of twenty. For one thing, it pleased his family. For another, he supposed that he could "do good in the world" and "start liberalizing the church from within." Yet another reason—the one he is most loath to confess—is "the internal suspicion that the decision to become a missionary was tainted by the fact that it would postpone his being drafted into the war" (121).

As things turned out, Booth proved to be a highly successful missionary, being made mission secretary and residing at mission headquarters in Chicago. This was an auspicious eventuality, because while there he took several courses at the University of Chicago, where he would return after his mission and military service to continue his education and ultimately take a faculty position.[9] Moreover, without his knowing its consequences, being a missionary forced Booth to develop a systematic equivocation whereby he used language in his lessons and sermons that simultaneously satisfied both his own doubting self and his ardently believing listeners.

He would eventually call this systematic equivocation "hypocrisy-upward," and from it would eventually emerge a complex theory of rhetoric that he would call "rhetorology" (xiv). The aim of this well-intentioned dissembling, he explains, is moral. It serves "the deepest of all human values: understanding—sympathetic, serious listening to others—which almost always requires at least some biting of tongues, some posing" (133). He attributes this valuable insight to his Mormon raising. He observed, "Just as your deepest faith—whether 'religious' or 'atheist' or 'agnostic'—penetrates all that you do, so what I sometimes call 'the good side of Mormonism' penetrates my life and will be with me till I die" (134).

In chapter 7, "The Puritan Preaches at the Luster While the Hypocrite Covers the Show," Booth says that he has experienced a "normal" degree of lust and unconsummated desire for attractive females throughout his life but asserts his fidelity to Phyllis both before and after marriage. He also speaks of his relationship with Phyllis as a "rescue." When he was drafted into the army shortly after becoming engaged to her, he was determined to be faithful to her. The exchange of frequent letters between him and Phyllis helped him ignore such abundant temptations as a French chambermaid who thanked him for a gift of soap by offering to go to bed with him. Believing that the sexual promiscuity of the contemporary era has produced little happiness and a great deal of strife, Booth writes an admonitory warning: "I can't think of any fully coherent way—other than happy marriage—to reconcile masculine lust with what is for me the supreme moral commandment: thou shalt not, in pursuit of your own current pleasure or profit, harm other people or your future Self. What I do not question—what produces not the slightest Self-Splits . . . is my slow discovery that monogamy, *sexually faithful* monogamy, is a much neglected rescue from life's many threatening disasters" (151–52). Unquestionably, Booth's Mormon conscience had something to do with his commitment to fidelity.

In chapter 8, "The Lover Becomes a Trapped Army Private," Booth interprets his two-year stint in the U.S. Army during World War II as a largely "choice-free" period. As a soldier, he writes, "you've lost all free choice about what you are to do hour by hour. . . . Every moment is decided by this or that officer's order, whether stupid, cruel, or wise. You are thus in one sense freed from the Self-Splits that faced you day by day when you were free. In training, as you sit on the ground waiting for an order or conduct a four-hour hike or practice with your rifle, you tend to think of only one split, and it's not *within* your Self. Instead, it is 'I am trapped and I want out; I want Phyllis'" (155).

Chronologically speaking, chapter 8 is the first to feature a suspension of his Splits—although, as we saw in chapter 3, he writes that years after his son had died, he realized that his loss had resulted in such a suspension, producing "a weird kind of total centering" (51). Chapter 8 also narrates a crucial transformation of belief on Booth's part deriving from an evasion of combat that predates his later escape from combat in the Battle of the Bulge that he speaks of in chapter 1. In chapter 8, Booth tells us that soon after his arrival in France, he and other soldiers, trained as "clerk/riflemen," were at a replacement center in northern France, awaiting assignment. One morning they were all ordered onto trucks, heading for the nearby front—all, that is, except Booth. When he had first been inducted into the army, an official had mistakenly recorded that he could type eighty words a minute. On the strength of this supposed proficiency, he was ordered to return to Paris for assignment as a clerk. On that cold ride he did a lot of thinking about "God, chance, and choice," concluding that it "is arrogance of the most unforgivable sort to think God would preserve me, without wife & children, and allow to be killed men with families." Despite his guilt, he found himself "exuberantly happy at being out of the worst part of the mess" (155). But the ultimate result was that he came to "the absolute, final decision to conclude my inner debates about God's existence: there is no God, because no God deserving our worship would commit an act like that. I had no choice but to pronounce myself an atheist" (155).

Going on, in chapter 9, "An Egalitarian Quarrels Scornfully with a Hypocritical Bourgeois," Booth upbraids himself for hypocritically pursuing a comfortable middle-class lifestyle in violation of his deeply felt egalitarian ideals. Ineluctably, he sees himself as an elitist. "The very act of writing a *Life* can be called anti-egalitarian," he writes (168). While EgalitarianB wants "his work to address everybody . . . the intellectual, especially VainB . . . wants to be admired at 'the top'" (171). He has sold out, he writes, "to the comforts of getting ahead, the pleasures of owning houses and cars and yachts that others cannot afford. We hypocrites surrender daily to violations of the ideal of true equality; I'm typing here on my expensive computer, sitting on a costly ergonomic chair. We're just back from a lovely vacation in Utah at our second home, having been able to afford a third 'senior citizen' seat on the plane for my cello. We've each paid more than $4,000 recently for hearing aids, without thinking very hard about what $8,500 would mean to this or that impoverished family." He concludes by admitting, "It's hardly surprising that I find such inner conflicts irresolvable" (176).

Moving ahead to chapter 14, titled "The Committed Father and Husband, as Lover, Shouts 'For Shame!' at All the Other Selves," we find Booth adversely judging his contribution to the wellbeing of the family he and Phyllis have established. At the start of their married life, Booth was determined to carry a full share of caring for their children. However, while a graduate student he quickly succumbed to the necessity of long hours of study, and after becoming a professor, he allowed teaching and writing to consume his time. Phyllis's hope for a career was "shoved aside by her half-successful husband and her duties with the children. Her friends were mainly my academic associates and their mates. Though . . . she came to love many of our common friends—especially those who played chamber music with us—her life often felt *subordinate*" (243). Booth derives comfort from the fact that later Phyllis achieved an impressive professional career of her own, taking a master's degree in human development and clinical psychology at the University of Chicago and being a key figure in the development of Theraplay, a sophisticated form of play therapy for children. He is also comforted to know that his grown daughters don't recall that he was particularly neglectful: "They remind me that I did most of the dishes, teaching them how to have fun doing it. I did most of the grocery shopping. And, they reassuringly claim, I did a lot of game playing. At bedtime I sang songs and read to them and made up fairy stories" (242). Nonetheless, he regrets not spending more time with them. "Nobody but VainB," he ruefully concludes, "would have suffered from the slight diminishment in my total publication record" (250).

Chapter 15, "The Man of Peace Tries to Tame the Slugger," adds anger to the list of deficiencies and shortcomings to which Booth confesses. He opens the chapter by describing what amounts to a tantrum on his part. While preparing a speech for a conference, he inadvertently lost ninety minutes of typing when his computer crashed. In a rage, he picked up a valuable reference book and threw it to the floor, severely damaging the spine. Telling us it was an oft-repeated outburst, he goes on to other instances of it. He recalls that while a boy he knocked down an uncle near his own age with an ax. He frequently got into fights as a boy—although he also characterizes himself as avoiding many fights by admitting in advance his opponent would win.

He grants that his propensity toward violence may surprise his readers, who may think of him "as an unusually peaceful, nonviolent man—a 'dialogist' or 'rhetorologist,' always working to achieve peaceful reconciliation between disputants through the pursuit of understanding" (252). He interprets his propensity toward violence as a part of his genetic heritage. He therefore takes "some comfort from the universality of hypocrisy about violence, with all human beings openly or secretly my siblings in this matter" (260). Nonetheless, he remains troubled with his inability to ignore the trespasses of others, even when they are minor. Speaking of himself in the third person, he sees himself as "a divided creature, aware that deep down there is a potential killer in him and that life itself, both a blessing and a curse, will finally kill him" (261).

I trust that by now my reader can see how Booth sets his contending Selves against each other. I will therefore proceed to chapter 17, the finale in which Booth intends to persuade us that he has figured out a way to harmonize conflicts among his seemingly irreconcilable Selves. The title of chapter 17, "Harmony at Last?," is put tentatively, as the question mark shows. Booth divides this chapter into three parts. He writes:

> This chapter begins with a brief summary of the innumerable moments of centering that might be called *temporary* harmonies. In each of them, the rivalry among Booths is briefly silenced, as some total concentration is achieved, blissful or tragic. Part two is an attempt to explain why no one can escape soul splits. At the heart of "things" is a strong conflict among three "absolutes": Supreme Being "orders" us to pursue Truth *but also* to pursue Beauty *and also* to pursue Goodness—the universal welfare of all God's creatures. Part three is my final quest for the most plausible harmony among these three inescapably conflicting human goals. (290)

Having outlined the chapter, Booth proceeds to a detailed development of its three parts. In the first of these, titled "Emotional Centerings," he offers a long list of what he calls "Temporary Blissful Centerings." Their point is, of course, that while he is experiencing them he is not aware of Splits. I will give three of them here by way of example:

- "Making love—not just having sex but *loving* my lifelong partner, Phyllis."
- "Writing a draft of something that feels good or even polishing . . . what was before just a messy paragraph or chapter."
- "Looking at a flower, or a shimmering lake, or a magnified photo of an insect, or a rainbow flash from a prism, feeling a flood of gratitude to the God/Nature that created such marvels." (292–93)

Booth also lists some other kinds of temporary centerings—"comic," "regrettable," "miserable," and "faked blissful." The most substantial of these are the miserable centerings imposed on Booth from time to time by the death of loved ones and close friends throughout his nearly eighty years. The most contemptible in Booth's opinion are the faked blissful centerings common to self-help books, which "never mention how much real good is done in the world by people who pretend to be harmoniously cheerful when they're actually torn apart" (298).

In the second part of chapter 17, titled "Dialogue among the Selves, Moving toward Harmony," Booth applies rhetorology—his special method for finding a common ground between conflicting forces, in this case, his Selves. He first warns the reader that in his search for harmony he sets special store by the term *plausible* in its meaning of "apparently valid, likely, or acceptable." That said, he asks, "What happens when this rhetorologist works to achieve real dialogue among a batch of rivaling Selves? He soon discovers that all of the disputes boil down to a simple conflict of three irrefutable, ultimate, universal values, oversimplified with the labels Truth, Goodness, and Beauty" (298). Booth has decided that by temperament he inclines more toward Goodness than toward Truth or Beauty, but he refuses to declare any of them superior to the others. Moreover, he regards them as "real" values, not mere "cultural constructs." In making that claim, he writes, "I am clearly invading the territory that all believers claim as their own." In short, rhetorology, applied to his conflicting Selves, "lands us in religious questions" (300).

Moving on to the third part of chapter 17, "Joining the Divine Chorus, in Spiritual Harmony," Booth undertakes to establish a harmony among the three great absolutes that he has declared to be "inescapably conflicting" values (290). How can it be managed? By a mystical vision of what he calls "the One." While reading Plato as a young man in the army, he has a remarkable dream that convinces him that "if he thinks long enough and hard enough about it, he will find the One that will harmonize Truth, Goodness, and Beauty" (301). Thereafter, thinking "long enough and hard enough" becomes something of an obsession. "That longing for a vision of the central One, totally harmonizing all the conflicts," Booth writes, "is revealed throughout my life" (302). Moreover, there are moments when people, including himself, "do feel illuminated by a sense of achieved harmony" (303). He is speaking of moments when "Supreme-Being-Itself seems in some mysterious way to *harmonize* what we cannot intellectually manage to harmonize" (303).

He draws comfort from the fact that, though he is mortal and will never achieve more than a fraction of the three great values, they will go on being discovered by others: "It was their actual existence in the total range of possibilities in Supreme Being that enabled any one of us to come along and discover them" (303). Herein lies a kind of immortality, the subsistence of the great absolute values, which are woven into the fabric of the universe, available for rediscovery by ongoing generations of human beings. Through evolution—"one of Supreme Being's cleverest creations"—other Selves on "this planet or on innumerable others" will come to know "there is a real difference between good and bad, and then *some* of them will engage in the quest for the difference and pursue harmony among the diverse goods" (304).

Although he believes no single person can "totally grasp the One," Booth hopes human beings will prove willing to "share diverse views of Him/Her/It" and thus enlarge a collective understanding. The chief point of his book, of course, is that he himself offers a view of "the One," which he is convinced he has experienced on a variety of occasions. He concludes his book by reporting one of these occasions, a mystical experience that occurs while he and Phyllis, on a visit to Utah, hike on a favorite trail on Mount Timpanogos. It was a fresh, resplendent morning and as they steadily mounted, they engaged in "blissful kissing" and felt a "spiritual ecstasy." It was a moment of total harmony, all his Self Splits being "wiped away." Writing about it four years later, he goes beyond the tentativeness of the term "plausible." It was, he says, an epiphany that "still seems not just a *plausible* harmony: it's the real thing" (307).

As I have said, Booth intends in chapter 17 to persuade his readers that he has figured out a way to harmonize the conflicts among his Selves. I take him at his word when he says he experienced a mystical epiphany while hiking with Phyllis on Mount Timpanogos. I do not doubt his sincerity when he says he has grasped not just a plausible but a real harmony among his conflicting Selves. He has arrived at a mystical resolution of the conflict through reasoning about it. I cited above his conviction—conceived following a remarkable dream while in the army—that "if he thinks long enough and hard enough about it, he will find the One that will harmonize Truth, Goodness, and Beauty" (301). This is what his autobiography has been about: an account of a lifetime of *long, hard thinking* that ends in harmony. This reconciliation of conceptual conflicts has prepared him for an intuition of the unity—the Oneness—of all things. It has prepared him, in short, for a mystical experience.

However, it appears that on a *practical* plane—in the everyday life to which he and Phyllis returned following their morning hike on Timpanogos—Booth has resolved few if any of his hitherto unresolved conflicts. Four years intervene between the mystical experience on Timpanogos and the finishing of the autobiography. There's little evidence that he returned to Chicago with a greater control over SluggerB, or with a lessened susceptibility to grief when a loved one or friend dies, or with a more generous funding of EgalitarianB's charitable donations than he formerly had. In short, for most, if not all, of Booth's readers, his mystical resolution to inner conflicts will prove unsatisfactory, if for no other reason than that most people don't have mystical experiences. Temporary blissful centerings are the sort that reality imposes on most of us.

Nonetheless, by no means do I consider Booth's attempt to create a new sort of autobiography a failure. I don't know whether would-be autobiographers will follow his lead in the future and concentrate upon their unresolved conflicts, treating them in an order determined randomly by free association. I doubt that I would if I had the task of writing my own autobiography again. So it's entirely possible that Booth has established a category in which his book will remain the sole example. But I am glad that someone of Booth's stature gave it a try. It is, as I said above, a daring innovation in organizational structure, demonstrating a spirit of enterprise and willingness to experiment on Booth's part. Moreover, Booth's style of writing is highly engaging. It passes adroitly back and forth between the formal and the colloquial in sentence structure and its diction is replete with humor, irony, and a wry self-deprecation.

I also like this book because I have unresolved conflicts enough—as I suspect most, if not all, people do—to find some degree of catharsis while reading it. An exceptional practitioner of introspection, Booth articulates impulses and drives that many of us overlook or ignore in ourselves. Moreover, I like his candor. I admit that I am shocked to learn that even as an adult he has to keep an impulse toward theft in check and that he sometimes succumbs to a chronic, difficult-to-control anger. But I admire the candor which drove him to admit such things in his autobiography. His conscience impels him toward confession. Booth shares with St. Augustine a strong ethical disposition and an extraordinarily sensitive conscience.

Booth owes his conscience, he tells us, to his Mormon upbringing. Herein, I believe, is the reason to consider his work as a Mormon autobiography even though some might argue that Booth's early declaration of atheism (later modified into a sort of Platonic religiosity) undermines his claim to be a Mormon. It would seem he rarely attended church. According to Neal Kramer, a former student of Booth's and presently a professor of English at BYU, Booth's non-Mormon students "assumed he must be one of the most admired and appreciated members of our congregation [in Chicago]. In a touch of Boothian irony, I had to admit that to many he was just another less active member."[10] Nonetheless, in a review of Booth's *The Company We Keep: The Ethics of Fiction*, Kramer praises Booth's book for rejuvenating "the once powerful idea that reading stories can indeed influence the development of character, our day-to-day ethical practices."[11] It says much that Mormon professors and students find, ethically speaking, a kindred spirit in Wayne Booth.

I will also point out that when invited to address Mormon groups, Booth spoke as an insider. For example, in a paper read at a conference on LDS culture at Utah Valley State College, he adopted the persona of a believer, speaking of "our scriptures" and introducing a point with the following phrase, "as the Lord puts it in D&C 41:5."[12]

In my opinion, Booth may be classified as a liberal Mormon. Liberal Mormons differ from their more orthodox brothers and sisters in some point or points of doctrine or practice yet still think of themselves as Mormon. If they advocate change, it will be of a progressive sort rather than the regressive return to polygamy advocated by fundamentalist Latter-day Saints. Although their numbers are relatively few, they exert a considerable influence on Mormon culture through annual Sunstone symposia in Salt Lake City and elsewhere and through publications such as *Sunstone* magazine and *Dialogue: A Journal of Mormon Thought*. Liberal Mormons bear the church no ill will and may even wish to see it flourish. The picture of Mormonism is not complete without them. I am such a Mormon, as are many of my friends, and I am proud to find myself in the company of a spirit as humane, intelligent, and erudite as Wayne Booth.

Notes

1. Leonard J. Arrington, *Adventures of a Church Historian* (Urbana: University of Illinois Press, 1998); Armand L. Mauss, *Shifting Borders and a Tattered Passport: Intellectual Journeys of a Mormon Academic* (Salt Lake City: University of Utah Press, 2012).
2. Wayne C. Booth, *My Many Selves: The Quest for a Plausible Harmony* (Logan: Utah State University Press, 2006). Page numbers from this work will be noted parenthetically within the text.
3. As an example of an abundantly documented autobiography, I can cite my own life's story, *A Rascal by Nature, A Christian by Yearning: A Mormon Autobiography* (Salt Lake City: University of Utah Press, 2006). I will add that I came by my personal copy of Booth's autobiography in Utah during the summer of 2006. I had been invited to read from my book at a summer home in Provo Canyon. After the reading, I was approached by Phyllis Barnes Booth, Wayne's widow, who, as it happened, was spending a few weeks in the nearby Booth summer home. Mrs. Booth presented me with a copy of his book with the following inscription: "Wayne admired your work very much. I know he would have wanted you to have a copy of this book." I was deeply honored.
4. Booth occupied an endowed chair, the George M. Pullman Distinguished Service Professor in English Language and Literature. He was the recipient of numerous honors and distinctions.

5. Wayne C. Booth, *The Rhetoric of Fiction* (Chicago: University of Chicago Press, 1961; 2nd ed., 1983).
6. Quoted in an obituary released from the University of Chicago News Office, Oct. 11, 2005, http://www-news.uchicago.edu/releases/05/051011.booth.shtml. I myself made good use of this book as a graduate student during the early 1960s.
7. Wayne C. Booth, *For the Love of It: Amateuring and Its Rivals* (Chicago: University of Chicago Press, 1999).
8. Booth first met Phyllis at a chamber concert at Brigham Young University soon after returning from his mission in 1944. "She was playing the viola in a Mozart flute quintet," he writes. "After the recital, my sister introduced me to Phyllis Barnes, and the three of us chatted a bit. A day or so later Phyllis played a violin solo at my missionary homecoming, and we went for a walk on 'lover's lane'" (149).
9. Booth's BA degree was awarded by BYU, Booth having transferred credits from the University of Chicago to the Utah institution in 1947. Phyllis Booth to Levi Peterson, email, March 21, 2013.
10. Neal W. Kramer, "Tribute to Wayne C. Booth, 1921–2005," *Dialogue: A Journal of Mormon Thought* 39, no. 1 (Spring 2006): vi.
11. Neal W. Kramer, "Review of *The Company We Keep: The Ethics of Fiction*," *BYU Studies* 30, no. 1 (Winter 1990).
12. Wayne Booth, "The Rhetoric of Hypocrisy: Virtuous and Vicious," *Dialogue: A Journal of Mormon Thought* 33, no, 1 (Spring 2000): 124.

Chapter 12 | Art and Artifice
The Role of Memoir in Mormon Identity Formation

Jana Riess

When Terry Tempest Williams's mother was dying, she revealed a secret. As Williams reclined with her, rubbing her mother's back, the dying woman confessed that she was leaving Williams, the family writer, all of her journals. She extracted a promise that her only daughter would wait until after her death to open them, and only then did she divulge their location. At the start of her memoir *When Women Were Birds*, Williams describes the discovery:

> On the next full moon I found myself alone in the family home. I kept expecting Mother to appear. Her absence became her presence. It was the right time to read her journals. They were exactly where she'd said they would be: three shelves of beautiful clothbound books; some floral, some paisley, others in solid colors. The spines of each were perfectly aligned against the lip of the shelves. I opened the first journal. It was empty. I opened the second journal. It was empty. I opened the third. It, too, was empty, as was the fourth, the fifth, the sixth—shelf after shelf after shelf, all my mother's journals were blank.[1]

Many readers, upon hearing this story, may think: What a crushing thing for a parent to do. Poor Terry Tempest Williams. We imagine the way her body would have literally deflated at the disappointment of her mother's empty journals. She could not unearth her mother from the ground, but for some few wild days of hope she had believed she could unearth her mother's spirit and drink once again from her wisdom.

Williams, however, had a different response, which was to wonder instead what her ever-thoughtful mother was trying to teach her from the grave. Her mother loved words and books. She had been raised as a Mormon and taught that leaving a record of her life for posterity was not just a nice thing to do but nearly a sacred obligation. Yet she had left behind only silence. Why?

Many people yearn to write a memoir. Some do so to leave something behind, a legacy of sorts. Some write in order to have the chance to explain themselves to others, while others do so in order to better understand who they are and where they have been. All of these motivations have been present throughout Mormon history. The Mormon story is both unique and not unique. After first outlining the role of "record-keeping" in Mormon history and theology, this chapter explores three tensions with Mormon memoir to assess what role the act of recording personal stories has played in Mormon identity formation. I begin with the notion of agenda, or memoir as propaganda, then consider memoir as a vehicle for recording transcendent religious experiences. Finally, I survey the tension between faith-promoting testimony and realism, as memoirists struggle with how much brokenness to reveal in the records they leave behind.

A Record-Keeping People

"All writers are vain, selfish, and lazy," George Orwell wrote in 1946, "and at the very bottom of their motives lies a mystery. Writing a book is a horrible, exhausting struggle, like a long bout of some painful illness. One would never undertake such a thing if one were not driven on by some demon whom one can neither resist nor understand."[2] If Orwell was correct that the act of writing a book is an epic struggle, it is important for readers to ascertain why any author would ever choose to embark on it. For Mormons, one answer to that question has been that they believe they are conveying vital truths about God and the religious life, and that they have a responsibility to communicate those truths to their peers and descendants.

Since the earliest days of LDS record keeping, Mormons have expressed a "desire to see things as they are, to find out true facts and store them up for the use of posterity," as Orwell put it. Mormons take this so much for granted—that their writing should be preserved for their children and even their great-great-great-grandchildren—that they may not realize that the drive to record themselves so thoroughly is unusual in the annals of religious groups. Some Mormons express guilt if they do *not* make a faithful record of their lives, a fact seen in the early pages of Armand Mauss's memoir, where he berates himself for not having kept anything other than a sporadic diary—and then proceeds to demonstrate that faithful journal keeping is not a prerequisite for successful intellectual autobiography.[3]

In this matter the Mormon psyche carries a scriptural burden from Jesus's visit to the Nephites. Whereas in the New Testament Jesus comes across as naively unaware of any obligation to record his teachings, in the Book of Mormon, he explicitly tells his disciples to write them down lest they become ephemera. He scrutinizes the written record they already possess and reminds his followers that there is an important story missing, one about Samuel the Lamanite and the saints rising from the dead. Duly chastised, the disciples agree to add that in.[4] It is crucial—even divinely prescribed—that their record be complete.

Jesus was talking about scriptures, and the importance of maintaining a written sacred book—a preoccupation that marks a good deal of the Book of Mormon.[5] But since many early members of the LDS Church saw themselves as inhabiting a glorious dispensation of sacred time,[6] the line between scripture and personal experience may have been somewhat permeable.[7] Holy moments became manifestations of God's new work on the earth, work that Mormons were commanded to share with the world. Mormon prophet Joseph Smith set an example by purchasing a journal in November 1832, in which he intended "to keep a minute account of all things that come under my observation." Like most diarists, his record keeping was more sporadic than he had initially hoped, but between his own efforts and those of his intimate scribes he managed to leave behind over 1,500 manuscript pages for posterity.[8] And although many Mormons' goals for regular journal keeping remain largely aspirational, they have managed to leave behind thousands of such documents, which are housed in university and church archives, the Library of Congress, or passed down from one generation to the next within a family. Mormons have kept journals and missionary diaries, and compiled life sketches and oral histories.

But another level is the crafting of memoir, a conscious sifting of one's experiences with a reader in mind, whether the memoir is intended for publication or just for family members. It can be instructive to assess how the writing of such memoirs reflects—and in turn helps to create—the author's own identity. Historian and memoirist Jill Ker Conway has noted that "Whether we are aware of it or not, our culture gives us an inner script by which we live our lives. . . . What makes the reading of autobiography so appealing is the chance it offers to see how this man or that woman whose public self interests us has negotiated the problem of self-awareness and has broken the internalized code a culture supplies about how life should be experienced."[9]

Agendas: Memoir as Propaganda

The privilege of any memoirist is to have the last word. We see this in Mormon memoir, whether it's Sonia Johnson's daughter congratulating her on getting to literally "write off" her ex-husband in *From Housewife to Heretic* or Lucy Mack Smith speculating at the end of her memoir on the possible eternal damnation of all who once persecuted her family.[10] This points to the first area of tension in Mormon memoir, which is about setting the record straight and asserting one's own voice—sometimes in the face of a nonbelieving culture outside the LDS Church, and sometimes in defense against what the author perceives to be misunderstandings *within* the church. Memoirs by definition espouse a unique point of view, and many—if not all—have propagandistic tendencies.

Lucy Mack Smith, mother of the prophet Joseph, addressed both of those audiences. When her *History* was published in 1855, it created a stir within the Mormon community because it seemed to state clearly that Joseph Smith wished someone in his direct family line to succeed him as prophet, rather than Brigham Young. (As Jan Shipps notes, Brigham Young went to some lengths to suppress the book both for that reason and because he believed it contained many historical inaccuracies.)[11] A belief in dynastic Smith family succession was an inconvenient point of view for the Utah church.

But if Lucy wrote her memoir with an agenda of supplanting the order of succession that had arisen internally within the LDS Church, her more obvious agenda was external, as she took on her family's enemies. Everything in Lucy's memoir, she said, was "true and will stand forever," and that included fierce accusations against those who had wronged her. She had reared six sons to manhood, she wrote, but only one survived, and the world would come to regret that injustice.[12] Her vehemence here far transcended George Orwell's rather charming notion that people might write memoirs because as successful adults they wanted to get back at, for example, a teacher who had failed to believe in their potential. Lucy's anger was palpable, and her memoir reveals that while hard experience had taught her not to expect justice in this life, she would taste its sweetness in the hereafter. Her memoir, she said, would "stand before God at that hour when small and great shall appear to answer at his bar for the deeds done in the body, whether they be good or evil, and there will I meet the persecutors of my family who are the enemies of the church and declare with a voice that shall penetrate the ears of every intelligence which shall be present on that momentous occasion."[13] Tellingly, Lucy did not at first say that *she* would stand before God, but that "it"—her memoir—would stand. It was an ethereal extension of her core being. It was her "testimony," a word she used repeatedly in various forms—her insistence upon its accuracy and significance thereby blurring the lines between legal and theological language.

Lucy's agenda of raining spite upon her enemies gave animus to the way she chose to present her life. Writing, as Orwell made clear, is often a form of propaganda. He insisted that "no book is genuinely free from political bias," noting that most writers have a "desire to push the world in a certain direction." In using the word *political*, he did not necessarily mean the urge to explicitly influence politics or the wheels of justice, but in the broader sense of putting forward a particular worldview and making a difference in the course of things.

Throughout Mormon history, and to the present day, one consistent agenda for the writing of memoir has been to persuade the reader of the theological truth of

Mormonism. The conversion narrative has been a popular form, as folklorist Eric Eliason has shown; Mormon conversion narratives, whether oral or written, tend to follow recognizable patterns that involve seeking spiritual truth in diverse places and being surprised to discover it in Mormonism. The convert has an epiphany or other confirming experience despite enduring opposition or persecution for the new belief.[14]

On the other end of the spectrum are deconversion narratives penned by ex-Mormons who desire to explain both their original affiliation with and subsequent defection from the church and to warn others about what they see as the shadow realities of Mormonism. Like the consistent performance of Mormon conversion narratives, what is most striking about these memoirs of defection and disaffection is how little they have changed in more than a century and a half. The basic tropes are the same, with the author generally establishing his or her rock-solid credentials of card-carrying Mormonism in the first half and then tearing down the religious and intellectual foundations of the faith in the second. Sometimes these critiques are hard-hittingly personal and involve accusations of physical or sexual abuse, as in Martha Nibley Beck's *Leaving the Saints,* and sometimes they emphasize the dangers inherent in leaving the fold of Mormonism or one of its offshoots, as in Carolyn Jessop's aptly titled *Escape.*[15]

Far more fascinating are the memoirs that occupy the middle ground, the ones written by people who are trying to be faithful but for one reason or another find some aspect of Mormonism difficult to understand—or to explain to others. One of the best Mormon memoirs of all time, *A Mormon Mother*, falls into this category. If there is an agenda to Annie Clark Tanner's telling of her life story, it is that she wished to explain to her children and grandchildren, who inhabited a church that had moved on from polygamy, what her personal life as a daughter and wife had been decades earlier in plural marriage. Though written in 1941 near the end of her life, Tanner focused on the turbulent years in the 1880s and 1890s when she was attempting to live as a second wife, often in secret.

The management of public and private selves in this memoir is a complex web; Tanner's presentation of herself is marked by the vast changes that took place in her belief system during the course of her life. From her girlhood as an obedient, literalist Mormon, she emerged a thoughtful adult who began to question the assumed superiority of male over female. From one who firmly embraced "the principle" to the point of extreme sacrifice, Tanner evolved into a person who valued the primacy of life experience over principles of doctrine. Her personal hardships with polygamy forced her to question the divine principle she had accepted unstintingly as a girl, and led her to the conclusion that "monogamous marriages are by far the more successful."[16] By titling her memoir *A Mormon Mother*, she highlighted her pride in the achievements of her ten children, for whose sake she was sometimes prompted to stand up to her husband and pursue a better life.

There is in Tanner's memoir a kind of politics or propaganda—not for or against Mormonism, but for a woman's right to make her own decisions and determine the course of her life. Indeed, one might say there is a subtle agenda to *all* of the Mormon memoirs that have been published since, whether it be Armand Mauss's *Shifting Borders and a Tattered Passport*, which builds a strong case for the compatibility of faithful scholarship alongside ecclesiastical service, or Joanna Brooks's heartfelt *The Book of Mormon Girl*, which simultaneously implores insiders to greater compassion for LGBT persons and outsiders to greater compassion for misunderstood and coarsely caricatured Latter-day Saints.[17]

In a contemporary example, Nicole Hardy's memoir *Confessions of a Latter-day Virgin* presents, in far more frank language than Tanner's ever could have, the difficulties of trying to live as a Mormon woman when the author does not fit the culture's norm. In Hardy's case, this is because as a single woman in a "married church" she didn't have a clear place, and as someone who was fairly certain she didn't want children, she sometimes felt like a leper. One Mother's Day at sacrament meeting, Hardy had an epiphany of self-definition. Hearing that "like Eve," her "motherhood began before [she was] even born" and that motherhood was the "essence" of her identity as a woman, Hardy decided she had had enough. She took refuge in the church hallway:

> My throat closes against the words I can't swallow, not one more time. Because it's not *true*, what they're telling me—what they've been telling me since I was a child. There cannot be only one way to be a woman. My identity cannot be something I've never felt.
>
> I try to steady myself with a hand on the wall, but these subversive thoughts only serve to increase my panic. I'm bent at the waist, nearly crippled by the possibility that what I've been taught is a lie. *I* have to be wrong, rather than the church, the Gospel, the prophet. I must be misunderstanding God's will, or his plan for me. I need to feel what I'm supposed to, *be* what I'm supposed to. I've been taught that the LDS gospel is absolute truth; if one lie is revealed, what then? How could I allow it?[18]

Through her memoir, Hardy describes gradually claiming the right to tell her own story—tentatively at first, then boldly in an op-ed in *The New York Times*, and then irrevocably in the form of her memoir. And in the telling of that story, she began to own her very identity. She would not be told, as she was on Mother's Day and on many other occasions growing up in LDS culture, that as a woman it was her destiny to be a mother. As she became more able to admit that she had never felt called to that vocation, she also became free to challenge other conventional wisdom, eventually to the point of leaving the LDS Church. Unlike the angry deconversion narratives found in other books, Hardy's memoir expresses affection for many aspects of her Mormon upbringing, especially her loving parents, and she finds a continuing faith in God and prayer. Through *telling* her story, she became able to *actualize* that story; she became the defining, agentive character not just in her memoir but also in her life.

While we may be tempted to dismiss propaganda as one-sided, and therefore of little use, Orwell upheld propaganda, ironically, as the most honest and powerful reason for writing. He noted that his own writing improved suddenly and dramatically in 1936, when he became deeply concerned about the Spanish Civil War. "Looking back through my work," he said a decade later, "I see that it is invariably where I lacked a *political* purpose that I wrote lifeless books and was betrayed into purple passages, sentences without meaning, decorative adjectives and humbug generally."[19] Propaganda, then, is a powerful reason to write memoir, whether to set the record straight or to give voice to religious transcendence.

Testimony: Memoir as a Tool for Promoting Faith

Nineteenth-century Mormon memoirists sought to articulate what they viewed as a veritable explosion of beauty: their *writing* may not have always been memorable, but the *experiences* they recorded were transcendent. For example, in 1877, during the course of her medical studies in the eastern United States, Romania Pratt, plural wife of Parley P. Pratt Jr., had the surprising opportunity of visiting the Hill Cumorah with other female students, none of whom was Mormon:

> How can expression be given to the sacred awe pervading the soul as one nears the hallowed ground, where of a certainty we know that angels trod,—perhaps your foot may press the very footprint of a celestial being. Slowly and deeply impressed I ascended the sacred mount accompanied by the other ladies who had no impression of the awe or solemnity of the occasion. As we neared the summit a flock of sheep were grazing quietly but fled at our approach and soon we stood on the top of that memorable hill which has been the theater of many a severe conflict, physically between mortals and spiritually between the angels of light and darkness.[20]

Mormon memoirists have sought to declare ineffable religious experiences by employing the crude beast of language, a deplorably inadequate tool for describing encounters with the divine. This is true of many people's general struggles with writing. Novelist and memoirist Ann Padgett, for example, says that in her head, her stories are works of indescribable beauty. The key word, though, is "indescribable," because her writing can never fully capture it. She compares her creative ideas to butterflies "whose wings were cut from the rose window in Notre Dame"; those same butterflies, however, are killed in the process of pinning them to the flat page. What she is left with feels two-dimensional and lifeless compared to the glorious beauty that was in her mind. As Padgett puts it, "The journey from the head to hand is perilous and lined with bodies."[21]

If that is true of the general writing process, how much more true when one is trying to capture transcendent, even divine, experiences? This has been the case from the beginnings of Mormon history, when Joseph Smith tried repeatedly to describe what has come to be called the First Vision. Many scholars have wondered aloud at the increasingly grandiose nature of the telling; the would-be prophet's theophany became more lavish and his age more tender with each recounting. A less cynical interpretation is that mere language proved grossly insufficient to capture beauty, to convey matchless awe, so Smith gamely kept trying. In his personal history he wanted to invite us in, to share an experience that, as Richard Bushman has noted, was first understood as a quietly personal conversion but grew into a startling call with far-reaching import.[22] Like Romania Pratt, Smith was conscious that few outside of his immediate community would likely give credence to his experiences. It is surely no accident that the canonized version of the First Vision is replete with defensive language about not being able to deny a genuine epiphany:

> I had *actually* seen a light, and in the midst of that light I saw two Personages, and they did *in reality* speak to me; and though I was hated and persecuted for saying that I had seen a vision, *yet it was true*; and while they were persecuting me, reviling me, and speaking all manner of evil against me falsely for so saying, *I was led to say* in my heart: Why persecute me for telling the truth? I have *actually* seen a vision; and who am I that I can withstand God, or why does the world think to make me deny what I have *actually* seen? *For I had seen a vision; I knew it, and I knew that God knew it, and I could not deny it, neither dared I do it*; at least I knew that by so doing I would offend God, and come under condemnation.[23]

Smith's use of words such as "actually" and "real" speaks to his deep desire to make his theophany understood in concrete terms, but almost in the same breath he relates that he was hated and persecuted for precisely that concreteness: he had seen and heard God, and that was unforgivable.

Most Latter-day Saint memoirs and journals submerged the divine within the quotidian, far more so than Smith. Mormons recorded the ups and downs of life (children's illnesses, business transactions, new bonnets, Sunday meetings) with the sacred squeezed between, and bestowing meaning upon, the everyday. Moments of grace and answers to prayer, when they came, arrived within the larger context of work and family life. In fact, anthropologist Tom Mould notes a general reluctance on the part of many Mormons to sensationalize their spiritual experiences or remove them from the round of the everyday. In his analysis of 441 Mormon oral testimonies, Mould found that only ten narrators used the heady word "revelation" in reference to their own experiences, and says that in seven of those ten cases, the interviewees were responding to Mould's own use of the term in framing his question. "While church members regularly use explicit scriptural terms when *discussing* personal revelation, they typically avoid them when *narrating* their experiences," he notes. Calling one's own spiritual promptings "revelations" might "suggest an authority one does not have, a decidedly immodest presentation of oneself to one's peers."[24] Instead, Mormons more commonly employ claims like "I was prompted" or "I was inspired to do something." Interestingly, this more subdued language is the norm not only for rank-and-file members but also for LDS General Authorities, who rarely pronounce outright in General Conference or other venues that they have had a revelation.[25]

There is in Mormon accounts an emphasis on the miraculous breaking in to the everyday. With that in mind, the consistent focus on Latter-day Saints' quotidian concerns only serves to underscore the sacred drama of their experiences. Although "solicited revelation" is the form of divine guidance that Mormons receive most often—answers to daily prayer, guidance about life's problems—it is not the genre that dominates Mormon *narratives* of the holy. In Mould's ethnographic and archival research, 80 percent of the narratives marked revelation that arrived unsolicited or seemingly out of the blue.[26] Therefore the telling of sacred experiences emphasizes dramatic manifestations even as it highlights that drama by noting the very commonplace situations in which the narrators found themselves before receiving their unsolicited theophanies. The telling is also heightened by the weight narrators often place on their own unsuitability for receiving such manifestations. In Mormon accounts of personal revelation, one persistent trope is often that of the individual's initial resistance to divine guidance. People tell of initially disbelieving a revelation, or of believing it but not acting upon it; such tales of doubt simultaneously highlight both the narrators' own spiritual humility and God's powerful work in cutting through their earlier skepticism.

Discovery: Balancing Faith and Realism

Mould observes that while Mormons' oral testimonies often highlight personal challenges faced when receiving inspiration, some of those specific details are muted when the same accounts make it into print. An oral testimony told to one's family or ward community undergoes certain changes when it is written down for a wider audience: it is often depersonalized, with specific facts removed to make it universal; and it is likely to have jettisoned the doubt or initial resistance that characterized an individual's response to divine guidance as recounted orally. Some of this transformation is surely due to the venue of publication. Mould, for example, explores Mormon written testimonies in the official church magazine *Ensign*. He notes that these *Ensign* accounts, unlike most Mormon oral testimonies, "display a uniformity of skill in hearing and obeying the Spirit. There is not a single mention of hesitation or delay in responding to the Spirit in the narratives of any of the twelve issues published in 2007."[27]

Such refinement of personal testimony is perhaps to be expected in an official church magazine, which would have a vested interest in publishing only triumphant stories of revelation clearly received and immediately implemented. Less clear is why such changes also often occur in unofficial Mormon memoirs, in which some writers chose to omit from their later crafted accounts whatever difficult experiences or crises of faith they might have recorded in their day-to-day journals or letters.

For example, Angelina Farley's struggles with plural marriage and grinding poverty were recounted in a colorful diary she kept in the mid- to late-nineteenth century. In its pages she described the intense jealousy she felt toward another of her husband's wives, Lydia, whose company he seemed to prefer. Angelina wrote that her own children were dressed in rags and that she was "heartsick to look about the room in which I spend my days." Her life, she wrote, was "filthy wearisome," and her spirits were not improved when her husband was "always with [Lydia] night and day, at home and abroad."[28]

But the rawness of Angelina's perspective is rendered more acute because she wrote of her quandary in a diary as events unfolded, without the benefit (or curse) of hindsight. As Paula Kelly Harline observes in *The Polygamous Wives Writing Club*, which draws on the writings of ordinary nineteenth-century plural wives, Angelina's diary showed that she "chose to transgress cultural expectations" that demanded she present herself as an ideal woman: quiet, infinitely patient, and willing to overlook any failings in her husband. Harline compares Angelina's diary to the more reticent accounts left by polygamous women who compiled memoirs later in life, such as Henrietta Williams.[29] Henrietta was seventy-three in 1900, approximately when she wrote her account of her life in polygamy. Unlike Angelina's anguished, immediate record, Henrietta's autobiography is "most notable for what it does *not* say about the younger wives" who gave her so much trouble earlier in her life. She mentioned her husband's second wife only a few times, and his third not at all.[30] Another woman living in polygamy, Elizabeth MacDonald, also left out a great deal from the record she made late in life. She emphasized her years living with her husband rather than the years apart, probably exaggerated the degree to which she and her sister-wives "lived mostly together," and failed to mention that her husband died in Mexico while living with another wife.[31]

These plural wives' records show a third tension in Mormon memoir, the balance between writing about the ideal and the real. Much of the dilemma—and the craft—of writing memoir lies in the kinds of decisions once outlined by Ralph Waldo Emerson, who noted that memoirs can be captivating "if only a man knew how to choose among what he calls his experiences that which is really his experience, and how to record truth truly."[32] What do authors choose to include, and what do they carefully omit? In Mormonism, these plural wives' tradition of selectivity has a prophetic imprimatur, though it came after their time. LDS President Spencer W. Kimball stated in 1975 that the very angels of heaven might quote from ordinary Mormons' memoirs, a fascinating (if pressure-filled) acknowledgment of the divine role accorded to record keeping in Mormon culture.[33] In his exhortation to keep a journal, however, President Kimball was clear that not every experience was worth recording. What he wanted Mormons to exclude is interesting:

> Your journal should contain your true self rather than a picture of you when you are "made up" for a public performance. There is a temptation to paint one's virtues in rich color and whitewash the vices, but there is also the opposite pitfall of accentuating the negative. Personally I have little respect for anyone who delves into the ugly phases of the life he is portraying, whether it be his own or another's. The truth should be told, but we should not emphasize the negative. Even a long life full of inspiring experiences can be brought to the dust by one ugly story.[34]

After a promising opening line in which Kimball encouraged Mormons to bare their "true selves," he then cautioned them not to "emphasize the negative." In Kimball's view, just one ugly story might be enough to invalidate a lifetime of inspiring events.

The challenge for Mormon memoirists, then, is to relate difficult circumstances or painful events while imparting a faith-promoting legacy to their descendants. President Kimball was talking about journal keeping, but the tendency to focus primarily on what is inspiring is perhaps even more pronounced in retrospectively crafted Mormon memoirs than in real-time journals. In a memoir, there is time to sift, modulate, and interpret. One example is *Bringing Elizabeth Home: A Memoir of Faith and Hope*, by Ed and Lois Smart, the parents of kidnapping victim Elizabeth Smart. This book espouses a thoughtful approach to faith and human free will, which Mormons call "agency." But in their explanations of how LDS theology allows for bad things to happen to good people, the Smarts steer away from dwelling on those bad things.

Kidnapping and predatory sexual abuse merely form the backdrop for this family's story of triumph over adversity and reunion in the face of terrible odds. It is an inspiring memoir, if an incomplete one. At the end of the book, the Smarts recount what happened when Elizabeth, home and safe for only a "couple of weeks," brought her family to see the campsite where she had been held captive months before:

> When we stood at the site, Elizabeth was free—free to do and say whatever she wanted. It was liberating and cathartic. More crucial to her was to prove that Brian and Wanda [her kidnappers] did not own her. There were no tears—she certainly didn't show any anguish about being there. It was like a cleansing for her. It is part of the healing. For us, it was bewildering. We didn't know what to expect. It was horrifying seeing the conditions she had to live under. On the other hand, it was glorious to see our daughter hold her head up in victory—to see her in control, knowing that she was a survivor in every sense of the word.[35]

Smart's own memoir, published a decade after her parents', delved into the themes of agency and control even more. Hers is not a victim's story, but a survivor's. From the opening epigraph, in which she quotes the Christian church father Origen ("The power of choosing good and evil is within the reach of all"), Smart's tale is one of choosing life. "After I had been raped and brutalized," she states at the beginning of her account, "there was something new inside my soul. There was a burning now inside me, a fierce determination that no matter what I had to do, *I was going to live!*"[36] Although she does not dwell on the details of her daily rape, neither does she shrink from relating that stark truth. Overall, however, her memoir focuses not on crime but on hope.

That hope is sometimes expressed in specifically Mormon ways, such as when Smart recites the story of suffering pioneers who died along the Mormon trail in the mid-nineteenth century. She remembers a little girl who prayed for some shoes to save her bloodied feet during the Mormons' frozen trek. Night after night the girl had begged God for them, and then one morning they appeared: brand-new shoes that fit her like a dream. In similar fashion, Smart remembers a day during her captivity when she was "so thirsty I thought I would die." Chained to a cable to prevent her from running away, she was at the mercy of her kidnappers for water, but they were so concerned about avoiding discovery that they did not dare venture from the campsite to fetch any. At night, Smart woke to witness a miracle:

> There was a yellow cup sitting beside my pillow. I leaned toward it, checking it in the moonlight. It was filled to the very brim with water. I stared at it

> a moment, not believing it was real. I reached out to touch it. The cup was cold. I pulled back my hand and looked around. Was I dreaming? Was I crazy? I quickly turned to Mitchell and Barzee. Neither of them had moved. I listened. A gentle breeze blew through the tops of the trees, swaying in the night.[37]

Smart drank the water, believing that it came from God since there was not a drop of water in the camp and she knew her captors would have provided for themselves before ever taking care of her. Why had God sent it, she wondered? Unlike the pioneer girl whose feet had nearly frozen, Smart's life was not in immediate danger, since her captors would certainly have obtained water for them all eventually. God had sent it "because he loved me. And he wanted me to know."[38] God had a plan for her, God was aware of her suffering, and God cared. That was enough.

Examining the Smart family memoirs raises the question: Are Mormons only to share stories that promote faith? If so, *what* promotes faith? Some people, perhaps including President Kimball, would prefer the exclusion of ugliness, criticism, or doubt. Others, particularly more recent Mormon memoirists, seem capable of including stories of brokenness and weakness while allowing readers to make their own judgments.

An example of this is the 2014 missionary memoir of Brigham Young University professor Craig Harline, whose *Way Below the Angels* combines humor and realism in recounting his mid-1970s mission to Belgium. The staunchly Catholic areas of Belgium where Harline served were not receptive to Mormon missionaries. Although he had begun his mission with glorious dreams of heroism—his initial baptismal goal was a whopping eighty-four converts—he soon realized he'd be lucky if he got to baptize a single person after two frustrating years of knocking on doors, bicycling in the rain, and chatting up Dutch-speaking Belgians on street corners. One day, worn down with the emptiness of his efforts, he retreated to his room and tried to pray. The words would not come. "Maybe this was the sort of emptiness the mystics said you had to feel before you could really feel God," he mused. On the other hand, "maybe the emptiness was all there was, rather than just some sort of lead-up to being filled by God. Maybe the void was it, period."[39]

What inspiration Harline received in that moment was not what he was expecting: merely the words *Just be yourself*, "a totally silent thought/feeling that calmly but overwhelmingly entered the emptiness inside." He was floored, and even a bit disappointed:

> Of all the thoughts/feelings in the universe that might've been lightning-bolted down to me, this was it? Of all the gems I might've found in church councils and scriptures and sacred history or God himself, this trite 1970s

> thing was all I actually got? No new magical proselyting techniques? No new dose of heroic resolve to get the faith necessary to make eighty-four converts?
>
> The biggest obstacle to my saying *yes* to this unexpected thought/feeling was that I'd never really stopped to consider who I was, had never even stopped to consider that I *needed* to consider it, because who I was supposed to be or more accurately supposed to become had already pretty much been laid out for me, my whole life long.[40]

Harline's modest thought/feeling *Just be yourself* was immediately followed by doubts that the message was really from God. Why would God not exhort him to become *better*, to grow into that special super-missionary Harline hoped was lying dormant somewhere inside of him? Receiving a revelation that he was supposed to simply be himself sounded like "some syrupy Hollywood idea," or even what the devil would have him believe. Surely only the devil would encourage a Mormon to stop progressing. Yet the idea persisted and was surprisingly radical. Harline writes that it may seem obvious that we would always want to only be ourselves, but it's actually not so clear, perhaps especially in the conformity-based context of Mormon missionary culture:

> It turns out you don't always want to be you, because you know very well all the spectacular failures and character flaws lurking around inside, and you think that maybe it'd be nicer to be someone else instead, who obviously doesn't have all those failures and flaws. . . . And you especially know that the people around you, a.k.a. your culture, don't really want you completely to be you either, but only the parts of you they approve of, especially the parts that are most like them, because that's what they're basically telling you all the time: *be more like us.*[41]

The triumphalist script of a standard Mormon missionary narrative would have Harline's modest revelation *Just be yourself* acting as the cornerstone of a subsequent transformation. The mission would begin succeeding as potential converts caught a whiff of the Holy Ghost and clamored to have that same spirit for themselves. But that's not what happened, at least not outwardly. What happened instead was that Harline, partly freed from the mask of needing to appear successful, began to love the Belgian people. In the end, he says, they "shaped my views without even ever trying to, more than I ever shaped theirs while actually trying."[42]

Harline's memoir is admirably conscious of the story he is *not* telling, which he calls the One True Missionary Story.[43] This is the victorious narrative all Mormons anticipate when they hear about someone else's mission. They expect to hear that those two years were the hardest the missionary had ever had, sure. But the next line of the accepted script is always that they were also the *best* years. Harline, by contrast, couldn't wait to go home and confesses in the book that he had nightmares for years that he was being called on another mission. In the epilogue he notes that he finally decided to write *Way Below the Angels* as he gradually discovered many such people "needing to talk out the rough stuff" about their missions and their lives—so many, in fact, that his memoir was "right in the middle of a flippin' zeitgeist."[44]

Harline's memoir highlights all three of the central points discussed in this essay. First, he freely admits to having constructed it as a form of propaganda—in his case, an intentional subversion of the narrative expectations of the One True Missionary Story. As such, its vulnerability opens the way for other Mormon life stories that wrestle with candid truth. However, the book manages to do this while meeting the second tension identified here, which is that even (or especially) in its truth-telling it manages to promote a deep religious faith. While there are no tidy answers in Harline's memoir, there are ineffable sacred experiences and a commitment to a Mormon understanding of God. Finally, this balance of faith and realism leads the author to the triumph of self-definition. His truth has been told; but as Spencer Kimball advocated, he has done so without an undue focus on the negative.

If there is a "zeitgeist" in Mormon memoir, one hopes that it will spawn more of these middle-ground stories, from the purely fun glimpses of LDS subculture (Elna Baker's *The New York Regional Mormon Singles Halloween Dance*) to the reflective and lovely (Phyllis Barber's *Raw Edges*).[45] As Mormonism becomes more accepted in the mainstream, it is likely there will also be more memoirs by Mormons who don't feel they have to write about Mormonism. What memoir teaches writers is that it can be deeply cathartic to choose how to tell their own story, and a large part of this empowerment is rejecting any script that may have been handed to them as a boilerplate. With that in mind, it is a great loss that Terry Tempest Williams's mother chose to leave behind only silence. We can respect her choice but also grieve it, and look to the future of Mormon memoir as a flowering of voices.

Notes

A portion of this paper was first presented at the Calvin Festival of Faith and Writing in Grand Rapids, Michigan, in April 2012, and another portion at the Mormon Studies conference at Claremont Graduate University on March 16, 2013.

1. Terry Tempest Williams, *When Women Were Birds: Fifty-Four Variations on Voice* (New York: Sarah Crichton Books/FSG, 2012), 3–4.
2. George Orwell, "Why I Write," in *The Orwell Reader: A Treasury of the Best of George Orwell*, introduced by Richard H. Rovere (New York: Harcourt, 1956), 390–96.

3. Armand L. Mauss, *Shifting Borders and a Tattered Passport: Intellectual Journeys of a Mormon Academic* (Salt Lake City: University of Utah Press, 2012), xiii–xiv. In this essay, the words "autobiography" and "memoir" are used more or less interchangeably, which is not how the words are used today but is consistent with the way Mormon writers used them in the nineteenth century. Today, a greater distinction is made between "memoir" as a crafted account of one particular aspect or time of life (a year spent in Nepal, for example, or a relationship with an alcoholic parent) versus "autobiography," which is an individual's account of his or her entire life.
4. See 3 Nephi 23:6, 11–13.
5. See, for example, the Book of Omni, as various narrators disclose their individual roles in maintaining the sacred records of their people.
6. See Jan Shipps, *Mormonism: The Story of a New Religious Tradition* (Urbana: University of Illinois Press, 1985), chapter 6, especially 125–27.
7. This is particularly important if it is indeed true that, as novelist Frederick Buechner has noted, "all theology, like all fiction, is at its heart autobiography, and that what a theologian is doing essentially is examining as honestly as he can the rough-and-tumble of his own experience with all its ups and downs, its mysteries and loose ends, and expressing in logical, abstract terms the truth about human life and God that he believes he has found implicit there." Frederick Buechner, *The Sacred Journey: A Memoir of Early Days* (San Francisco: HarperCollins, 1982), 1.
8. The Joseph Smith Papers, "Introduction to the Journals," online at http://josephsmithpapers.org/doc/series-introduction-for-the-journals-series.
9. Jill Ker Conway, *When Memory Speaks: Reflections on Autobiography* (New York: Alfred A. Knopf, 1998), 7, 17.
10. Sonia Johnson, *From Housewife to Heretic: One Woman's Spiritual Awakening and Her Excommunication from the Mormon Church* (Garden City, NY: Doubleday & Company, 1981), Lucy Mack Smith, *The Revised and Enhanced History of Joseph Smith by His Mother*, edited by Scot Facer Proctor and Maurine Jensen Proctor (Salt Lake City: Bookcraft, 1996).
11. Shipps, *Mormonism*, 99–102.
12. Smith, *Revised and Enhanced History*, 459–60.
13. Ibid., 460.
14. Eric A. Eliason, "Toward the Folkloristic Study of Latter-day Saint Conversion Narratives," *BYU Studies* 38, no. 1 (1999): 137–50.
15. Martha Nibley Beck, *Leaving the Saints: How I Lost the Mormons and Found My Faith* (New York: Broadway Books, 2005); Carolyn Jessop with Laura Palmer, *Escape* (New York: Broadway Books, 2007).
16. Annie Clark Tanner, *A Mormon Mother* (Salt Lake City: Tanner Trust Fund, University of Utah Library, 1983), 272.
17. Mauss, *Shifting Borders and a Tattered Passport*; Joanna Brooks, *The Book of Mormon Girl: A Memoir of an American Faith* (New York: Free Press, 2012).
18. Nicole Hardy, *Confessions of a Latter-day Virgin: A Memoir* (New York: Hyperion, 2013), 101–2.
19. Orwell, "Why I Write," 396.

20. Memoir of Romania B. Pratt, M.D., March 19, 1881, Salt Lake City, Utah; http://jared.pratt-family.org/parley_family_histories/romania_bunnell_memoirs.html.
21. Ann Padgett, *This Is the Story of a Happy Marriage* (New York: HarperCollins, 2013), 24–25.
22. See Richard Bushman, *Joseph Smith, Rough Stone Rolling: A Cultural Biography of Mormonism's Founder* (New York: Knopf, 2005), 40–41.
23. Joseph Smith History 1:25, emphases added.
24. Tom Mould, *Still, the Small Voice: Narrative, Personal Revelation, and the Mormon Folk Tradition* (Logan: Utah State University Press, 2011), 77.
25. Ibid., 78–80.
26. Ibid., 144, 152.
27. Ibid., 358.
28. Paula Kelly Harline, *The Polygamous Wives Writing Club: From the Diaries of Mormon Pioneer Women* (New York: Oxford University Press, 2014), 61, 63.
29. Ibid., 68.
30. Ibid., 70.
31. Ibid., chapter 4.
32. Ralph Waldo Emerson, quoted in Henry Miller, *Tropic of Cancer* (New York: Grove Press, 1961), epigraph.
33. Spencer W. Kimball, "The Angels May Quote from It," *New Era* (October 1975), online at https://www.lds.org/new-era/2003/02/the-angels-may-quote-from-it?lang=eng.
34. Ibid.
35. Ed and Lois Smart with Laura Morton, *Bringing Elizabeth Home: A Journey of Faith and Hope* (New York: Doubleday, 2003), 198.
36. Elizabeth Smart, *My Story* (New York: St. Martin's Press, 2013), 6.
37. Ibid., 130.
38. Ibid., 131.
39. Craig Harline, *Way Below the Angels: The Pretty Clearly Troubled but Not Even Close to Tragic Confessions of a Real Live Mormon Missionary* (Grand Rapids, MI: Eerdmans, 2014), 119.
40. Ibid., 120.
41. Ibid., 122.
42. Ibid., 238.
43. Ibid., 258.
44. Ibid., 285.
45. Elna Baker, *The New York Regional Mormon Singles Halloween Dance* (New York: Plume, 2009); Phyllis Barber, *Raw Edges: A Memoir* (Reno: University of Nevada Press, 2009).

Coda | A Man of His Time and Place

An Appreciation of Armand Mauss and the California Mormons

Claudia Bushman

Many years ago I read *The Angel and the Beehive*, Armand Mauss's pathbreaking sociological study of the Church of Jesus Christ of Latter-day Saints. He had conceptualized the story as the church's serial magnetic attraction to two opposing forces: the need to remain true to the church's mystical, sensational history and to adapt to the modern world. When I read the book I was struck by how clearly his model explained the church that I had grown up in and what it had come to be. Changes that had made no sense to me, that I certainly regretted, that I felt had been mistakes, made complete sense in his system. The things that I and others had valued in the church were throwaways as we moved into the promised globalism of the late twentieth century. I did what I had never done before or since. I wrote him a fan letter.

My husband Richard and I had always known Armand and Ruth Mauss, but not well. Moving in the same circles, we have always been aware of them. And I had probably met him long ago when we were much younger, because we come from almost exactly the same world. We are children of Utah's outmigration whose families settled in northern California. As the LDS Church of the past had attempted to establish Mormon villages in sparsely settled outlands, our little congregations supplied Mormon villages for us in California.

Armand and I didn't live in Utah but we lived very much in Mormonism, where intensive programs involved us heavily in Zion most of the days of the year. Armand was Utah-born, but his parents left the home state when he was very young as part of the great Mormon diaspora between the two World Wars. His family moved to Southern California where the first stake outside the original Deseret plat was founded and then moved on to Oakland in the San Francisco Bay Area. My family followed the same trajectory, my father and mother coming as single young people in the 1920s, meeting and marrying in Los Angeles, then settling in Oakland where I was born. They later moved to San Francisco across the bay. But before that my father was bishop of Oakland's Dimond Ward, an offshoot of the ward where Armand's father was bishop.

His father, the eldest of nine children, and my father, the eldest of ten, both left school early to work, no other options being available. Both of our fathers rose above their beginnings and brought family members along with them. A large part of the education that helped them both to get ahead came from serving Mormon missions and leading LDS congregations.

Armand and I are not Utahans. We have never been Utahans. We are California Mormons. In our time, California Mormons were more independent than Utah Mormons; they were grateful for the distance that separated them from Salt Lake City. They paid less homage to old church families. They were less pious, less judgmental, more aware of living in and negotiating with the secular world. Mormons, being rarer away from our central Zion, clung together. They valued each other more because they were a rarer commodity. They provided a nurturing village for the children.

California Mormons remain cooler in style, bearing less effusive testimonies. They do not stand to sing "Oh Ye Mountains High" and try to avoid singing it at all. They are loyal and reliable. They are the real Mormon pioneers as all California Mormons know. Didn't Sam Brannan, the leader of two hundred-plus Mormons on the ship *Brooklyn*, leave New York, sail around the horn, and land in Yerba Buena, later San Francisco, doubling the population in 1846, a full year before Brigham Young proclaimed the desolate Salt Lake Valley to be "the place"? Had not Brigham Young called the California Mormons "home" at the time of the Utah War, California's Mormon roots would be more visible. The vestiges are still there.

So Armand grew up in a double culture: church and its multiple activities, the small Mormon community, against the sharp striving of the Californians, people of every nation streaming into the Golden State with the hopes of making it big or at least better. Armand saw the opportunities to get ahead that had not been available for his father. He could compare his sharp mind to those of his own peers and be confident that he measured up. He went to good schools with people of all stripes in the very shadow of the great University of California at Berkeley, which was blessedly cheap in his day. He could have gone right through those gates. But temporarily leaving secular culture, he chose to go on a mission. As he says:

> I was a religious boy despite my rebellious tendencies, and I had been reared in a California Mormon community that had richly nurtured me socially, intellectually, and spiritually. The Oakland Ward, where I had lived for more than the previous decade, had a membership drawn from the working and lower-middle classes, with very few members of greater social status. All were hardworking, earnest, and (for the most part) religiously devout. From amongst them had come my most important ecclesiastical leaders, teachers,

> and youth counselors—all devoted volunteers, of course. I could not and would not let them down.[1]

What a perfect picture of the Mormon Church of the 1940s and 1950s. Noisy apostates and naysayers were generally invisible in those days.

It happened that Armand went to the New England states for his mission, becoming one of the young lieutenants of S. Dilworth Young, the old Boy Scout leader who sent his elders out for months at a time "without purse or scrip." The mission increased Armand's native sharpness to deal with difficulties while also putting his Mormon beliefs, which had been unquestioned, under scrutiny compared to the knowledge of the world. From then on he was more careful about the beliefs that he proclaimed. Even while on a mission, he made his own decisions. As he later wrote:

> While still a young adult, I learned to recognize and appreciate the human fallibility in all our leaders, and thus to keep my expectations for their performance quite modest. That attitude has blessed me with a certain immunity against disillusionment, which for many Saints has followed their confrontations with the human failings of leaders from the greatest to the least. My loyalty to the Church as an institution, therefore, has never depended on my assessments of the teachings or behavior of any particular leaders at either the local or the general level.[2]

In his way he kept his distance both from the church he had grown up in and from the university life he was training to join.

After his mission, instead of enrolling in the University of California, Armand chose adventure and went to Japan where his father had been called to be the church's mission president. During his four and a half years there, from the summer of 1949 to the end of 1953, Armand graduated from a Jesuit university, served two and a half years of a four-year enlistment in the United States Air Force, found a bride, and produced two children. He describes his meeting with Ruth Elinor Hathaway, a petite young blonde from southeastern Idaho also in the Air Force on duty in Tokyo. Conducting a church meeting in 1950, he immediately noticed her "broad, fetching smile, set off by charming dimples."[3] The relationship deepened, and as the country exploded in spring cherry blossoms, they were married the following year.

What do we make of this trajectory? Here is a smart young man in a hurry who knows where he is going, very much involved in learning and ambitious about getting ahead. He is adventurous and confident with many years of training to go. He is quick on his feet, adjusting to circumstances. And yet very much an LDS young man, he succumbs to dimples and cherry blossoms. Was there any concern about beginning a family when he had so much school ahead?

Back to his academic life in 1955, he enrolled as a graduate student at UC-Berkeley in pursuit of a general secondary teaching credential and a master's degree in Asian and U.S. history. He had the G.I. Bill to help him, but nevertheless he embarked on a ferocious schedule of school and toil to support his growing clan. He worked as a night watchman and a janitor, and taught in middle school, high school, and junior college. He could have stopped at any of those places but did not. He not only endured, he persisted, and he prevailed.

Think of the labors of that life, full-time work plus full-time or part-time school. How many people do we know who have washed out of such a regime, their ambition tempered by the labor? With his MA in hand he accepted a position in a ward bishopric, planning a rest from his double labors of work and school. That was 1957, when he was twenty-nine. Yet, after those five years of time off from school, when he could have continued as a community college professor, he went back to school and worked on. During this period, the Mauss family ranks swelled. A truly fitting tribute would give Ruth the credit she deserves for this successful family of ten.

Would a young man today, planning an extensive training period toward a doctorate and a modest income as a professor, a young man without a trust fund, have had or chosen to have eight children? This large progeny may well have resulted from the outspoken LDS Church beliefs of the times. The church not only discouraged birth control for its members, it did not even allow birth control information to be disseminated until the 1970s. *Roe v. Wade* was not decided until 1973. Whatever the reasons, a grand family resulted. It was a heavy load, even for Armand.

So back to UC in 1962, entirely self-supporting. No big fellowships, no support packages. He found it expedient to change his field to sociology where he could study part-time. He expected some adjustments moving from history, but not as many as he found. He had troubles with the sociological concept that truth and reality are socially constructed. What now seems to be merely an inconvenient truth newly challenged his religious faith, but he gradually accepted the "social constructionist" way of understanding reality. The double work burden was assuaged by his efficiency in freeing time for his graduate classes. In 1967, when he was ABD (all but dissertation), he took a job at Utah State University, where he was, for the only time in his career, surrounded by Mormons at work. Here was a new challenge: dividing the LDS religion from the Mormon individuals with whom he associated, some of high church office and some unfriendly. Even when he worked with Mormons, Armand had to divide himself from Mormonism. Even in Zion he remained a California Mormon. He soon moved to Washington State University, his primary academic home for the remainder of his career, where he had the more advanced technical support needed to complete the statistical portions of his dissertation.

In reflecting on this early stage of his career, Mauss identifies himself as a young apologist for the LDS Church. That might be a surprise to some after the measured skepticism and coolness of his later discourse. His relationships with church authority have always been distanced and respectful. He is never slavish and wonders if his attitude has kept him from higher church office. But he also admits to tense relationships with sociology colleagues because of his candid, self-promoting, perhaps combative or abrasive style. He has felt tensions in both of his major membership groups. He was, and is, a very tough grader, both at school and at church, of students and colleagues. No sentimentality here.

Still, he has played the academic game and won it: winning grants, doing research, publishing in the required journals, ascending to respected senior status, although he has not always found satisfaction in the timely topics that it was wise for him to explore. He wanted to return to religious studies, especially on Mormons. Instead of working together, his two lives had worked in opposition to each other. He worked this divided life toward a synthesis that he eventually achieved during the 1980s. He had paid off his apprenticeship to academia and earned the right to do what he wanted. He phased out the professional activities related to deviant behavior, social problems, and alcohol studies and jumped into Mormon studies with both feet.

Mauss's important book, *The Angel and the Beehive*, resulted from the marriage of his years of experience in and observation of Mormonism and his sociological skills. This was Mauss's first solo-authored book, published in 1994 when he was sixty-six, rather late in his career. He had been working with the ideas and the methods for a long time, but rather than wearing out, he had been sharpening his tools all the time. He saw strange changes in the LDS Church in top-down requirements that juiced up the priesthood at the expense of the auxiliaries, that emphasized obedience to authority and discouraged independent groups. Gradually, as the strictures of "correlation" became apparent, he continued to observe, searching for a sociological model that would explain what was happening. He wondered how the church could be headed toward secularization and assimilation into the general American culture while at the same time resisting that assimilation and striving to maintain its distinctive and peculiar traits. He saw that a new generation of conservative leaders was trying to move the church back toward original beliefs, a process that he called retrenchment. He was finally able to come up with a theoretical explanation for this anomaly. He was able to see the contradictory counterforces operating on the LDS Church in sociological terms. That's the conundrum that he was able to explicate so brilliantly. That was the explanation that galvanized readers like me.

Armand's tenacity and his ability to build and plant where he is located has allowed him to make indelible marks on Mormon thought and on independent Mormon organizations. I have been in a position to see his potent effect on two of these organizations—*Dialogue: A Journal of Mormon Thought* and Claremont Graduate University's Mormon studies program. I think he is largely responsible for the financial and editorial strength of *Dialogue* today. During a long term as board chairman, he pressed for professional standards and fiscal responsibility with several boards and editors, promising a future to a little journal that could very well have cashed out by now. In an emotional meeting with the dying Eugene England, he promised to "save *Dialogue*," and with some help from others, he has done it.

He has been the most faithful person in the creation of the Mormon studies program at Claremont. He has served as professor, advisor, donor, fundraiser, negotiator, financial watchdog, and active Mormon Studies Council member. He has served with many other potent leaders who have moved on to other church assignments and I think he is the only one of the original group left standing. Thanks again to his tenacity, many young and older students have had the opportunity to study Mormonism at a traditional school of religion. Many community members have had the chance to experience academic treatments of Mormonism in a context other than church itself.

So he has been a man of considerable gifts who with long labor and discipline has honed those gifts to make serious contributions. His frankness and intensity are not always politic but they give him a formidable authenticity and undeniable authority. The three major books he has written in what would have been his retirement years have all added to the Mormon studies canon, significantly influencing a generation of students and the future of the discipline. His activities and dedication to organizations that have benefited from his interest and labor will change the conversation for generations to come. He and Ruth have peopled his landscape with their multitudinous progeny. They will leave gifts to the future in many forms.

And to think that this successful life all results from his being a California Mormon.

Notes

1. Armand L. Mauss, *Shifting Borders and a Tattered Passport* (Salt Lake City: University of Utah Press, 2012), 7–8.
2. Ibid., 169.
3. Ibid., 15.

Contributors

Matthew Bowman is associate professor of history at Henderson State University. He is the author of *The Mormon People: The Making of an American Faith*, and *The Urban Pulpit: New York City and the Fate of Liberal Evangelicalism*. Currently he is working on a study of the meanings of the word "Christian" in American politics.

Claudia L. Bushman is a social and cultural historian now retired from teaching to finish up her assorted life work which includes oral histories and autobiography. She is the author or editor of several books, including *Contemporary Mormonism: Latter-day Saints in Modern America* and, with Caroline Kline, *Mormon Women Have Their Say: Essays from the Claremont Oral History Collection*. She is currently writing a study of Harriet Hanson Robinson in and out of Boston in 1870.

Richard Bushman is Gouverneur Morris Professor, Emeritus, at Columbia University and author of *Joseph Smith: Rough Stone Rolling* and other books in early American history. He occupied the Howard W. Hunter Chair in Mormon Studies at Claremont Graduate University from 2008 to 2011. He lives in New York City with his wife, Claudia Bushman.

Wilfried Decoo is a native Belgian, linguist and educator, and emeritus professor at the University of Antwerp and Brigham Young University. Among his publications are *Crisis on Campus* and *Systemization in Foreign Language Teaching*. He has published a number of articles on Mormonism in Europe in *BYU Studies*, *Dialogue*, and the *Journal of Mormon History*.

Patrick Q. Mason is Howard W. Hunter Chair of Mormon Studies and associate professor of religion at Claremont Graduate University. He is the author of *The Mormon Menace: Violence and Anti-Mormonism in the Postbellum South*, and coeditor of *War and Peace in Our Time: Mormon Perspectives*.

Michael McBride is professor of economics at the University of California, Irvine, director of the Experimental Social Science Laboratory, and faculty affiliate of the UC Irvine Religious Studies Program. His research uses game theory and experimental methods to study collective action, conflict, and religion. His research has appeared in the *Journal of Economic Theory*, the *Journal of Public Economics*, the *American Journal of Sociology*, and the *Journal of Economic Behavior and Organization*.

Quincy D. Newell researches and writes about American religions, focusing on the religious history of the American West. She is the author of *Constructing Lives at Mission San Francisco: Native Californians and Hispanic Colonists, 1776–1821*; the coeditor of *New Perspectives in Mormon Studies: Creating and Crossing Boundaries*; and the author of numerous book chapters and journal articles. After more than a decade on the religious studies faculty at the University of Wyoming, Newell now teaches American religious history at Hamilton College.

Levi S. Peterson, now retired, was a professor of English at Weber State University. He is the author of two collections of short stories, *The Canyons of Grace* and *Night Soil*; two novels, *The Backslider* and *Aspen Marooney*; a biography, *Juanita Brooks: The Life Story of a Courageous Historian of the Mountain Meadows Massacre*; and an autobiography, *A Rascal by Nature, A Christian by Yearning*.

W. Paul Reeve is the author of *Religion of a Different Color: Race and the Mormon Struggle for Whiteness* and *Making Space on the Western Frontier: Mormons, Miners, and Southern Paiutes*, and coeditor of two additional books. He is an associate professor and the director of graduate studies in the History Department at the University of Utah where he teaches courses on Utah history, Mormon history, and the history of the U.S. West.

Jana Riess has a PhD in American religious history from Columbia University and has worked for many years as an editor in the publishing industry. She is the author or coauthor of numerous books, including *Flunking Sainthood* and *Mormonism for Dummies*. She blogs about Mormonism for Religion News Service and has taught at Barnard College and Miami University of Ohio.

Gary Shepherd is professor emeritus of sociology at Oakland University, and Gordon Shepherd is professor of sociology at the University of Central Arkansas. The brothers have coauthored a number of books and articles throughout their careers. Their most recent collaborations are *Binding Earth and Heaven: Patriarchal Blessings in the Prophetic Development of Early Mormonism*, *A Kingdom Transformed: Early Mormonism and the Modern LDS Church*, and *Voices for Equality: Ordain Women and Resurgent Mormon Feminism.*

Jan Shipps, author of *Mormonism: The Story of a New Religious Tradition* and *Sojourner in the Promised Land: Forty Years among the Mormons*, is professor emerita of religious studies and history at Indiana University–Purdue University Indianapolis.

Shinji Takagi is professor emeritus of economics at Osaka University, Osaka, Japan. He is the author of nearly two hundred publications in international economics and related fields, including most recently *Conquering the Fear of Freedom: Japanese Exchange Rate Policy Since 1945*. His contributions in Mormon history have previously appeared in the *Journal of Mormon History*, *BYU Studies*, and the *Journal of the Book of Mormon and Other Restoration Scripture.*

Walter van Beek is emeritus professor of anthropology of religion at Tilburg University, and senior researcher at the African Studies Center, Leiden, both in the Netherlands. His main research area is West Africa, where he has done anthropological field research among the Kapsiki/Higi of North Cameroon and northeastern Nigeria, and among the Dogon of Mali. His recent publications include *The Forge and the Funeral: The Smith in Kapsiki/Higi Culture*, and an edited volume with William Olson, *Evil in Africa: Anthropology of the Everyday*. He has published on Mormonism in the Netherlands and Africa in *Dialogue* and the *International Journal of Mormon Studies.*

Index

Page numbers in italics refer to figures and tables.